JUSTICE LEAGUE
BEYOND

IN GODS WE TRUST

DEREK FRIDOLFS   JT KRUL   DUSTIN NGUYEN
WRITERS

HOWARD PORTER   BEN CALDWELL   JORGE CORONA   DUSTIN NGUYEN
FIONA STAPLES   MARCUS TO   DEREK FRIDOLFS   LIVESAY
ARTISTS

CARRIE STRACHAN   RANDY MAYOR   NICK FILARDI
JOHN KALISZ   IAN HERRING
COLORISTS

SAIDA TEMOFONTE
LETTERER

KHARY RANDOLPH & EMILIO LOPEZ
COLLECTION COVER ARTISTS

SUPERMAN CREATED BY JERRY SIEGEL AND JOE SHUSTER
BY SPECIAL ARRANGEMENT WITH THE JERRY SIEGEL FAMILY

Alex Antone Ben Abernathy Editors – Original Series

Robin Wildman Editor

Robbin Brosterman Design Director – Books

Curtis King Jr. Publication Design

Hank Kanalz Senior VP – Vertigo and Integrated Publishing

Diane Nelson President

Dan DiDio and **Jim Lee** Co-Publishers

Geoff Johns Chief Creative Officer

John Rood Executive VP – Sales, Marketing and Business Development

Amy Genkins Senior VP – Business and Legal Affairs

Nairi Gardiner Senior VP – Finance

Jeff Boison VP – Publishing Planning

Mark Chiarello VP – Art Direction and Design

John Cunningham VP – Marketing

Terri Cunningham VP – Editorial Administration

Alison Gill Senior VP – Manufacturing and Operations

Jay Kogan VP – Business and Legal Affairs, Publishing

Jack Mahan VP – Business Affairs, Talent

Nick Napolitano VP – Manufacturing Administration

Sue Pohja VP – Book Sales

Courtney Simmons Senior VP – Publicity

Bob Wayne Senior VP – Sales

JUSTICE LEAGUE BEYOND: IN GODS WE TRUST
Published by DC Comics. Cover and compilation Copyright © 2014
DC Comics. All Rights Reserved.
Originally published in digital comic form as JUSTICE LEAGUE BEYOND
DIGITAL CHAPTERS 17-25, SUPERMAN BEYOND DIGITAL CHAPTERS 11-20
© 2013 DC Comics. All Rights Reserved. All characters, their distinctive
likenesses and related elements featured in this publication are
trademarks of DC Comics. The stories, characters and incidents featured
in this publication are entirely fictional. DC Comics does not read
or accept unsolicited ideas, stories or artwork.

DC Comics, 1700 Broadway, New York, NY 10019
A Warner Bros. Entertainment Company.
Printed by RR Donnelley, Salem, VA, USA. 2/7/14. First Printing.
ISBN: 978-1-4012-4754-6

Library of Congress Cataloging-in-Publication Data

Fridolfs, Derek.
  Justice League Beyond : In Gods We Trust / Derek Fridolfs, JT Krul, Howard Porter.
    pages cm
  ISBN 978-1-4012-4754-6 (pbk.)
  1. Graphic novels. i. Krul, J. T. ii. Title.
  PN6728.J87F77 2014
  741.5'973—dc23
                        2013045686

SUSTAINABLE
FORESTRY
INITIATIVE

Certified Chain of Custody
At Least 20% Certified Forest Content
www.sfiprogram.org
SFI-01042
APPLIES TO TEXT STOCK ONLY

JUSTICE LEAGUE
BEYOND

ORIGINS:
MICRON

WRITTEN BY
DEREK FRIDOLFS
AND **DUSTIN NGUYEN**

ART AND COLORS BY
FIONA STAPLES

THERE ARE TWO IMPORTANT INDIVIDUALS WHO MADE ME WHO I AM. MY MOM AND BRUCE WAYNE... BUT IT'S NOT WHAT YOU THINK.

BEFORE I WAS BORN, *WAYNE ENTERPRISES* WAS THE LEADING TECHNOLOGY INDUSTRY IN GOTHAM. WHICH MEANS IT WAS ALSO A HUGE TARGET FOR CORPORATE SABOTAGE.

BUT IT CAME WITH THE BEST IN SECURITY.

KRRSHHH

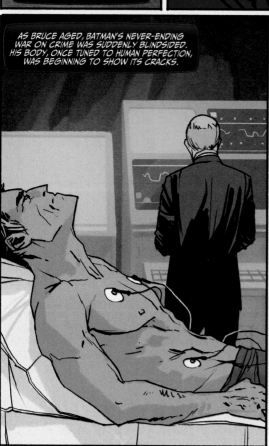

AS BRUCE AGED, BATMAN'S NEVER-ENDING WAR ON CRIME WAS SUDDENLY BLINDSIDED. HIS BODY, ONCE TUNED TO HUMAN PERFECTION, WAS BEGINNING TO SHOW ITS CRACKS.

FOR IT WASN'T THE JOKER, TWO-FACE, OR THE PENGUIN THAT KILLED THE BATMAN. IT WAS THE STRESSES PUT ON A WEAK, DETERIORATING HEART.

BUT EVEN THAT WASN'T GOING TO STOP HIM, IF HE COULD HELP IT.

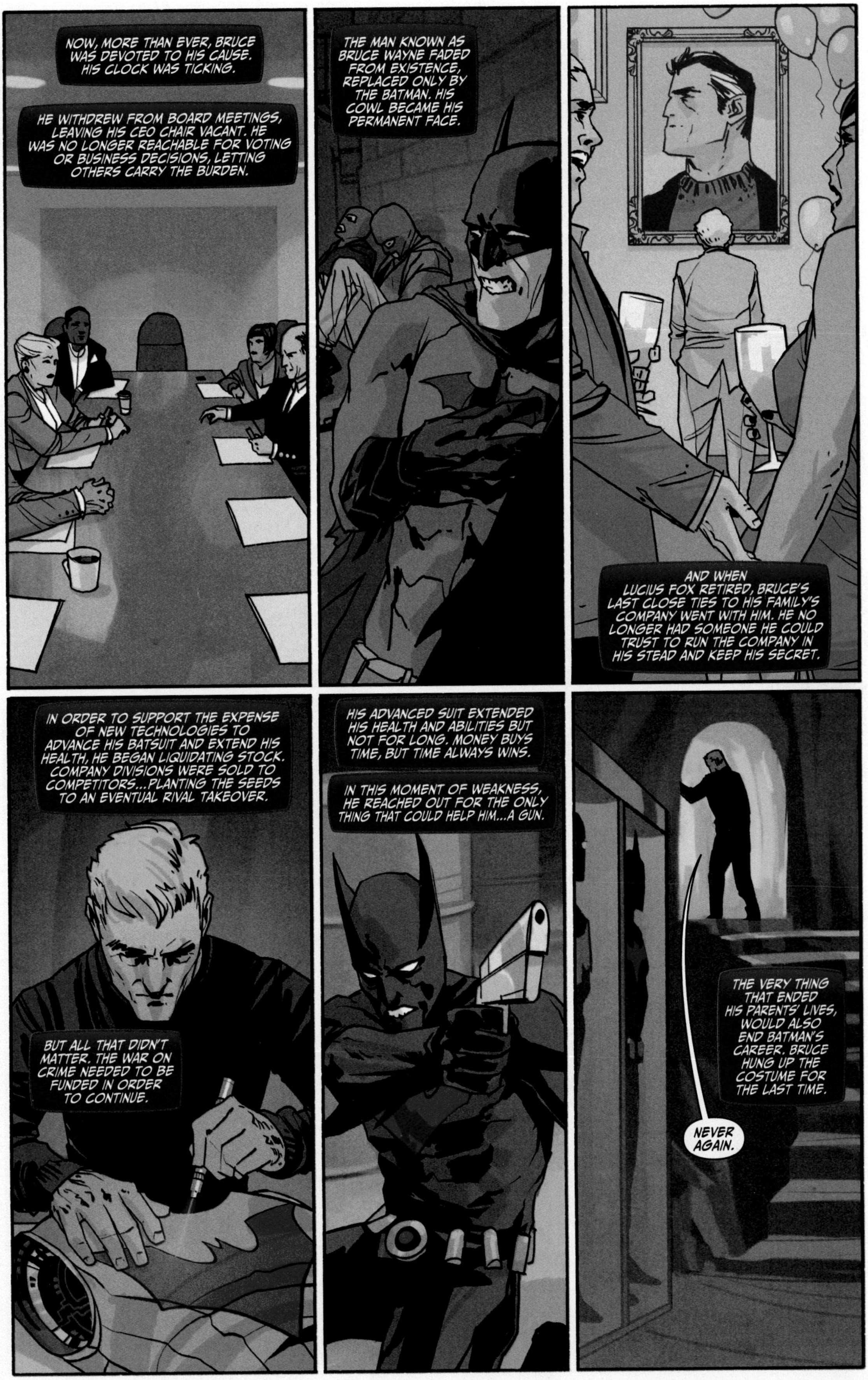
NOW, MORE THAN EVER, BRUCE WAS DEVOTED TO HIS CAUSE. HIS CLOCK WAS TICKING.
HE WITHDREW FROM BOARD MEETINGS, LEAVING HIS CEO CHAIR VACANT. HE WAS NO LONGER REACHABLE FOR VOTING OR BUSINESS DECISIONS, LETTING OTHERS CARRY THE BURDEN.
THE MAN KNOWN AS BRUCE WAYNE FADED FROM EXISTENCE, REPLACED ONLY BY THE BATMAN. HIS COWL BECAME HIS PERMANENT FACE.
AND WHEN LUCIUS FOX RETIRED, BRUCE'S LAST CLOSE TIES TO HIS FAMILY'S COMPANY WENT WITH HIM. HE NO LONGER HAD SOMEONE HE COULD TRUST TO RUN THE COMPANY IN HIS STEAD AND KEEP HIS SECRET.
IN ORDER TO SUPPORT THE EXPENSE OF NEW TECHNOLOGIES TO ADVANCE HIS BATSUIT AND EXTEND HIS HEALTH, HE BEGAN LIQUIDATING STOCK. COMPANY DIVISIONS WERE SOLD TO COMPETITORS...PLANTING THE SEEDS TO AN EVENTUAL RIVAL TAKEOVER.
BUT ALL THAT DIDN'T MATTER. THE WAR ON CRIME NEEDED TO BE FUNDED IN ORDER TO CONTINUE.
HIS ADVANCED SUIT EXTENDED HIS HEALTH AND ABILITIES BUT NOT FOR LONG. MONEY BUYS TIME, BUT TIME ALWAYS WINS.
IN THIS MOMENT OF WEAKNESS, HE REACHED OUT FOR THE ONLY THING THAT COULD HELP HIM...A GUN.
THE VERY THING THAT ENDED HIS PARENTS' LIVES, WOULD ALSO END BATMAN'S CAREER. BRUCE HUNG UP THE COSTUME FOR THE LAST TIME.
NEVER AGAIN.

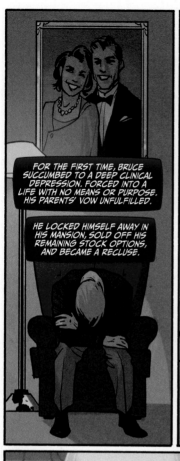

FOR THE FIRST TIME, BRUCE SUCCUMBED TO A DEEP CLINICAL DEPRESSION. FORCED INTO A LIFE WITH NO MEANS OR PURPOSE. HIS PARENTS' VOW UNFULFILLED.

HE LOCKED HIMSELF AWAY IN HIS MANSION, SOLD OFF HIS REMAINING STOCK OPTIONS, AND BECAME A RECLUSE.

AFTER A HISTORY OF FAILED TAKEOVER ATTEMPTS FROM DAGGETT INDUSTRIES AND EVEN LEXCORP, IT WAS SHREWD INDUSTRIALIST DEREK POWERS WHO FINALLY SUCCEEDED.

ACQUIRING A MAJORITY SHARE, HE MERGED HIS OWN COMPANY IN THE BUYOUT TO FORM WAYNE-POWERS ENTERPRISES.

IN THE EARLY DAYS OF THE TRANSITION, AN ENTERPRISING SCIENTIST CAME TO THE FOREFRONT. NOBU OTAKA, THE HEAD OF THE RESEARCH DEPARTMENT, WAS GIVING A TOUR TO VISITING COLLEAGUES AND REPORTERS.

HE WAS SHARING HIS THEORIES ON VIBRASPACE, WHEREIN ATOMS AND MOLECULES COULD VIBRATE IN SUCH A WAY AS TO PASS THROUGH EACH OTHER, AND ALSO CHANGE SHAPE AND DIMENSION.

SADLY HE WOULD NOT HAVE LONG TO SHARE HIS IDEAS.

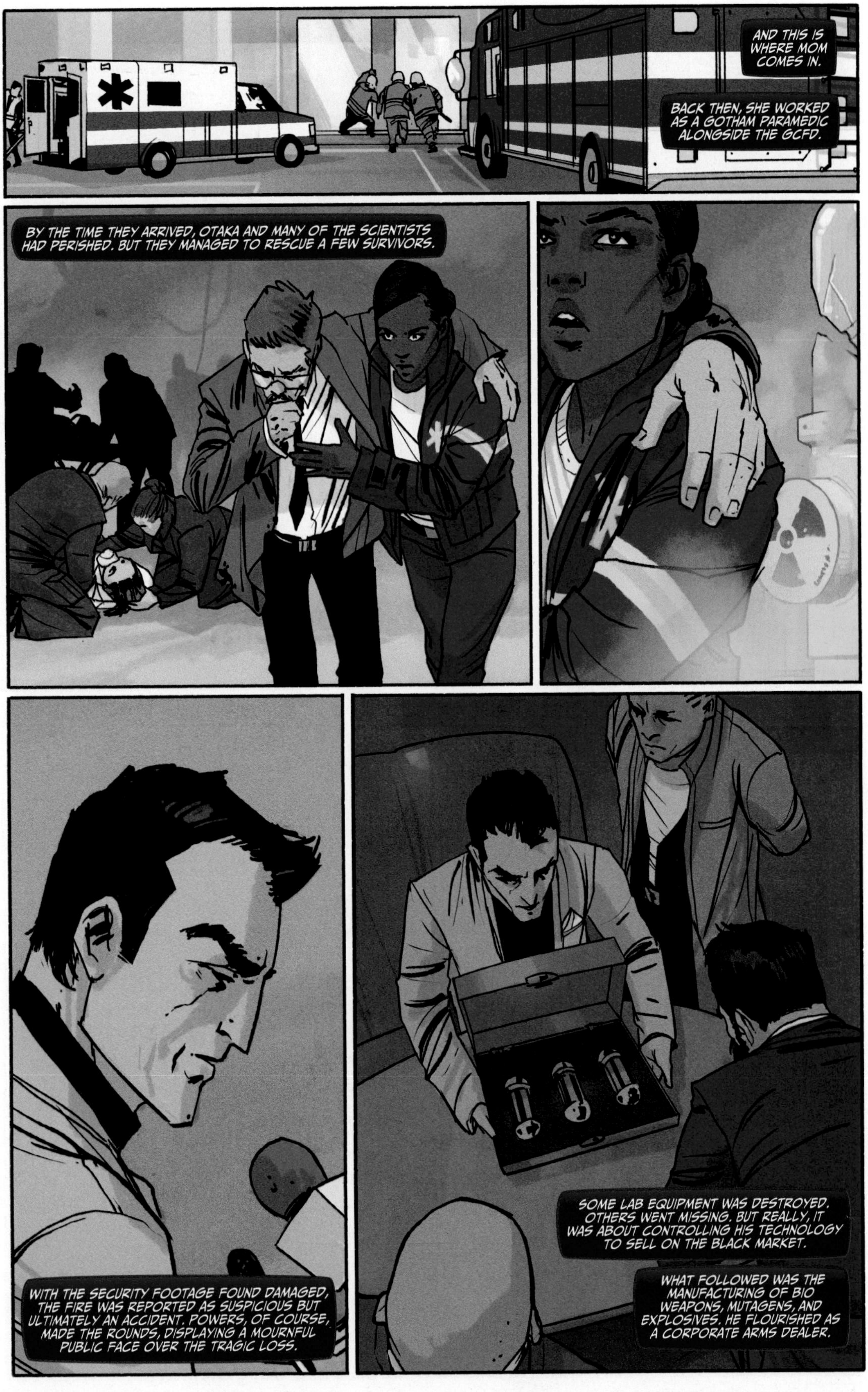
AND THIS IS WHERE MOM COMES IN.
BACK THEN, SHE WORKED AS A GOTHAM PARAMEDIC ALONGSIDE THE GCFD.
BY THE TIME THEY ARRIVED, OTAKA AND MANY OF THE SCIENTISTS HAD PERISHED. BUT THEY MANAGED TO RESCUE A FEW SURVIVORS.
WITH THE SECURITY FOOTAGE FOUND DAMAGED, THE FIRE WAS REPORTED AS SUSPICIOUS BUT ULTIMATELY AN ACCIDENT. POWERS, OF COURSE, MADE THE ROUNDS, DISPLAYING A MOURNFUL PUBLIC FACE OVER THE TRAGIC LOSS.
SOME LAB EQUIPMENT WAS DESTROYED. OTHERS WENT MISSING. BUT REALLY, IT WAS ABOUT CONTROLLING HIS TECHNOLOGY TO SELL ON THE BLACK MARKET.
WHAT FOLLOWED WAS THE MANUFACTURING OF BIO WEAPONS, MUTAGENS, AND EXPLOSIVES. HE FLOURISHED AS A CORPORATE ARMS DEALER.

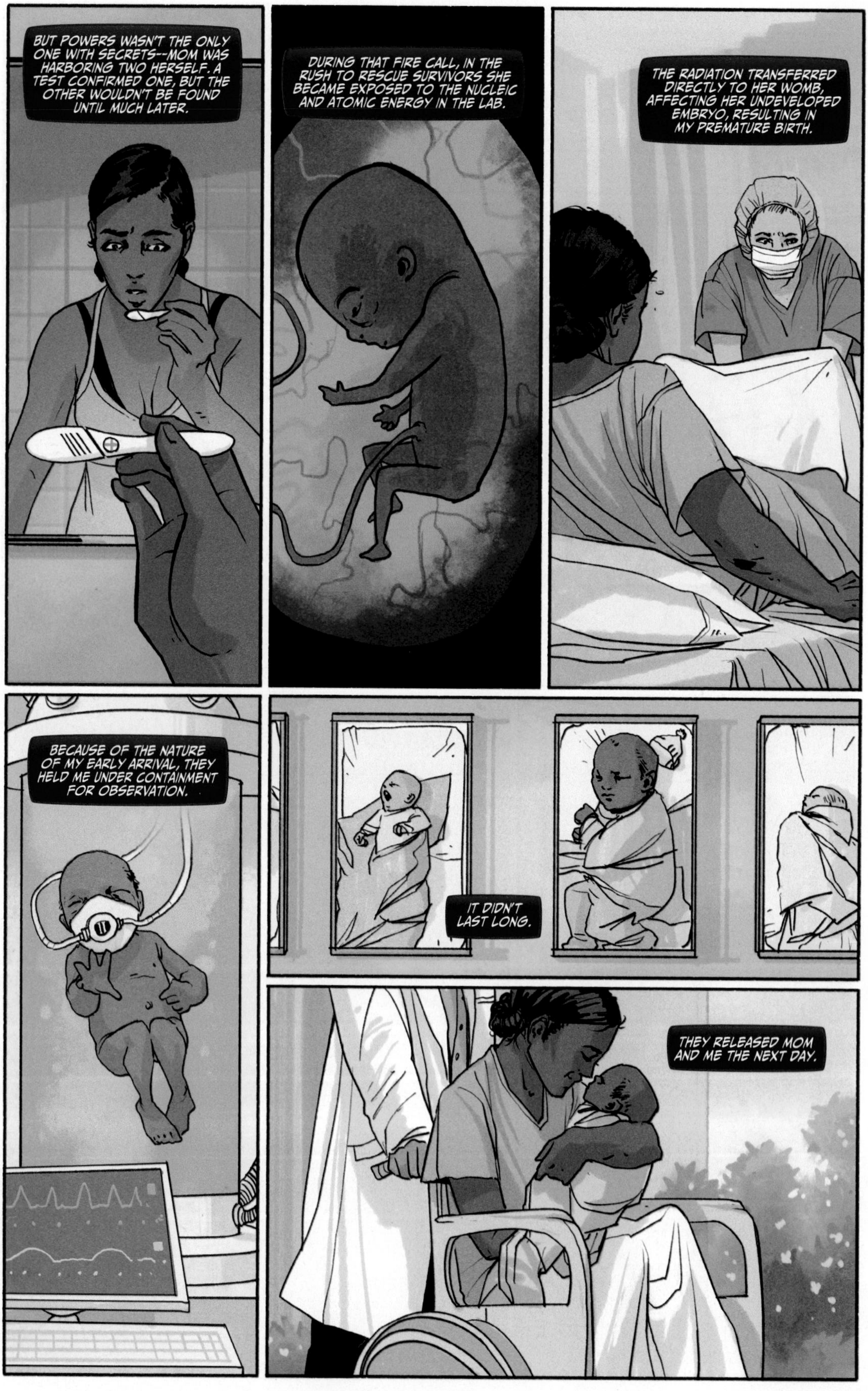
BUT POWERS WASN'T THE ONLY ONE WITH SECRETS--MOM WAS HARBORING TWO HERSELF. A TEST CONFIRMED ONE, BUT THE OTHER WOULDN'T BE FOUND UNTIL MUCH LATER.
DURING THAT FIRE CALL, IN THE RUSH TO RESCUE SURVIVORS SHE BECAME EXPOSED TO THE NUCLEIC AND ATOMIC ENERGY IN THE LAB.
THE RADIATION TRANSFERRED DIRECTLY TO HER WOMB, AFFECTING HER UNDEVELOPED EMBRYO, RESULTING IN MY PREMATURE BIRTH.
BECAUSE OF THE NATURE OF MY EARLY ARRIVAL, THEY HELD ME UNDER CONTAINMENT FOR OBSERVATION.
IT DIDN'T LAST LONG.
THEY RELEASED MOM AND ME THE NEXT DAY.

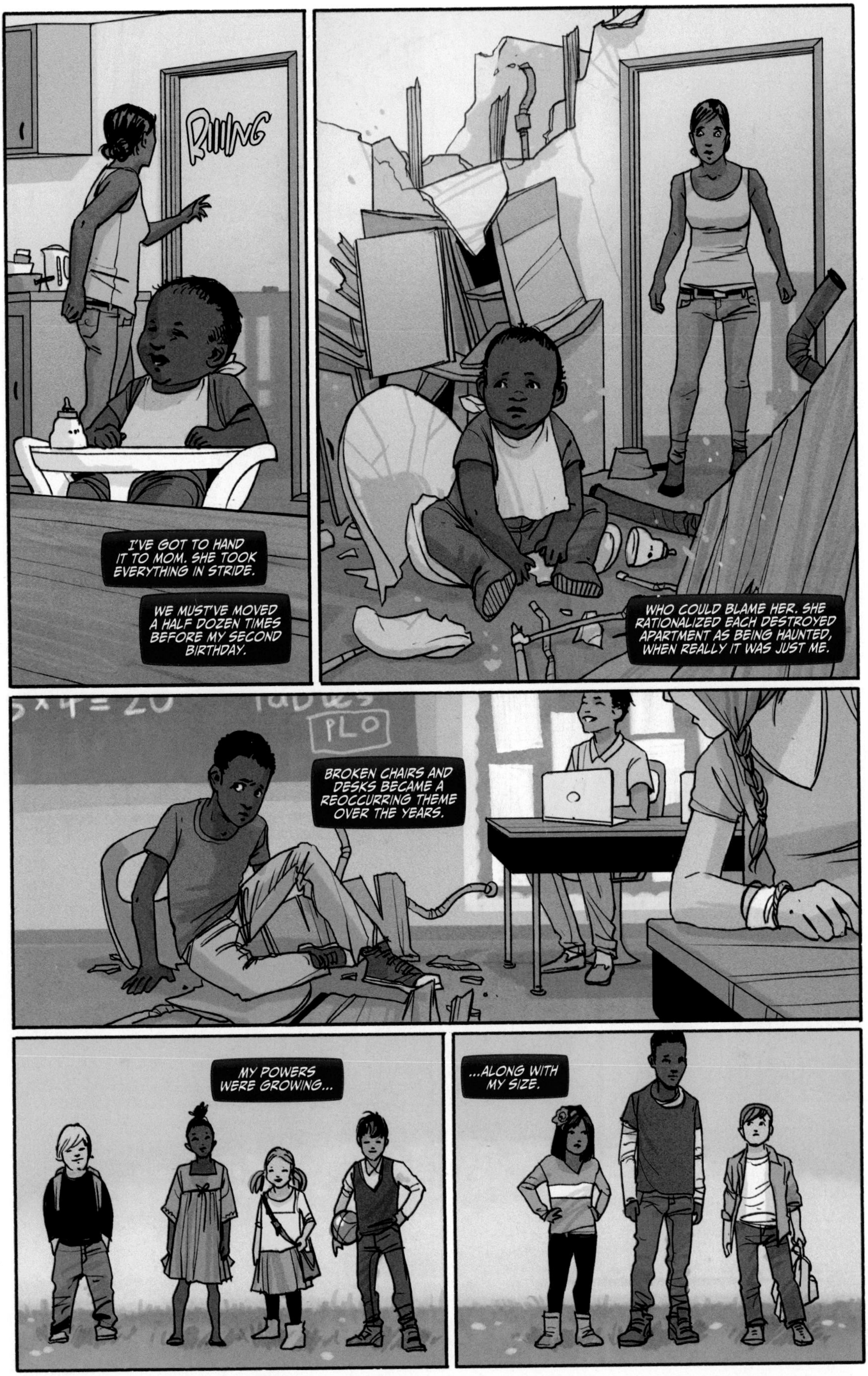
RIIIING
I'VE GOT TO HAND IT TO MOM. SHE TOOK EVERYTHING IN STRIDE.
WE MUST'VE MOVED A HALF DOZEN TIMES BEFORE MY SECOND BIRTHDAY.
WHO COULD BLAME HER. SHE RATIONALIZED EACH DESTROYED APARTMENT AS BEING HAUNTED, WHEN REALLY IT WAS JUST ME.
PLO
BROKEN CHAIRS AND DESKS BECAME A REOCCURRING THEME OVER THE YEARS.
MY POWERS WERE GROWING...
...ALONG WITH MY SIZE.

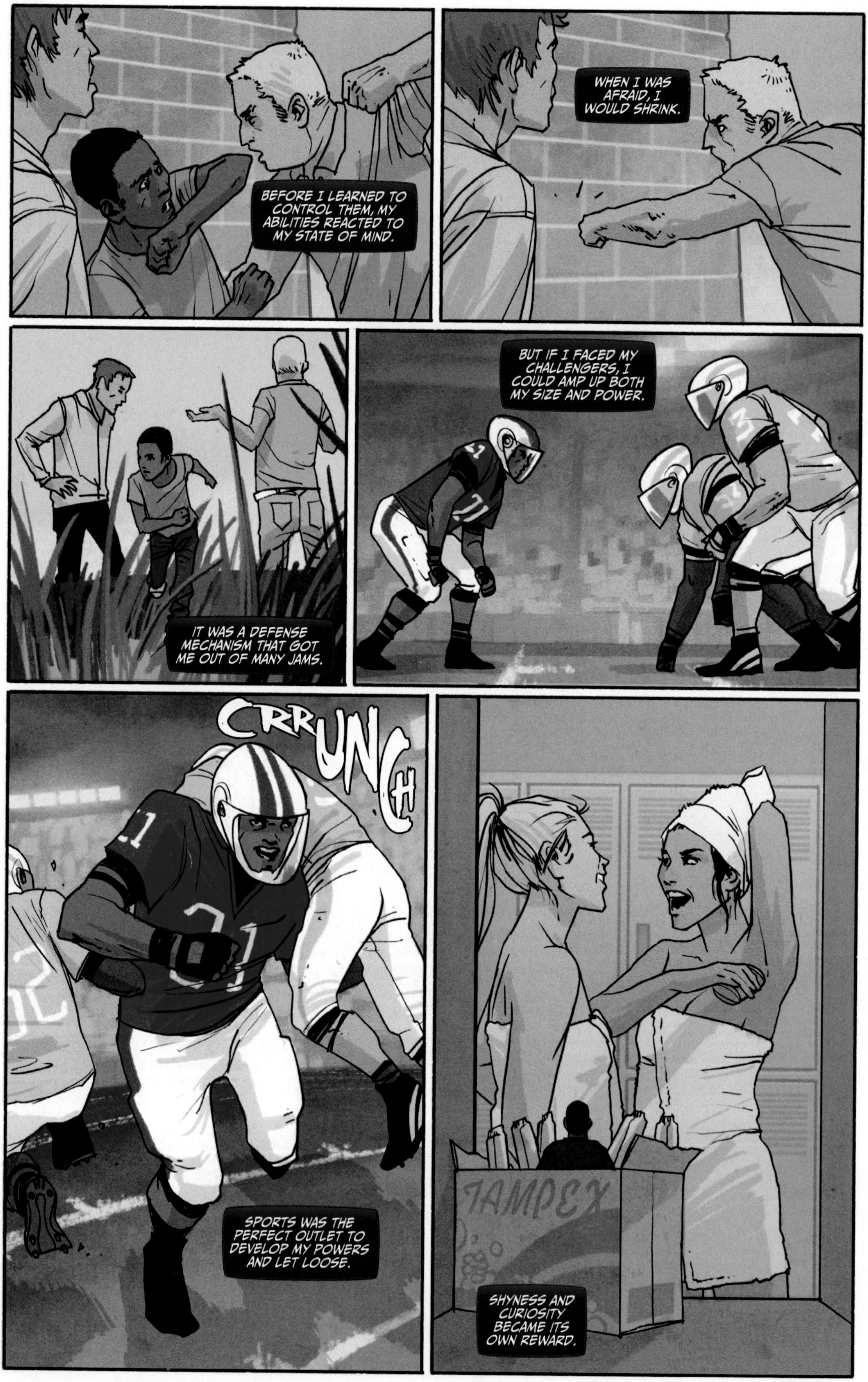
BEFORE I LEARNED TO CONTROL THEM, MY ABILITIES REACTED TO MY STATE OF MIND.
WHEN I WAS AFRAID, I WOULD SHRINK.
IT WAS A DEFENSE MECHANISM THAT GOT ME OUT OF MANY JAMS.
BUT IF I FACED MY CHALLENGERS, I COULD AMP UP BOTH MY SIZE AND POWER.
CRRUNCH
SPORTS WAS THE PERFECT OUTLET TO DEVELOP MY POWERS AND LET LOOSE.
TAMPEX
SHYNESS AND CURIOSITY BECAME ITS OWN REWARD.

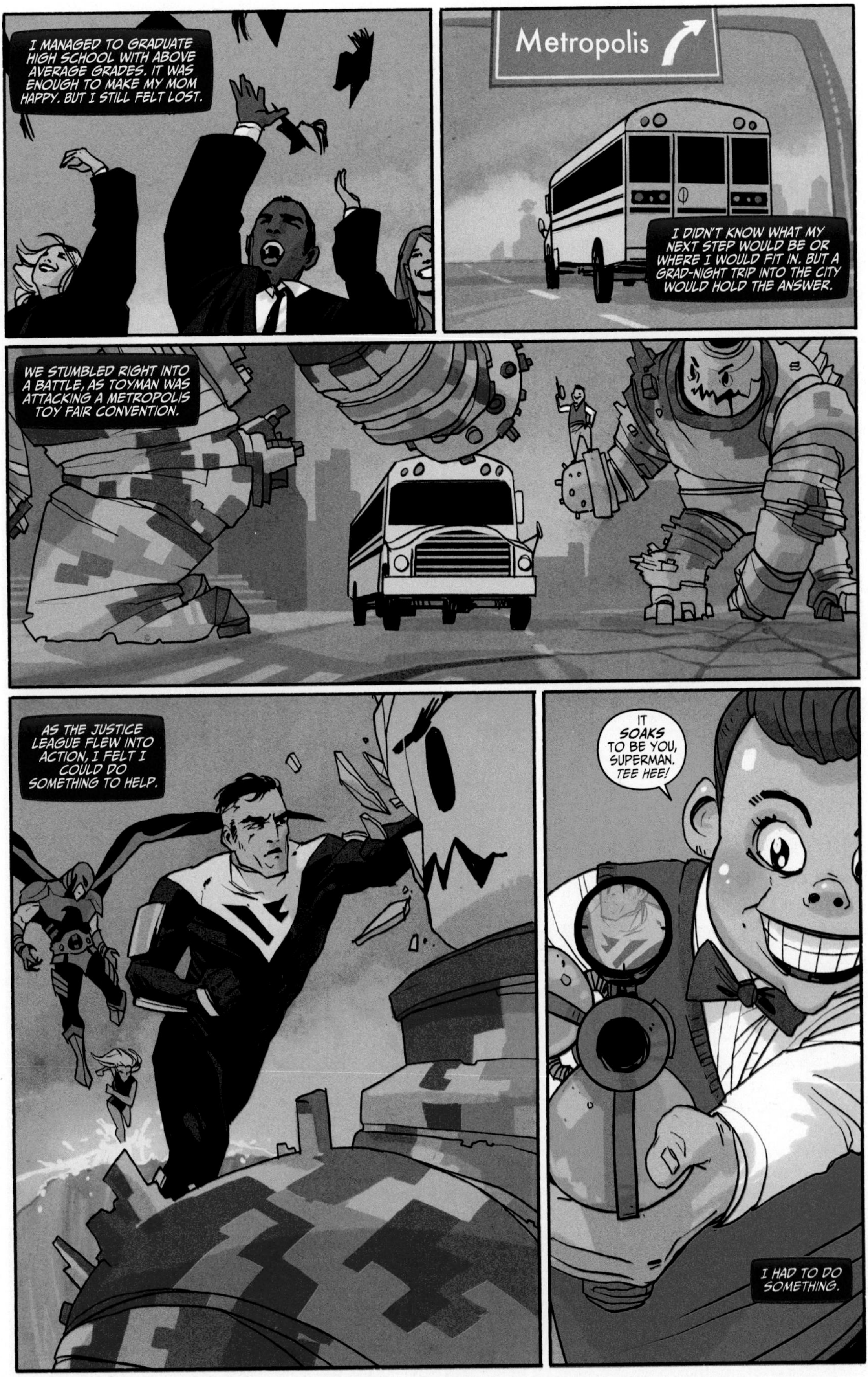
I MANAGED TO GRADUATE HIGH SCHOOL WITH ABOVE AVERAGE GRADES. IT WAS ENOUGH TO MAKE MY MOM HAPPY. BUT I STILL FELT LOST.
Metropolis
I DIDN'T KNOW WHAT MY NEXT STEP WOULD BE OR WHERE I WOULD FIT IN. BUT A GRAD-NIGHT TRIP INTO THE CITY WOULD HOLD THE ANSWER.
WE STUMBLED RIGHT INTO A BATTLE, AS TOYMAN WAS ATTACKING A METROPOLIS TOY FAIR CONVENTION.
AS THE JUSTICE LEAGUE FLEW INTO ACTION, I FELT I COULD DO SOMETHING TO HELP.
IT SOAKS TO BE YOU, SUPERMAN. TEE HEE!
I HAD TO DO SOMETHING.

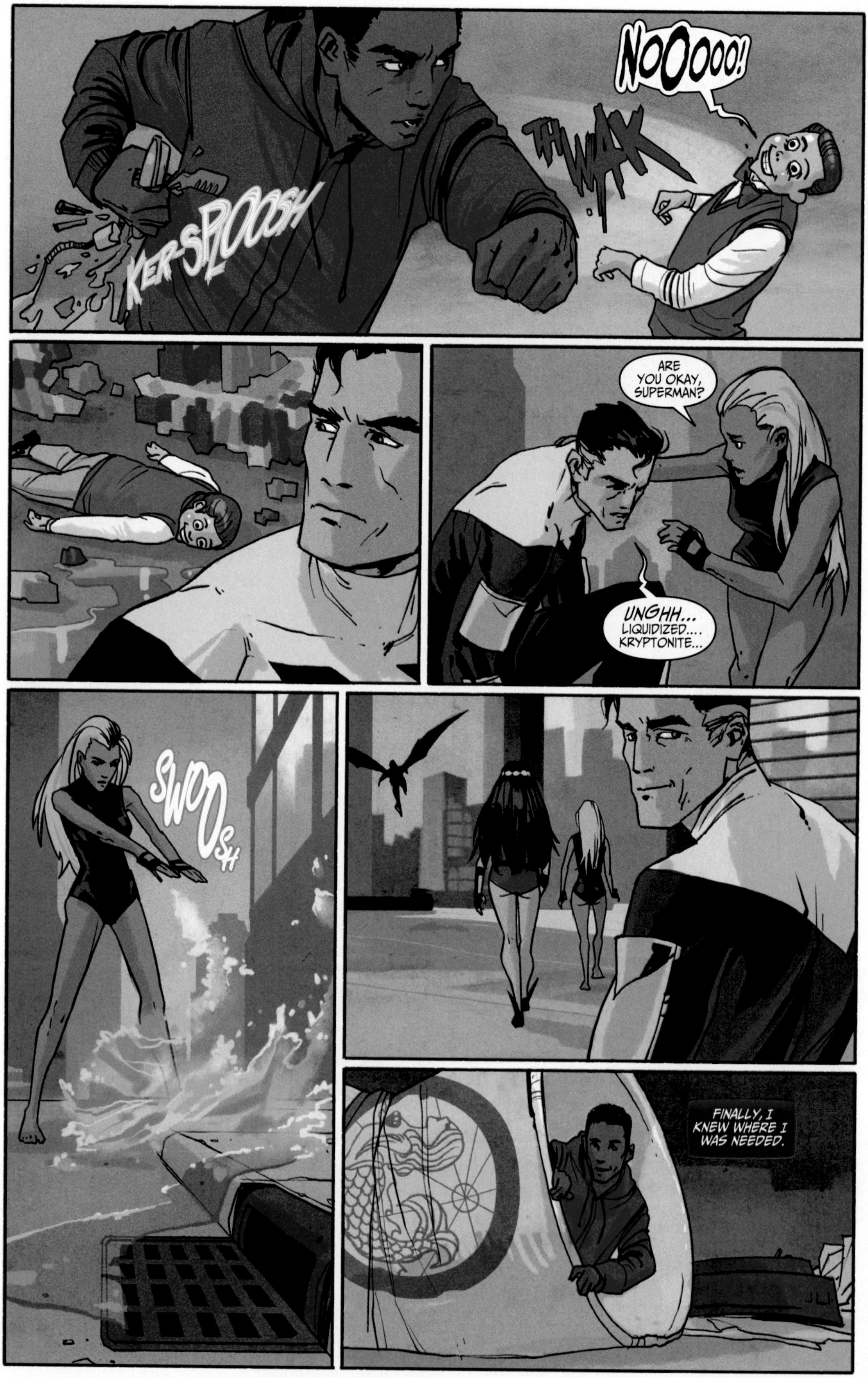
KER-SPLOOOSH
THWAK
NOOOOO!
ARE YOU OKAY, SUPERMAN?
UNGHH... LIQUIDIZED.... KRYPTONITE...
SWOOSH
FINALLY, I KNEW WHERE I WAS NEEDED.

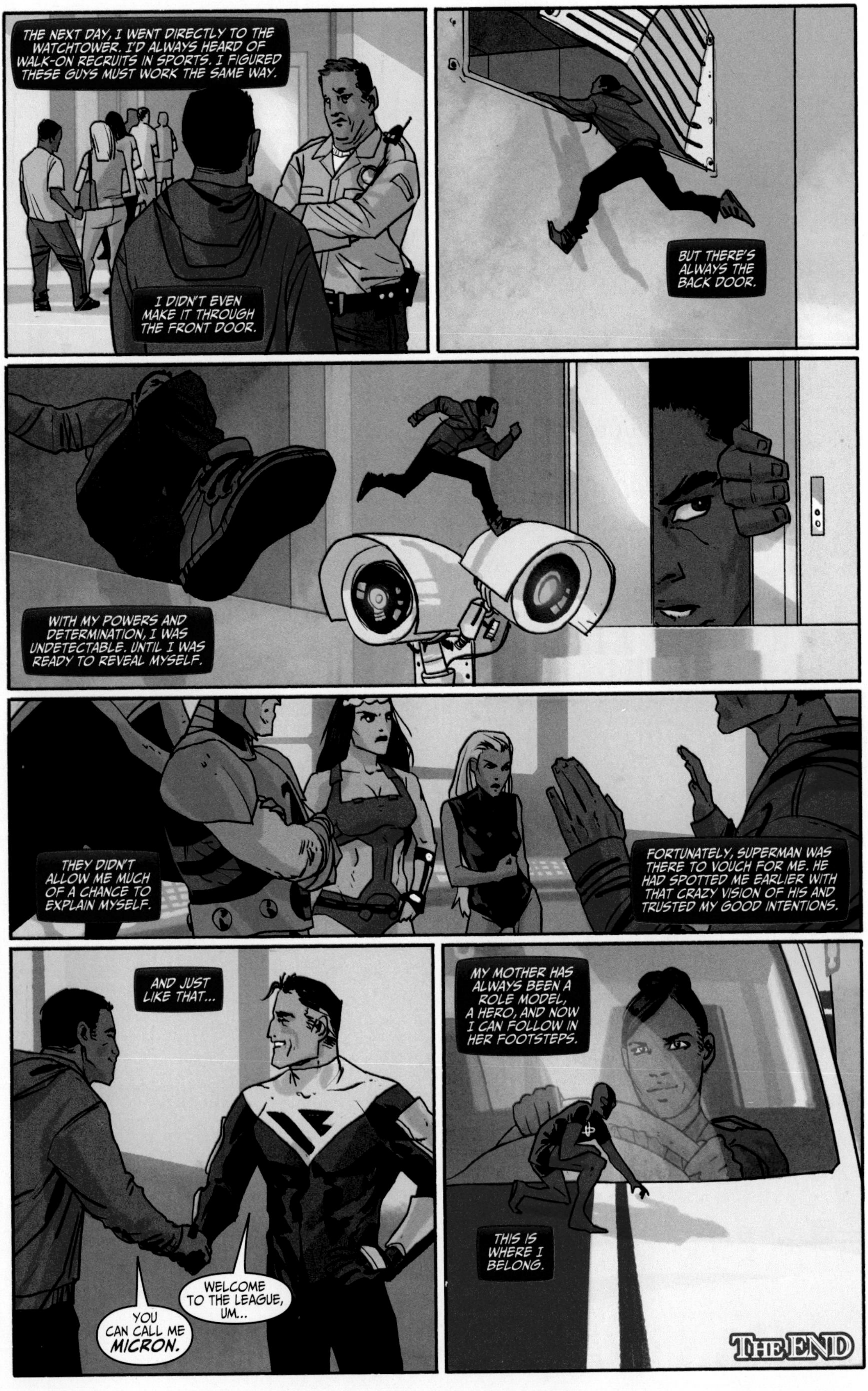
THE NEXT DAY, I WENT DIRECTLY TO THE WATCHTOWER. I'D ALWAYS HEARD OF WALK-ON RECRUITS IN SPORTS. I FIGURED THESE GUYS MUST WORK THE SAME WAY.
I DIDN'T EVEN MAKE IT THROUGH THE FRONT DOOR.
BUT THERE'S ALWAYS THE BACK DOOR.
WITH MY POWERS AND DETERMINATION, I WAS UNDETECTABLE. UNTIL I WAS READY TO REVEAL MYSELF.
THEY DIDN'T ALLOW ME MUCH OF A CHANCE TO EXPLAIN MYSELF.
FORTUNATELY, SUPERMAN WAS THERE TO VOUCH FOR ME. HE HAD SPOTTED ME EARLIER WITH THAT CRAZY VISION OF HIS AND TRUSTED MY GOOD INTENTIONS.
AND JUST LIKE THAT...
WELCOME TO THE LEAGUE, UM...
YOU CAN CALL ME MICRON.
MY MOTHER HAS ALWAYS BEEN A ROLE MODEL, A HERO, AND NOW I CAN FOLLOW IN HER FOOTSTEPS.
THIS IS WHERE I BELONG.
THE END

JUSTICE LEAGUE
BEYOND

FLASHDRIVE

WRITTEN BY
DEREK FRIDOLFS

PENCILS BY
JORGE CORONA

INKS BY
DEREK FRIDOLFS

COLORS BY
RANDY MAYOR and **NICK FILARDI**

ORIGINS:
THE FLASH

WRITTEN BY
DEREK FRIDOLFS

ART BY
MARCUS TO

COLORS BY
IAN HERRING

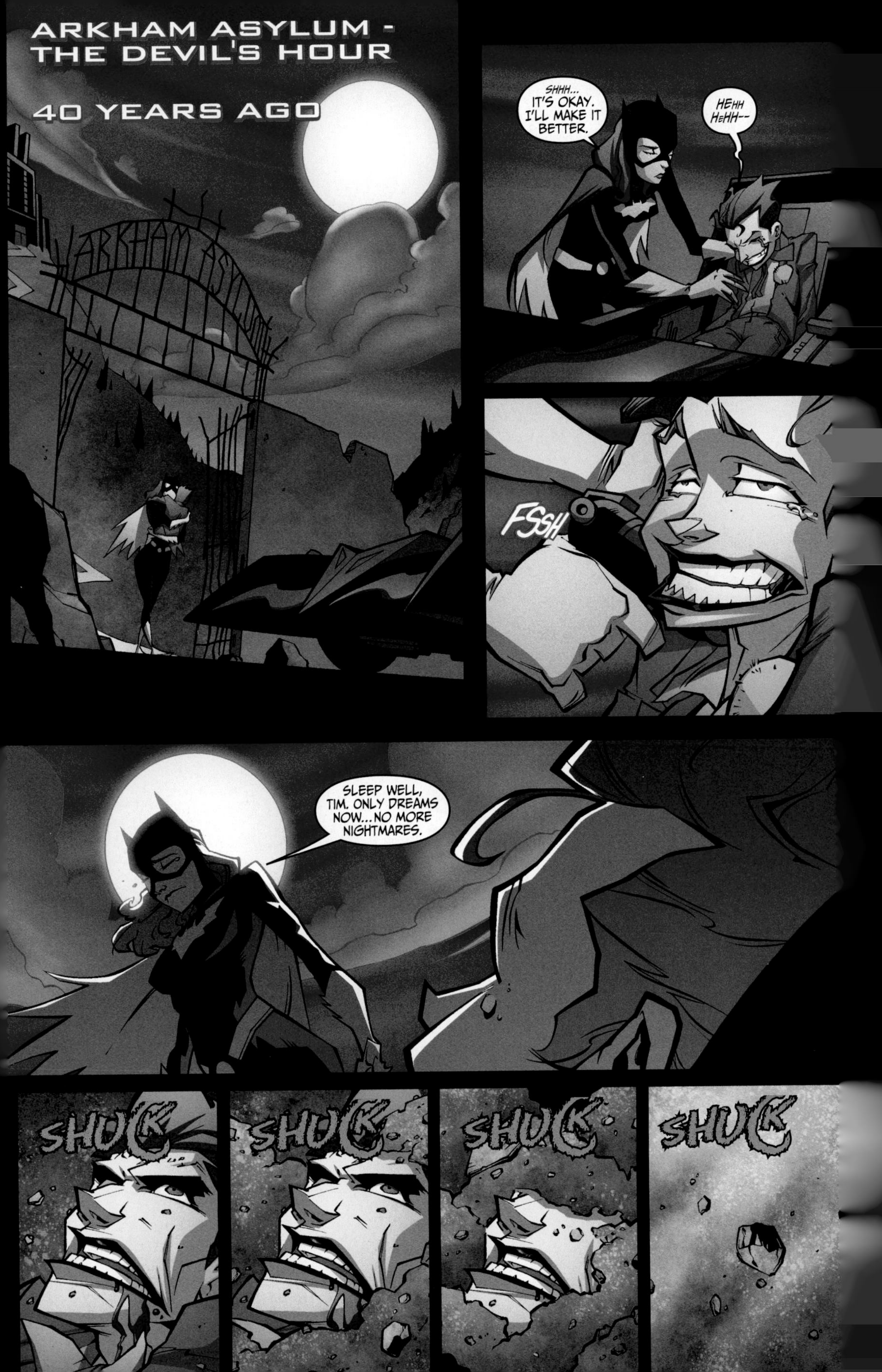
ARKHAM ASYLUM - THE DEVIL'S HOUR
40 YEARS AGO
ARKHAM ASYLUM
SHHH... IT'S OKAY. I'LL MAKE IT BETTER.
HEHH HEHH--
FSSH
SLEEP WELL, TIM. ONLY DREAMS NOW...NO MORE NIGHTMARES.
SHUCK
SHUCK
SHUCK
SHUCK

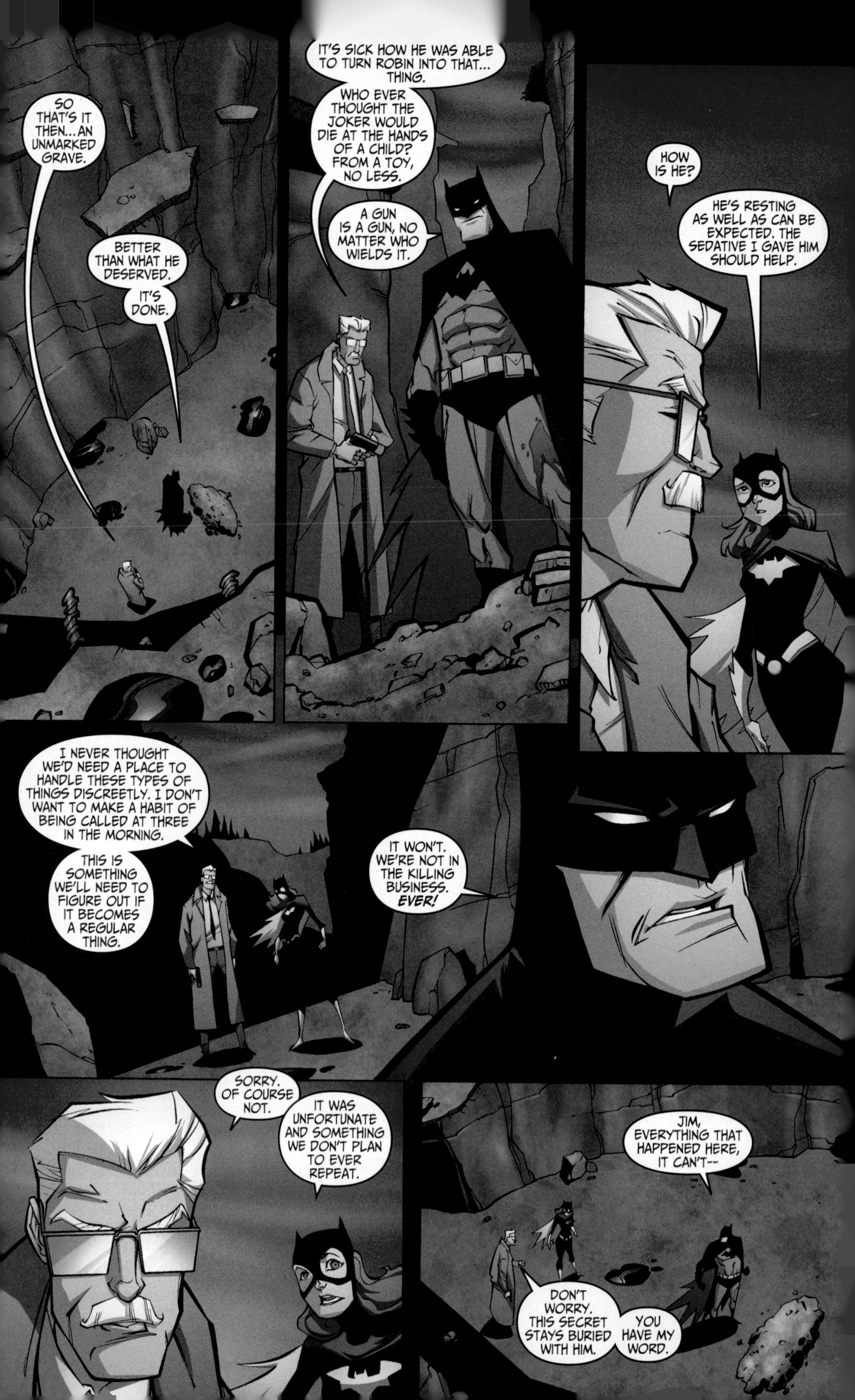
SO THAT'S IT THEN...AN UNMARKED GRAVE.
BETTER THAN WHAT HE DESERVED.
IT'S DONE.
IT'S SICK HOW HE WAS ABLE TO TURN ROBIN INTO THAT... THING.
WHO EVER THOUGHT THE JOKER WOULD DIE AT THE HANDS OF A CHILD? FROM A TOY, NO LESS.
A GUN IS A GUN, NO MATTER WHO WIELDS IT.
HOW IS HE?
HE'S RESTING AS WELL AS CAN BE EXPECTED. THE SEDATIVE I GAVE HIM SHOULD HELP.
I NEVER THOUGHT WE'D NEED A PLACE TO HANDLE THESE TYPES OF THINGS DISCREETLY. I DON'T WANT TO MAKE A HABIT OF BEING CALLED AT THREE IN THE MORNING.
THIS IS SOMETHING WE'LL NEED TO FIGURE OUT IF IT BECOMES A REGULAR THING.
IT WON'T. WE'RE NOT IN THE KILLING BUSINESS. *EVER!*
SORRY. OF COURSE NOT.
IT WAS UNFORTUNATE AND SOMETHING WE DON'T PLAN TO EVER REPEAT.
JIM, EVERYTHING THAT HAPPENED HERE, IT CAN'T--
DON'T WORRY. THIS SECRET STAYS BURIED WITH HIM.
YOU HAVE MY WORD.

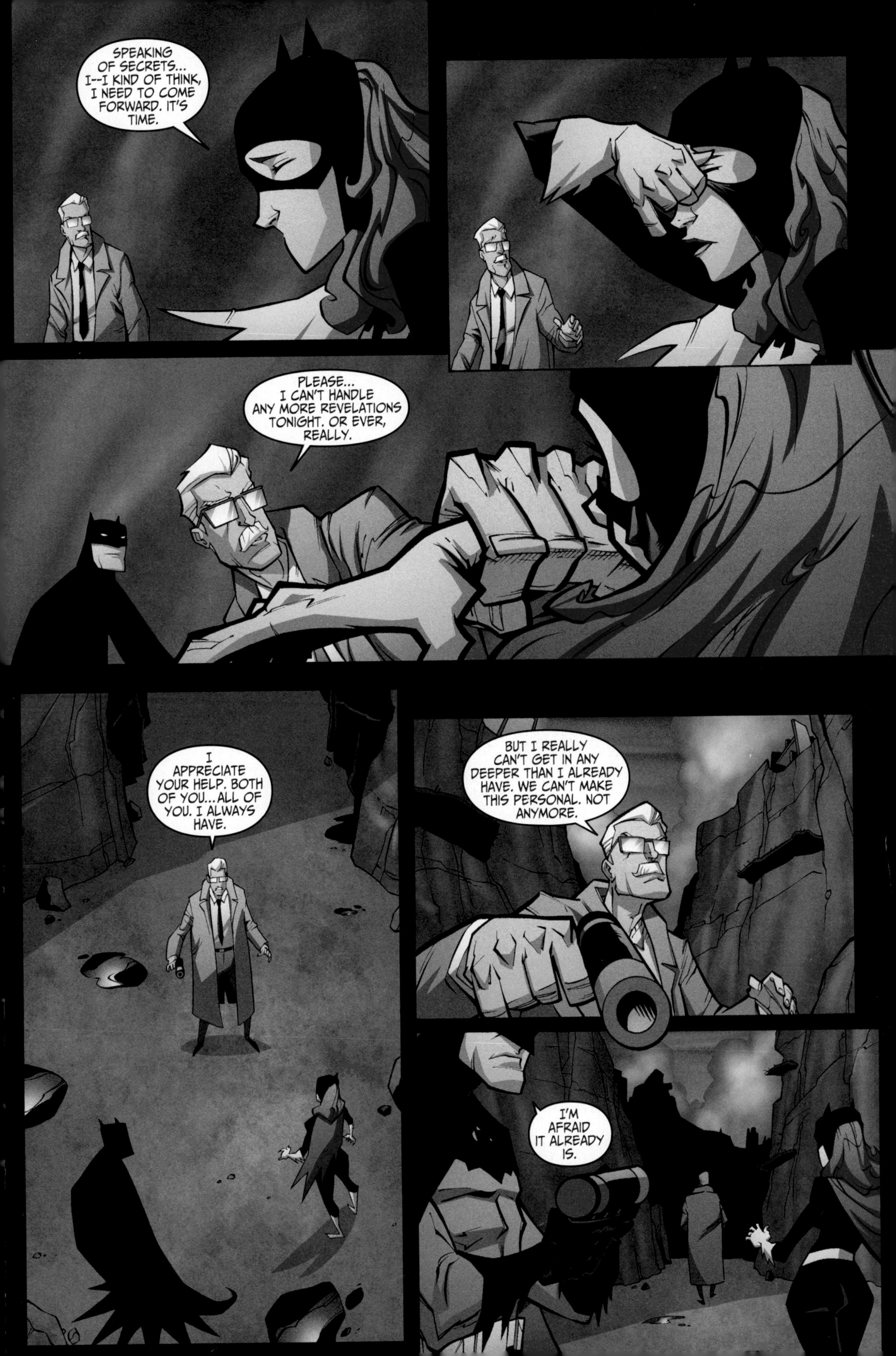
SPEAKING OF SECRETS... I--I KIND OF THINK, I NEED TO COME FORWARD. IT'S TIME.
PLEASE... I CAN'T HANDLE ANY MORE REVELATIONS TONIGHT. OR EVER, REALLY.
I APPRECIATE YOUR HELP. BOTH OF YOU...ALL OF YOU. I ALWAYS HAVE.
BUT I REALLY CAN'T GET IN ANY DEEPER THAN I ALREADY HAVE. WE CAN'T MAKE THIS PERSONAL. NOT ANYMORE.
I'M AFRAID IT ALREADY IS.

JIM IS RIGHT.

ABOUT NOT MAKING THIS PERSONAL?

NO. THAT WE NEED SOMETHING IN PLACE TO DEAL WITH THESE TYPES OF SITUATIONS.

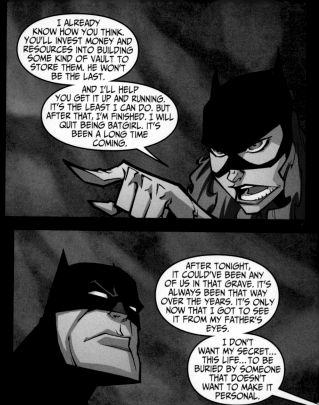

I ALREADY KNOW HOW YOU THINK. YOU'LL INVEST MONEY AND RESOURCES INTO BUILDING SOME KIND OF VAULT TO STORE THEM. HE WON'T BE THE LAST.

AND I'LL HELP YOU GET IT UP AND RUNNING. IT'S THE LEAST I CAN DO. BUT AFTER THAT, I'M FINISHED. I WILL QUIT BEING BATGIRL. IT'S BEEN A LONG TIME COMING.

AFTER TONIGHT, IT COULD'VE BEEN ANY OF US IN THAT GRAVE. IT'S ALWAYS BEEN THAT WAY OVER THE YEARS. IT'S ONLY NOW THAT I GOT TO SEE IT FROM MY FATHER'S EYES.

I DON'T WANT MY SECRET... THIS LIFE...TO BE BURIED BY SOMEONE THAT DOESN'T WANT TO MAKE IT PERSONAL.

IS THIS ABOUT THAT INCIDENT WITH SCARECROW, WHERE YOU THOUGHT YOU DIED, PITTING YOUR FATHER AGAINST ME?

I WON'T LIE. THAT WAS THE FIRST STEP. TONIGHT WAS THE LAST.

I'VE...ALREADY PASSED SOME EARLY ENTRANCE EXAMS. I PLAN TO ENROLL IN THE ACADEMY IN THE FALL.

TO BECOME A REAL LAW OFFICER. NOT A VIGILANTE.

I'M SORRY.

I UNDERSTAND.

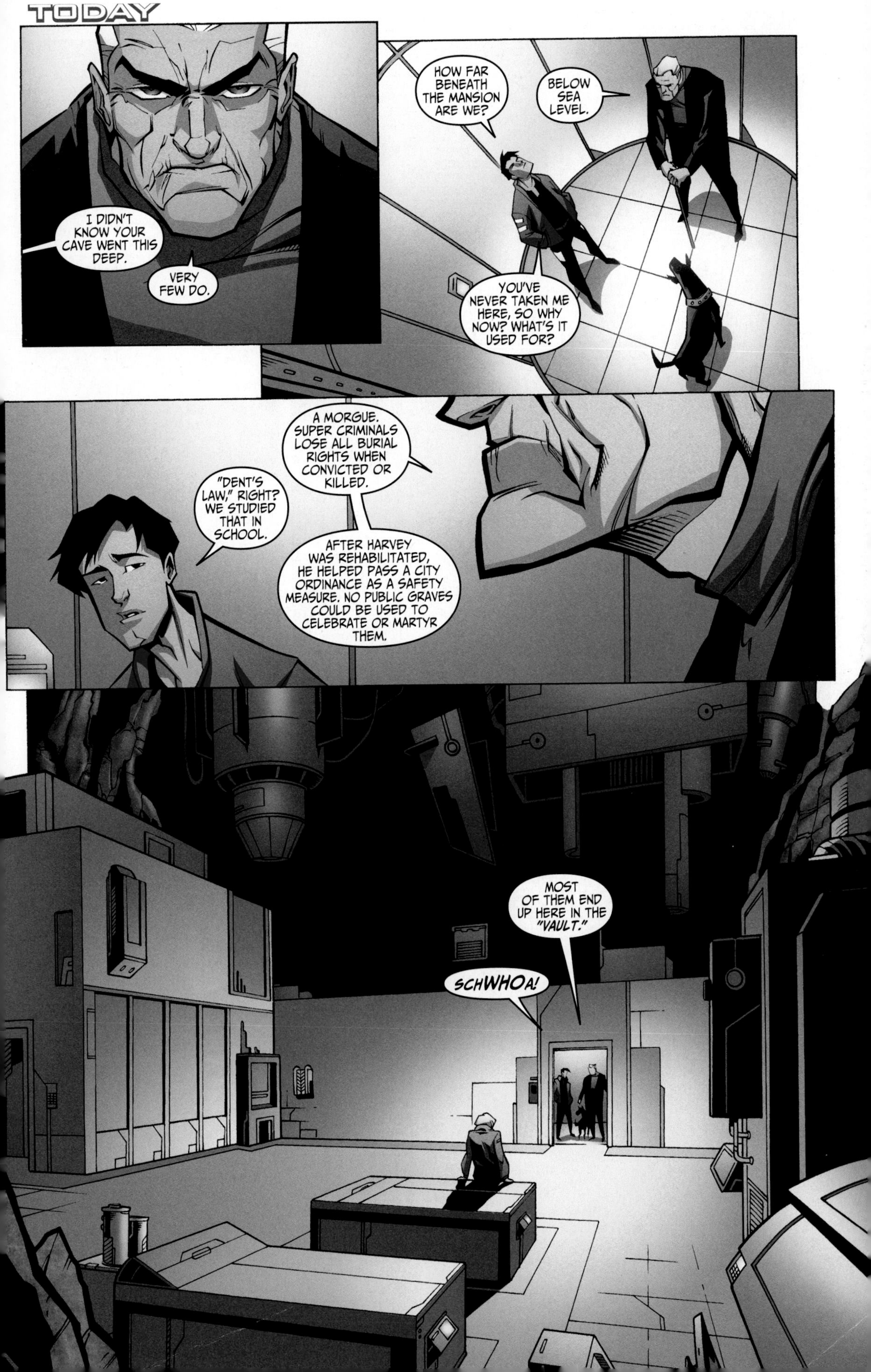
TODAY
I DIDN'T KNOW YOUR CAVE WENT THIS DEEP.
VERY FEW DO.
HOW FAR BENEATH THE MANSION ARE WE?
BELOW SEA LEVEL.
YOU'VE NEVER TAKEN ME HERE, SO WHY NOW? WHAT'S IT USED FOR?
A MORGUE. SUPER CRIMINALS LOSE ALL BURIAL RIGHTS WHEN CONVICTED OR KILLED.
"DENT'S LAW," RIGHT? WE STUDIED THAT IN SCHOOL.
AFTER HARVEY WAS REHABILITATED, HE HELPED PASS A CITY ORDINANCE AS A SAFETY MEASURE. NO PUBLIC GRAVES COULD BE USED TO CELEBRATE OR MARTYR THEM.
MOST OF THEM END UP HERE IN THE "VAULT."
SCHWHOA!

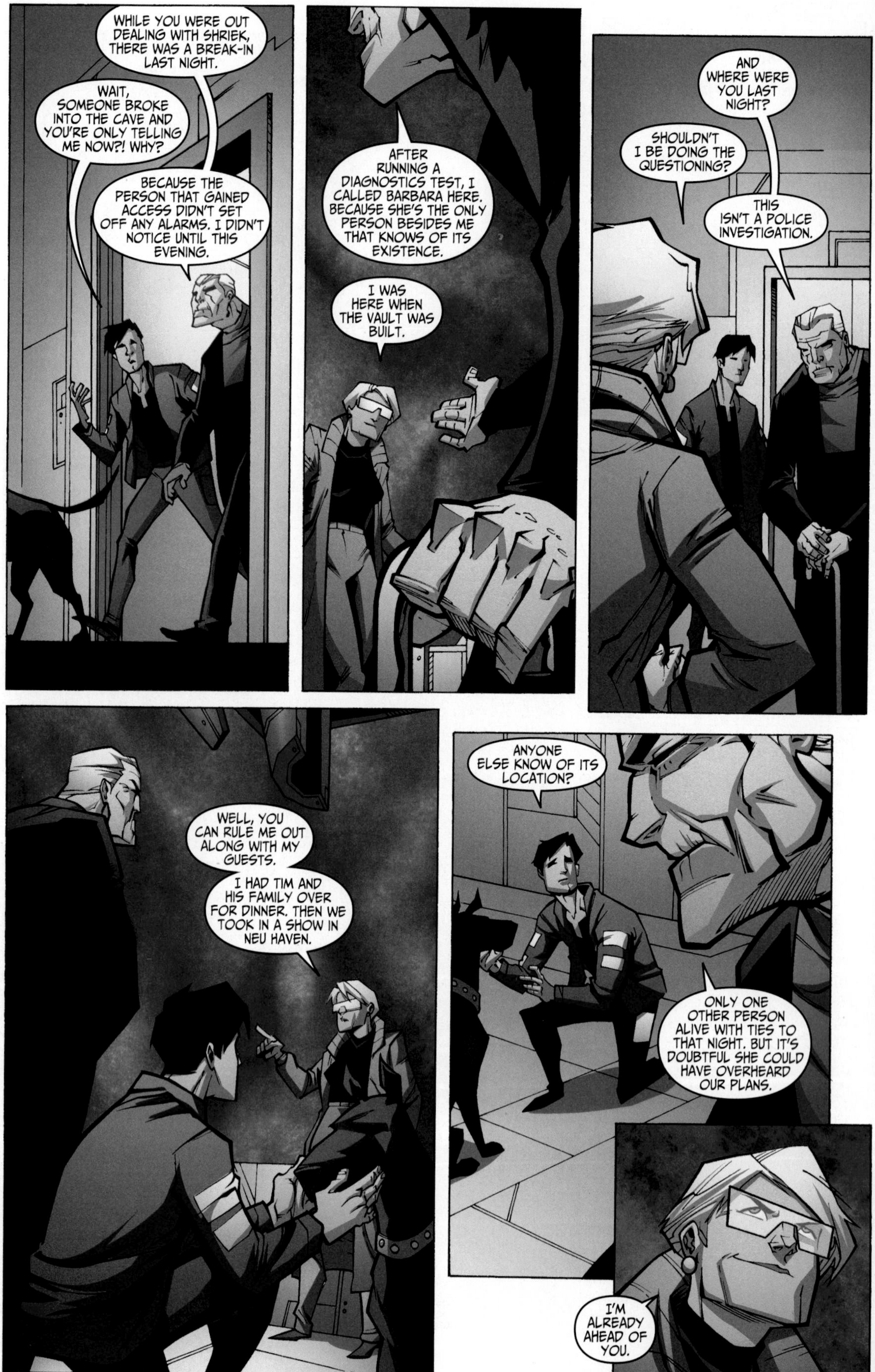
WHILE YOU WERE OUT DEALING WITH SHRIEK, THERE WAS A BREAK-IN LAST NIGHT.
WAIT, SOMEONE BROKE INTO THE CAVE AND YOU'RE ONLY TELLING ME NOW?! WHY?
BECAUSE THE PERSON THAT GAINED ACCESS DIDN'T SET OFF ANY ALARMS. I DIDN'T NOTICE UNTIL THIS EVENING.
AFTER RUNNING A DIAGNOSTICS TEST, I CALLED BARBARA HERE. BECAUSE SHE'S THE ONLY PERSON BESIDES ME THAT KNOWS OF ITS EXISTENCE.
I WAS HERE WHEN THE VAULT WAS BUILT.
AND WHERE WERE YOU LAST NIGHT?
SHOULDN'T I BE DOING THE QUESTIONING?
THIS ISN'T A POLICE INVESTIGATION.
WELL, YOU CAN RULE ME OUT ALONG WITH MY GUESTS.
I HAD TIM AND HIS FAMILY OVER FOR DINNER. THEN WE TOOK IN A SHOW IN NEU HAVEN.
ANYONE ELSE KNOW OF ITS LOCATION?
ONLY ONE OTHER PERSON ALIVE WITH TIES TO THAT NIGHT. BUT IT'S DOUBTFUL SHE COULD HAVE OVERHEARD OUR PLANS.
I'M ALREADY AHEAD OF YOU.

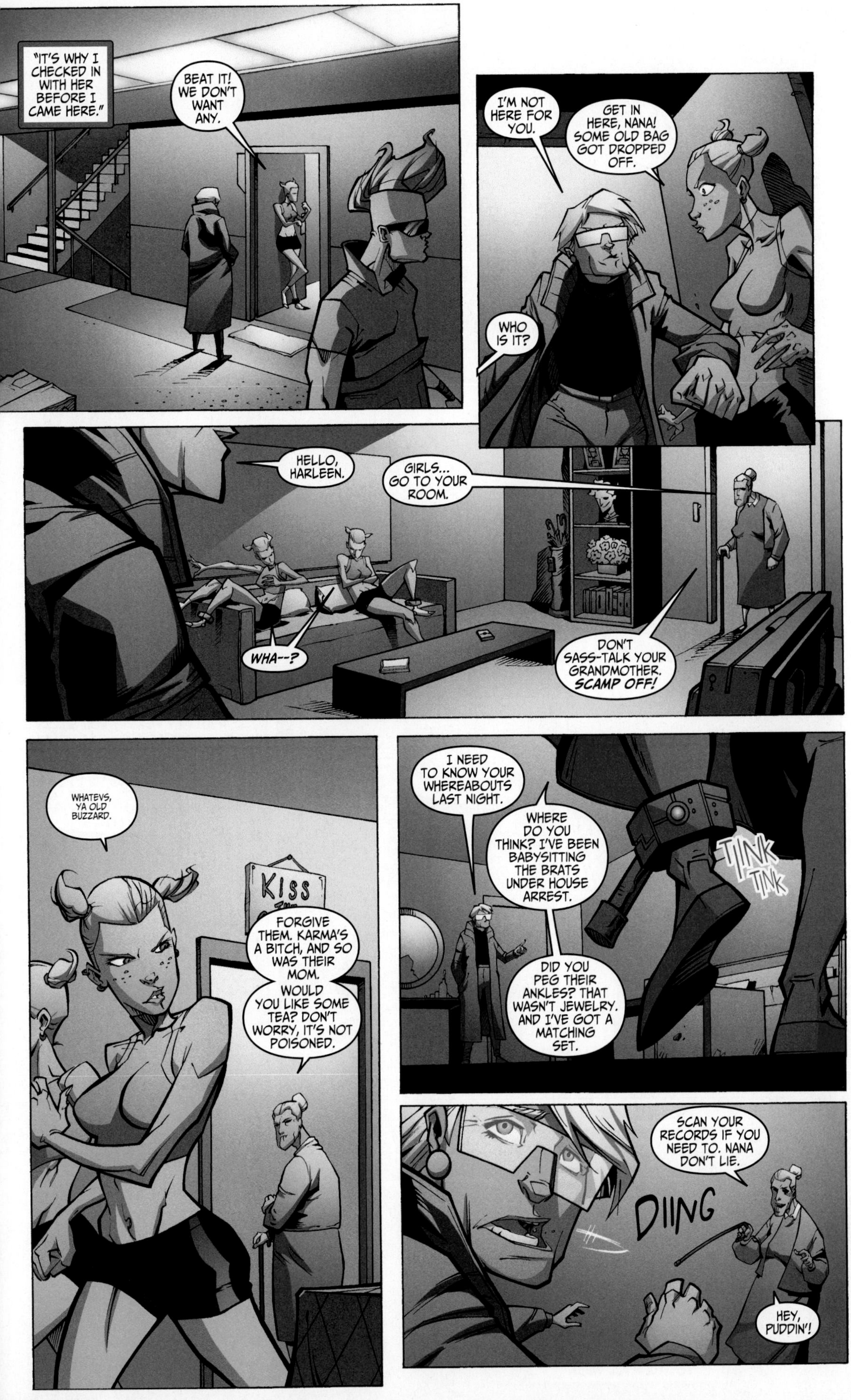
"IT'S WHY I CHECKED IN WITH HER BEFORE I CAME HERE."
BEAT IT! WE DON'T WANT ANY.
I'M NOT HERE FOR YOU.
GET IN HERE, NANA! SOME OLD BAG GOT DROPPED OFF.
WHO IS IT?
HELLO, HARLEEN.
GIRLS... GO TO YOUR ROOM.
WHA--?
DON'T SASS-TALK YOUR GRANDMOTHER. SCAMP OFF!
WHATEVS, YA OLD BUZZARD.
KISS
FORGIVE THEM. KARMA'S A BITCH, AND SO WAS THEIR MOM.
WOULD YOU LIKE SOME TEA? DON'T WORRY, IT'S NOT POISONED.
I NEED TO KNOW YOUR WHEREABOUTS LAST NIGHT.
WHERE DO YOU THINK? I'VE BEEN BABYSITTING THE BRATS UNDER HOUSE ARREST.
TINK TINK
DID YOU PEG THEIR ANKLES? THAT WASN'T JEWELRY. AND I'VE GOT A MATCHING SET.
SCAN YOUR RECORDS IF YOU NEED TO. NANA DON'T LIE.
DIING
HEY, PUDDIN'!

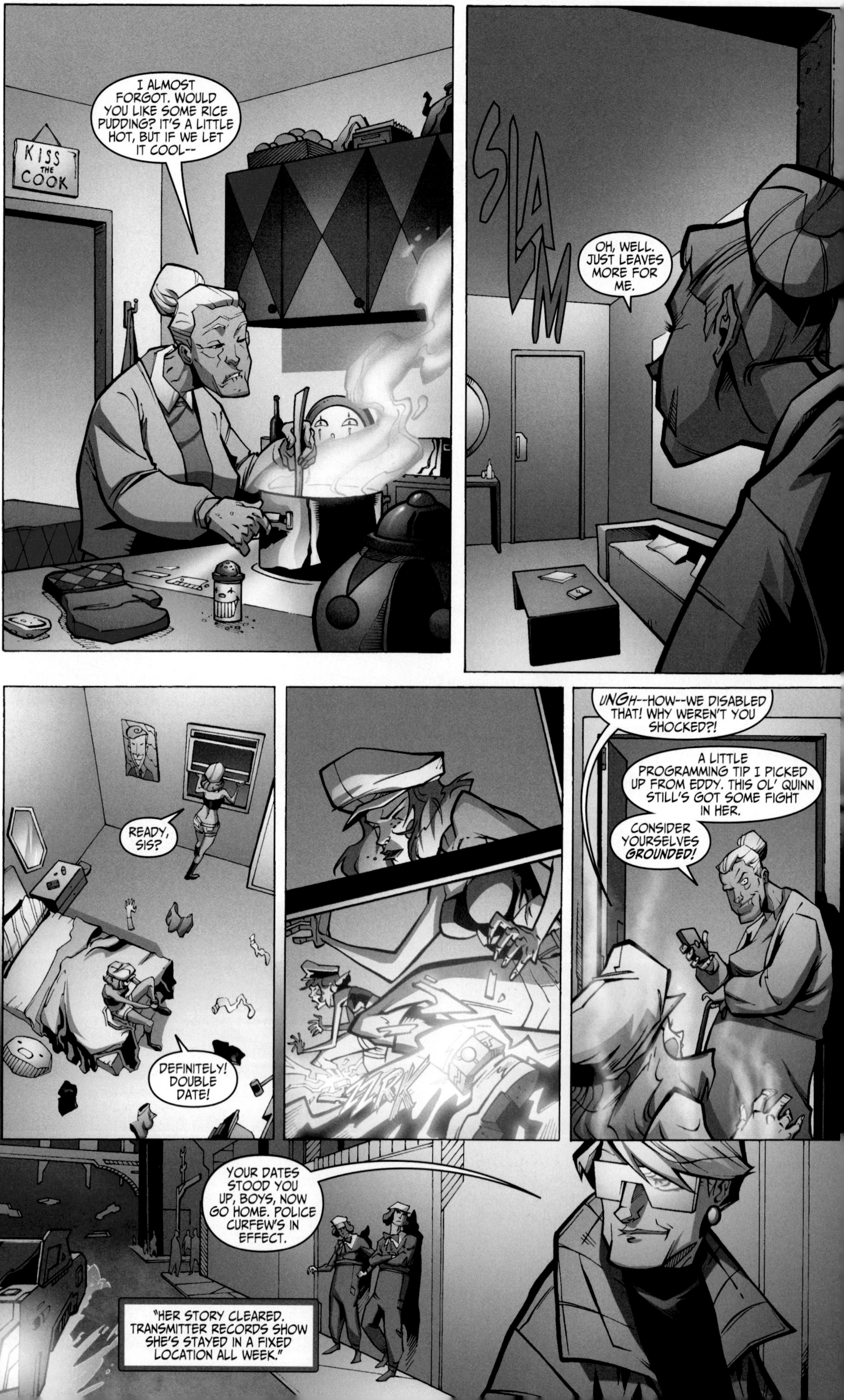
KISS THE COOK
I ALMOST FORGOT. WOULD YOU LIKE SOME RICE PUDDING? IT'S A LITTLE HOT, BUT IF WE LET IT COOL--
SLAM
OH, WELL. JUST LEAVES MORE FOR ME.
READY, SIS?
DEFINITELY! DOUBLE DATE!
ZZRK
UNGH--HOW--WE DISABLED THAT! WHY WEREN'T YOU SHOCKED?!
A LITTLE PROGRAMMING TIP I PICKED UP FROM EDDY. THIS OL' QUINN STILL'S GOT SOME FIGHT IN HER.
CONSIDER YOURSELVES GROUNDED!
YOUR DATES STOOD YOU UP, BOYS, NOW GO HOME. POLICE CURFEW'S IN EFFECT.
"HER STORY CLEARED. TRANSMITTER RECORDS SHOW SHE'S STAYED IN A FIXED LOCATION ALL WEEK."

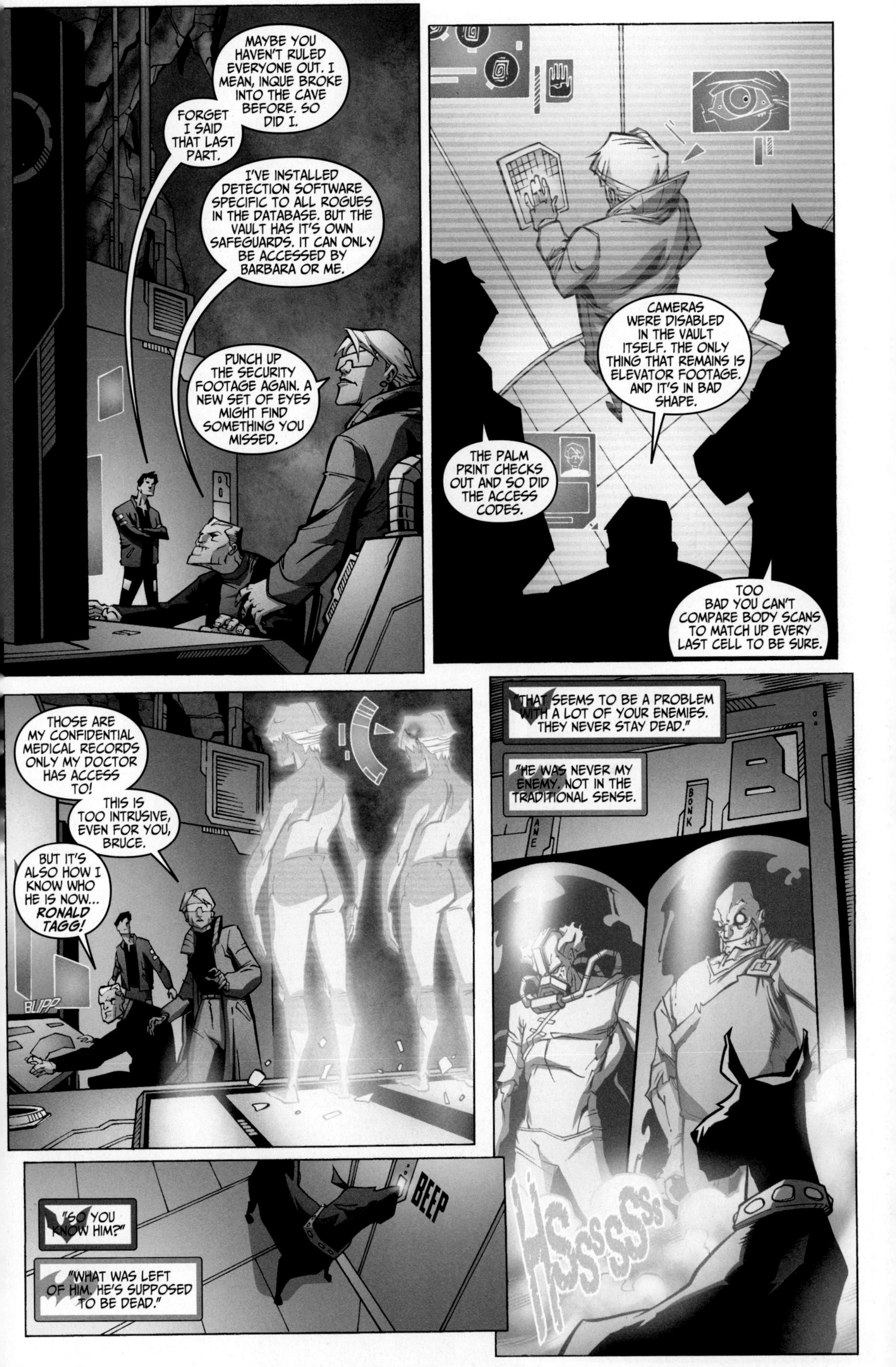
MAYBE YOU HAVEN'T RULED EVERYONE OUT. I MEAN, INQUE BROKE INTO THE CAVE BEFORE. SO DID I.
FORGET I SAID THAT LAST PART.
I'VE INSTALLED DETECTION SOFTWARE SPECIFIC TO ALL ROGUES IN THE DATABASE. BUT THE VAULT HAS IT'S OWN SAFEGUARDS. IT CAN ONLY BE ACCESSED BY BARBARA OR ME.
PUNCH UP THE SECURITY FOOTAGE AGAIN. A NEW SET OF EYES MIGHT FIND SOMETHING YOU MISSED.
CAMERAS WERE DISABLED IN THE VAULT ITSELF. THE ONLY THING THAT REMAINS IS ELEVATOR FOOTAGE. AND IT'S IN BAD SHAPE.
THE PALM PRINT CHECKS OUT AND SO DID THE ACCESS CODES.
TOO BAD YOU CAN'T COMPARE BODY SCANS TO MATCH UP EVERY LAST CELL TO BE SURE.
THOSE ARE MY CONFIDENTIAL MEDICAL RECORDS ONLY MY DOCTOR HAS ACCESS TO!
THIS IS TOO INTRUSIVE, EVEN FOR YOU, BRUCE.
BUT IT'S ALSO HOW I KNOW WHO HE IS NOW... ***RONALD TAGG!***
BLIPP
BEEP
"SO YOU KNOW HIM?"
"WHAT WAS LEFT OF HIM. HE'S SUPPOSED TO BE DEAD."
"THAT SEEMS TO BE A PROBLEM WITH A LOT OF YOUR ENEMIES. THEY NEVER STAY DEAD."
"HE WAS NEVER MY ENEMY. NOT IN THE TRADITIONAL SENSE.
BONK
HISSSSSSS

"TAGG WORKED AT A MUSEUM DEVOTED TO SUPERHEROES IN GOTHAM. WHEN IT LOST ITS FUNDING, HE LOST HIS JOB.

"HE TURNED UP NEXT AS A PAPARAZZO, TRYING TO CAPTURE BATMAN IN ACTION. GOOD AT BLENDING INTO A CROWD.

"A BAD INFORMANT LED HIM TO AN ELDERLY KARL HELLFERN, LIVING UNDER AN ASSUMED NAME. KARL HAD GIVEN UP HIS DOCTOR DEATH IDENTITY OVER TWENTY YEARS AGO.

"WITNESSES SAW TAGG BREAK INTO HELLFERN'S CONDO, FOLLOWED BY AN EXPLOSION IN HIS BASEMENT LAB. THERE WERE NO SURVIVORS.

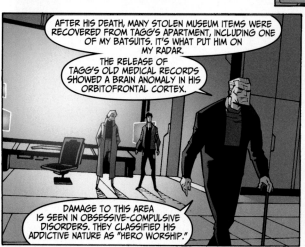

AFTER HIS DEATH, MANY STOLEN MUSEUM ITEMS WERE RECOVERED FROM TAGG'S APARTMENT, INCLUDING ONE OF MY BATSUITS. IT'S WHAT PUT HIM ON MY RADAR.

THE RELEASE OF TAGG'S OLD MEDICAL RECORDS SHOWED A BRAIN ANOMALY IN HIS ORBITOFRONTAL CORTEX.

DAMAGE TO THIS AREA IS SEEN IN OBSESSIVE-COMPULSIVE DISORDERS. THEY CLASSIFIED HIS ADDICTIVE NATURE AS "HERO WORSHIP."

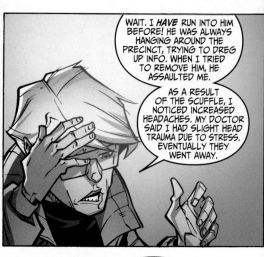

WAIT. I *HAVE* RUN INTO HIM BEFORE! HE WAS ALWAYS HANGING AROUND THE PRECINCT, TRYING TO DREG UP INFO. WHEN I TRIED TO REMOVE HIM, HE ASSAULTED ME.

AS A RESULT OF THE SCUFFLE, I NOTICED INCREASED HEADACHES. MY DOCTOR SAID I HAD SLIGHT HEAD TRAUMA DUE TO STRESS. EVENTUALLY THEY WENT AWAY.

THERE'S NO TELLING WHAT TYPES OF CHEMICALS TAGG WAS EXPOSED TO IN THAT EXPLOSION. BUT THE ANOMALY IN HIS BRAIN, I'VE SEEN IT BEFORE IN RUDY JONES... THE PARASITE. IT'S NOT AN EXACT MATCH, BUT IT DOES SHARE SIMILARITIES.

THE PARASITE WAS ABLE TO DRAIN ITS VICTIM'S POWER IN ORDER TO GET STRONGER. TAGG SEEMS TO DOWNLOAD EVERYTHING FROM ANYONE HE COMES IN CONTACT WITH...MEMORIES AND ATTRIBUTES. MAYBE EVEN A FALSE VISUAL.

IT EXPLAINS HOW HE WAS ABLE TO GET IN. EVERYTHING I KNOW, HE'D KNOW.

HE HAD ACCESS TO EVERYONE IN THIS VAULT. HE'S COLLECTING AND HE HASN'T STOPPED THERE.

I PUT A SPECIAL ADDITIVE IN THE EMBALMING FLUID. EVEN THE SLIGHTEST AMOUNT OF EXPOSURE TO HIS BODY COULD BE TRACKED.

I JUST ACCESSED THE LEAGUE'S CITADEL SATELLITE TO PINPOINT HIS LOCATION. HE'S IN CENTRAL CITY. THE REOPENING OF THE FLASH MUSEUM IS THIS WEEKEND.

TERRY... CALL THE LEAGUE!

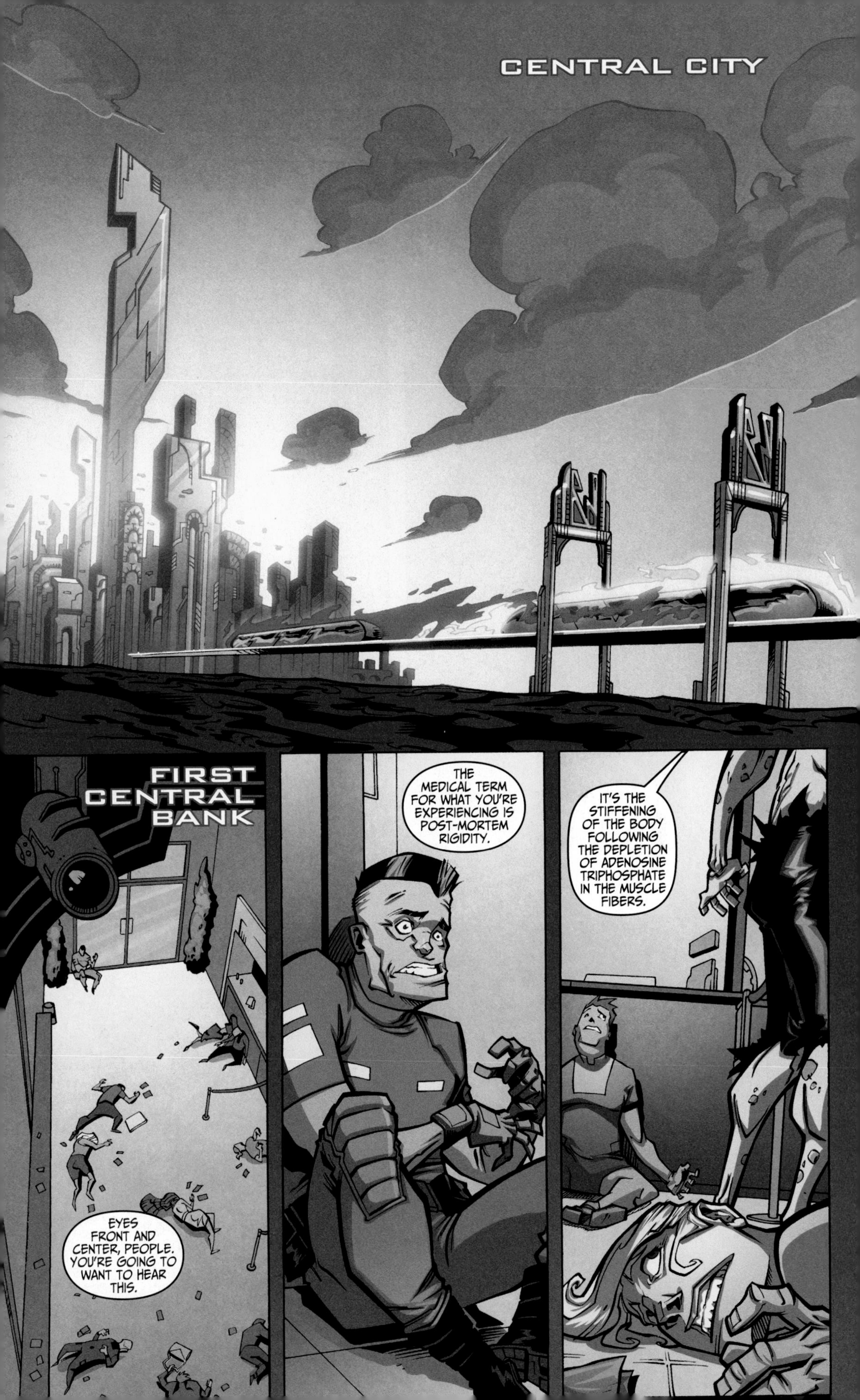
CENTRAL CITY
FIRST CENTRAL BANK
EYES FRONT AND CENTER, PEOPLE. YOU'RE GOING TO WANT TO HEAR THIS.
THE MEDICAL TERM FOR WHAT YOU'RE EXPERIENCING IS POST-MORTEM RIGIDITY.
IT'S THE STIFFENING OF THE BODY FOLLOWING THE DEPLETION OF ADENOSINE TRIPHOSPHATE IN THE MUSCLE FIBERS.

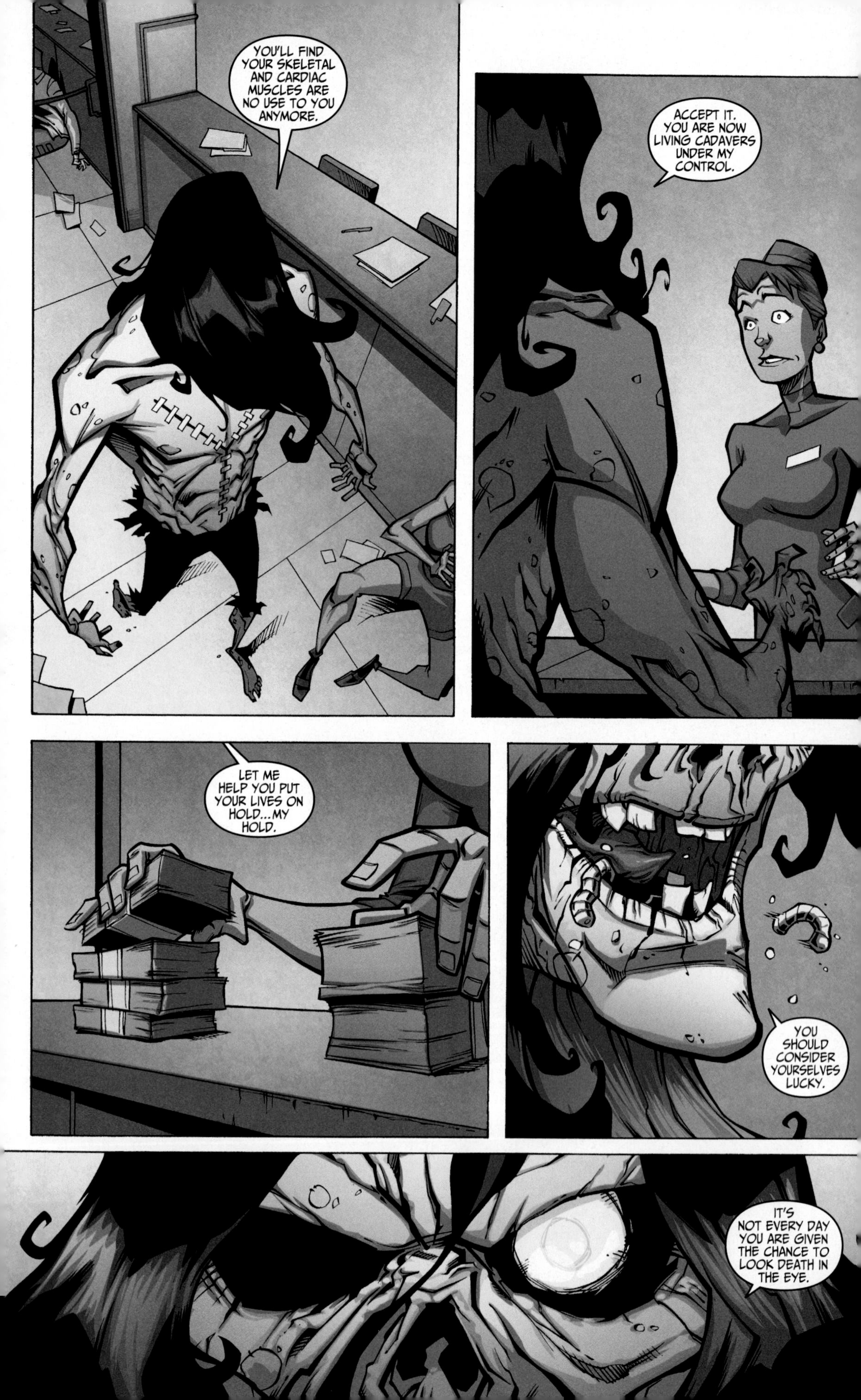
YOU'LL FIND YOUR SKELETAL AND CARDIAC MUSCLES ARE NO USE TO YOU ANYMORE.
ACCEPT IT. YOU ARE NOW LIVING CADAVERS UNDER MY CONTROL.
LET ME HELP YOU PUT YOUR LIVES ON HOLD...MY HOLD.
YOU SHOULD CONSIDER YOURSELVES LUCKY.
IT'S NOT EVERY DAY YOU ARE GIVEN THE CHANCE TO LOOK DEATH IN THE EYE.

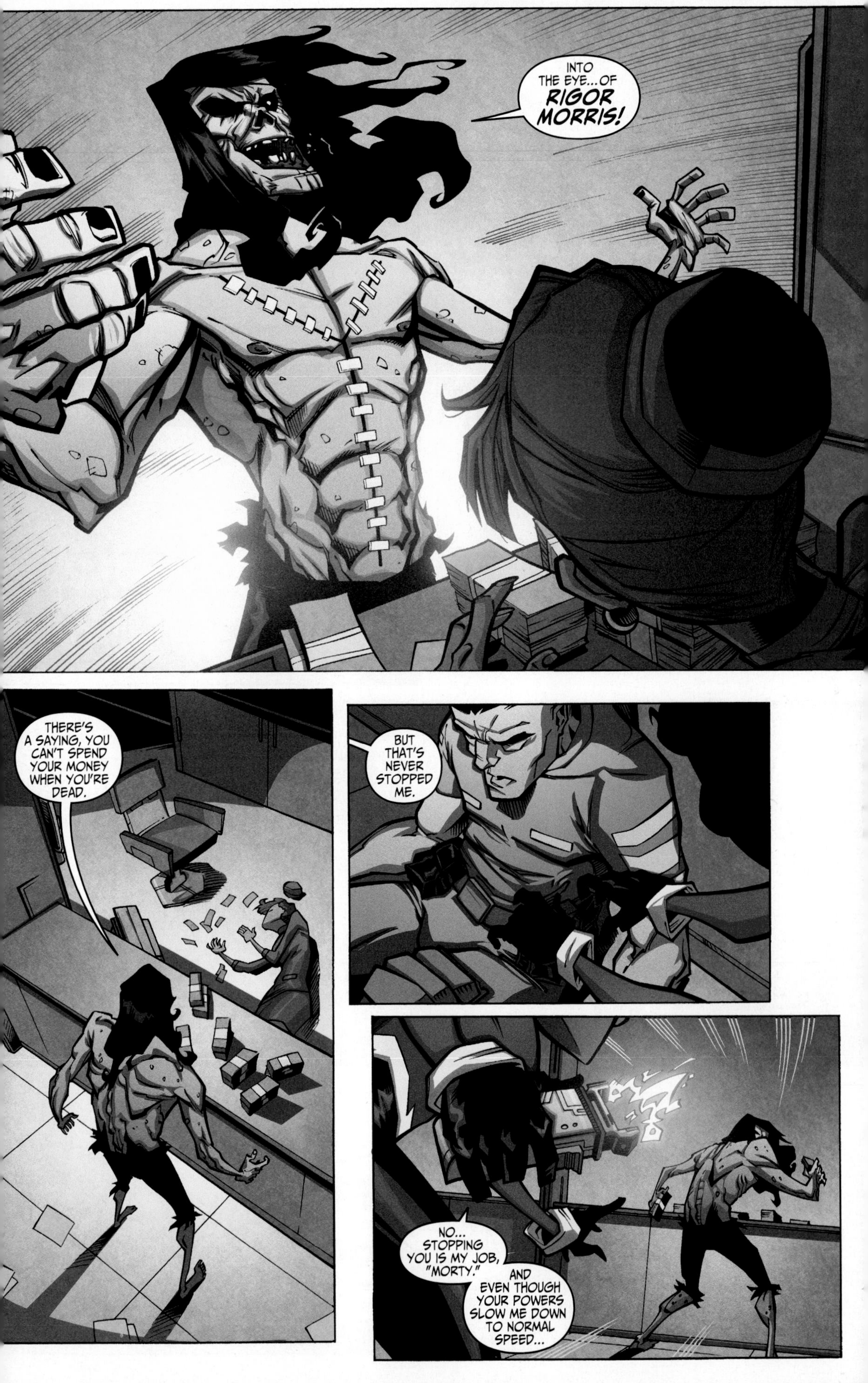
INTO THE EYE...OF RIGOR MORRIS!
THERE'S A SAYING, YOU CAN'T SPEND YOUR MONEY WHEN YOU'RE DEAD.
BUT THAT'S NEVER STOPPED ME.
NO... STOPPING YOU IS MY JOB, "MORTY."
AND EVEN THOUGH YOUR POWERS SLOW ME DOWN TO NORMAL SPEED...

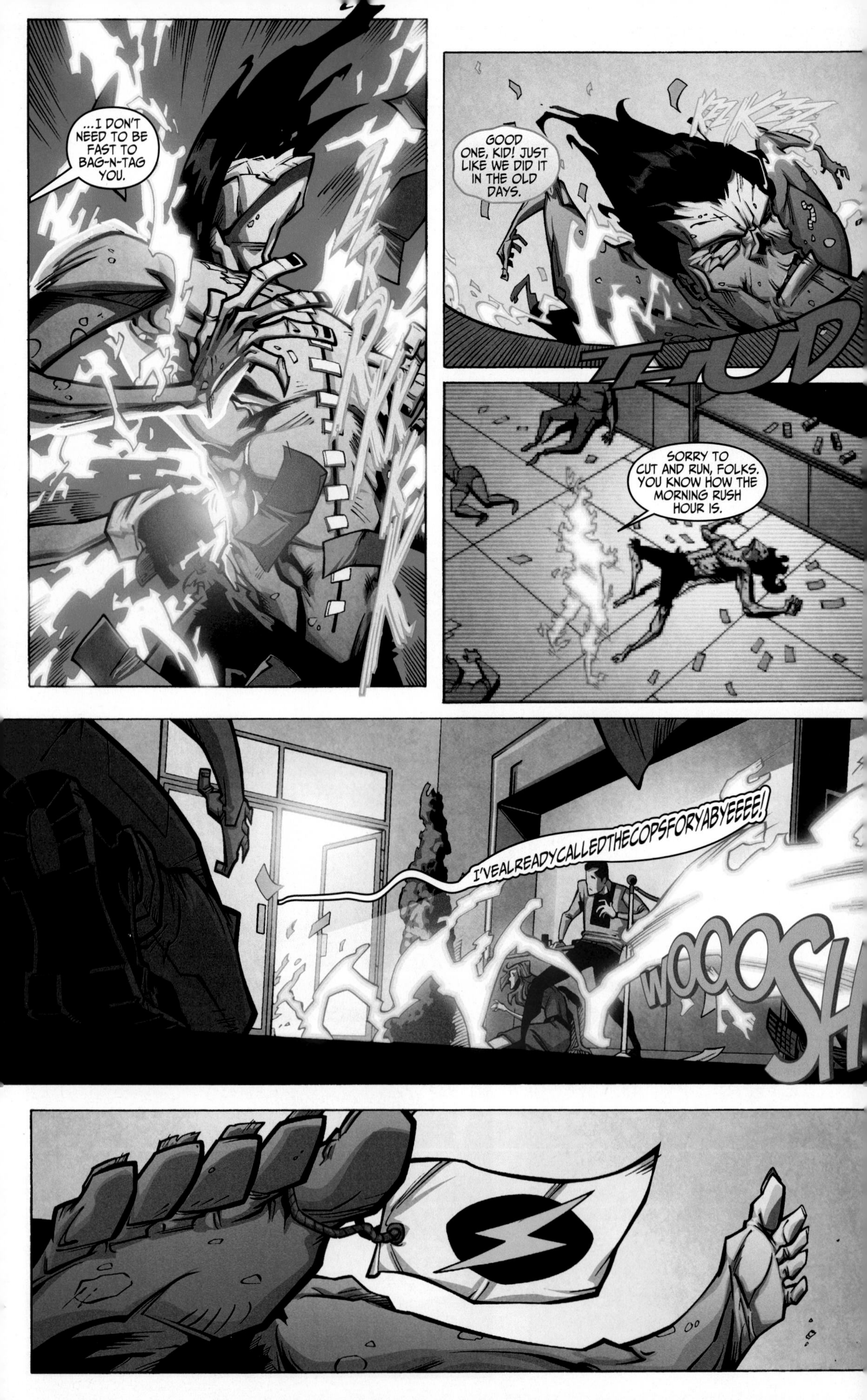
...I DON'T NEED TO BE FAST TO BAG-N-TAG YOU.
ZZRRRRRRKK
GOOD ONE, KID! JUST LIKE WE DID IT IN THE OLD DAYS.
KZZKZZZ
THUD
SORRY TO CUT AND RUN, FOLKS. YOU KNOW HOW THE MORNING RUSH HOUR IS.
I'VEALREADYCALLEDTHECOPSFORYABYEEEE!
WOOOSH

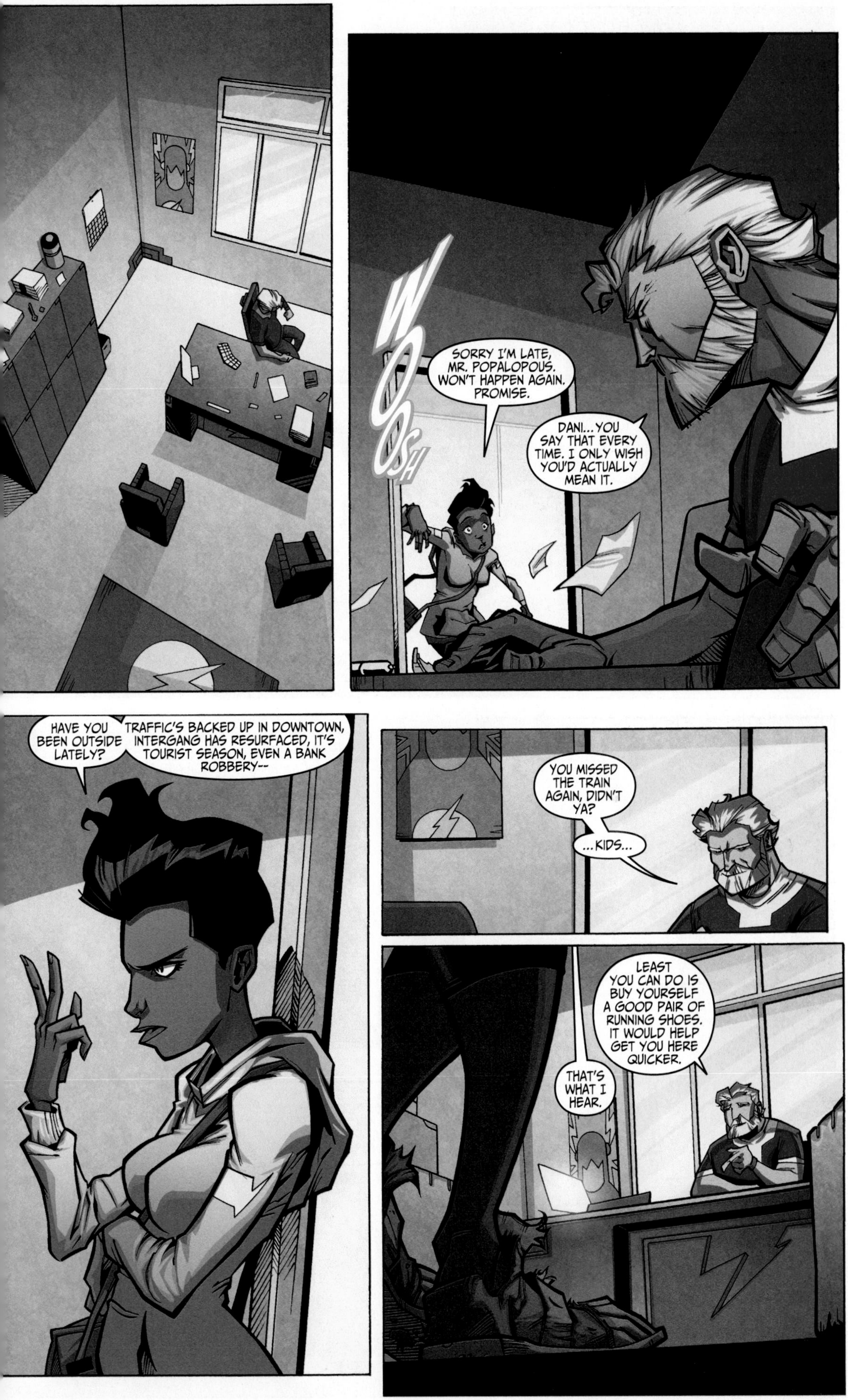
WOOOSH
SORRY I'M LATE, MR. POPALOPOUS. WON'T HAPPEN AGAIN. PROMISE.
DANI...YOU SAY THAT EVERY TIME. I ONLY WISH YOU'D ACTUALLY MEAN IT.
HAVE YOU BEEN OUTSIDE LATELY?
TRAFFIC'S BACKED UP IN DOWNTOWN, INTERGANG HAS RESURFACED, IT'S TOURIST SEASON, EVEN A BANK ROBBERY--
YOU MISSED THE TRAIN AGAIN, DIDN'T YA?
...KIDS...
LEAST YOU CAN DO IS BUY YOURSELF A GOOD PAIR OF RUNNING SHOES. IT WOULD HELP GET YOU HERE QUICKER.
THAT'S WHAT I HEAR.

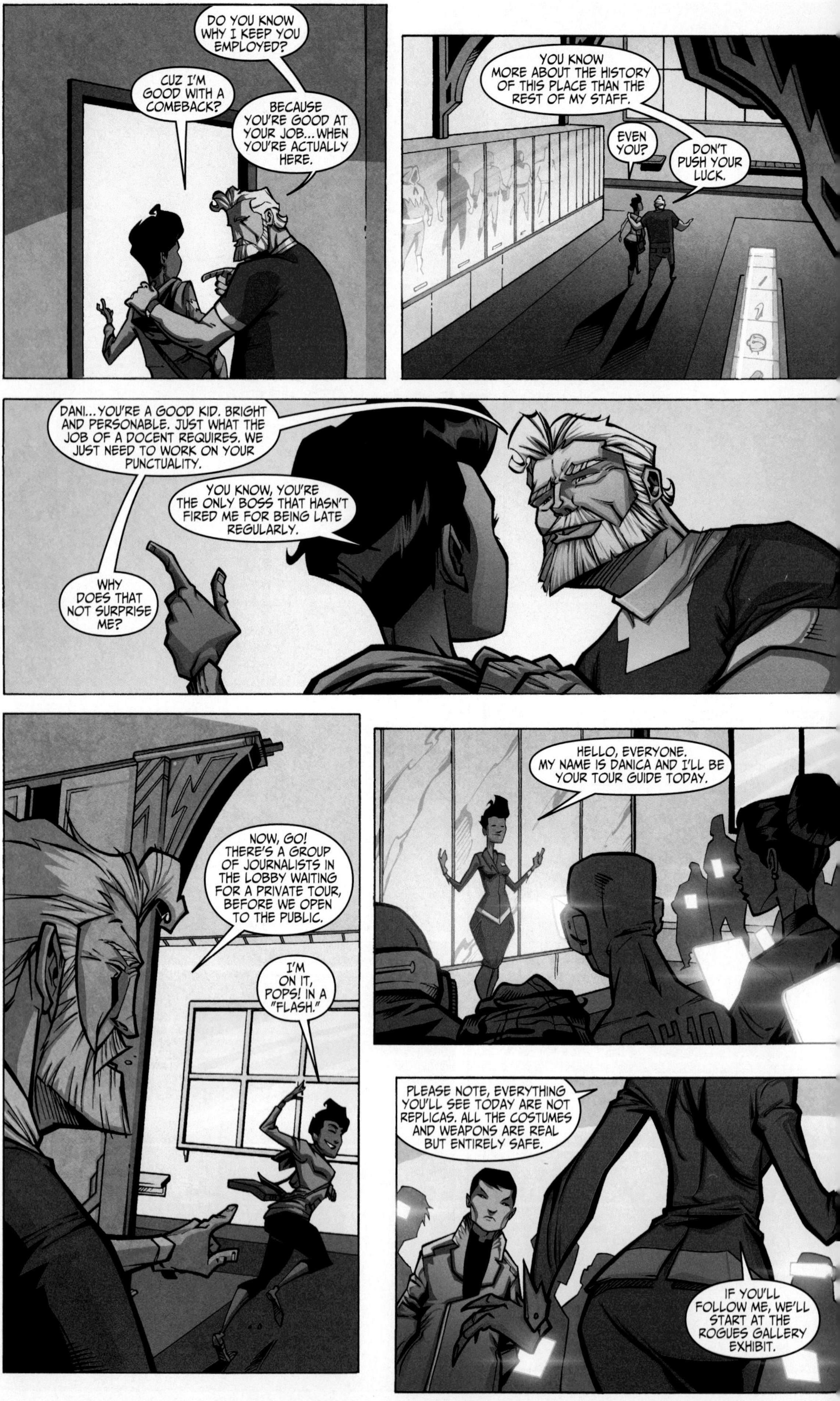
DO YOU KNOW WHY I KEEP YOU EMPLOYED?
CUZ I'M GOOD WITH A COMEBACK?
BECAUSE YOU'RE GOOD AT YOUR JOB...WHEN YOU'RE ACTUALLY HERE.
YOU KNOW MORE ABOUT THE HISTORY OF THIS PLACE THAN THE REST OF MY STAFF.
EVEN YOU?
DON'T PUSH YOUR LUCK.
DANI...YOU'RE A GOOD KID. BRIGHT AND PERSONABLE. JUST WHAT THE JOB OF A DOCENT REQUIRES. WE JUST NEED TO WORK ON YOUR PUNCTUALITY.
YOU KNOW, YOU'RE THE ONLY BOSS THAT HASN'T FIRED ME FOR BEING LATE REGULARLY.
WHY DOES THAT NOT SURPRISE ME?
NOW, GO! THERE'S A GROUP OF JOURNALISTS IN THE LOBBY WAITING FOR A PRIVATE TOUR, BEFORE WE OPEN TO THE PUBLIC.
I'M ON IT, POPS! IN A "FLASH."
HELLO, EVERYONE. MY NAME IS DANICA AND I'LL BE YOUR TOUR GUIDE TODAY.
PLEASE NOTE, EVERYTHING YOU'LL SEE TODAY ARE NOT REPLICAS. ALL THE COSTUMES AND WEAPONS ARE REAL BUT ENTIRELY SAFE.
IF YOU'LL FOLLOW ME, WE'LL START AT THE ROGUES GALLERY EXHIBIT.

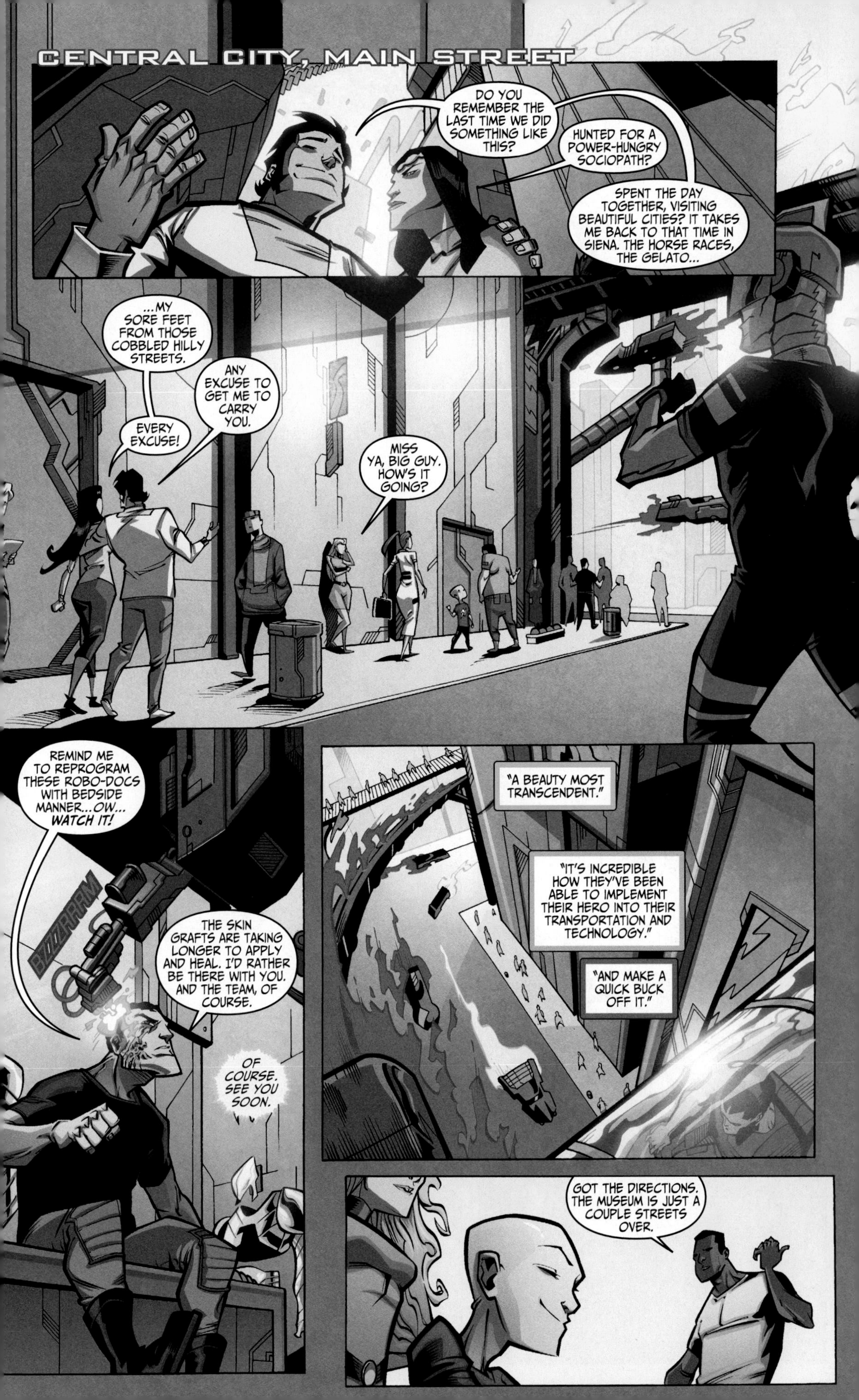
CENTRAL CITY, MAIN STREET
DO YOU REMEMBER THE LAST TIME WE DID SOMETHING LIKE THIS?
HUNTED FOR A POWER-HUNGRY SOCIOPATH?
SPENT THE DAY TOGETHER, VISITING BEAUTIFUL CITIES? IT TAKES ME BACK TO THAT TIME IN SIENA. THE HORSE RACES, THE GELATO...
...MY SORE FEET FROM THOSE COBBLED HILLY STREETS.
ANY EXCUSE TO GET ME TO CARRY YOU.
EVERY EXCUSE!
MISS YA, BIG GUY. HOW'S IT GOING?
REMIND ME TO REPROGRAM THESE ROBO-DOCS WITH BEDSIDE MANNER...OW... WATCH IT!
BZZRRRM
THE SKIN GRAFTS ARE TAKING LONGER TO APPLY AND HEAL. I'D RATHER BE THERE WITH YOU. AND THE TEAM, OF COURSE.
OF COURSE. SEE YOU SOON.
"A BEAUTY MOST TRANSCENDENT."
"IT'S INCREDIBLE HOW THEY'VE BEEN ABLE TO IMPLEMENT THEIR HERO INTO THEIR TRANSPORTATION AND TECHNOLOGY."
"AND MAKE A QUICK BUCK OFF IT."
GOT THE DIRECTIONS. THE MUSEUM IS JUST A COUPLE STREETS OVER.

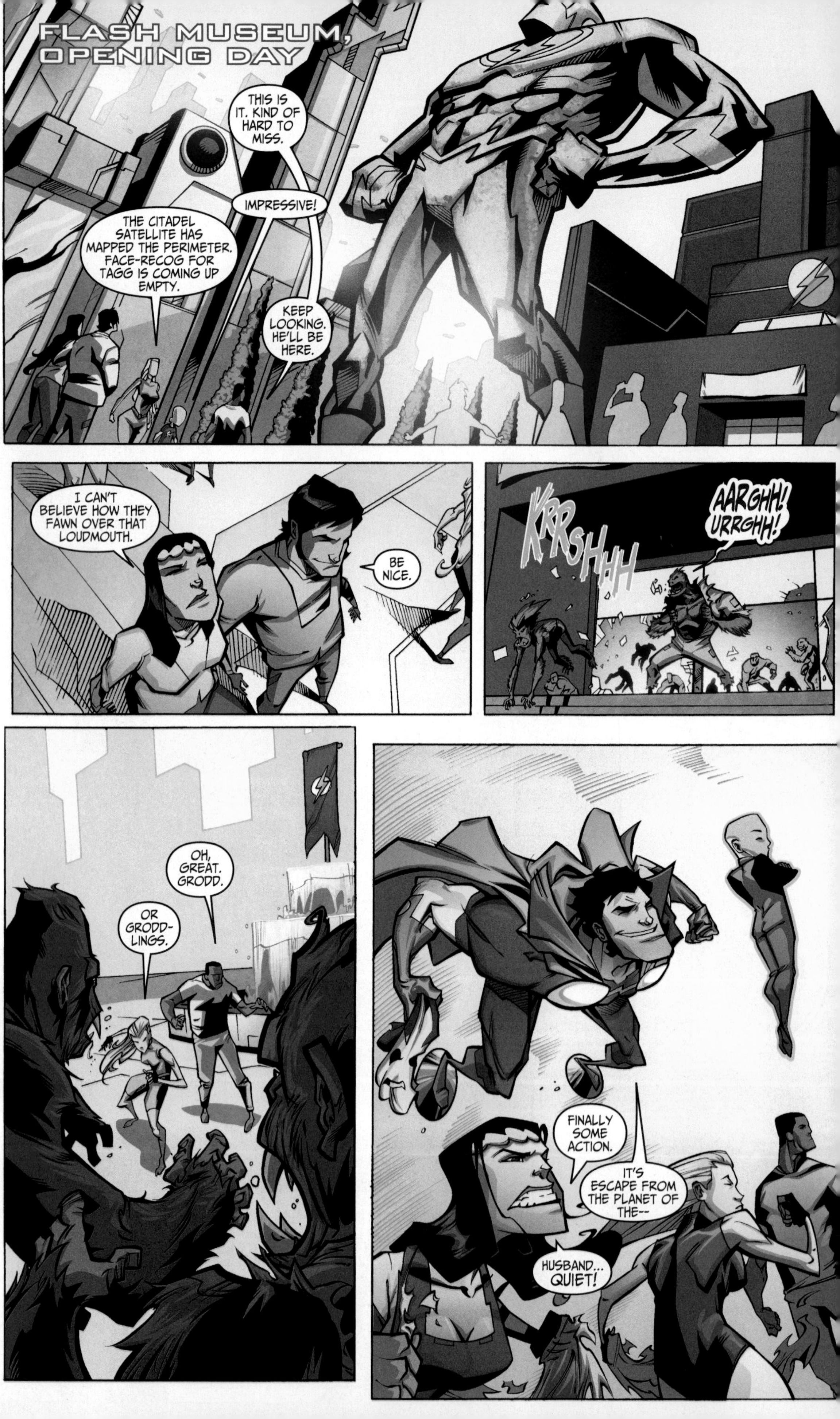
FLASH MUSEUM, OPENING DAY
THIS IS IT. KIND OF HARD TO MISS.
IMPRESSIVE!
THE CITADEL SATELLITE HAS MAPPED THE PERIMETER. FACE-RECOG FOR TAGG IS COMING UP EMPTY.
KEEP LOOKING. HE'LL BE HERE.
I CAN'T BELIEVE HOW THEY FAWN OVER THAT LOUDMOUTH.
BE NICE.
KRRSHHH
AARGHH! URRGHH!
OH, GREAT. GRODD.
OR GRODD-LINGS.
FINALLY SOME ACTION.
IT'S ESCAPE FROM THE PLANET OF THE--
HUSBAND... QUIET!

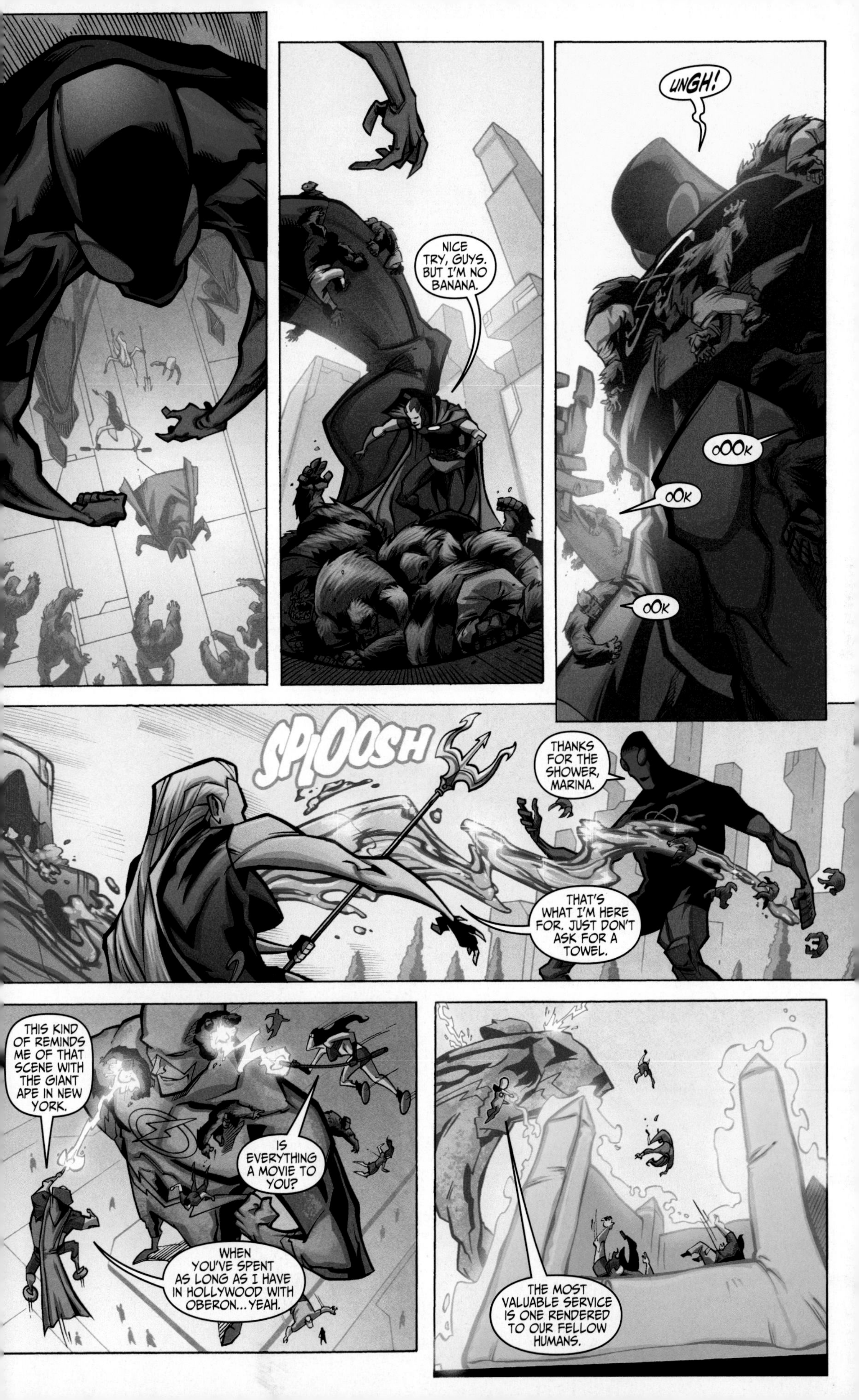

NICE TRY, GUYS. BUT I'M NO BANANA.
UNGH!
OOOK
OOK
OOK
SPLOOSH
THANKS FOR THE SHOWER, MARINA.
THAT'S WHAT I'M HERE FOR. JUST DON'T ASK FOR A TOWEL.
THIS KIND OF REMINDS ME OF THAT SCENE WITH THE GIANT APE IN NEW YORK.
IS EVERYTHING A MOVIE TO YOU?
WHEN YOU'VE SPENT AS LONG AS I HAVE IN HOLLYWOOD WITH OBERON...YEAH.
THE MOST VALUABLE SERVICE IS ONE RENDERED TO OUR FELLOW HUMANS.

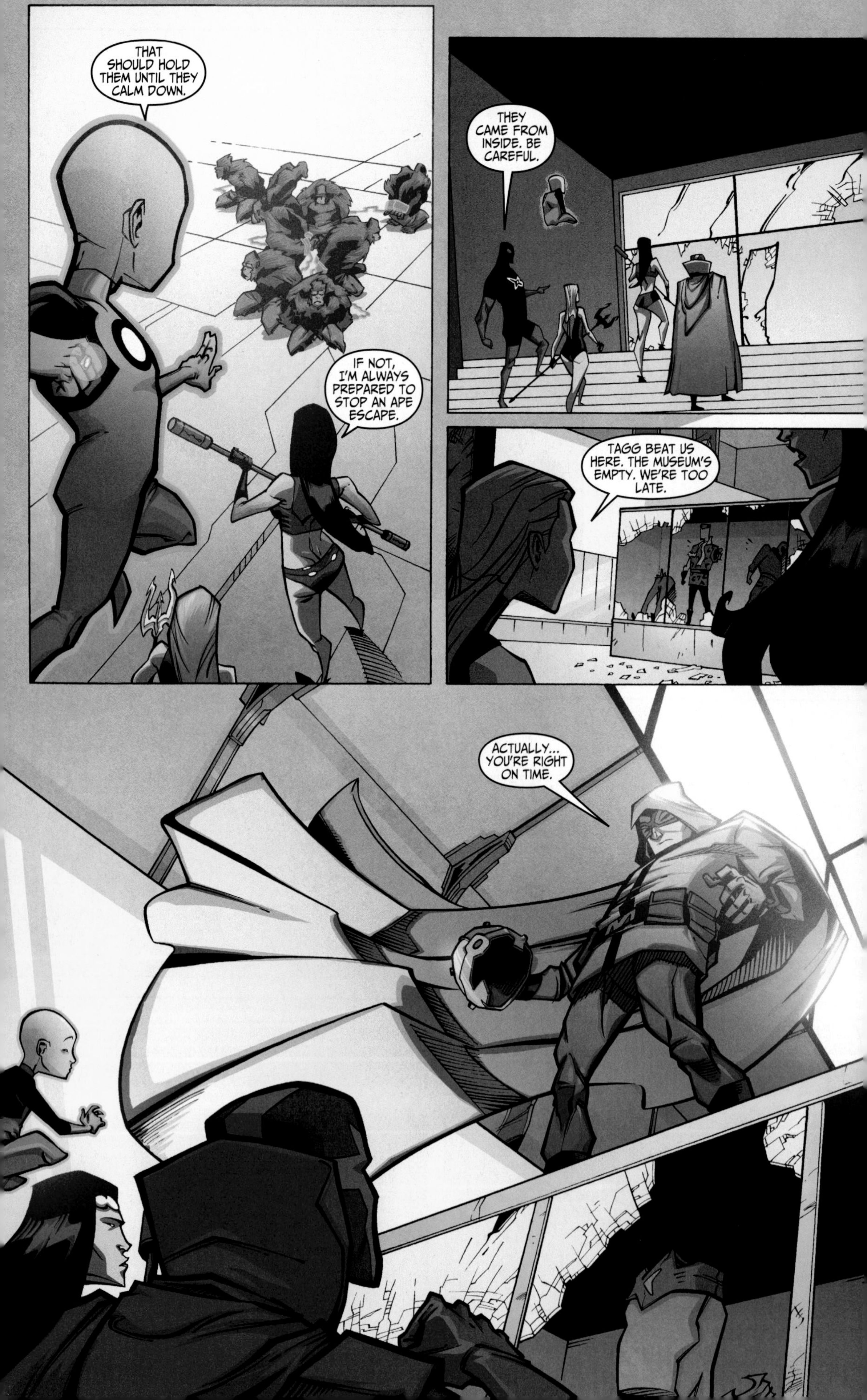
THAT SHOULD HOLD THEM UNTIL THEY CALM DOWN.
IF NOT, I'M ALWAYS PREPARED TO STOP AN APE ESCAPE.
THEY CAME FROM INSIDE. BE CAREFUL.
TAGG BEAT US HERE. THE MUSEUM'S EMPTY. WE'RE TOO LATE.
ACTUALLY... YOU'RE RIGHT ON TIME.

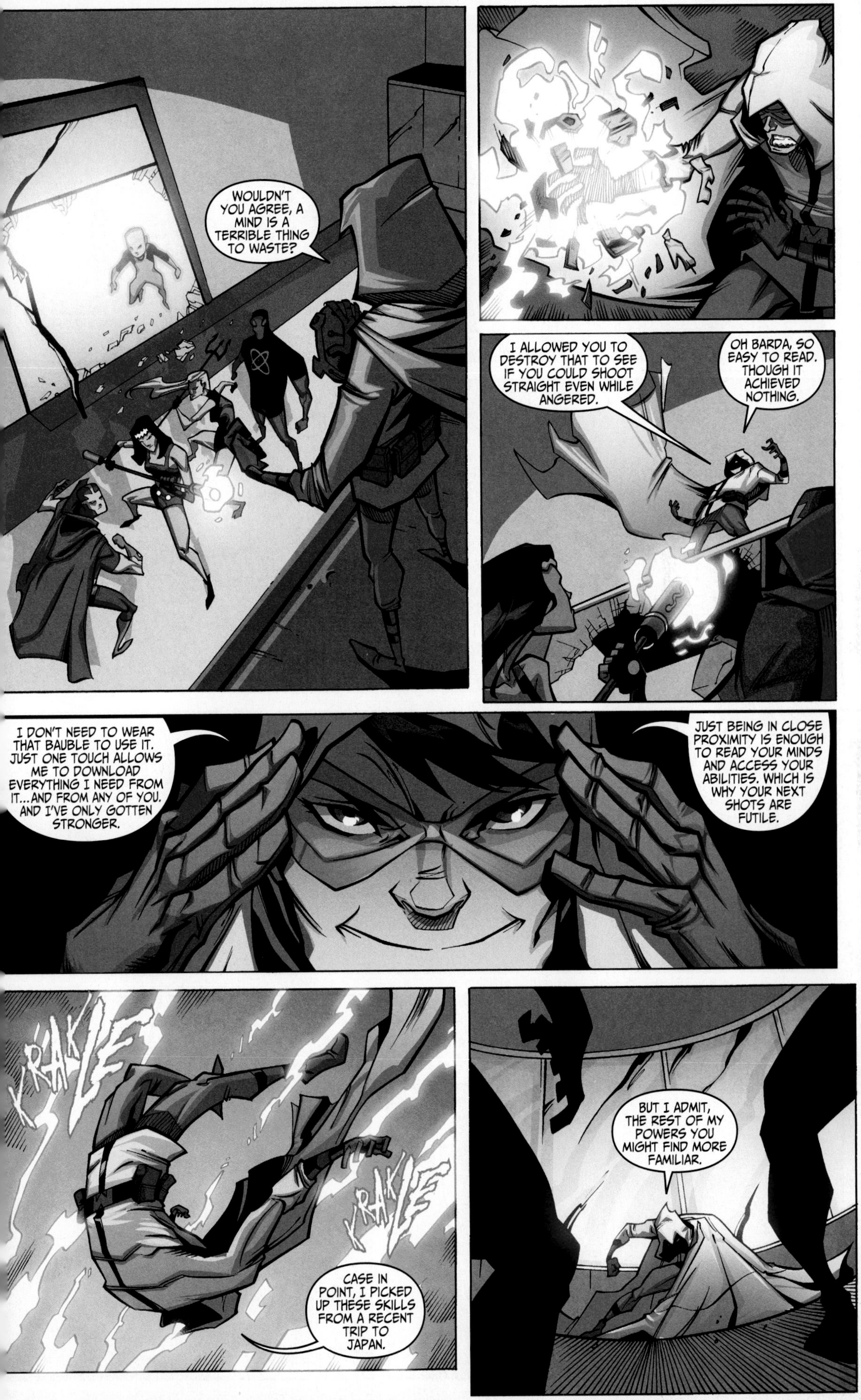
WOULDN'T YOU AGREE, A MIND IS A TERRIBLE THING TO WASTE?
I ALLOWED YOU TO DESTROY THAT TO SEE IF YOU COULD SHOOT STRAIGHT EVEN WHILE ANGERED.
OH BARDA, SO EASY TO READ. THOUGH IT ACHIEVED NOTHING.
I DON'T NEED TO WEAR THAT BAUBLE TO USE IT. JUST ONE TOUCH ALLOWS ME TO DOWNLOAD EVERYTHING I NEED FROM IT...AND FROM ANY OF YOU. AND I'VE ONLY GOTTEN STRONGER.
JUST BEING IN CLOSE PROXIMITY IS ENOUGH TO READ YOUR MINDS AND ACCESS YOUR ABILITIES. WHICH IS WHY YOUR NEXT SHOTS ARE FUTILE.
K'RAKLE
K'RAKLE
CASE IN POINT, I PICKED UP THESE SKILLS FROM A RECENT TRIP TO JAPAN.
BUT I ADMIT, THE REST OF MY POWERS YOU MIGHT FIND MORE FAMILIAR.

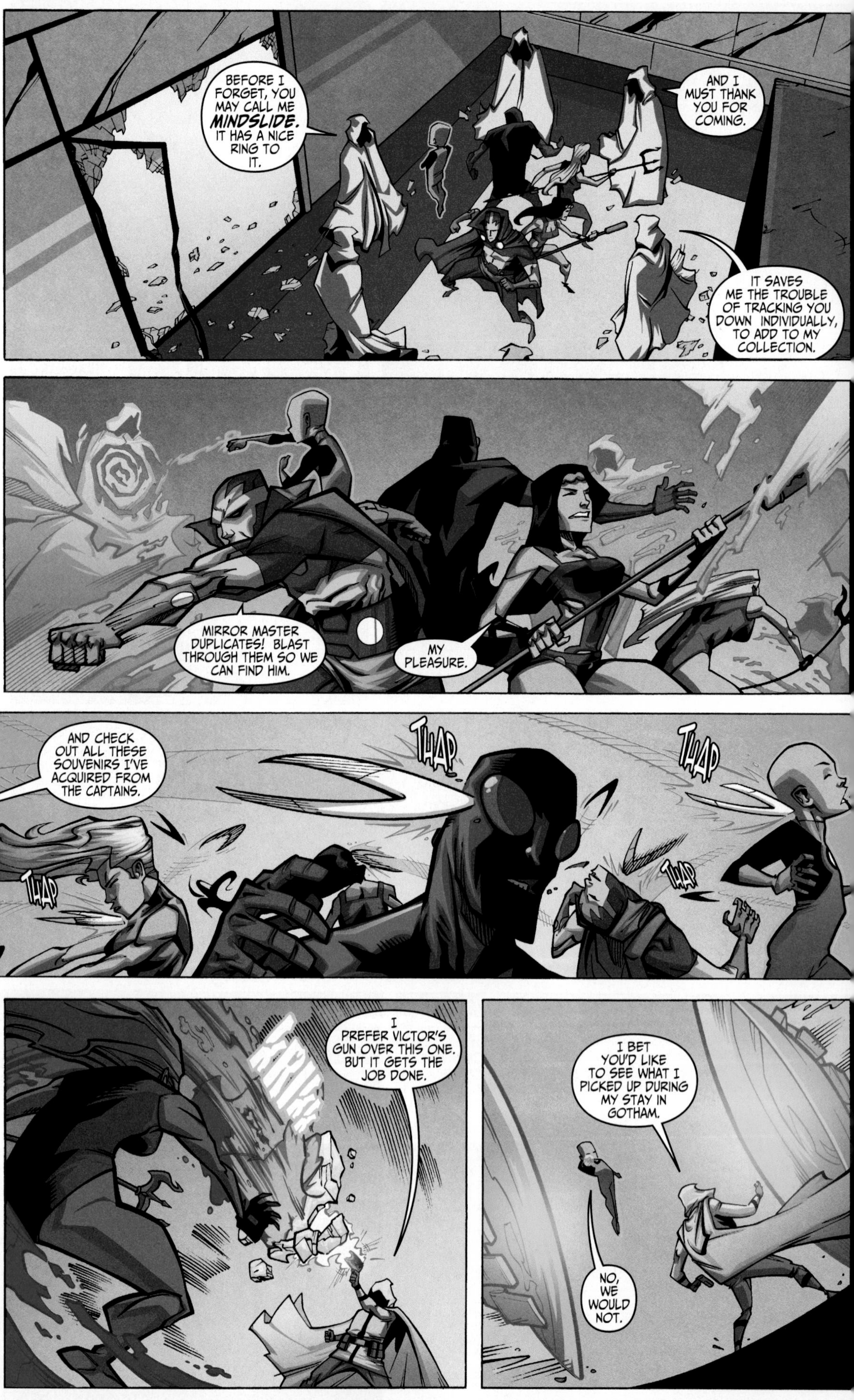
BEFORE I FORGET, YOU MAY CALL ME MINDSLIDE. IT HAS A NICE RING TO IT.
AND I MUST THANK YOU FOR COMING.
IT SAVES ME THE TROUBLE OF TRACKING YOU DOWN INDIVIDUALLY, TO ADD TO MY COLLECTION.
MIRROR MASTER DUPLICATES! BLAST THROUGH THEM SO WE CAN FIND HIM.
MY PLEASURE.
AND CHECK OUT ALL THESE SOUVENIRS I'VE ACQUIRED FROM THE CAPTAINS.
THAP
THAP
THAP
THAP
I PREFER VICTOR'S GUN OVER THIS ONE. BUT IT GETS THE JOB DONE.
I BET YOU'D LIKE TO SEE WHAT I PICKED UP DURING MY STAY IN GOTHAM.
NO, WE WOULD NOT.

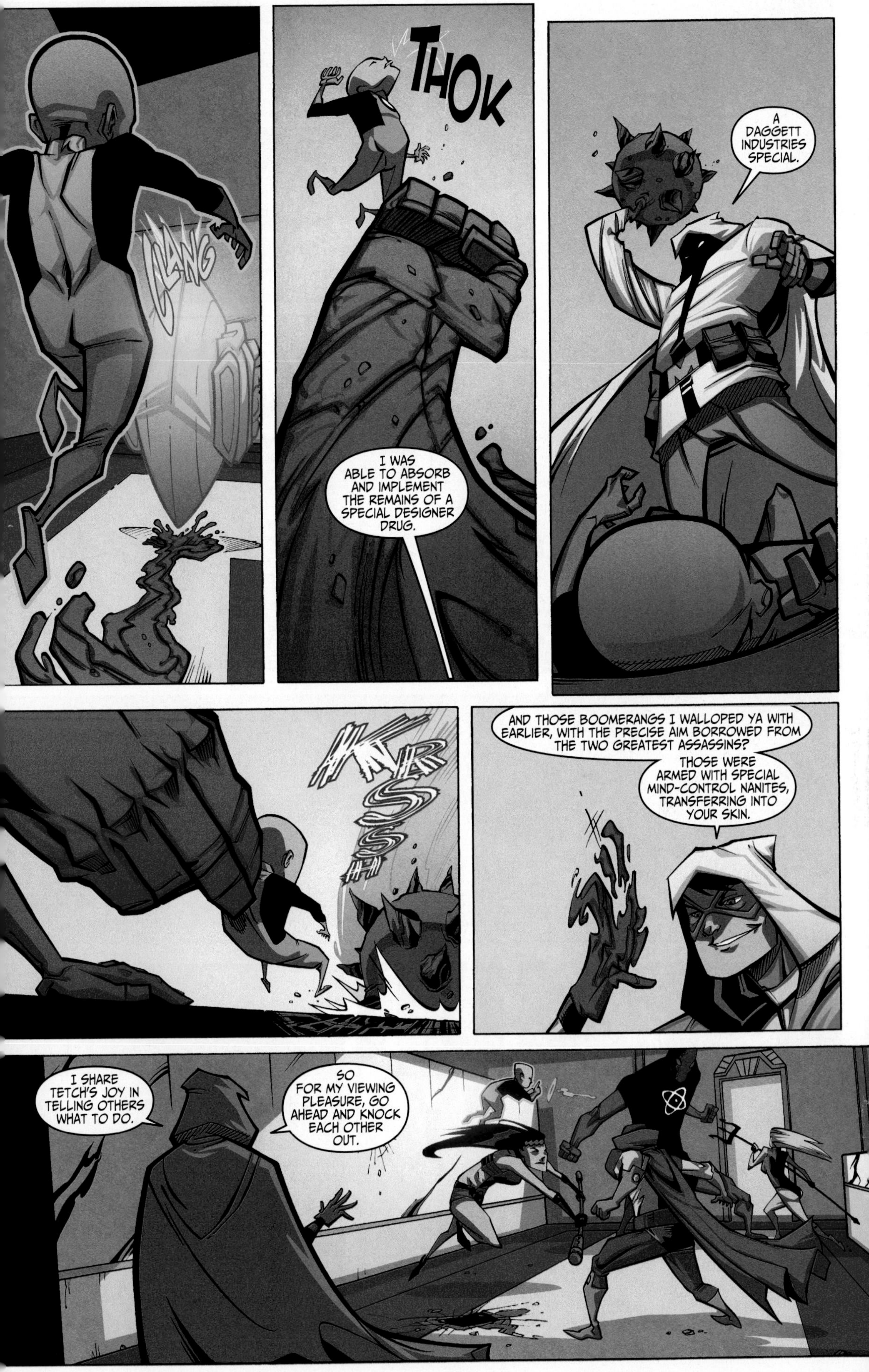
CLANG
THOK
I WAS ABLE TO ABSORB AND IMPLEMENT THE REMAINS OF A SPECIAL DESIGNER DRUG.
A DAGGETT INDUSTRIES SPECIAL.
KRSSSH
AND THOSE BOOMERANGS I WALLOPED YA WITH EARLIER, WITH THE PRECISE AIM BORROWED FROM THE TWO GREATEST ASSASSINS?
THOSE WERE ARMED WITH SPECIAL MIND-CONTROL NANITES, TRANSFERRING INTO YOUR SKIN.
I SHARE TETCH'S JOY IN TELLING OTHERS WHAT TO DO.
SO FOR MY VIEWING PLEASURE, GO AHEAD AND KNOCK EACH OTHER OUT.

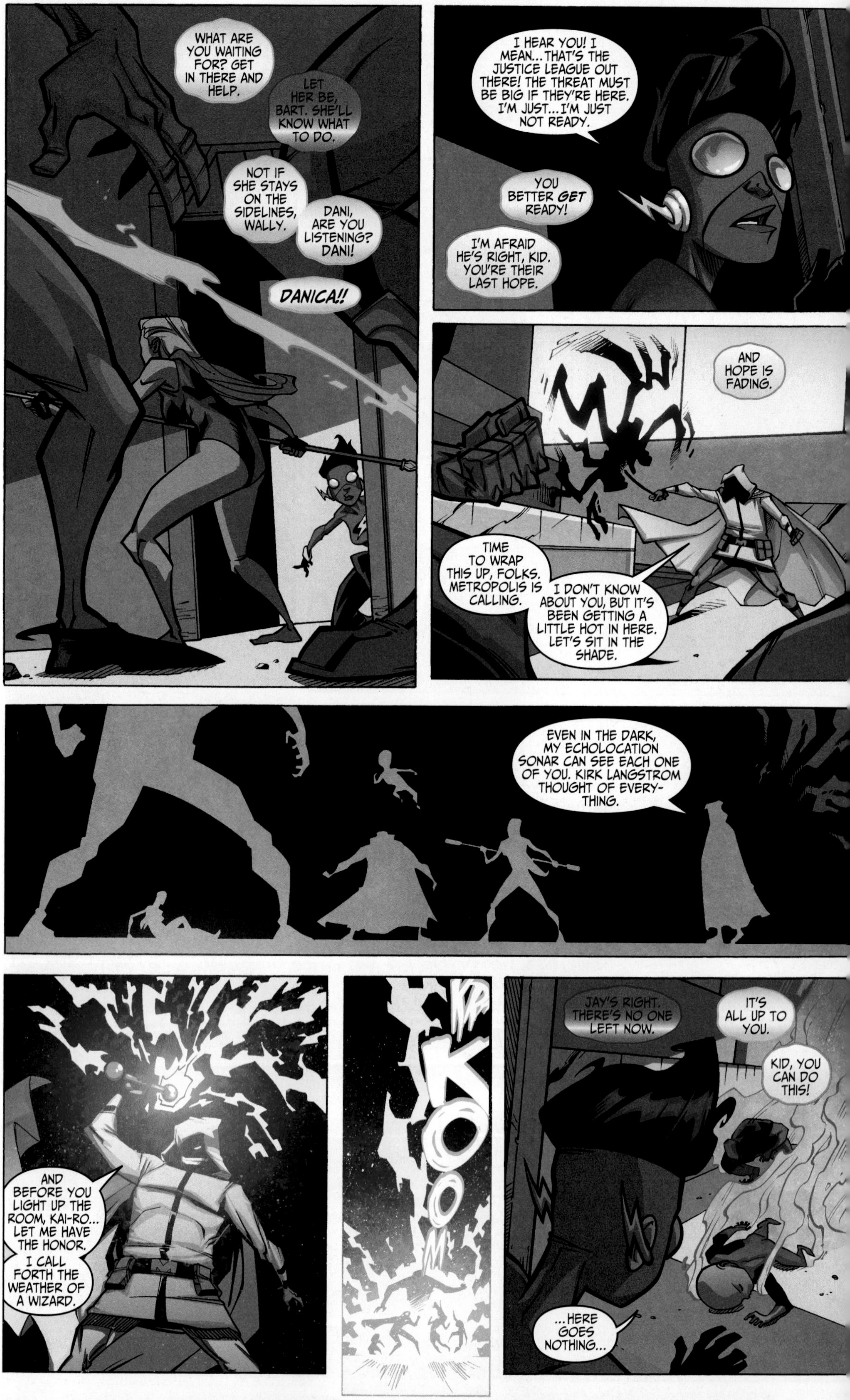
WHAT ARE YOU WAITING FOR? GET IN THERE AND HELP.
LET HER BE, BART. SHE'LL KNOW WHAT TO DO.
NOT IF SHE STAYS ON THE SIDELINES, WALLY.
DANI, ARE YOU LISTENING? DANI!
DANICA!!
I HEAR YOU! I MEAN... THAT'S THE JUSTICE LEAGUE OUT THERE! THE THREAT MUST BE BIG IF THEY'RE HERE. I'M JUST... I'M JUST NOT READY.
YOU BETTER GET READY!
I'M AFRAID HE'S RIGHT, KID. YOU'RE THEIR LAST HOPE.
AND HOPE IS FADING.
TIME TO WRAP THIS UP, FOLKS. METROPOLIS IS CALLING.
I DON'T KNOW ABOUT YOU, BUT IT'S BEEN GETTING A LITTLE HOT IN HERE. LET'S SIT IN THE SHADE.
EVEN IN THE DARK, MY ECHOLOCATION SONAR CAN SEE EACH ONE OF YOU. KIRK LANGSTROM THOUGHT OF EVERY-THING.
AND BEFORE YOU LIGHT UP THE ROOM, KAI-RO... LET ME HAVE THE HONOR.
I CALL FORTH THE WEATHER OF A WIZARD.
KRA-KOOOOM
JAY'S RIGHT. THERE'S NO ONE LEFT NOW.
IT'S ALL UP TO YOU.
KID, YOU CAN DO THIS!
...HERE GOES NOTHING...

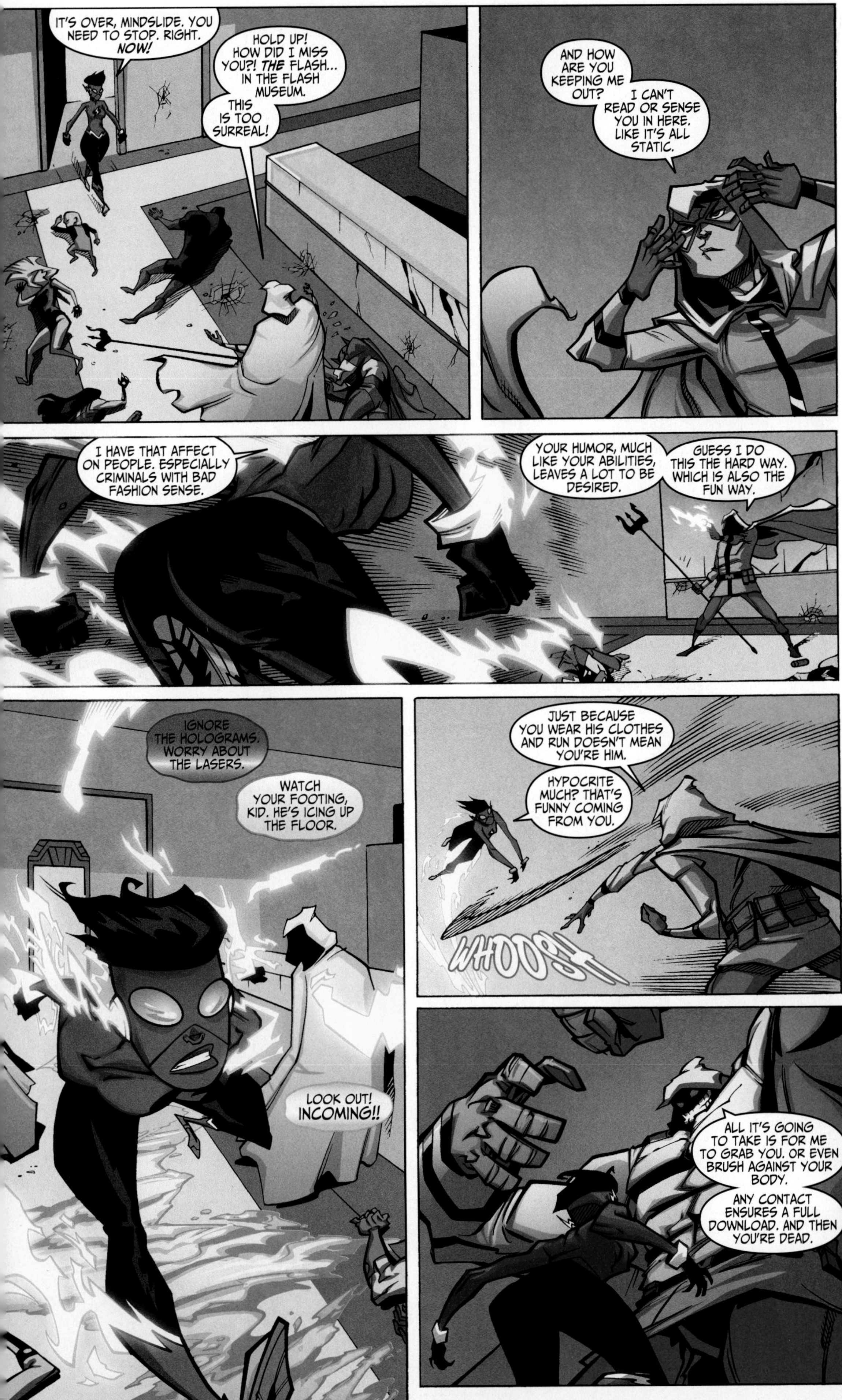
IT'S OVER, MINDSLIDE. YOU NEED TO STOP. RIGHT. NOW!
HOLD UP! HOW DID I MISS YOU?! THE FLASH... IN THE FLASH MUSEUM.
THIS IS TOO SURREAL!
AND HOW ARE YOU KEEPING ME OUT?
I CAN'T READ OR SENSE YOU IN HERE. LIKE IT'S ALL STATIC.
I HAVE THAT AFFECT ON PEOPLE. ESPECIALLY CRIMINALS WITH BAD FASHION SENSE.
YOUR HUMOR, MUCH LIKE YOUR ABILITIES, LEAVES A LOT TO BE DESIRED.
GUESS I DO THIS THE HARD WAY. WHICH IS ALSO THE FUN WAY.
IGNORE THE HOLOGRAMS. WORRY ABOUT THE LASERS.
WATCH YOUR FOOTING, KID. HE'S ICING UP THE FLOOR.
LOOK OUT! INCOMING!!
JUST BECAUSE YOU WEAR HIS CLOTHES AND RUN DOESN'T MEAN YOU'RE HIM.
HYPOCRITE MUCH? THAT'S FUNNY COMING FROM YOU.
WHOOSH
ALL IT'S GOING TO TAKE IS FOR ME TO GRAB YOU. OR EVEN BRUSH AGAINST YOUR BODY.
ANY CONTACT ENSURES A FULL DOWNLOAD. AND THEN YOU'RE DEAD.

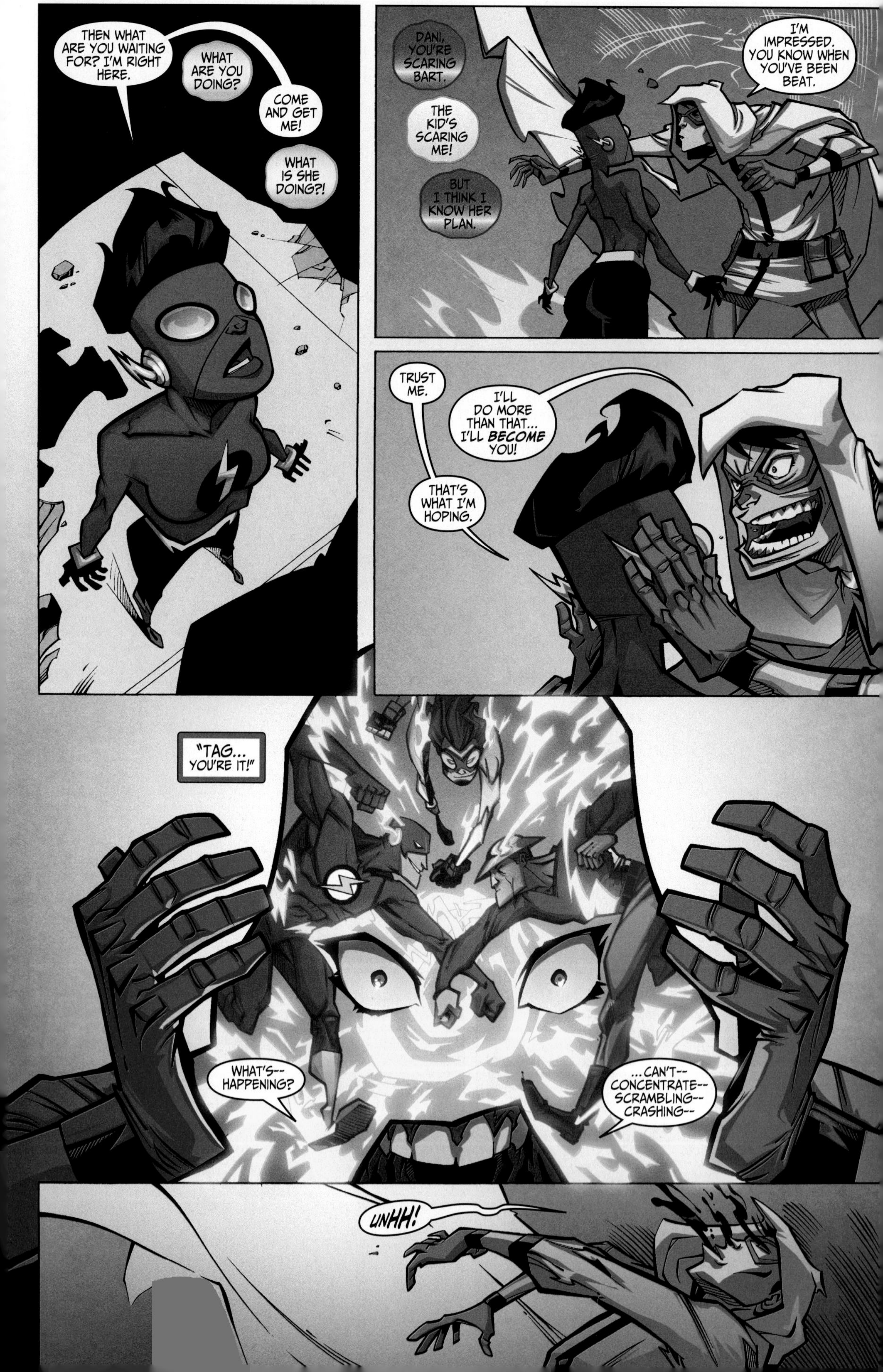
THEN WHAT ARE YOU WAITING FOR? I'M RIGHT HERE.
WHAT ARE YOU DOING?
COME AND GET ME!
WHAT IS SHE DOING?!
DANI, YOU'RE SCARING BART.
THE KID'S SCARING ME!
BUT I THINK I KNOW HER PLAN.
I'M IMPRESSED. YOU KNOW WHEN YOU'VE BEEN BEAT.
TRUST ME.
I'LL DO MORE THAN THAT... I'LL *BECOME* YOU!
THAT'S WHAT I'M HOPING.
"TAG... YOU'RE IT!"
WHAT'S--HAPPENING?
...CAN'T--CONCENTRATE--SCRAMBLING--CRASHING--
UNHH!

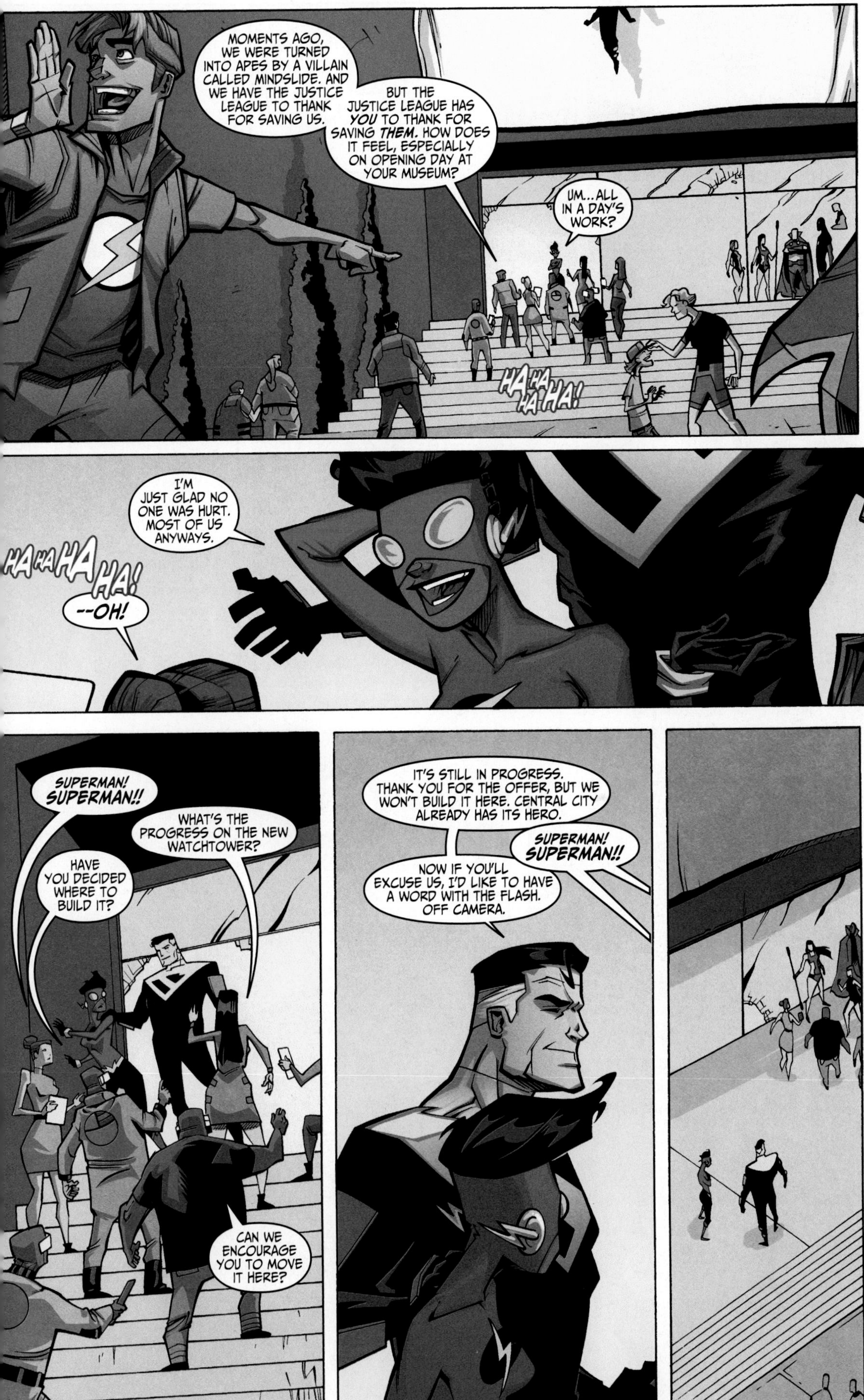

MOMENTS AGO, WE WERE TURNED INTO APES BY A VILLAIN CALLED MINDSLIDE. AND WE HAVE THE JUSTICE LEAGUE TO THANK FOR SAVING US.
BUT THE JUSTICE LEAGUE HAS *YOU* TO THANK FOR SAVING *THEM*. HOW DOES IT FEEL, ESPECIALLY ON OPENING DAY AT YOUR MUSEUM?
UM...ALL IN A DAY'S WORK?
HA HA HA HA!
I'M JUST GLAD NO ONE WAS HURT. MOST OF US ANYWAYS.
HA HA HA HA!
--OH!
SUPERMAN! SUPERMAN!!
WHAT'S THE PROGRESS ON THE NEW WATCHTOWER?
HAVE YOU DECIDED WHERE TO BUILD IT?
CAN WE ENCOURAGE YOU TO MOVE IT HERE?
IT'S STILL IN PROGRESS. THANK YOU FOR THE OFFER, BUT WE WON'T BUILD IT HERE. CENTRAL CITY ALREADY HAS ITS HERO.
SUPERMAN! SUPERMAN!!
NOW IF YOU'LL EXCUSE US, I'D LIKE TO HAVE A WORD WITH THE FLASH. OFF CAMERA.

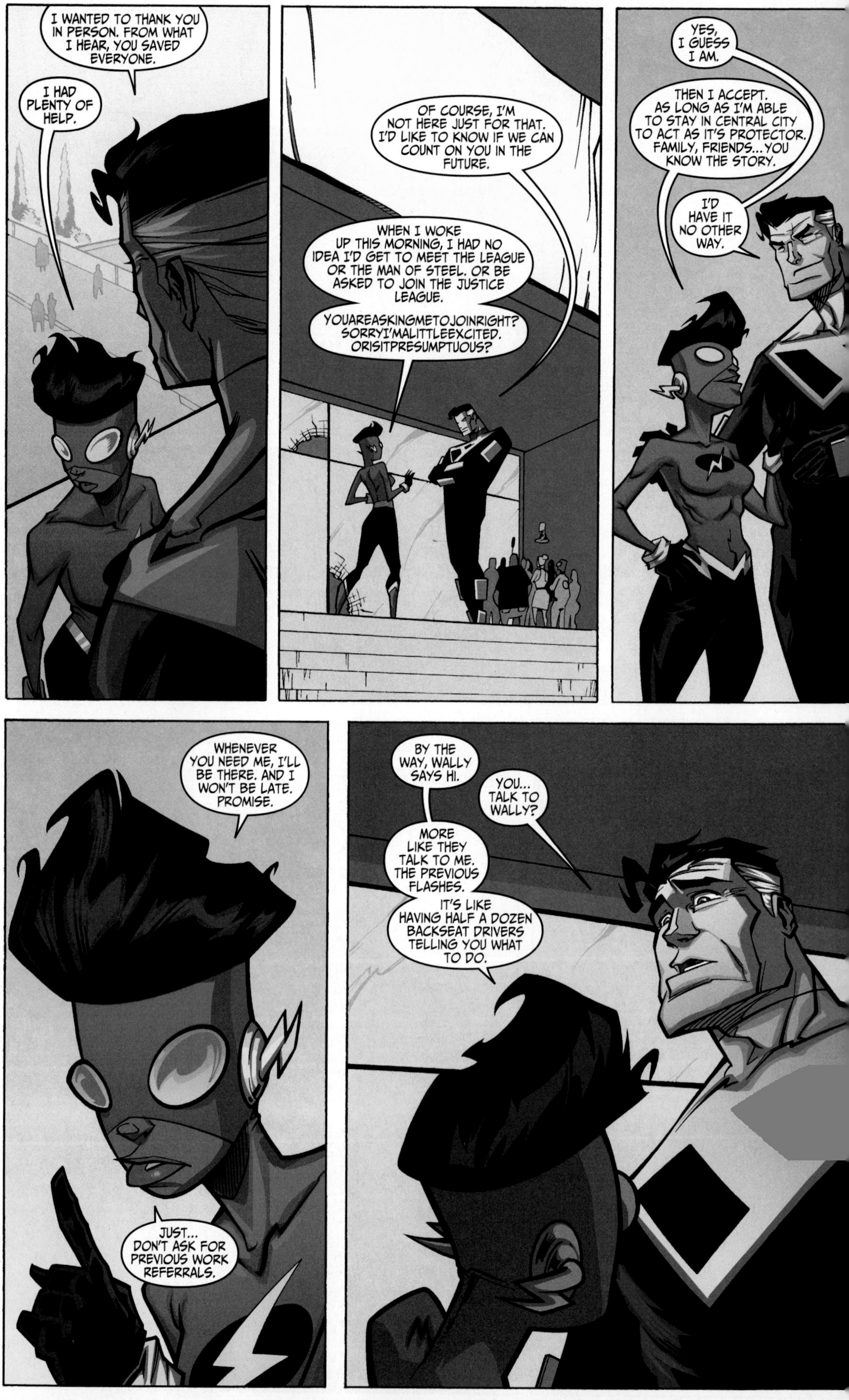
I WANTED TO THANK YOU IN PERSON. FROM WHAT I HEAR, YOU SAVED EVERYONE.
I HAD PLENTY OF HELP.
OF COURSE, I'M NOT HERE JUST FOR THAT. I'D LIKE TO KNOW IF WE CAN COUNT ON YOU IN THE FUTURE.
WHEN I WOKE UP THIS MORNING, I HAD NO IDEA I'D GET TO MEET THE LEAGUE OR THE MAN OF STEEL. OR BE ASKED TO JOIN THE JUSTICE LEAGUE.
YOUAREASKINGMETOJOINRIGHT? SORRYI'MALITTLEEXCITED. ORISITPRESUMPTUOUS?
YES, I GUESS I AM.
THEN I ACCEPT. AS LONG AS I'M ABLE TO STAY IN CENTRAL CITY TO ACT AS IT'S PROTECTOR. FAMILY, FRIENDS... YOU KNOW THE STORY.
I'D HAVE IT NO OTHER WAY.
WHENEVER YOU NEED ME, I'LL BE THERE. AND I WON'T BE LATE. PROMISE.
JUST... DON'T ASK FOR PREVIOUS WORK REFERRALS.
BY THE WAY, WALLY SAYS HI.
YOU... TALK TO WALLY?
MORE LIKE THEY TALK TO ME. THE PREVIOUS FLASHES.
IT'S LIKE HAVING HALF A DOZEN BACKSEAT DRIVERS TELLING YOU WHAT TO DO.

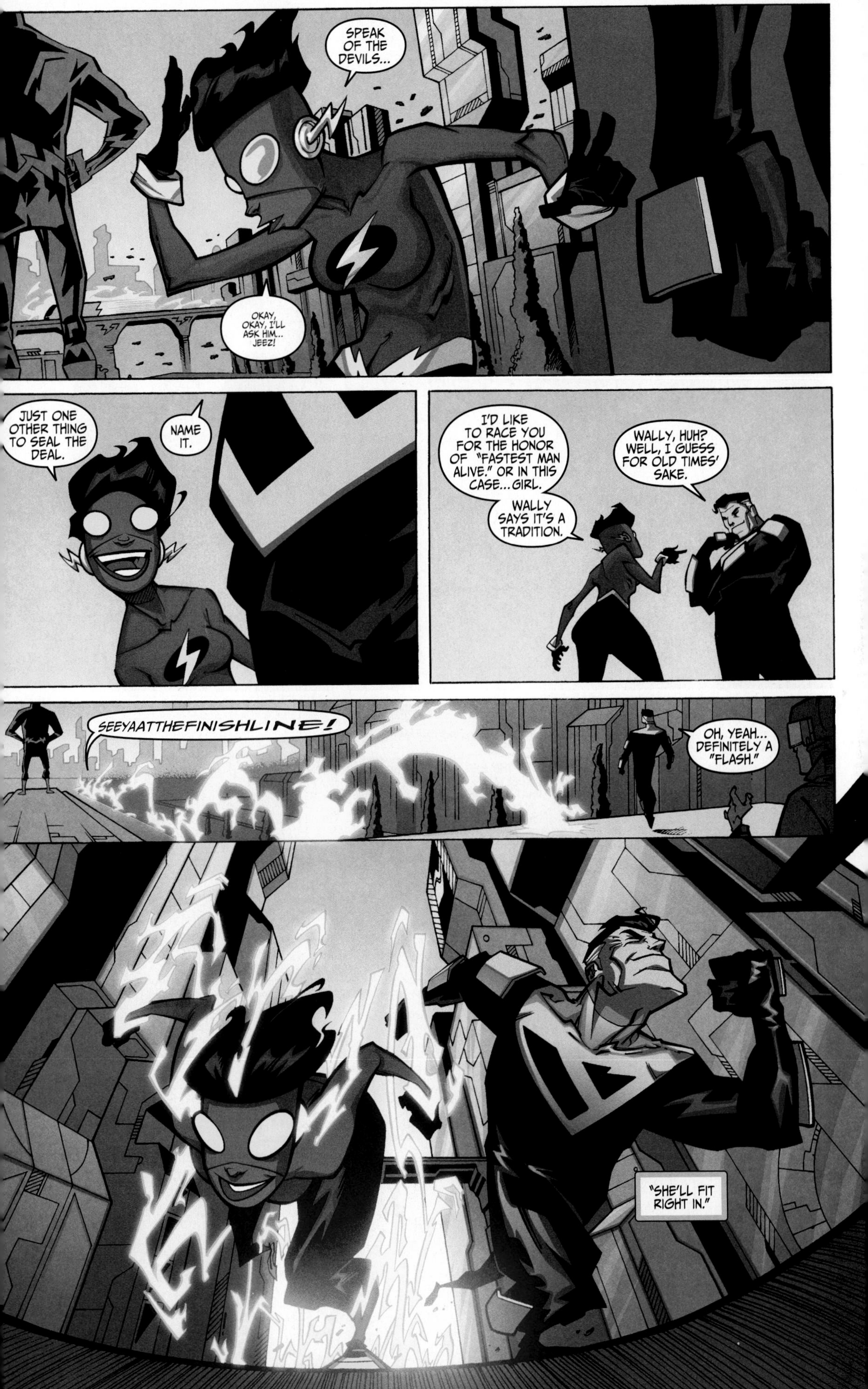
SPEAK OF THE DEVILS...
OKAY, OKAY, I'LL ASK HIM... JEEZ!
JUST ONE OTHER THING TO SEAL THE DEAL.
NAME IT.
I'D LIKE TO RACE YOU FOR THE HONOR OF "FASTEST MAN ALIVE." OR IN THIS CASE... GIRL.
WALLY SAYS IT'S A TRADITION.
WALLY, HUH? WELL, I GUESS FOR OLD TIMES' SAKE.
SEEYAATTHEFINISHLINE!
OH, YEAH... DEFINITELY A "FLASH."
"SHE'LL FIT RIGHT IN."

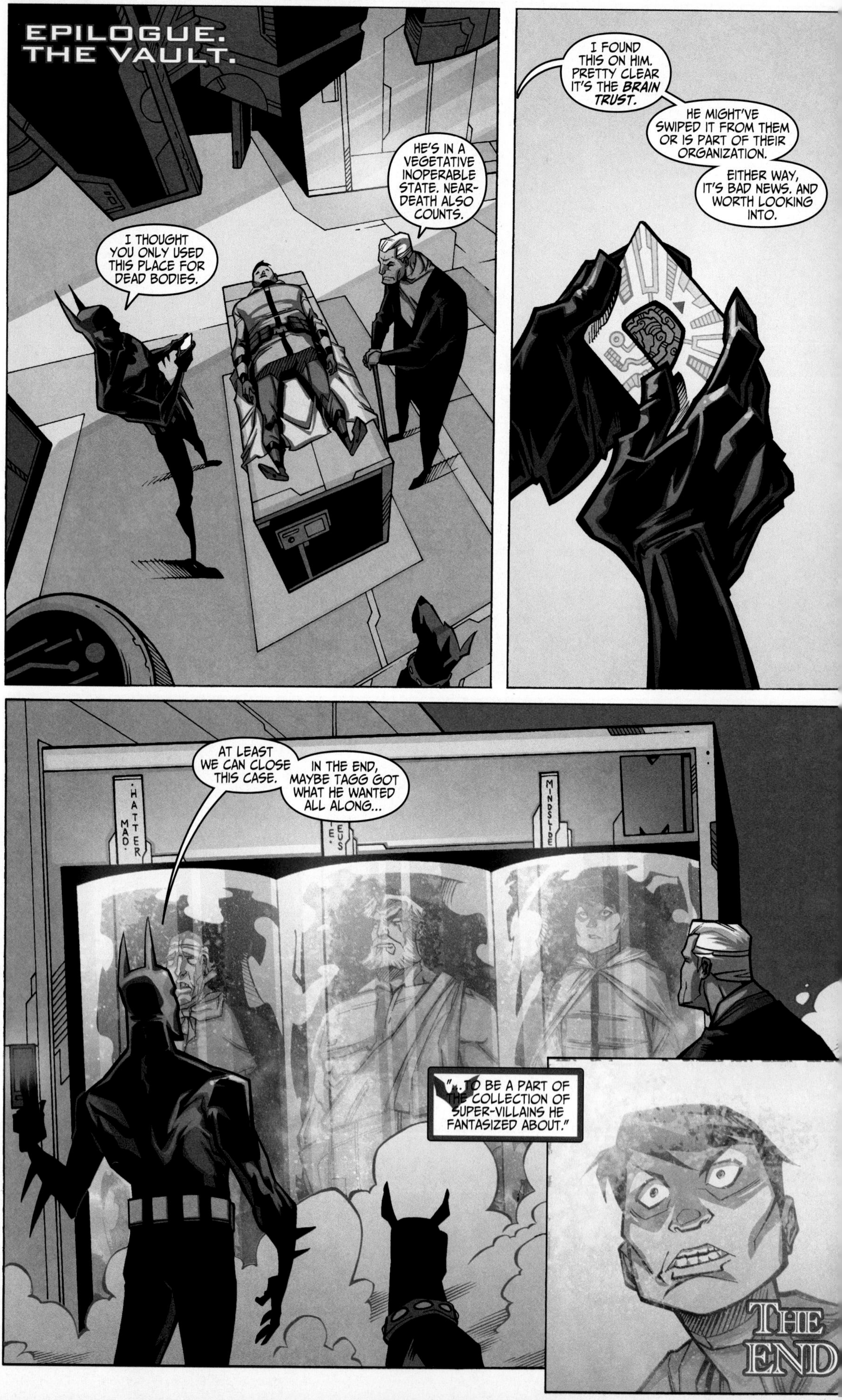
EPILOGUE. THE VAULT.
I THOUGHT YOU ONLY USED THIS PLACE FOR DEAD BODIES.
HE'S IN A VEGETATIVE INOPERABLE STATE. NEAR-DEATH ALSO COUNTS.
I FOUND THIS ON HIM. PRETTY CLEAR IT'S THE BRAIN TRUST.
HE MIGHT'VE SWIPED IT FROM THEM OR IS PART OF THEIR ORGANIZATION.
EITHER WAY, IT'S BAD NEWS. AND WORTH LOOKING INTO.
AT LEAST WE CAN CLOSE THIS CASE.
IN THE END, MAYBE TAGG GOT WHAT HE WANTED ALL ALONG...
MAD HATTER
MINDSLIDE
"...TO BE A PART OF THE COLLECTION OF SUPER-VILLAINS HE FANTASIZED ABOUT."
THE END

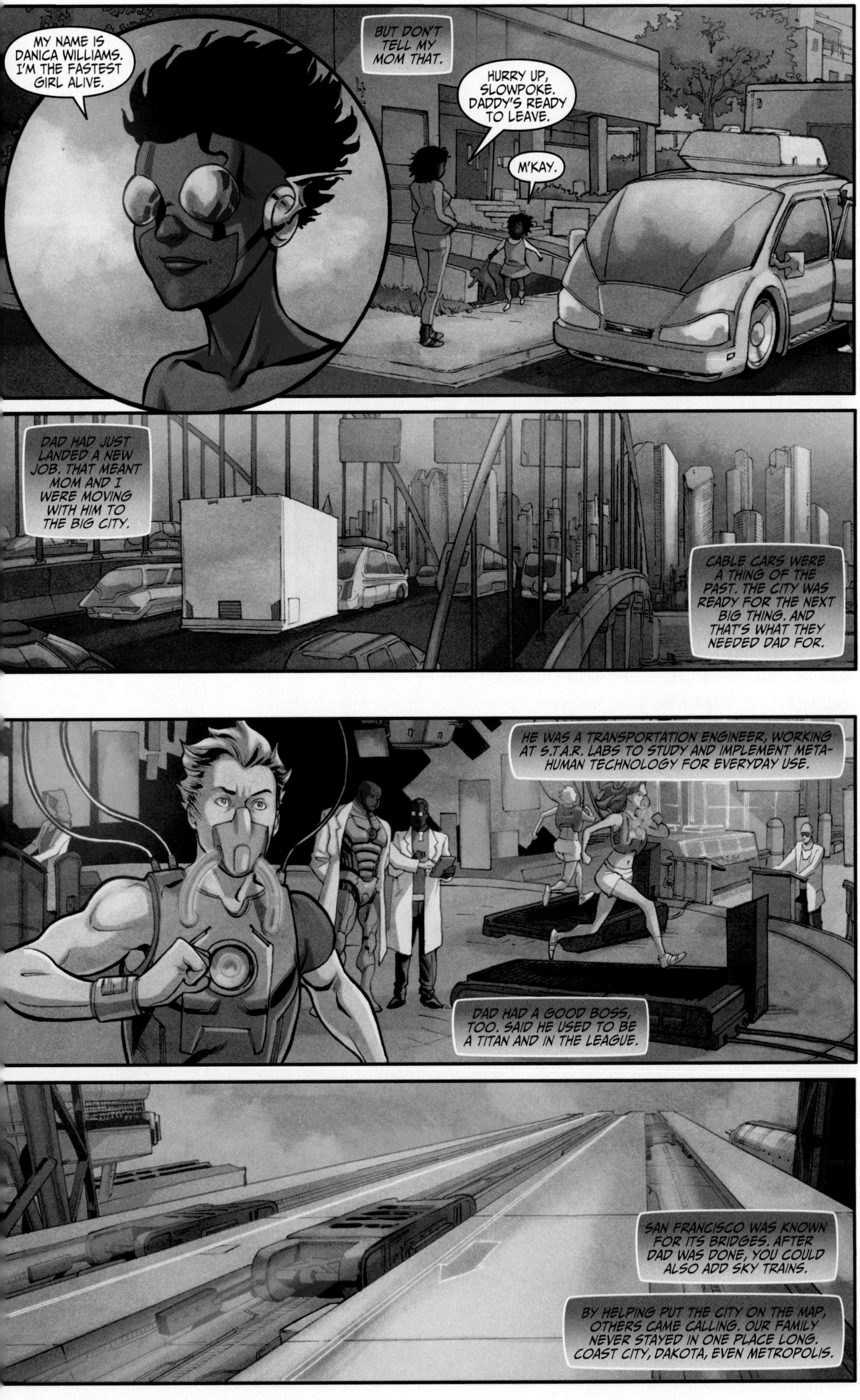
MY NAME IS DANICA WILLIAMS. I'M THE FASTEST GIRL ALIVE.
BUT DON'T TELL MY MOM THAT.
HURRY UP, SLOWPOKE. DADDY'S READY TO LEAVE.
M'KAY.
DAD HAD JUST LANDED A NEW JOB. THAT MEANT MOM AND I WERE MOVING WITH HIM TO THE BIG CITY.
CABLE CARS WERE A THING OF THE PAST. THE CITY WAS READY FOR THE NEXT BIG THING. AND THAT'S WHAT THEY NEEDED DAD FOR.
HE WAS A TRANSPORTATION ENGINEER, WORKING AT S.T.A.R. LABS TO STUDY AND IMPLEMENT META-HUMAN TECHNOLOGY FOR EVERYDAY USE.
DAD HAD A GOOD BOSS, TOO. SAID HE USED TO BE A TITAN AND IN THE LEAGUE.
SAN FRANCISCO WAS KNOWN FOR ITS BRIDGES. AFTER DAD WAS DONE, YOU COULD ALSO ADD SKY TRAINS.
BY HELPING PUT THE CITY ON THE MAP, OTHERS CAME CALLING. OUR FAMILY NEVER STAYED IN ONE PLACE LONG. COAST CITY, DAKOTA, EVEN METROPOLIS.

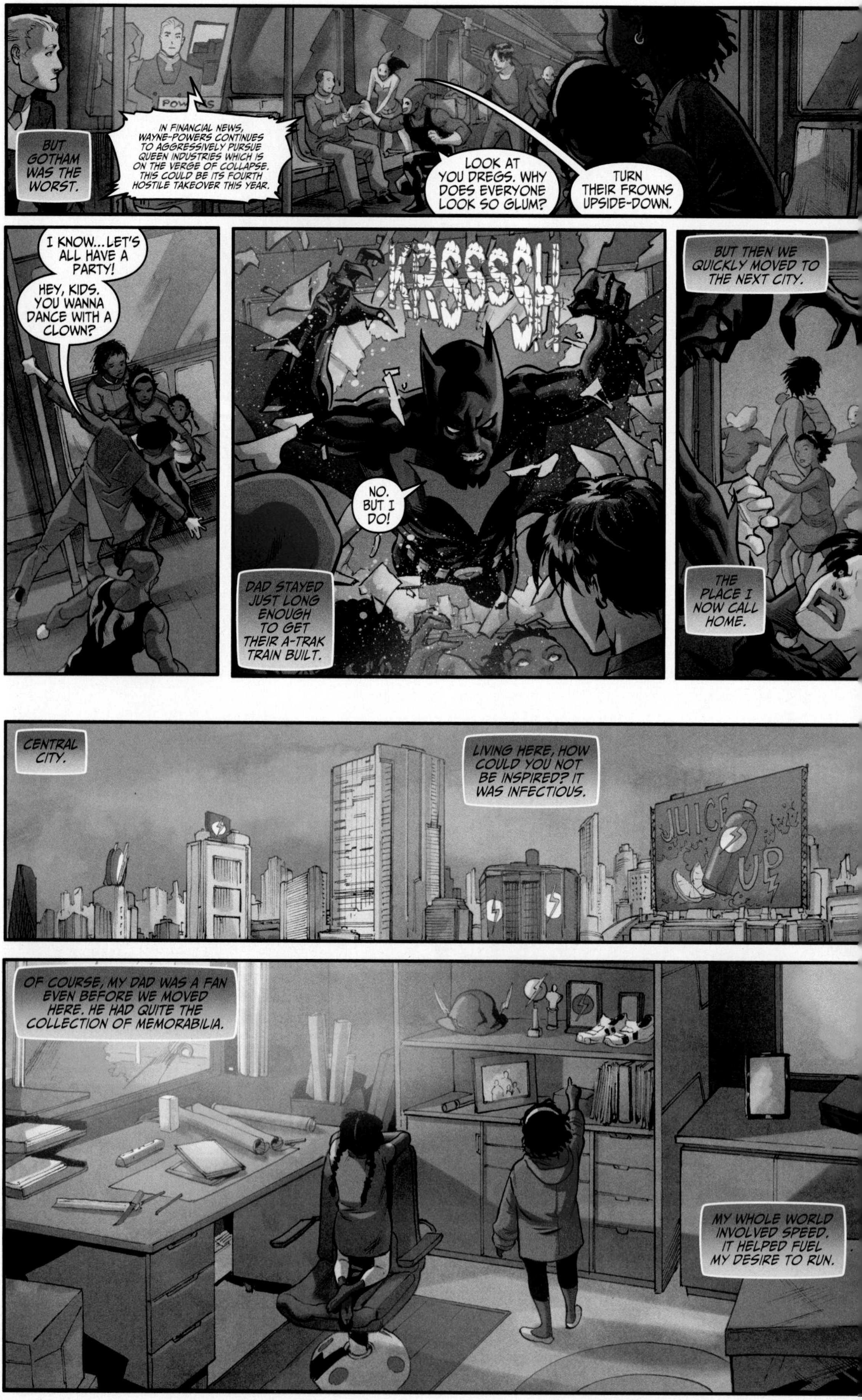
BUT GOTHAM WAS THE WORST.
IN FINANCIAL NEWS, WAYNE-POWERS CONTINUES TO AGGRESSIVELY PURSUE QUEEN INDUSTRIES WHICH IS ON THE VERGE OF COLLAPSE. THIS COULD BE ITS FOURTH HOSTILE TAKEOVER THIS YEAR.
LOOK AT YOU DREGS. WHY DOES EVERYONE LOOK SO GLUM?
TURN THEIR FROWNS UPSIDE-DOWN.
I KNOW...LET'S ALL HAVE A PARTY!
HEY, KIDS. YOU WANNA DANCE WITH A CLOWN?
KRSSSH!!
NO. BUT I DO!
DAD STAYED JUST LONG ENOUGH TO GET THEIR A-TRAK TRAIN BUILT.
BUT THEN WE QUICKLY MOVED TO THE NEXT CITY.
THE PLACE I NOW CALL HOME.
CENTRAL CITY.
LIVING HERE, HOW COULD YOU NOT BE INSPIRED? IT WAS INFECTIOUS.
JUICE UP
OF COURSE, MY DAD WAS A FAN EVEN BEFORE WE MOVED HERE. HE HAD QUITE THE COLLECTION OF MEMORABILIA.
MY WHOLE WORLD INVOLVED SPEED. IT HELPED FUEL MY DESIRE TO RUN.

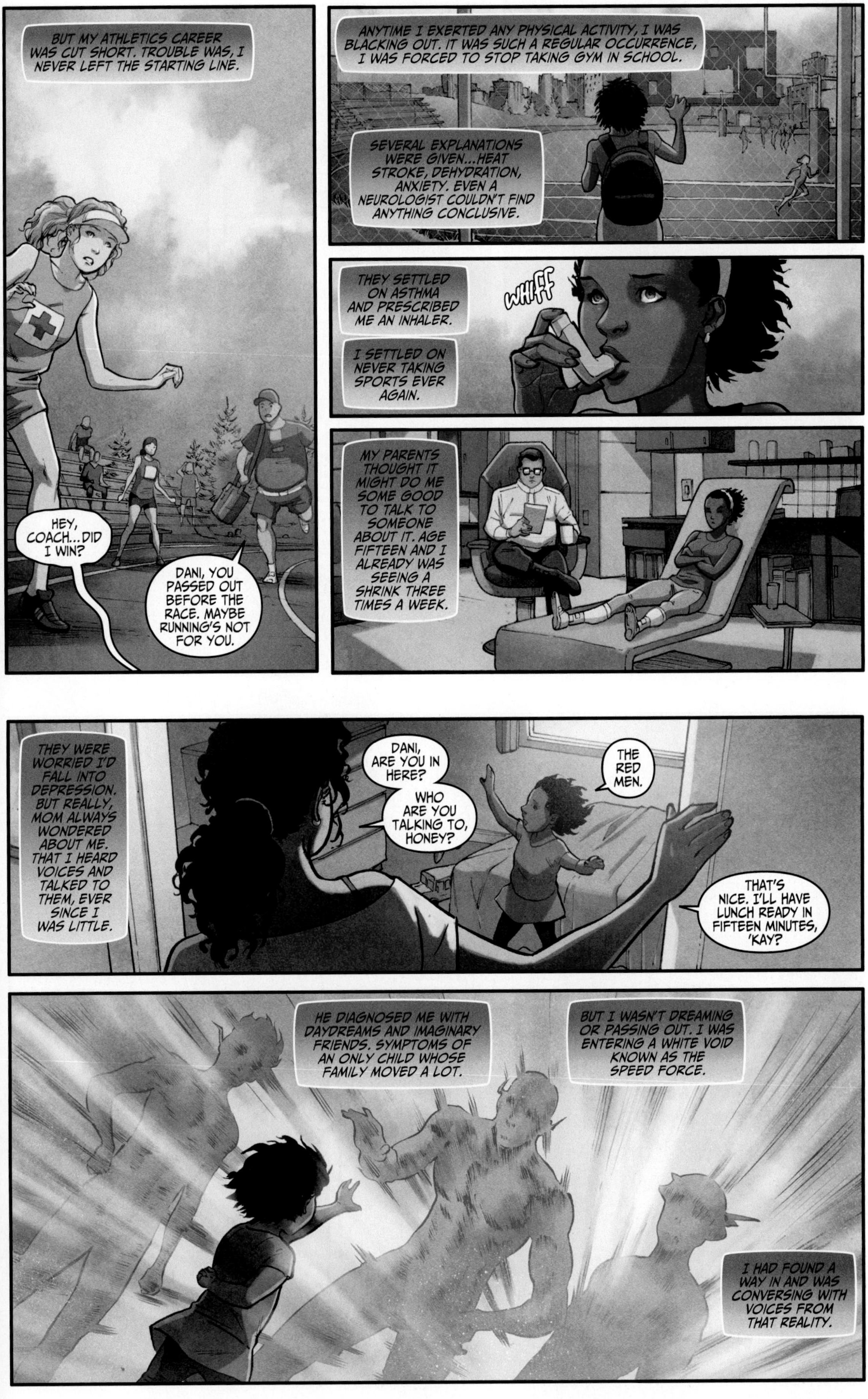
BUT MY ATHLETICS CAREER WAS CUT SHORT. TROUBLE WAS, I NEVER LEFT THE STARTING LINE.
HEY, COACH...DID I WIN?
DANI, YOU PASSED OUT BEFORE THE RACE. MAYBE RUNNING'S NOT FOR YOU.
ANYTIME I EXERTED ANY PHYSICAL ACTIVITY, I WAS BLACKING OUT. IT WAS SUCH A REGULAR OCCURRENCE, I WAS FORCED TO STOP TAKING GYM IN SCHOOL.
SEVERAL EXPLANATIONS WERE GIVEN...HEAT STROKE, DEHYDRATION, ANXIETY. EVEN A NEUROLOGIST COULDN'T FIND ANYTHING CONCLUSIVE.
THEY SETTLED ON ASTHMA AND PRESCRIBED ME AN INHALER.
WHIFF
I SETTLED ON NEVER TAKING SPORTS EVER AGAIN.
MY PARENTS THOUGHT IT MIGHT DO ME SOME GOOD TO TALK TO SOMEONE ABOUT IT. AGE FIFTEEN AND I ALREADY WAS SEEING A SHRINK THREE TIMES A WEEK.
THEY WERE WORRIED I'D FALL INTO DEPRESSION. BUT REALLY, MOM ALWAYS WONDERED ABOUT ME. THAT I HEARD VOICES AND TALKED TO THEM, EVER SINCE I WAS LITTLE.
DANI, ARE YOU IN HERE?
WHO ARE YOU TALKING TO, HONEY?
THE RED MEN.
THAT'S NICE. I'LL HAVE LUNCH READY IN FIFTEEN MINUTES, 'KAY?
HE DIAGNOSED ME WITH DAYDREAMS AND IMAGINARY FRIENDS. SYMPTOMS OF AN ONLY CHILD WHOSE FAMILY MOVED A LOT.
BUT I WASN'T DREAMING OR PASSING OUT. I WAS ENTERING A WHITE VOID KNOWN AS THE SPEED FORCE.
I HAD FOUND A WAY IN AND WAS CONVERSING WITH VOICES FROM THAT REALITY.

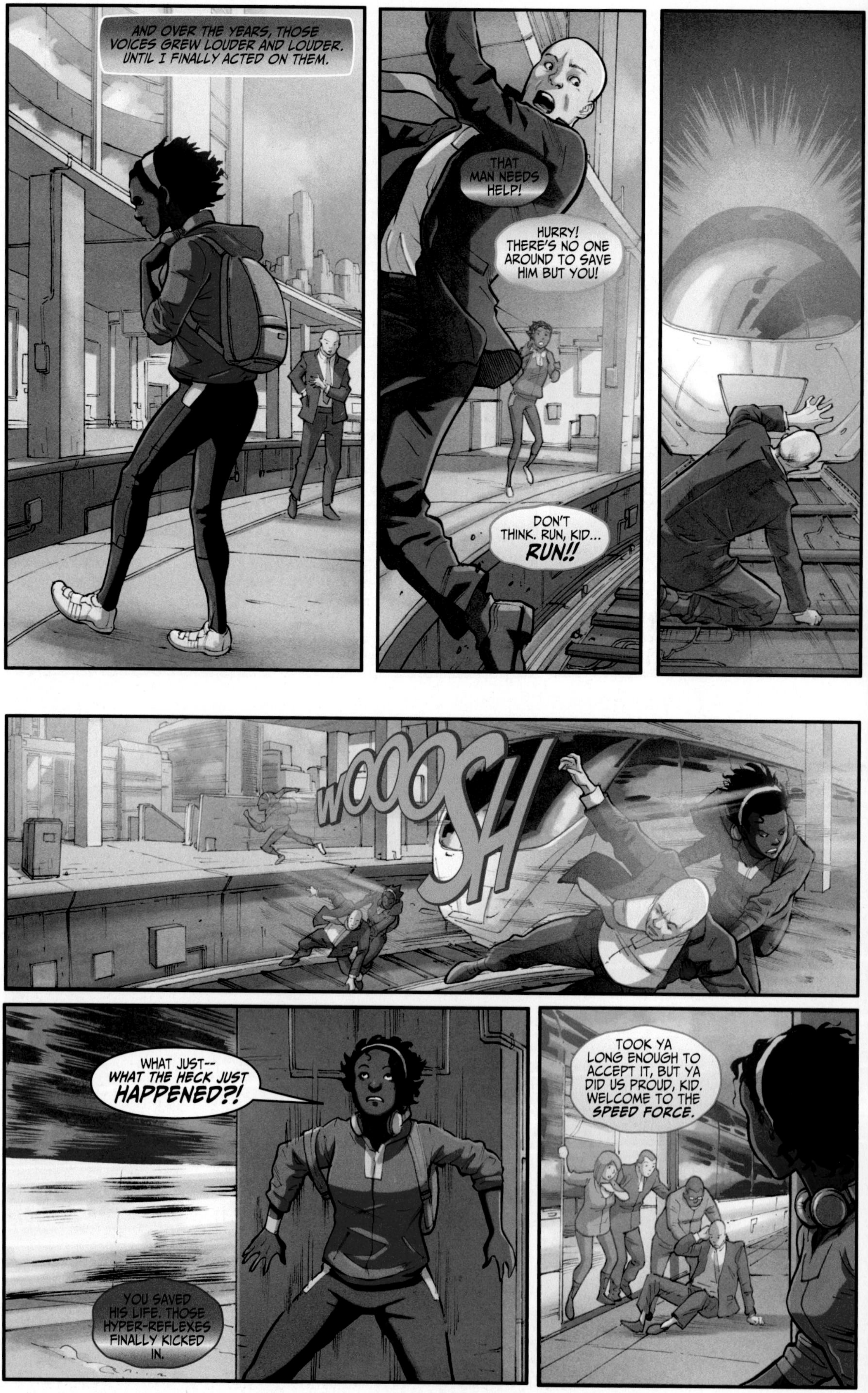
AND OVER THE YEARS, THOSE VOICES GREW LOUDER AND LOUDER. UNTIL I FINALLY ACTED ON THEM.
THAT MAN NEEDS HELP!
HURRY! THERE'S NO ONE AROUND TO SAVE HIM BUT YOU!
DON'T THINK. RUN, KID... RUN!!
WOOOSH
WHAT JUST-- WHAT THE HECK JUST HAPPENED?!
YOU SAVED HIS LIFE. THOSE HYPER-REFLEXES FINALLY KICKED IN.
TOOK YA LONG ENOUGH TO ACCEPT IT, BUT YA DID US PROUD, KID. WELCOME TO THE SPEED FORCE.

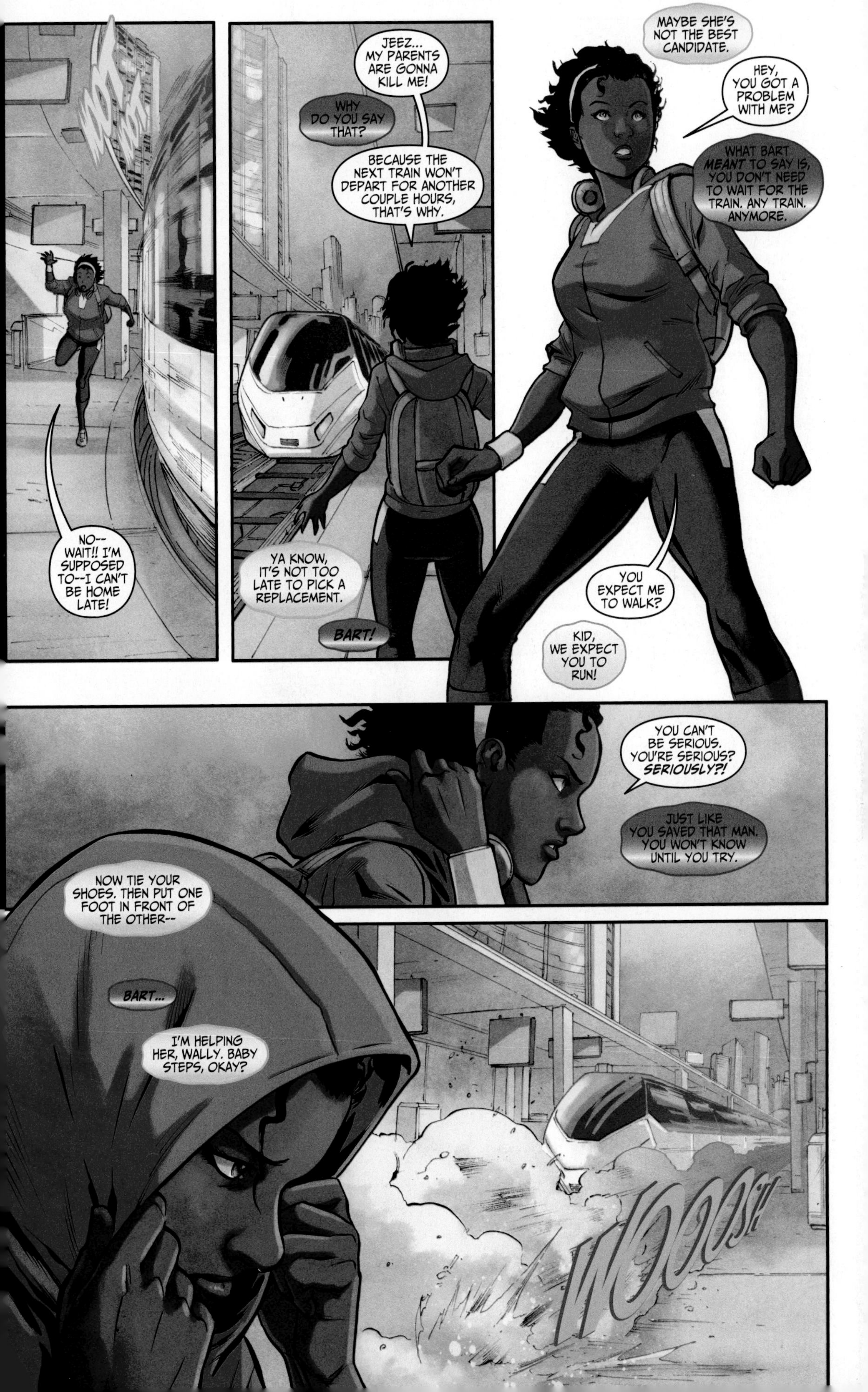
NO-- WAIT!! I'M SUPPOSED TO--I CAN'T BE HOME LATE!
JEEZ... MY PARENTS ARE GONNA KILL ME!
WHY DO YOU SAY THAT?
BECAUSE THE NEXT TRAIN WON'T DEPART FOR ANOTHER COUPLE HOURS, THAT'S WHY.
YA KNOW, IT'S NOT TOO LATE TO PICK A REPLACEMENT.
BART!
MAYBE SHE'S NOT THE BEST CANDIDATE.
HEY, YOU GOT A PROBLEM WITH ME?
WHAT BART MEANT TO SAY IS, YOU DON'T NEED TO WAIT FOR THE TRAIN. ANY TRAIN. ANYMORE.
YOU EXPECT ME TO WALK?
KID, WE EXPECT YOU TO RUN!
YOU CAN'T BE SERIOUS. YOU'RE SERIOUS? SERIOUSLY?!
JUST LIKE YOU SAVED THAT MAN. YOU WON'T KNOW UNTIL YOU TRY.
NOW TIE YOUR SHOES. THEN PUT ONE FOOT IN FRONT OF THE OTHER--
BART...
I'M HELPING HER, WALLY. BABY STEPS, OKAY?
WOOOSH

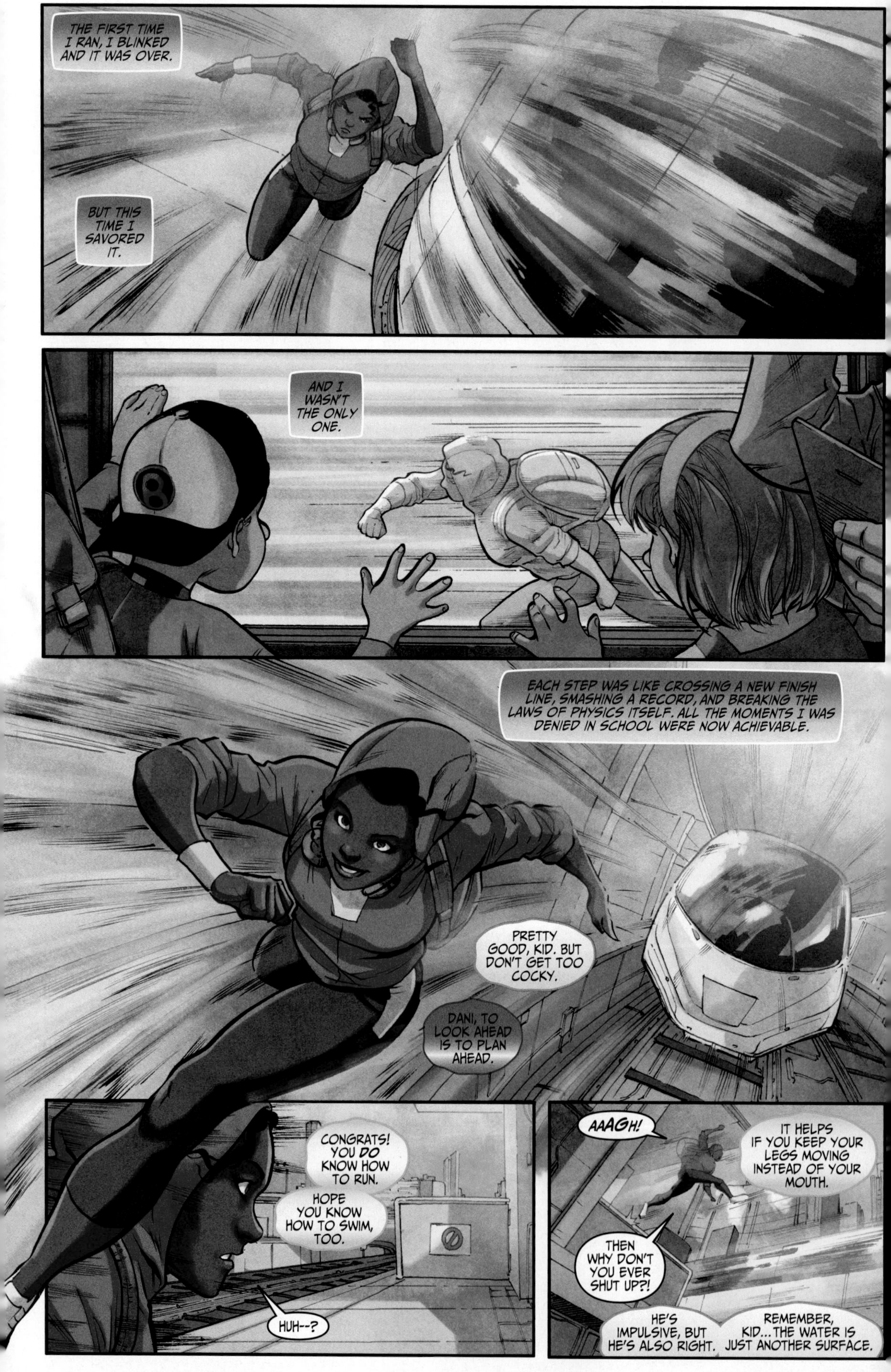
THE FIRST TIME I RAN, I BLINKED AND IT WAS OVER.
BUT THIS TIME I SAVORED IT.
AND I WASN'T THE ONLY ONE.
EACH STEP WAS LIKE CROSSING A NEW FINISH LINE, SMASHING A RECORD, AND BREAKING THE LAWS OF PHYSICS ITSELF. ALL THE MOMENTS I WAS DENIED IN SCHOOL WERE NOW ACHIEVABLE.
PRETTY GOOD, KID. BUT DON'T GET TOO COCKY.
DANI, TO LOOK AHEAD IS TO PLAN AHEAD.
CONGRATS! YOU DO KNOW HOW TO RUN.
HOPE YOU KNOW HOW TO SWIM, TOO.
HUH--?
AAAGH!
IT HELPS IF YOU KEEP YOUR LEGS MOVING INSTEAD OF YOUR MOUTH.
THEN WHY DON'T YOU EVER SHUT UP?!
HE'S IMPULSIVE, BUT HE'S ALSO RIGHT.
REMEMBER, KID... THE WATER IS JUST ANOTHER SURFACE.

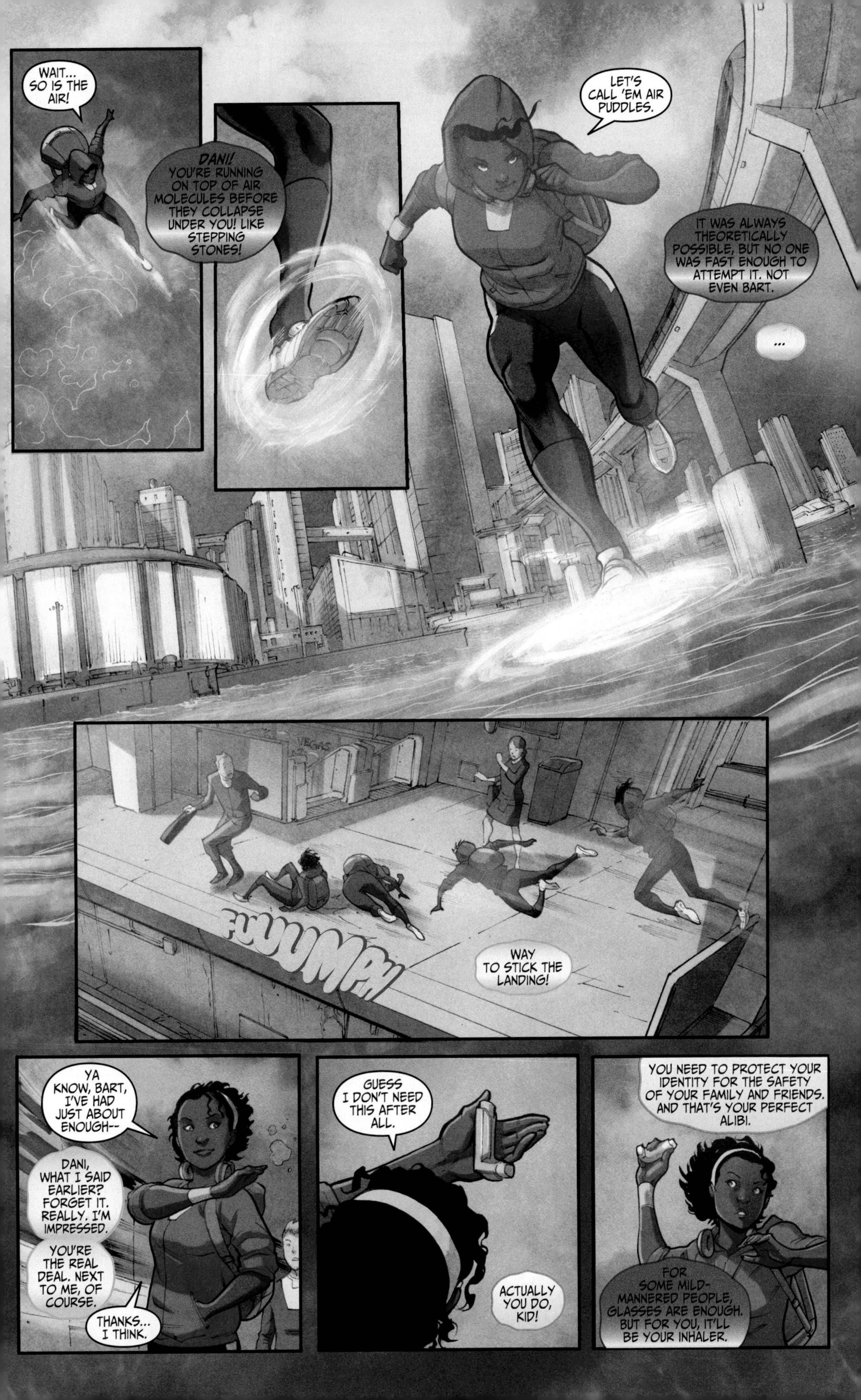
WAIT... SO IS THE AIR!
DANI! YOU'RE RUNNING ON TOP OF AIR MOLECULES BEFORE THEY COLLAPSE UNDER YOU! LIKE STEPPING STONES!
LET'S CALL 'EM AIR PUDDLES.
IT WAS ALWAYS THEORETICALLY POSSIBLE, BUT NO ONE WAS FAST ENOUGH TO ATTEMPT IT. NOT EVEN BART.
...
FUUUMPH
WAY TO STICK THE LANDING!
YA KNOW, BART, I'VE HAD JUST ABOUT ENOUGH--
DANI, WHAT I SAID EARLIER? FORGET IT. REALLY. I'M IMPRESSED.
YOU'RE THE REAL DEAL. NEXT TO ME, OF COURSE.
THANKS... I THINK.
GUESS I DON'T NEED THIS AFTER ALL.
ACTUALLY YOU DO, KID!
YOU NEED TO PROTECT YOUR IDENTITY FOR THE SAFETY OF YOUR FAMILY AND FRIENDS. AND THAT'S YOUR PERFECT ALIBI.
FOR SOME MILD-MANNERED PEOPLE, GLASSES ARE ENOUGH. BUT FOR YOU, IT'LL BE YOUR INHALER.

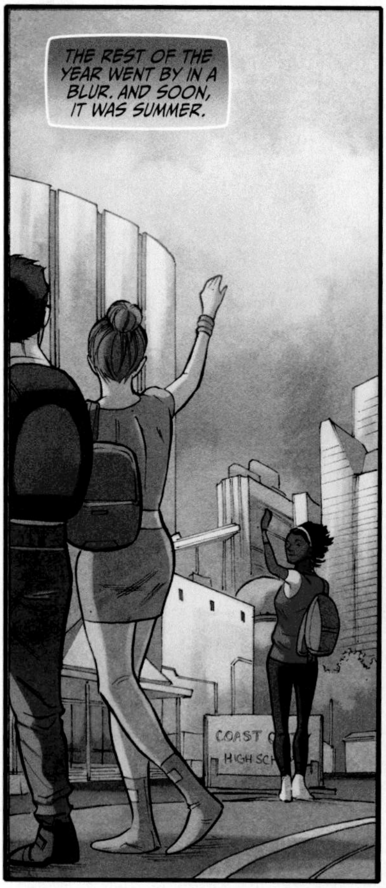
THE REST OF THE YEAR WENT BY IN A BLUR. AND SOON, IT WAS SUMMER.

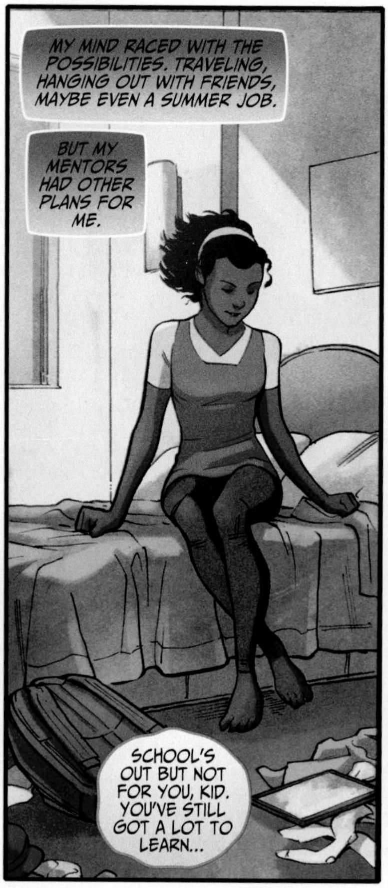
MY MIND RACED WITH THE POSSIBILITIES. TRAVELING, HANGING OUT WITH FRIENDS, MAYBE EVEN A SUMMER JOB.
BUT MY MENTORS HAD OTHER PLANS FOR ME.
SCHOOL'S OUT BUT NOT FOR YOU, KID. YOU'VE STILL GOT A LOT TO LEARN...

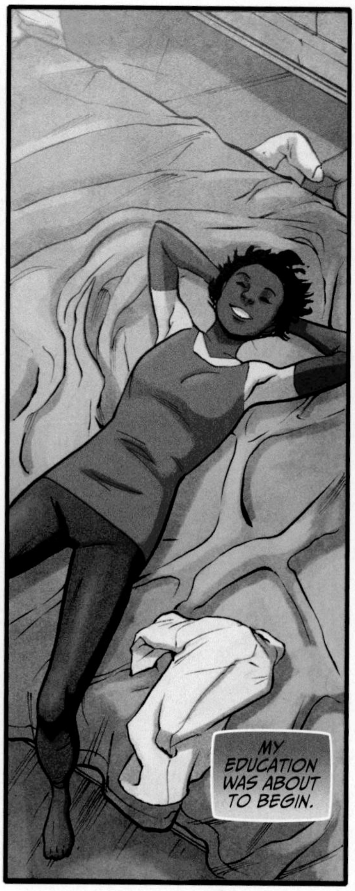
MY EDUCATION WAS ABOUT TO BEGIN.

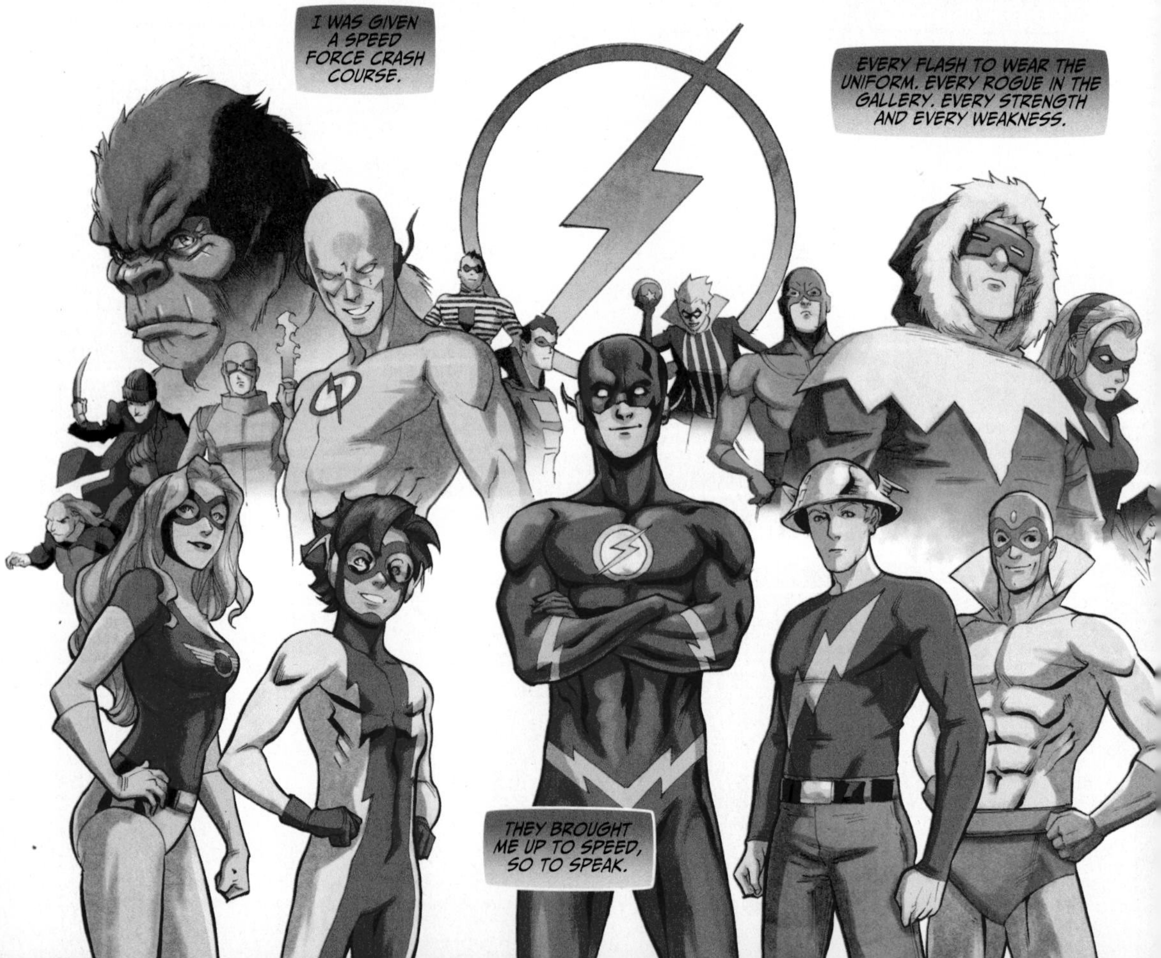
I WAS GIVEN A SPEED FORCE CRASH COURSE.
EVERY FLASH TO WEAR THE UNIFORM. EVERY ROGUE IN THE GALLERY. EVERY STRENGTH AND EVERY WEAKNESS.
THEY BROUGHT ME UP TO SPEED, SO TO SPEAK.

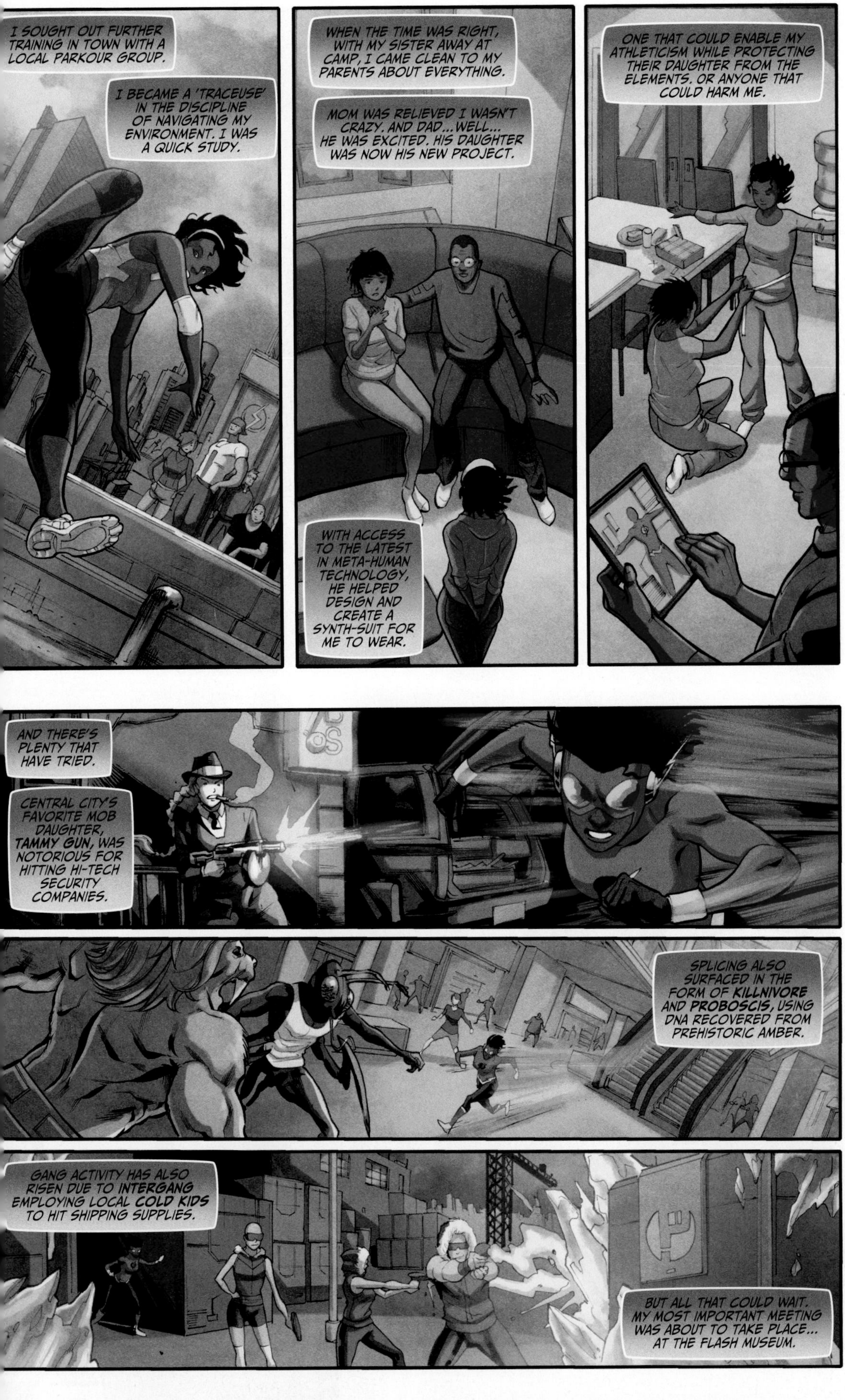
I SOUGHT OUT FURTHER TRAINING IN TOWN WITH A LOCAL PARKOUR GROUP.
I BECAME A 'TRACEUSE' IN THE DISCIPLINE OF NAVIGATING MY ENVIRONMENT. I WAS A QUICK STUDY.
WHEN THE TIME WAS RIGHT, WITH MY SISTER AWAY AT CAMP, I CAME CLEAN TO MY PARENTS ABOUT EVERYTHING.
MOM WAS RELIEVED I WASN'T CRAZY. AND DAD...WELL... HE WAS EXCITED. HIS DAUGHTER WAS NOW HIS NEW PROJECT.
WITH ACCESS TO THE LATEST IN META-HUMAN TECHNOLOGY, HE HELPED DESIGN AND CREATE A SYNTH-SUIT FOR ME TO WEAR.
ONE THAT COULD ENABLE MY ATHLETICISM WHILE PROTECTING THEIR DAUGHTER FROM THE ELEMENTS. OR ANYONE THAT COULD HARM ME.
AND THERE'S PLENTY THAT HAVE TRIED.
CENTRAL CITY'S FAVORITE MOB DAUGHTER, **TAMMY GUN**, WAS NOTORIOUS FOR HITTING HI-TECH SECURITY COMPANIES.
SPLICING ALSO SURFACED IN THE FORM OF **KILLNIVORE** AND **PROBOSCIS**, USING DNA RECOVERED FROM PREHISTORIC AMBER.
GANG ACTIVITY HAS ALSO RISEN DUE TO **INTERGANG** EMPLOYING LOCAL **COLD KIDS** TO HIT SHIPPING SUPPLIES.
BUT ALL THAT COULD WAIT. MY MOST IMPORTANT MEETING WAS ABOUT TO TAKE PLACE... AT THE FLASH MUSEUM.

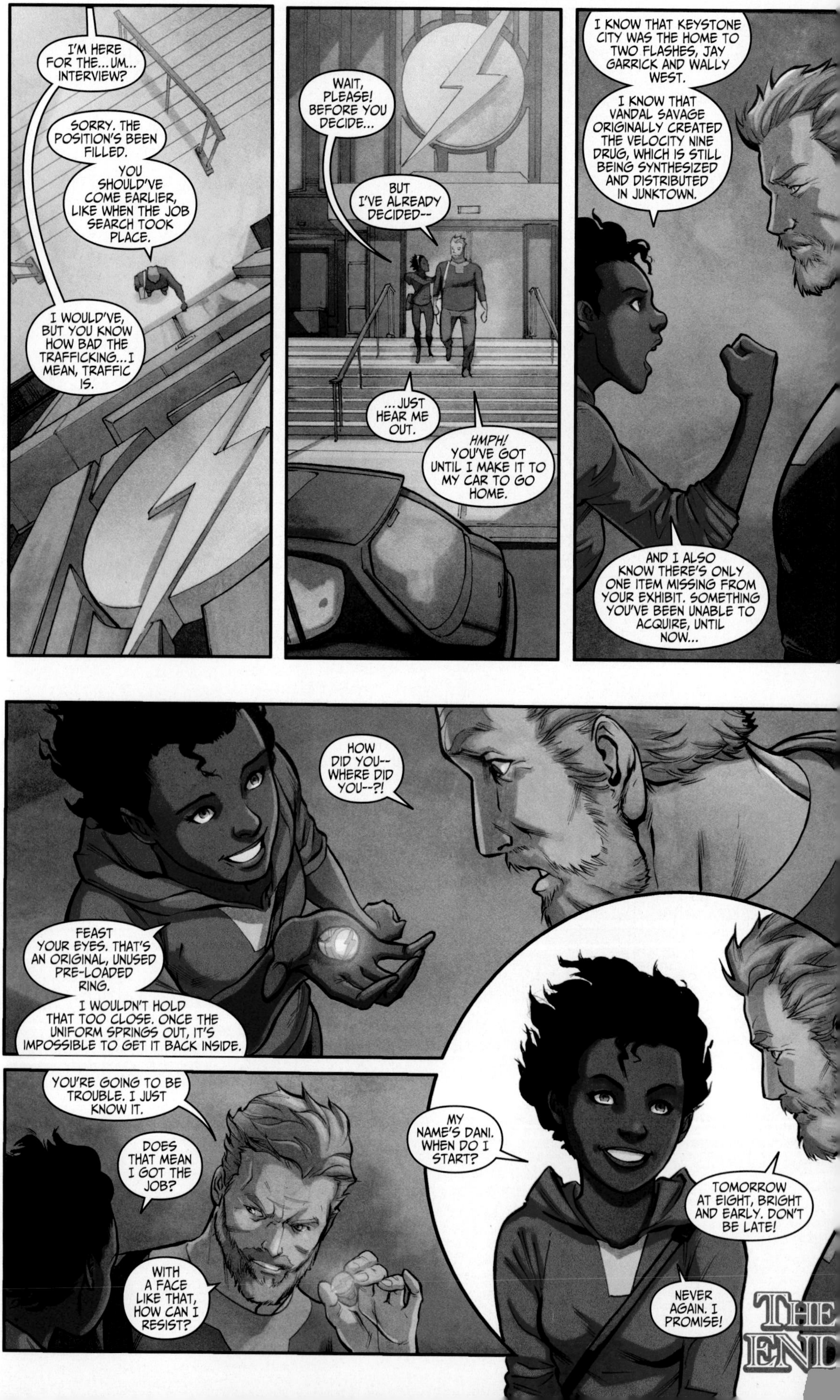

I'M HERE FOR THE...UM... INTERVIEW?
SORRY. THE POSITION'S BEEN FILLED.
YOU SHOULD'VE COME EARLIER, LIKE WHEN THE JOB SEARCH TOOK PLACE.
I WOULD'VE, BUT YOU KNOW HOW BAD THE TRAFFICKING...I MEAN, TRAFFIC IS.
WAIT, PLEASE! BEFORE YOU DECIDE...
BUT I'VE ALREADY DECIDED--
...JUST HEAR ME OUT.
HMPH! YOU'VE GOT UNTIL I MAKE IT TO MY CAR TO GO HOME.
I KNOW THAT KEYSTONE CITY WAS THE HOME TO TWO FLASHES, JAY GARRICK AND WALLY WEST.
I KNOW THAT VANDAL SAVAGE ORIGINALLY CREATED THE VELOCITY NINE DRUG, WHICH IS STILL BEING SYNTHESIZED AND DISTRIBUTED IN JUNKTOWN.
AND I ALSO KNOW THERE'S ONLY ONE ITEM MISSING FROM YOUR EXHIBIT. SOMETHING YOU'VE BEEN UNABLE TO ACQUIRE, UNTIL NOW...
HOW DID YOU-- WHERE DID YOU--?!
FEAST YOUR EYES. THAT'S AN ORIGINAL, UNUSED PRE-LOADED RING.
I WOULDN'T HOLD THAT TOO CLOSE. ONCE THE UNIFORM SPRINGS OUT, IT'S IMPOSSIBLE TO GET IT BACK INSIDE.
YOU'RE GOING TO BE TROUBLE. I JUST KNOW IT.
DOES THAT MEAN I GOT THE JOB?
WITH A FACE LIKE THAT, HOW CAN I RESIST?
MY NAME'S DANI. WHEN DO I START?
TOMORROW AT EIGHT, BRIGHT AND EARLY. DON'T BE LATE!
NEVER AGAIN. I PROMISE!
THE END

JUSTICE LEAGUE BEYOND

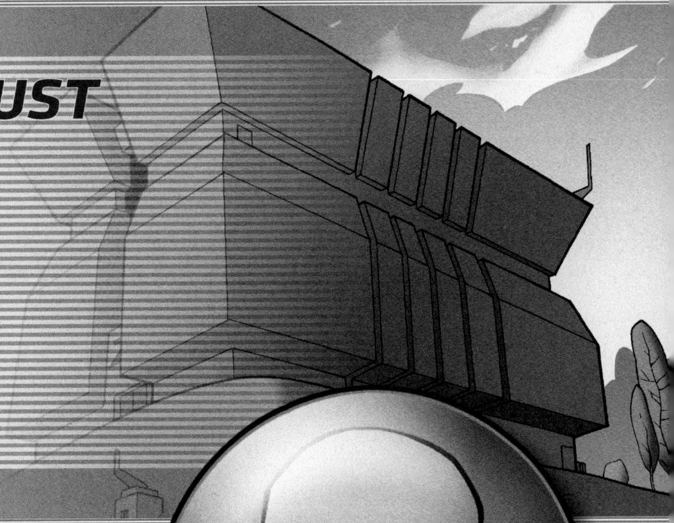

IN GODS WE TRUST

WRITTEN BY
DEREK FRIDOLFS
PENCILS BY
BEN CALDWELL
INKS BY
DEREK FRIDOLFS
COLORS BY
RANDY MAYOR

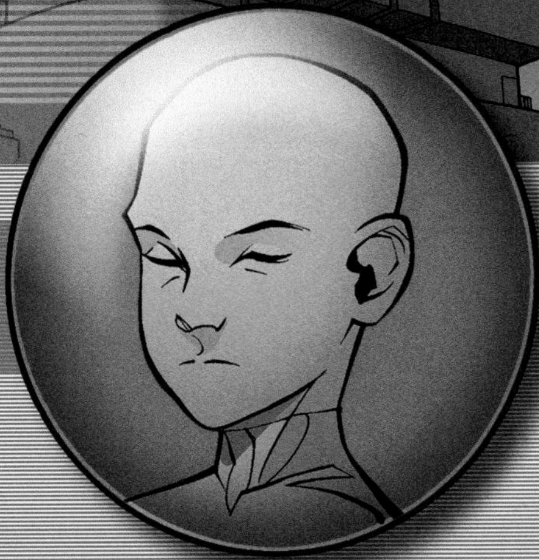

ORIGINS: GREEN LANTERN

WRITTEN BY
DEREK FRIDOLFS
AND DUSTIN NGUYEN
PENCILS BY
DUSTIN NGUYEN
INKS BY
DEREK FRIDOLFS
COLORS BY
JOHN KALISZ

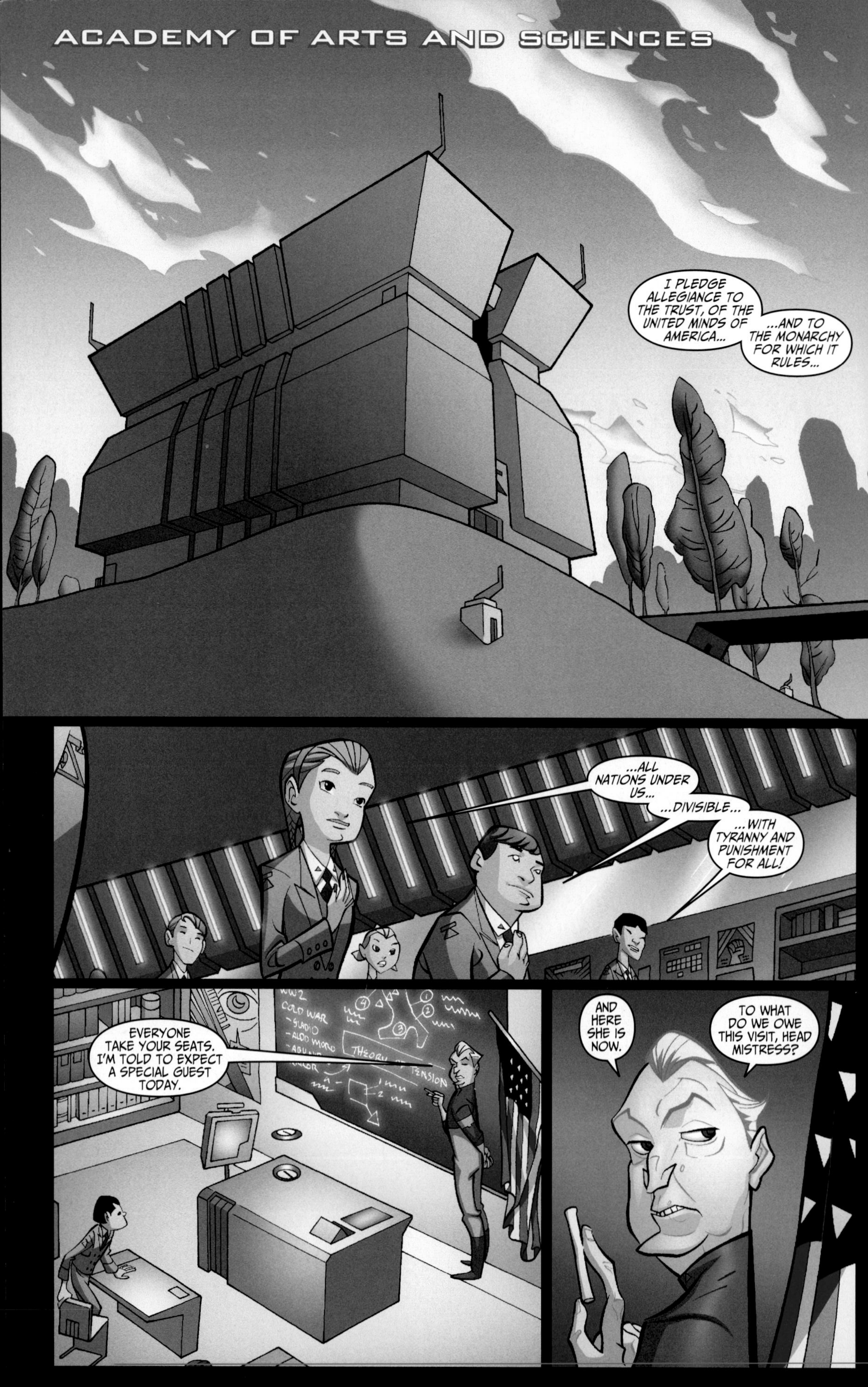
ACADEMY OF ARTS AND SCIENCES
I PLEDGE ALLEGIANCE TO THE TRUST, OF THE UNITED MINDS OF AMERICA...
...AND TO THE MONARCHY FOR WHICH IT RULES...
...ALL NATIONS UNDER US...
...DIVISIBLE...
...WITH TYRANNY AND PUNISHMENT FOR ALL!
EVERYONE TAKE YOUR SEATS. I'M TOLD TO EXPECT A SPECIAL GUEST TODAY.
AND HERE SHE IS NOW.
TO WHAT DO WE OWE THIS VISIT, HEAD MISTRESS?

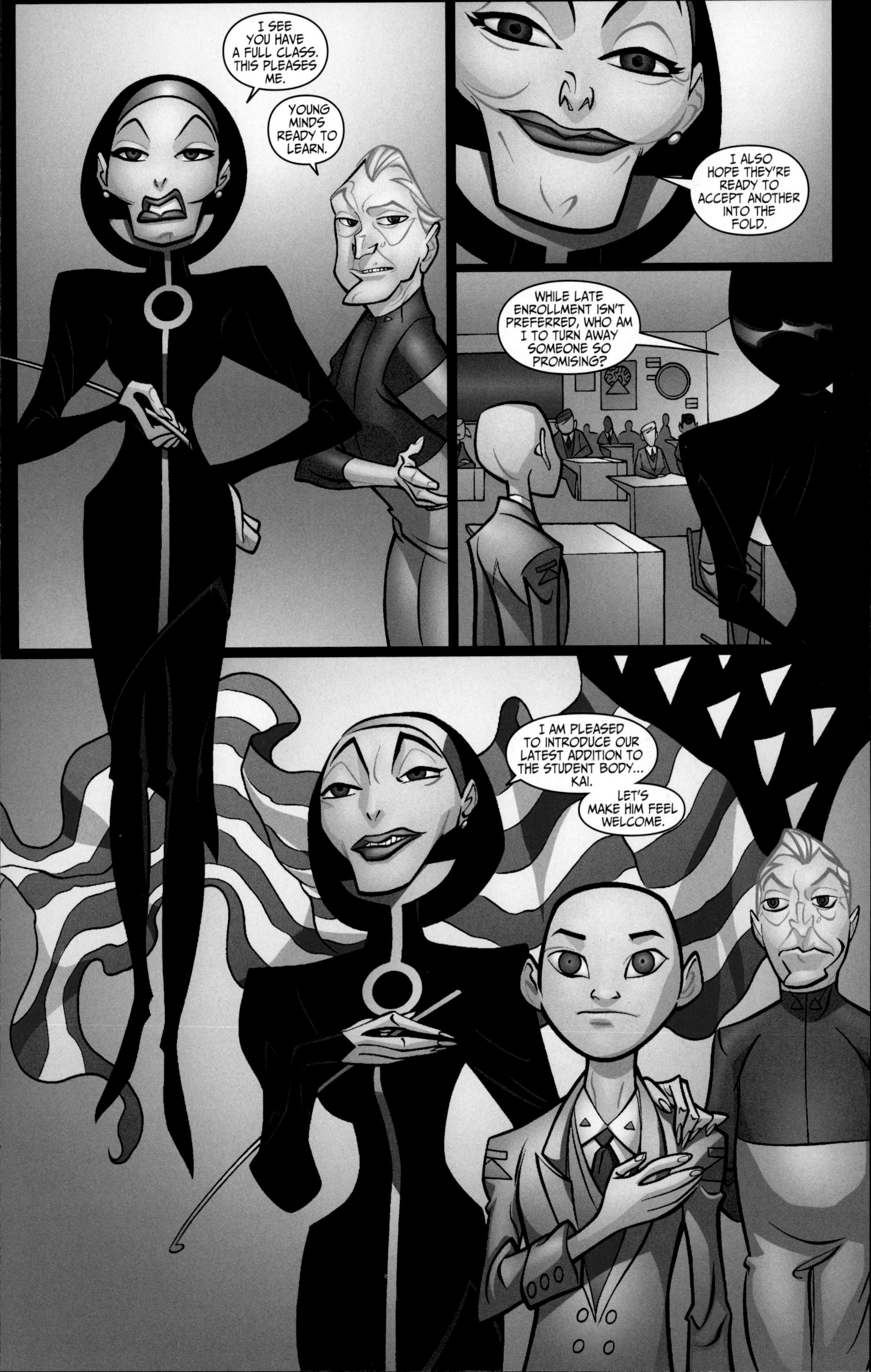
I SEE YOU HAVE A FULL CLASS. THIS PLEASES ME.
YOUNG MINDS READY TO LEARN.
I ALSO HOPE THEY'RE READY TO ACCEPT ANOTHER INTO THE FOLD.
WHILE LATE ENROLLMENT ISN'T PREFERRED, WHO AM I TO TURN AWAY SOMEONE SO PROMISING?
I AM PLEASED TO INTRODUCE OUR LATEST ADDITION TO THE STUDENT BODY... KAI.
LET'S MAKE HIM FEEL WELCOME.

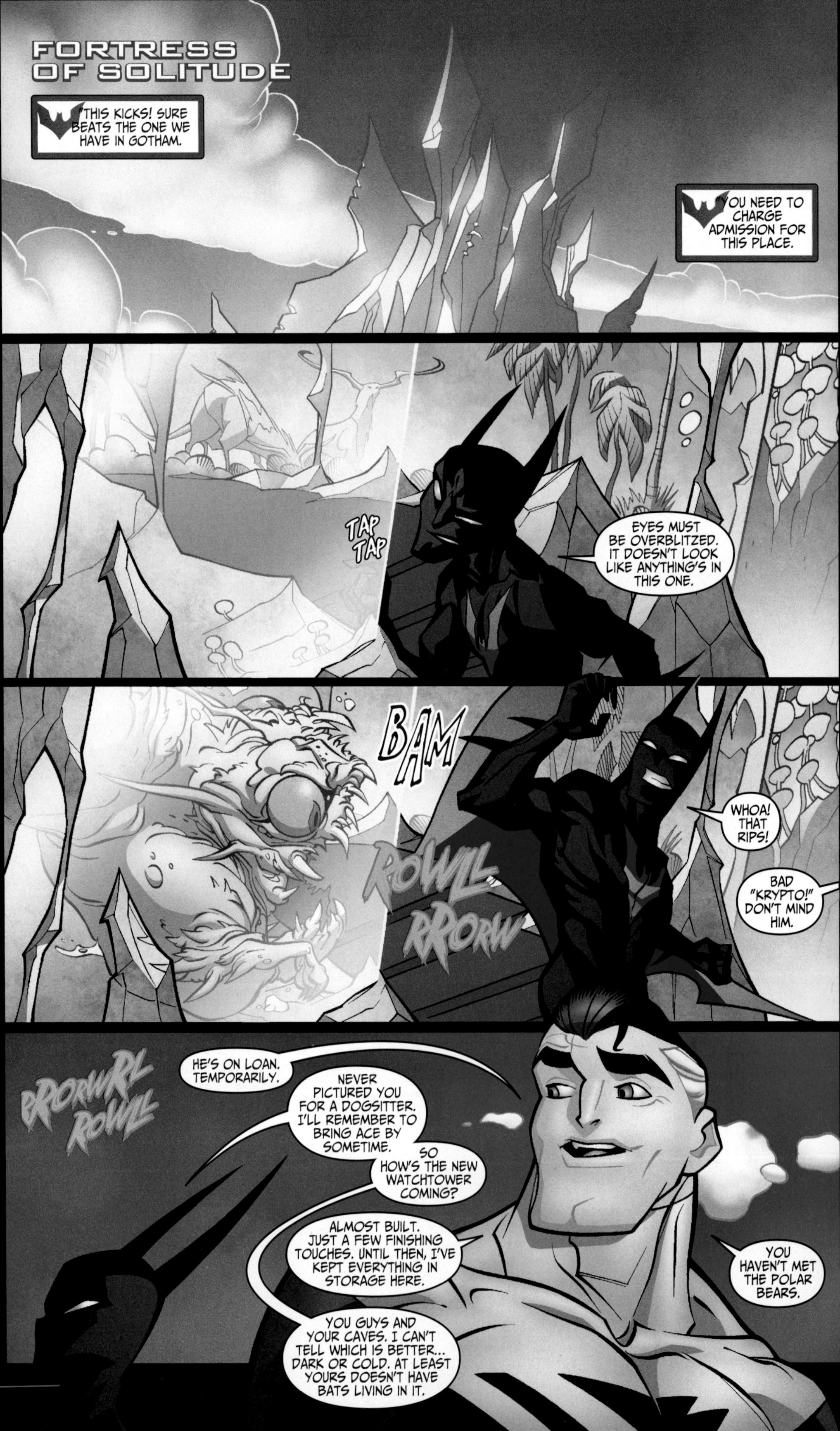
FORTRESS OF SOLITUDE
"THIS KICKS! SURE BEATS THE ONE WE HAVE IN GOTHAM.
"YOU NEED TO CHARGE ADMISSION FOR THIS PLACE.
TAP TAP
EYES MUST BE OVERBLITZED. IT DOESN'T LOOK LIKE ANYTHING'S IN THIS ONE.
BAM
ROWLL RRORW
WHOA! THAT RIPS!
BAD "KRYPTO!" DON'T MIND HIM.
RRORWRL ROWLL
HE'S ON LOAN. TEMPORARILY.
NEVER PICTURED YOU FOR A DOGSITTER. I'LL REMEMBER TO BRING ACE BY SOMETIME.
SO HOW'S THE NEW WATCHTOWER COMING?
ALMOST BUILT. JUST A FEW FINISHING TOUCHES. UNTIL THEN, I'VE KEPT EVERYTHING IN STORAGE HERE.
YOU HAVEN'T MET THE POLAR BEARS.
YOU GUYS AND YOUR CAVES. I CAN'T TELL WHICH IS BETTER... DARK OR COLD. AT LEAST YOURS DOESN'T HAVE BATS LIVING IN IT.

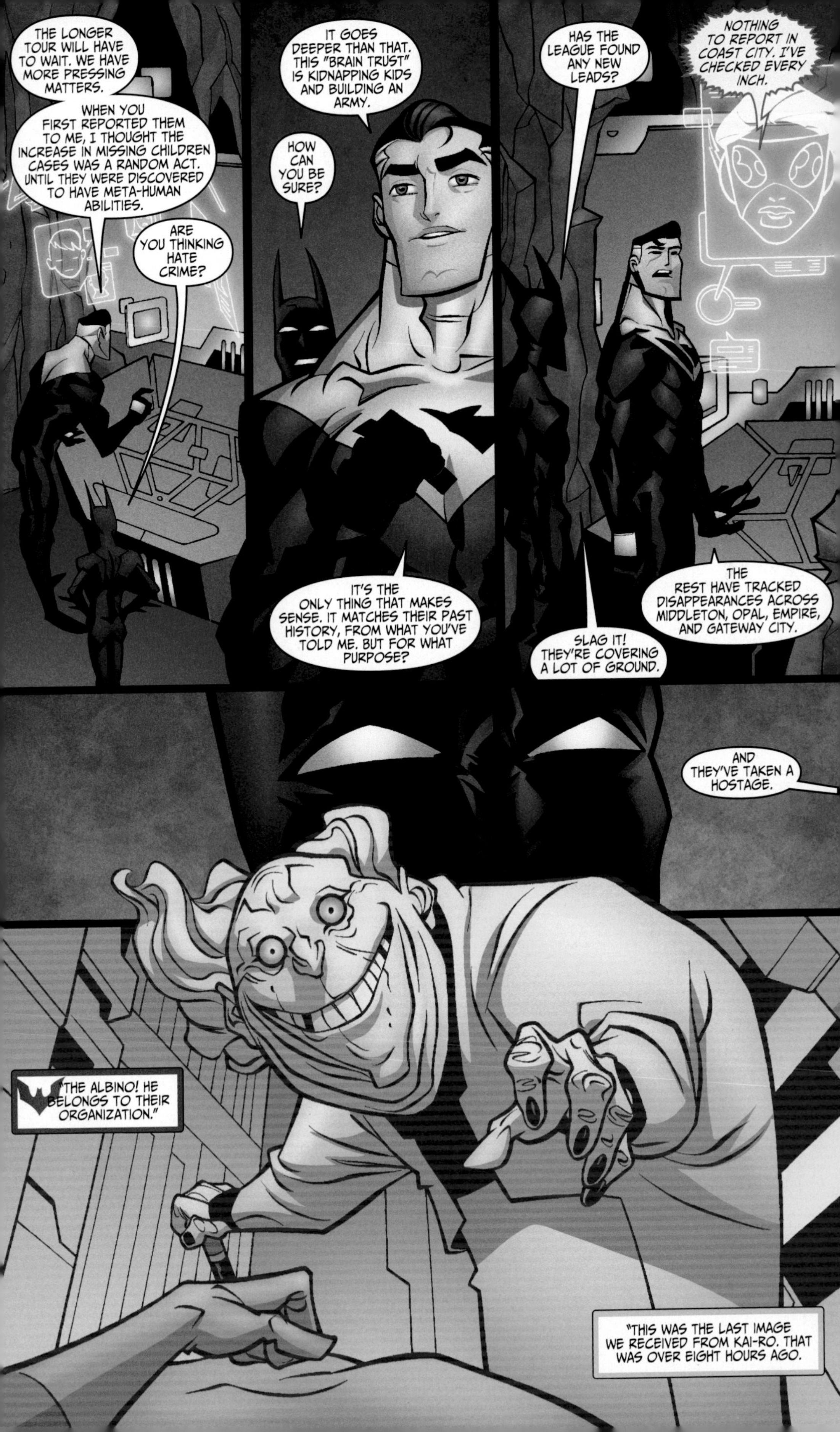
THE LONGER TOUR WILL HAVE TO WAIT. WE HAVE MORE PRESSING MATTERS.
WHEN YOU FIRST REPORTED THEM TO ME, I THOUGHT THE INCREASE IN MISSING CHILDREN CASES WAS A RANDOM ACT. UNTIL THEY WERE DISCOVERED TO HAVE META-HUMAN ABILITIES.
ARE YOU THINKING HATE CRIME?
IT GOES DEEPER THAN THAT. THIS "BRAIN TRUST" IS KIDNAPPING KIDS AND BUILDING AN ARMY.
HOW CAN YOU BE SURE?
IT'S THE ONLY THING THAT MAKES SENSE. IT MATCHES THEIR PAST HISTORY, FROM WHAT YOU'VE TOLD ME. BUT FOR WHAT PURPOSE?
HAS THE LEAGUE FOUND ANY NEW LEADS?
NOTHING TO REPORT IN COAST CITY. I'VE CHECKED EVERY INCH.
THE REST HAVE TRACKED DISAPPEARANCES ACROSS MIDDLETON, OPAL, EMPIRE, AND GATEWAY CITY.
SLAG IT! THEY'RE COVERING A LOT OF GROUND.
AND THEY'VE TAKEN A HOSTAGE.
"THE ALBINO! HE BELONGS TO THEIR ORGANIZATION."
"THIS WAS THE LAST IMAGE WE RECEIVED FROM KAI-RO. THAT WAS OVER EIGHT HOURS AGO.

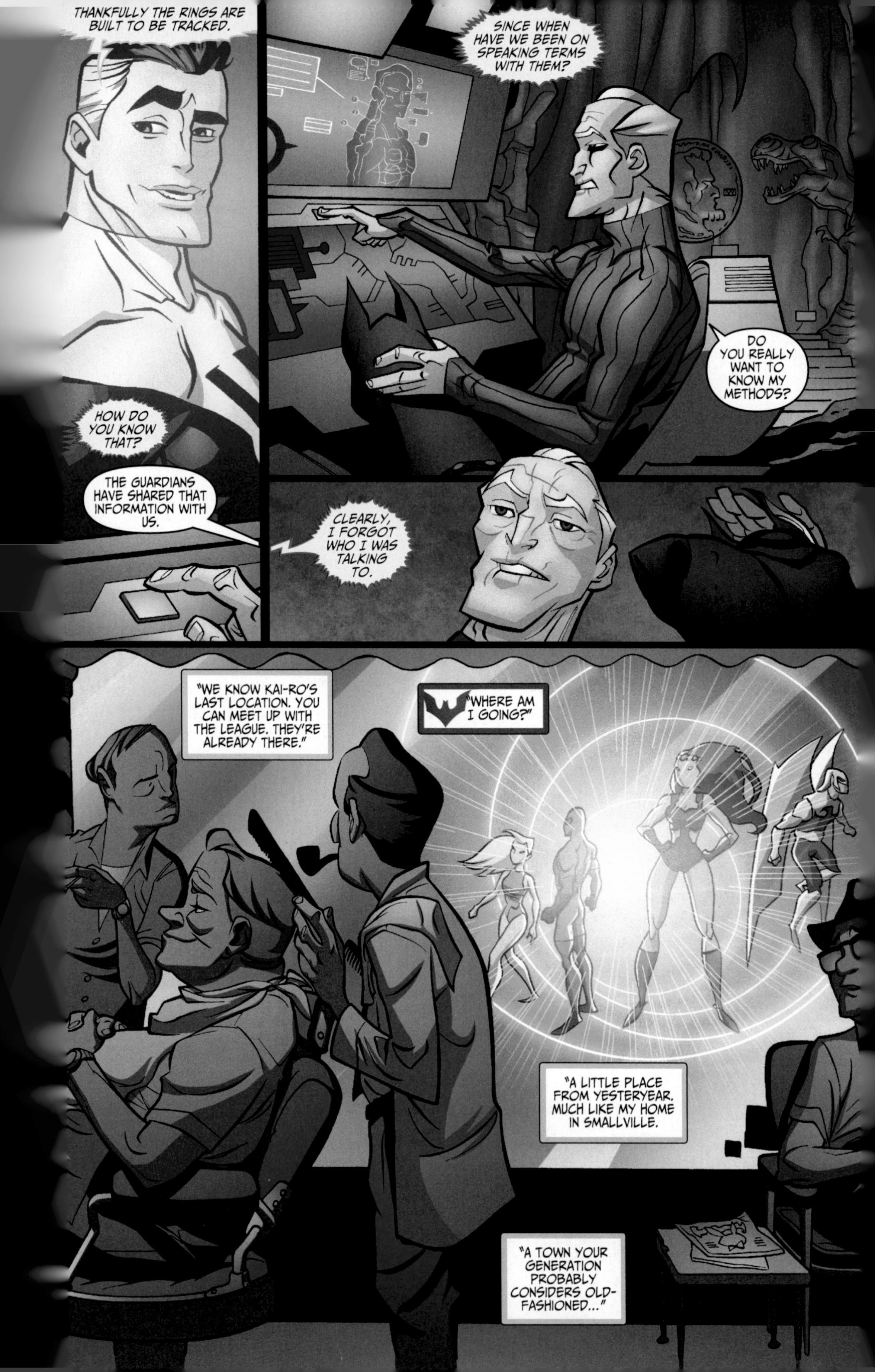
THANKFULLY THE RINGS ARE BUILT TO BE TRACKED.
SINCE WHEN HAVE WE BEEN ON SPEAKING TERMS WITH THEM?
DO YOU REALLY WANT TO KNOW MY METHODS?
HOW DO YOU KNOW THAT?
THE GUARDIANS HAVE SHARED THAT INFORMATION WITH US.
CLEARLY, I FORGOT WHO I WAS TALKING TO.
"WE KNOW KAI-RO'S LAST LOCATION. YOU CAN MEET UP WITH THE LEAGUE. THEY'RE ALREADY THERE."
"WHERE AM I GOING?"
"A LITTLE PLACE FROM YESTERYEAR. MUCH LIKE MY HOME IN SMALLVILLE.
"A TOWN YOUR GENERATION PROBABLY CONSIDERS OLD-FASHIONED..."

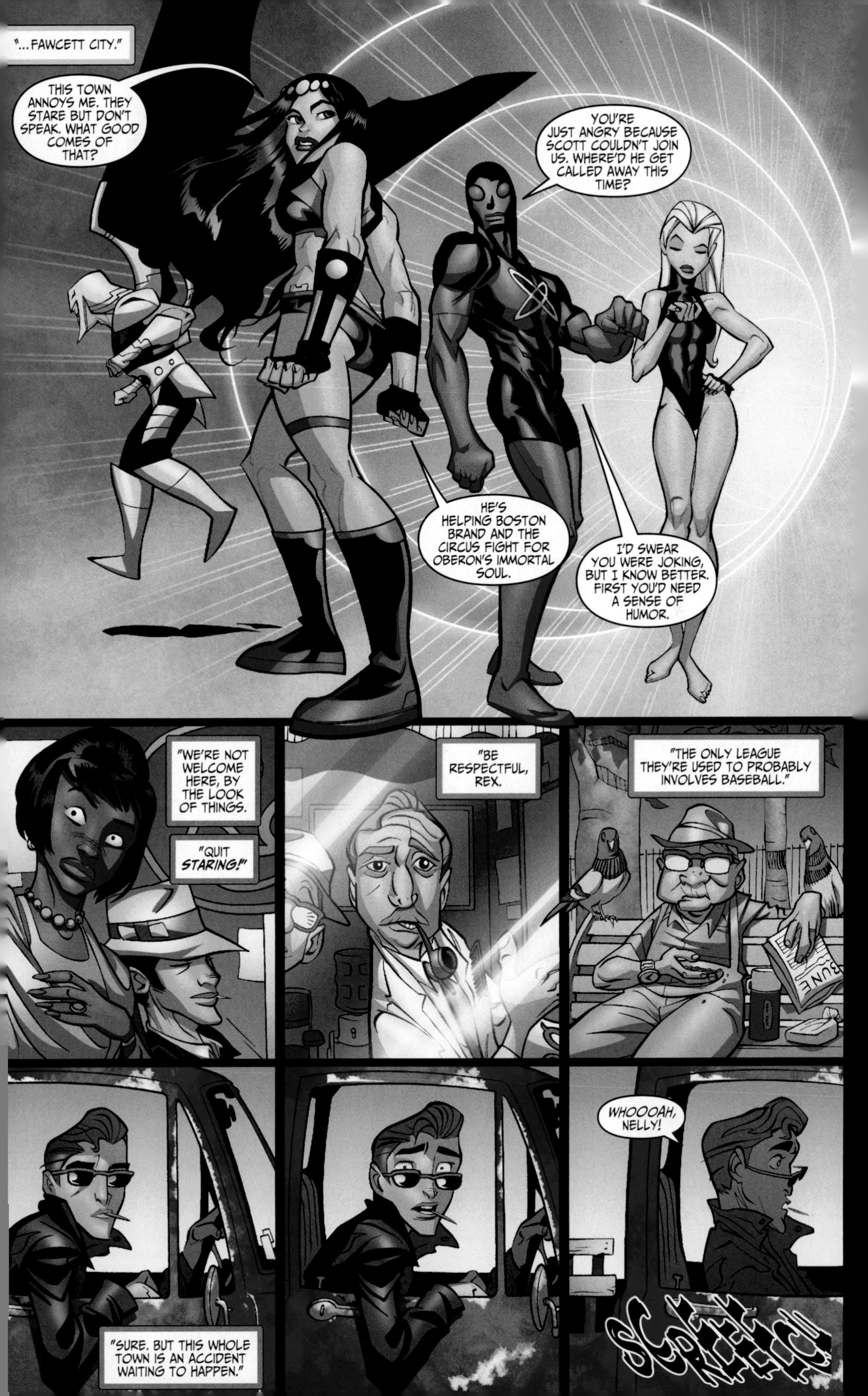
"...FAWCETT CITY."
THIS TOWN ANNOYS ME. THEY STARE BUT DON'T SPEAK. WHAT GOOD COMES OF THAT?
YOU'RE JUST ANGRY BECAUSE SCOTT COULDN'T JOIN US. WHERE'D HE GET CALLED AWAY THIS TIME?
HE'S HELPING BOSTON BRAND AND THE CIRCUS FIGHT FOR OBERON'S IMMORTAL SOUL.
I'D SWEAR YOU WERE JOKING, BUT I KNOW BETTER. FIRST YOU'D NEED A SENSE OF HUMOR.
"WE'RE NOT WELCOME HERE, BY THE LOOK OF THINGS.
"QUIT STARING!"
"BE RESPECTFUL, REX.
"THE ONLY LEAGUE THEY'RE USED TO PROBABLY INVOLVES BASEBALL."
"SURE. BUT THIS WHOLE TOWN IS AN ACCIDENT WAITING TO HAPPEN."
WHOOOAH, NELLY!
SCREEECH!

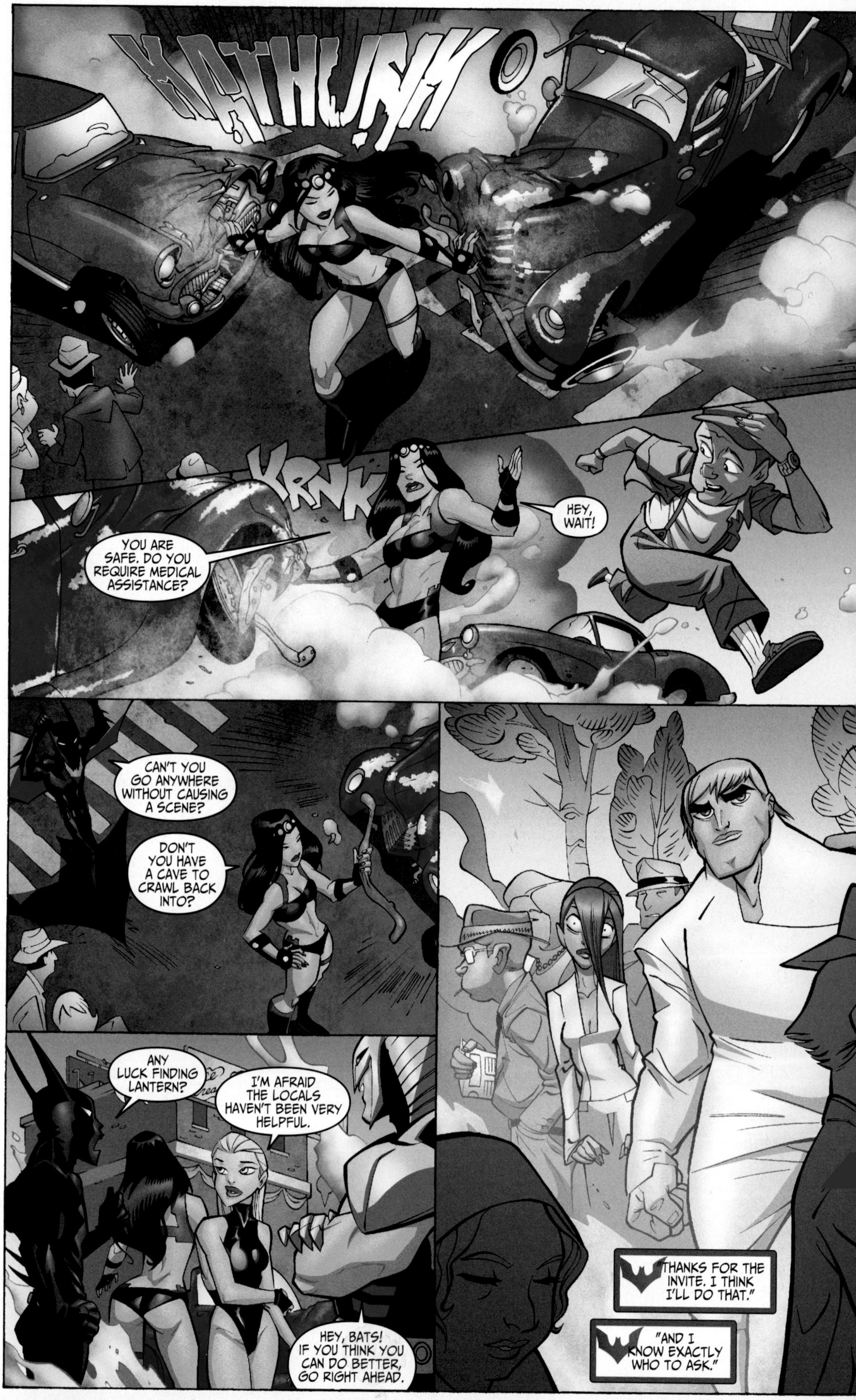
KRATHUNK!
KRNK
YOU ARE SAFE. DO YOU REQUIRE MEDICAL ASSISTANCE?
HEY, WAIT!
CAN'T YOU GO ANYWHERE WITHOUT CAUSING A SCENE?
DON'T YOU HAVE A CAVE TO CRAWL BACK INTO?
ANY LUCK FINDING LANTERN?
I'M AFRAID THE LOCALS HAVEN'T BEEN VERY HELPFUL.
HEY, BATS! IF YOU THINK YOU CAN DO BETTER, GO RIGHT AHEAD.
"THANKS FOR THE INVITE. I THINK I'LL DO THAT."
"AND I KNOW EXACTLY WHO TO ASK."

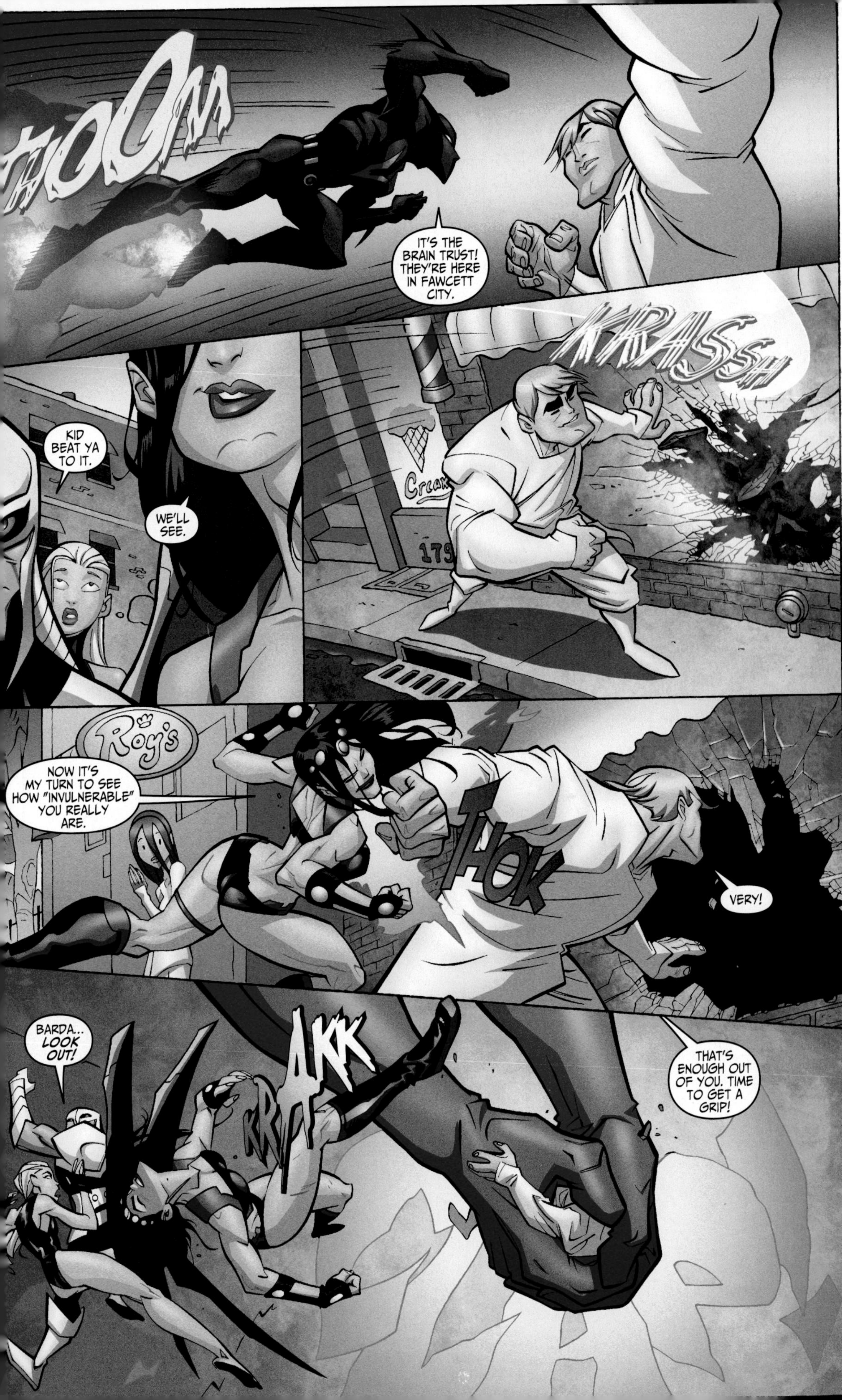
THOOM
IT'S THE BRAIN TRUST! THEY'RE HERE IN FAWCETT CITY.
KRASSSH
KID BEAT YA TO IT.
WE'LL SEE.
NOW IT'S MY TURN TO SEE HOW "INVULNERABLE" YOU REALLY ARE.
THOK
VERY!
BARDA... **LOOK OUT!**
AKK
KRA
THAT'S ENOUGH OUT OF YOU. TIME TO GET A GRIP!

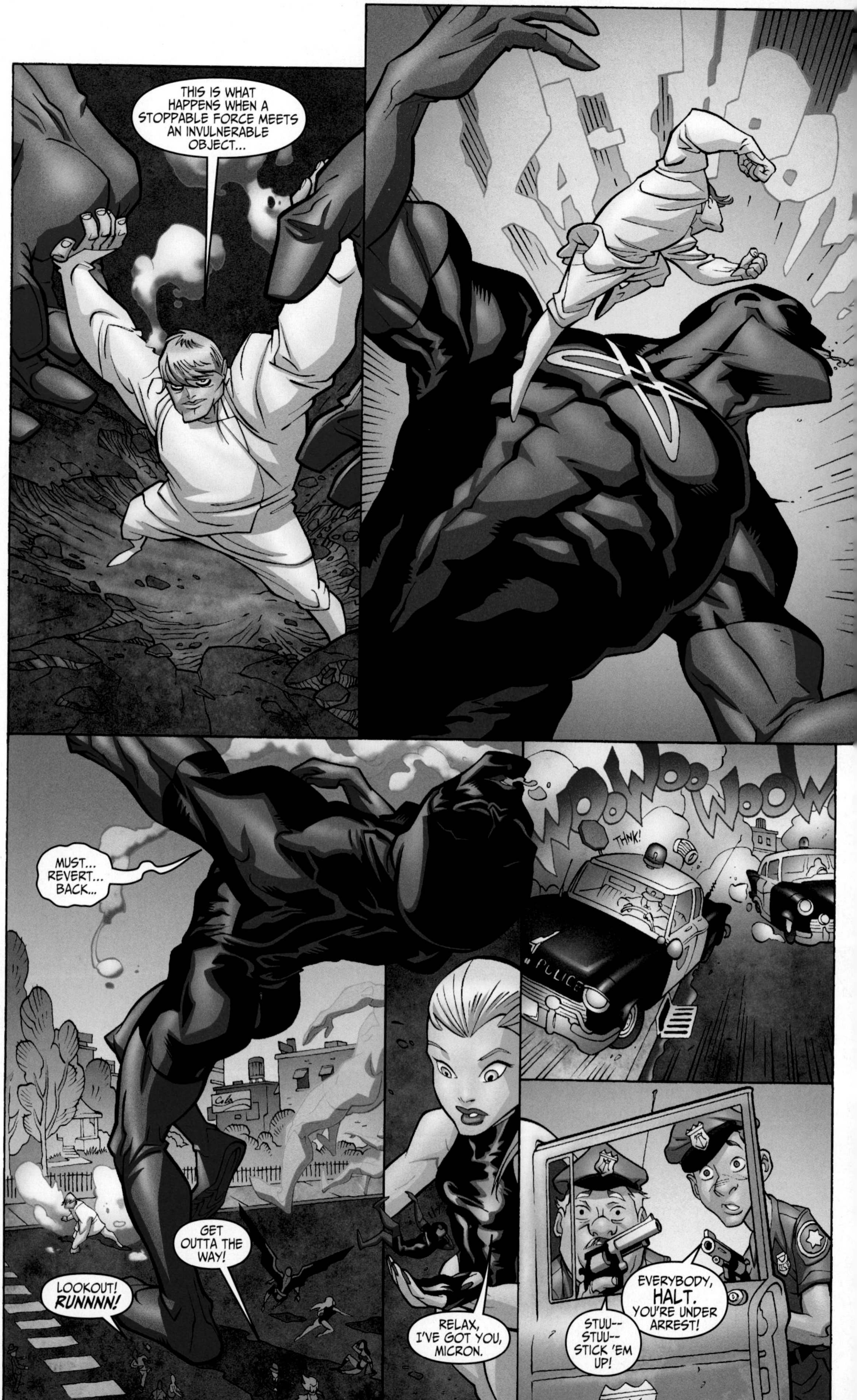
THIS IS WHAT HAPPENS WHEN A STOPPABLE FORCE MEETS AN INVULNERABLE OBJECT...
MUST... REVERT... BACK...
GET OUTTA THE WAY!
LOOKOUT! RUNNNN!
THNK!
RELAX, I'VE GOT YOU, MICRON.
POLICE
EVERYBODY, HALT. YOU'RE UNDER ARREST!
STUU-- STUU-- STICK 'EM UP!

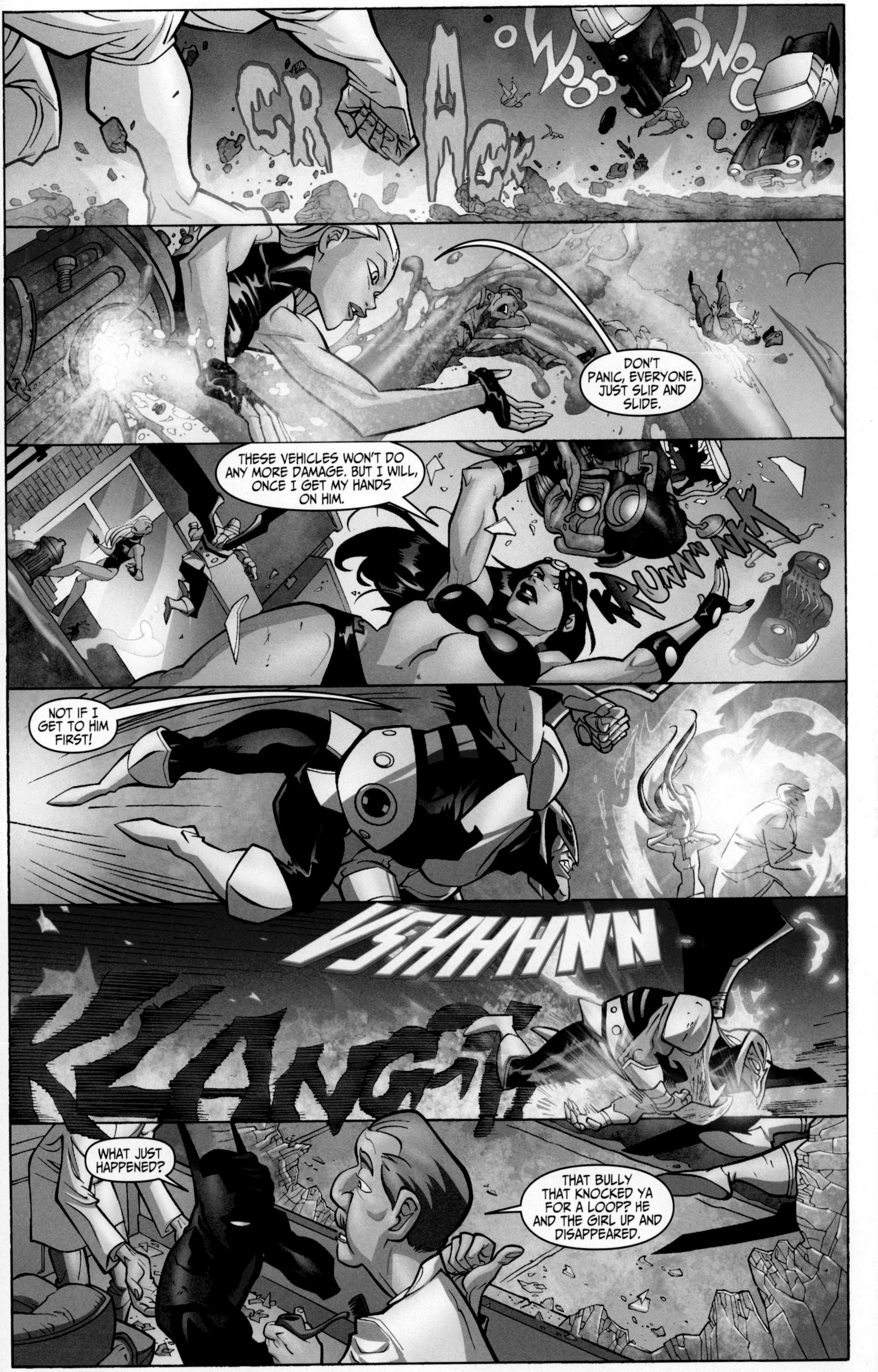
CRACK
WOOOONOOO
DON'T PANIC, EVERYONE. JUST SLIP AND SLIDE.
THESE VEHICLES WON'T DO ANY MORE DAMAGE. BUT I WILL, ONCE I GET MY HANDS ON HIM.
KRUNNNNKK
NOT IF I GET TO HIM FIRST!
VSHHHNN
KLANGH
WHAT JUST HAPPENED?
THAT BULLY THAT KNOCKED YA FOR A LOOP? HE AND THE GIRL UP AND DISAPPEARED.

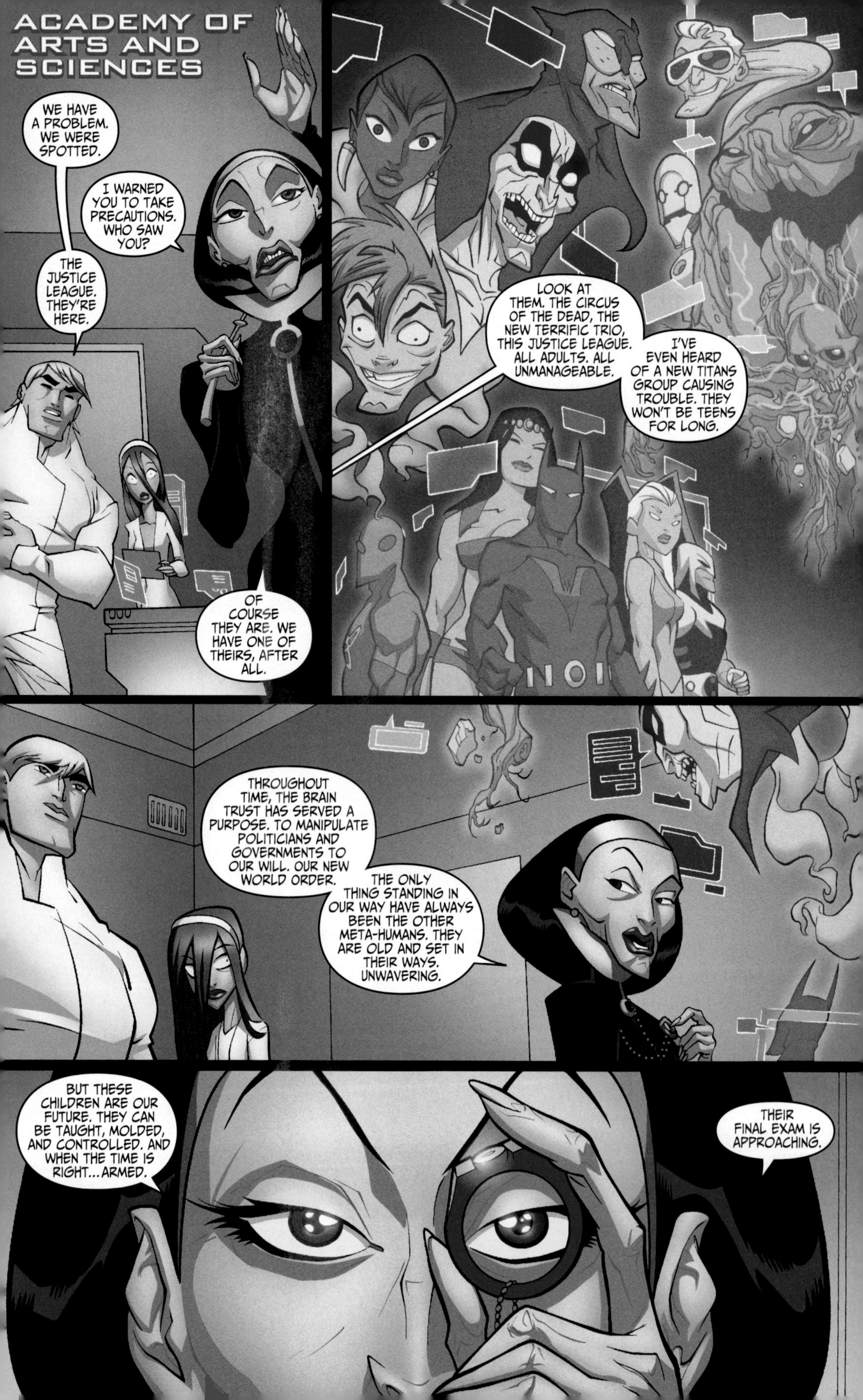
ACADEMY OF ARTS AND SCIENCES
WE HAVE A PROBLEM. WE WERE SPOTTED.
I WARNED YOU TO TAKE PRECAUTIONS. WHO SAW YOU?
THE JUSTICE LEAGUE. THEY'RE HERE.
OF COURSE THEY ARE. WE HAVE ONE OF THEIRS, AFTER ALL.
LOOK AT THEM. THE CIRCUS OF THE DEAD, THE NEW TERRIFIC TRIO, THIS JUSTICE LEAGUE. ALL ADULTS. ALL UNMANAGEABLE.
I'VE EVEN HEARD OF A NEW TITANS GROUP CAUSING TROUBLE. THEY WON'T BE TEENS FOR LONG.
THROUGHOUT TIME, THE BRAIN TRUST HAS SERVED A PURPOSE. TO MANIPULATE POLITICIANS AND GOVERNMENTS TO OUR WILL. OUR NEW WORLD ORDER.
THE ONLY THING STANDING IN OUR WAY HAVE ALWAYS BEEN THE OTHER META-HUMANS. THEY ARE OLD AND SET IN THEIR WAYS. UNWAVERING.
BUT THESE CHILDREN ARE OUR FUTURE. THEY CAN BE TAUGHT, MOLDED, AND CONTROLLED. AND WHEN THE TIME IS RIGHT...ARMED.
THEIR FINAL EXAM IS APPROACHING.

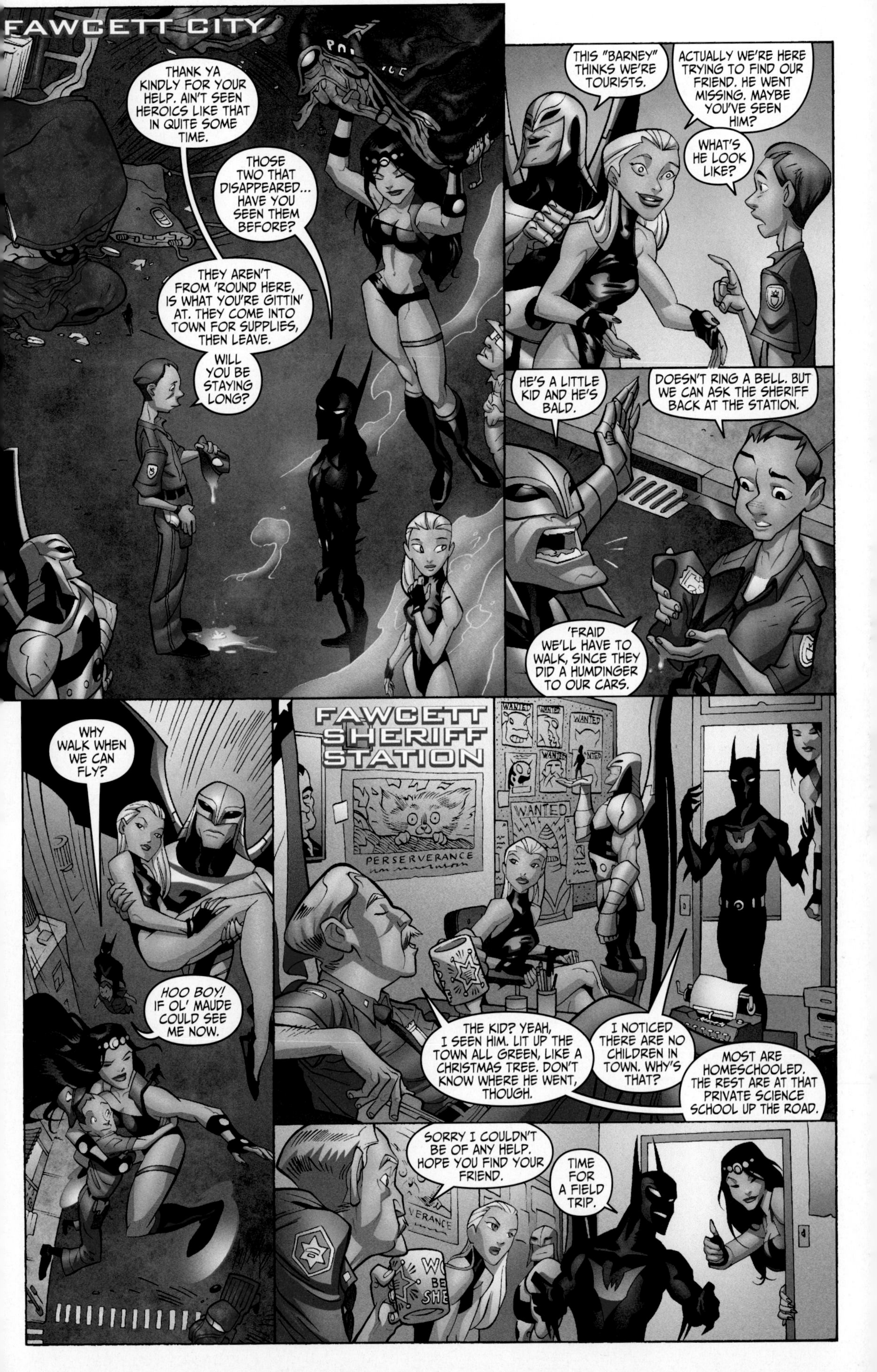
FAWCETT CITY
THANK YA KINDLY FOR YOUR HELP. AIN'T SEEN HEROICS LIKE THAT IN QUITE SOME TIME.
THOSE TWO THAT DISAPPEARED... HAVE YOU SEEN THEM BEFORE?
THEY AREN'T FROM 'ROUND HERE, IS WHAT YOU'RE GITTIN' AT. THEY COME INTO TOWN FOR SUPPLIES, THEN LEAVE.
WILL YOU BE STAYING LONG?
THIS "BARNEY" THINKS WE'RE TOURISTS.
ACTUALLY WE'RE HERE TRYING TO FIND OUR FRIEND. HE WENT MISSING. MAYBE YOU'VE SEEN HIM?
WHAT'S HE LOOK LIKE?
HE'S A LITTLE KID AND HE'S BALD.
DOESN'T RING A BELL. BUT WE CAN ASK THE SHERIFF BACK AT THE STATION.
'FRAID WE'LL HAVE TO WALK, SINCE THEY DID A HUMDINGER TO OUR CARS.
WHY WALK WHEN WE CAN FLY?
HOO BOY! IF OL' MAUDE COULD SEE ME NOW.
FAWCETT SHERIFF STATION
WANTED
PERSERVERANCE
THE KID? YEAH, I SEEN HIM. LIT UP THE TOWN ALL GREEN, LIKE A CHRISTMAS TREE. DON'T KNOW WHERE HE WENT, THOUGH.
I NOTICED THERE ARE NO CHILDREN IN TOWN. WHY'S THAT?
MOST ARE HOMESCHOOLED. THE REST ARE AT THAT PRIVATE SCIENCE SCHOOL UP THE ROAD.
SORRY I COULDN'T BE OF ANY HELP. HOPE YOU FIND YOUR FRIEND.
TIME FOR A FIELD TRIP.

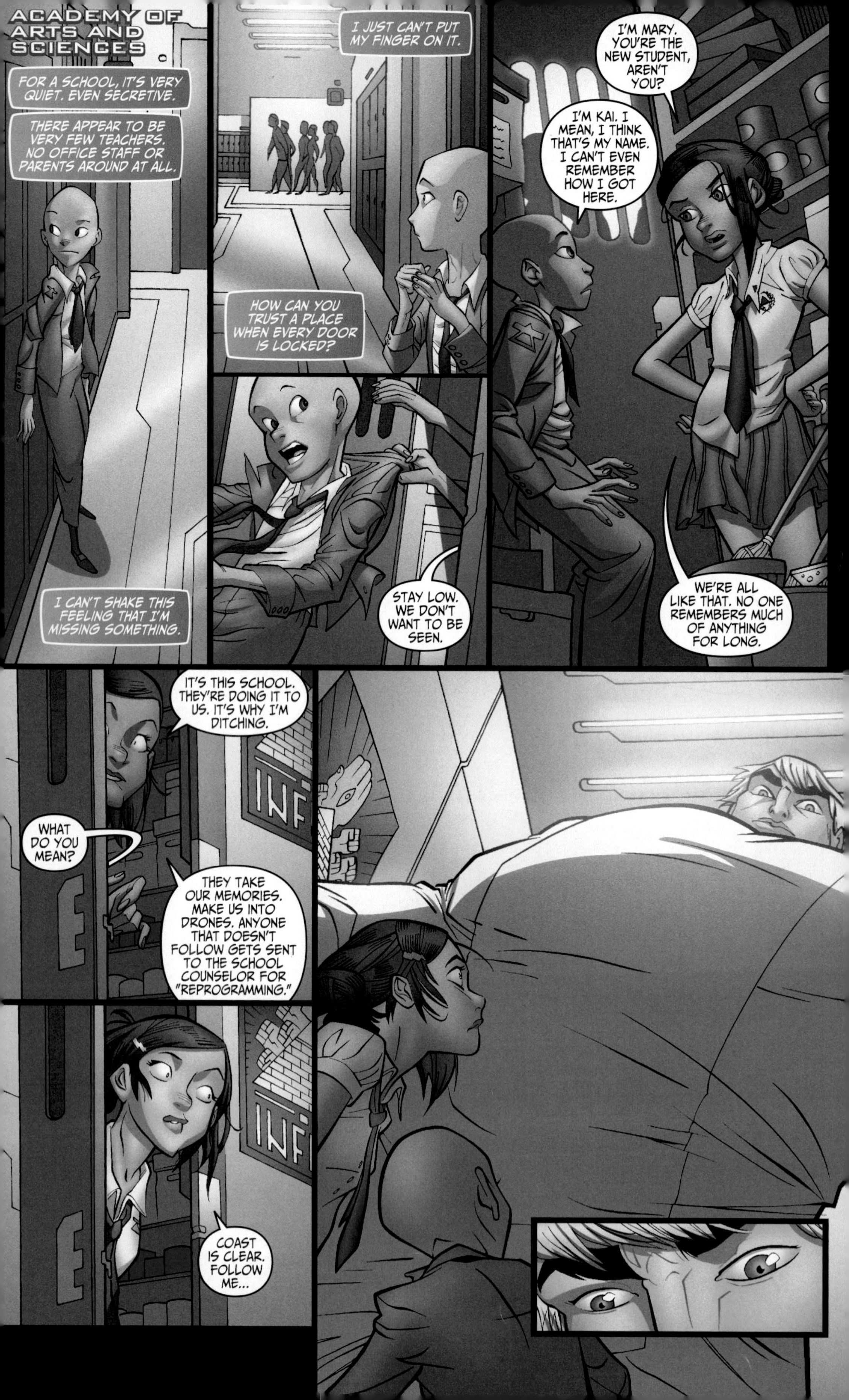
ACADEMY OF ARTS AND SCIENCES
FOR A SCHOOL, IT'S VERY QUIET. EVEN SECRETIVE.
THERE APPEAR TO BE VERY FEW TEACHERS. NO OFFICE STAFF OR PARENTS AROUND AT ALL.
I CAN'T SHAKE THIS FEELING THAT I'M MISSING SOMETHING.
I JUST CAN'T PUT MY FINGER ON IT.
HOW CAN YOU TRUST A PLACE WHEN EVERY DOOR IS LOCKED?
STAY LOW. WE DON'T WANT TO BE SEEN.
I'M MARY. YOU'RE THE NEW STUDENT, AREN'T YOU?
I'M KAI. I MEAN, I THINK THAT'S MY NAME. I CAN'T EVEN REMEMBER HOW I GOT HERE.
WE'RE ALL LIKE THAT. NO ONE REMEMBERS MUCH OF ANYTHING FOR LONG.
IT'S THIS SCHOOL. THEY'RE DOING IT TO US. IT'S WHY I'M DITCHING.
WHAT DO YOU MEAN?
THEY TAKE OUR MEMORIES. MAKE US INTO DRONES. ANYONE THAT DOESN'T FOLLOW GETS SENT TO THE SCHOOL COUNSELOR FOR "REPROGRAMMING."
COAST IS CLEAR. FOLLOW ME...

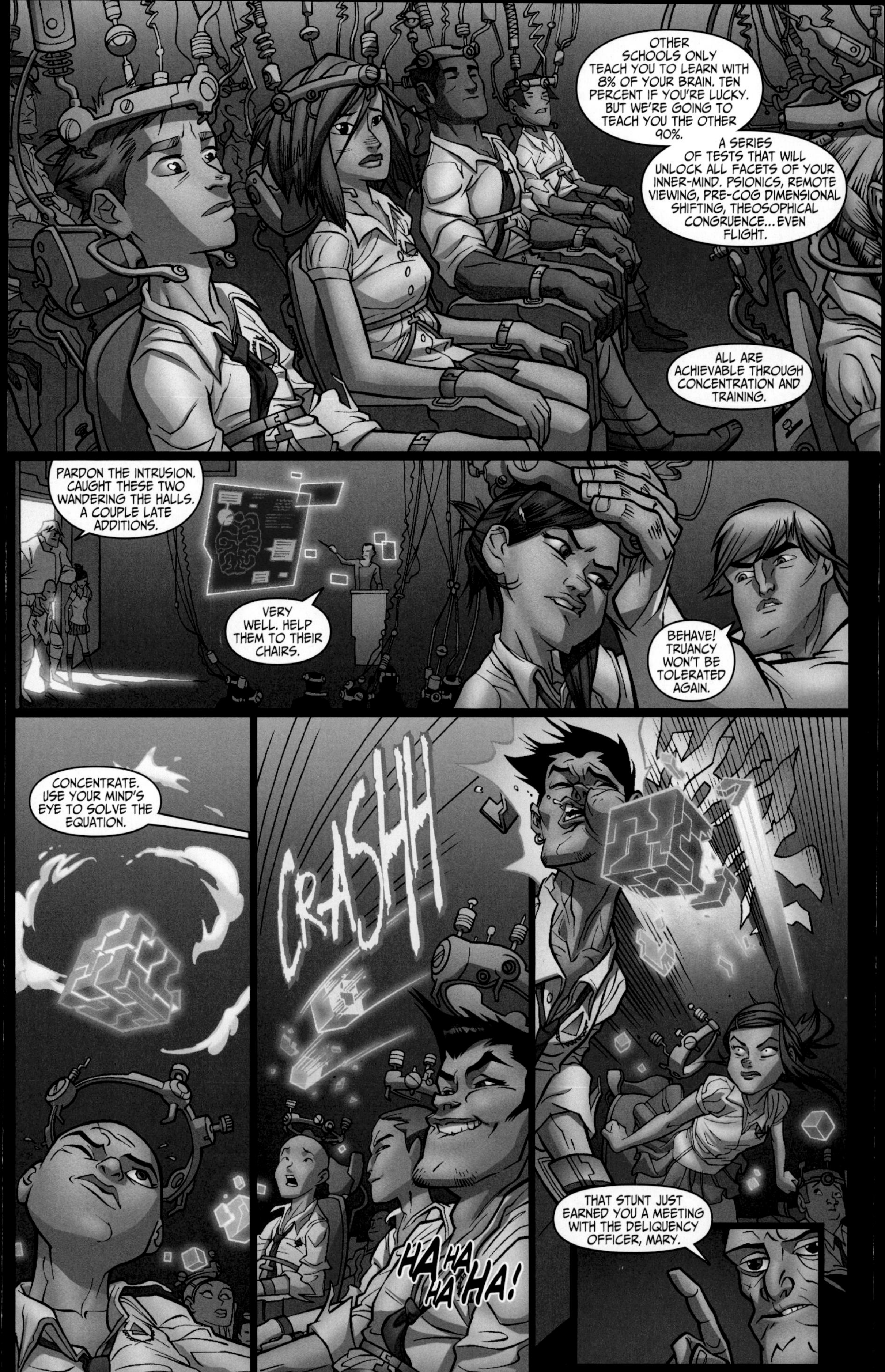
OTHER SCHOOLS ONLY TEACH YOU TO LEARN WITH 8% OF YOUR BRAIN. TEN PERCENT IF YOU'RE LUCKY. BUT WE'RE GOING TO TEACH YOU THE OTHER 90%.
A SERIES OF TESTS THAT WILL UNLOCK ALL FACETS OF YOUR INNER-MIND. PSIONICS, REMOTE VIEWING, PRE-COG DIMENSIONAL SHIFTING, THEOSOPHICAL CONGRUENCE... EVEN FLIGHT.
ALL ARE ACHIEVABLE THROUGH CONCENTRATION AND TRAINING.
PARDON THE INTRUSION. CAUGHT THESE TWO WANDERING THE HALLS. A COUPLE LATE ADDITIONS.
VERY WELL. HELP THEM TO THEIR CHAIRS.
BEHAVE! TRUANCY WON'T BE TOLERATED AGAIN.
CONCENTRATE. USE YOUR MIND'S EYE TO SOLVE THE EQUATION.
CRASHH
HA HA HA HA!
THAT STUNT JUST EARNED YOU A MEETING WITH THE DELIQUENCY OFFICER, MARY.

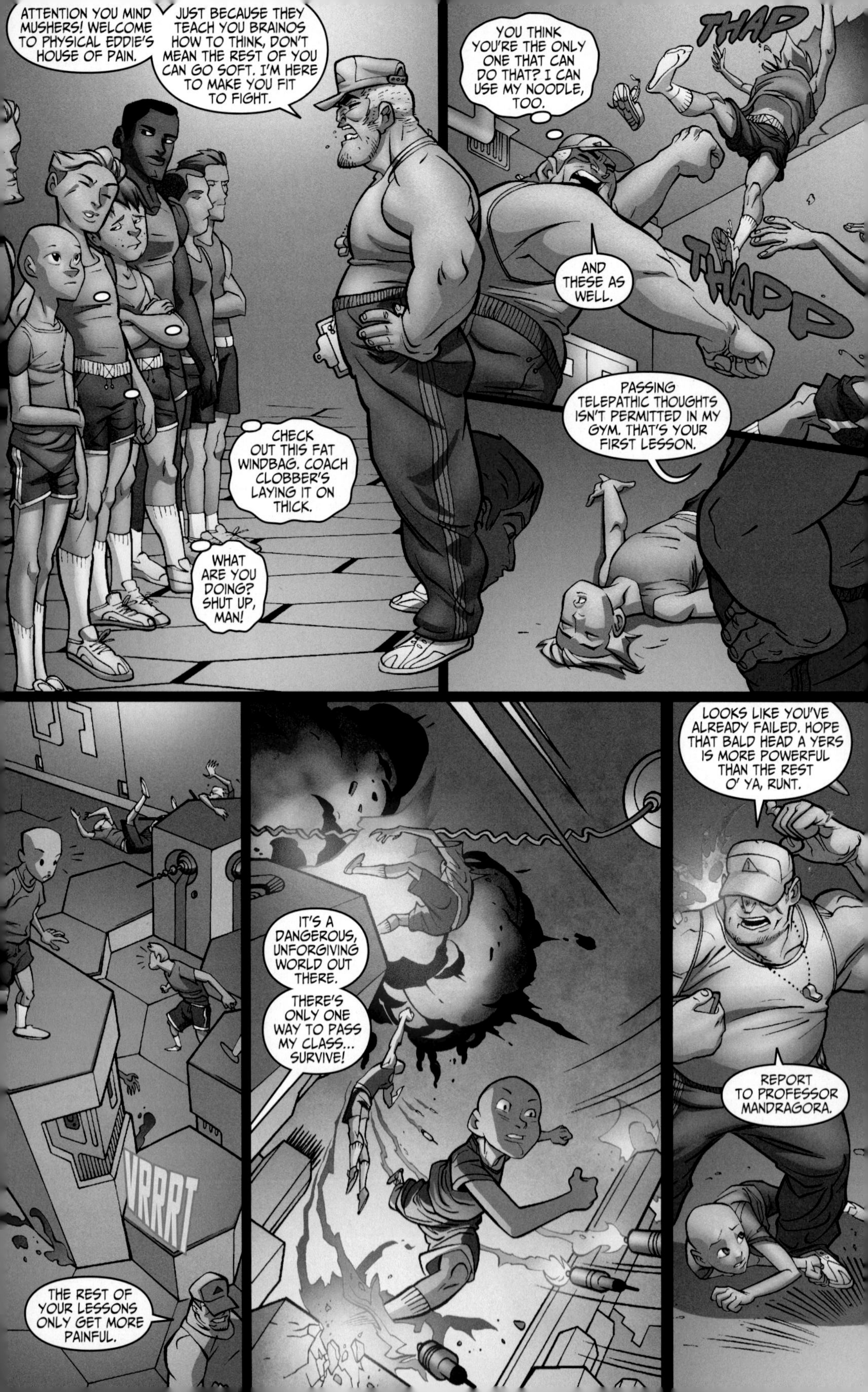
ATTENTION YOU MIND MUSHERS! WELCOME TO PHYSICAL EDDIE'S HOUSE OF PAIN.
JUST BECAUSE THEY TEACH YOU BRAINOS HOW TO THINK, DON'T MEAN THE REST OF YOU CAN GO SOFT. I'M HERE TO MAKE YOU FIT TO FIGHT.
CHECK OUT THIS FAT WINDBAG. COACH CLOBBER'S LAYING IT ON THICK.
WHAT ARE YOU DOING? SHUT UP, MAN!
YOU THINK YOU'RE THE ONLY ONE THAT CAN DO THAT? I CAN USE MY NOODLE, TOO.
THAP
AND THESE AS WELL.
THAPP
PASSING TELEPATHIC THOUGHTS ISN'T PERMITTED IN MY GYM. THAT'S YOUR FIRST LESSON.
VRRRT
THE REST OF YOUR LESSONS ONLY GET MORE PAINFUL.
IT'S A DANGEROUS, UNFORGIVING WORLD OUT THERE.
THERE'S ONLY ONE WAY TO PASS MY CLASS... SURVIVE!
LOOKS LIKE YOU'VE ALREADY FAILED. HOPE THAT BALD HEAD A YERS IS MORE POWERFUL THAN THE REST O' YA, RUNT.
REPORT TO PROFESSOR MANDRAGORA.

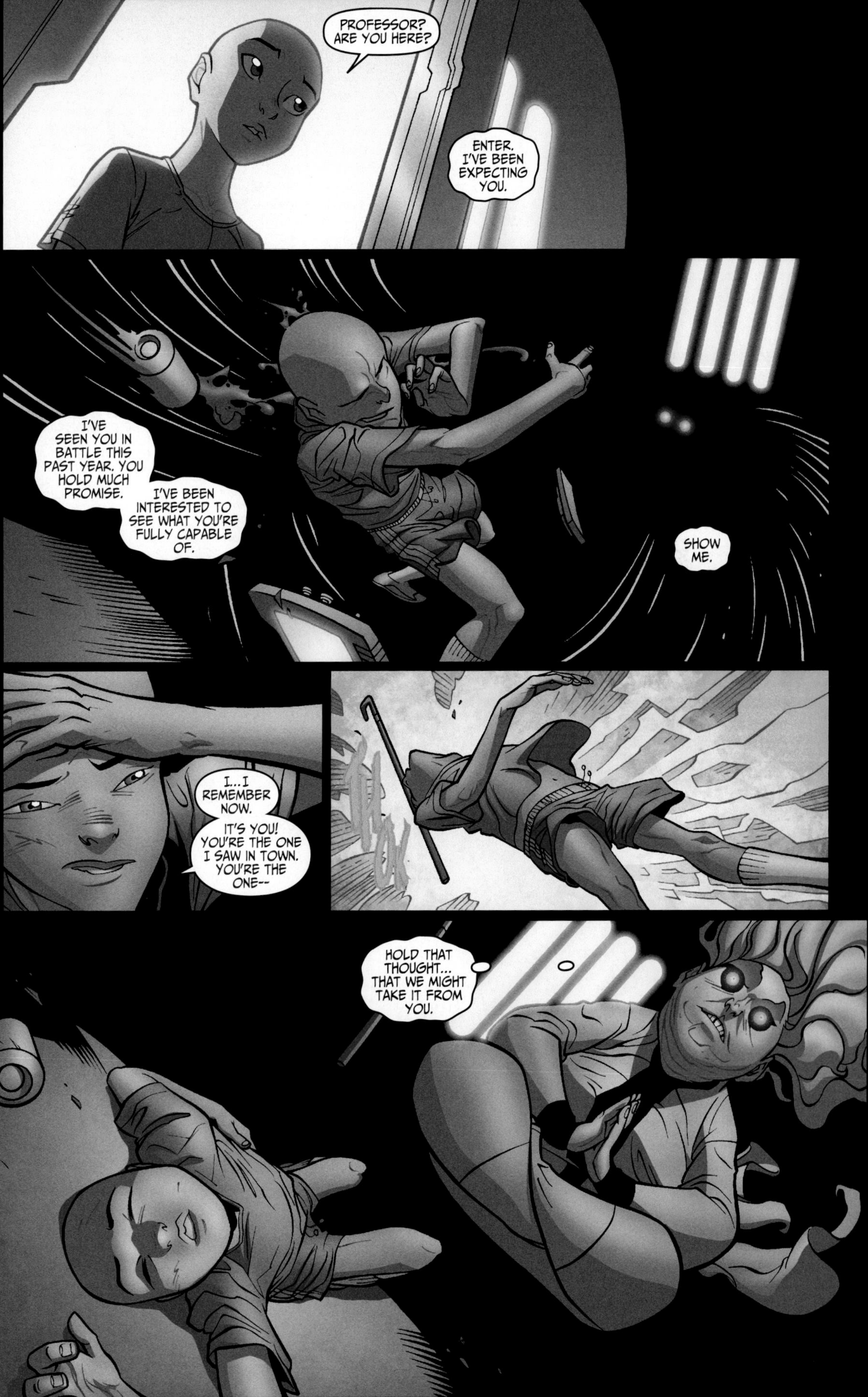
PROFESSOR? ARE YOU HERE?
ENTER. I'VE BEEN EXPECTING YOU.
I'VE SEEN YOU IN BATTLE THIS PAST YEAR. YOU HOLD MUCH PROMISE.
I'VE BEEN INTERESTED TO SEE WHAT YOU'RE FULLY CAPABLE OF.
SHOW ME.
I...I REMEMBER NOW.
IT'S YOU! YOU'RE THE ONE I SAW IN TOWN. YOU'RE THE ONE--
HOLD THAT THOUGHT... THAT WE MIGHT TAKE IT FROM YOU.

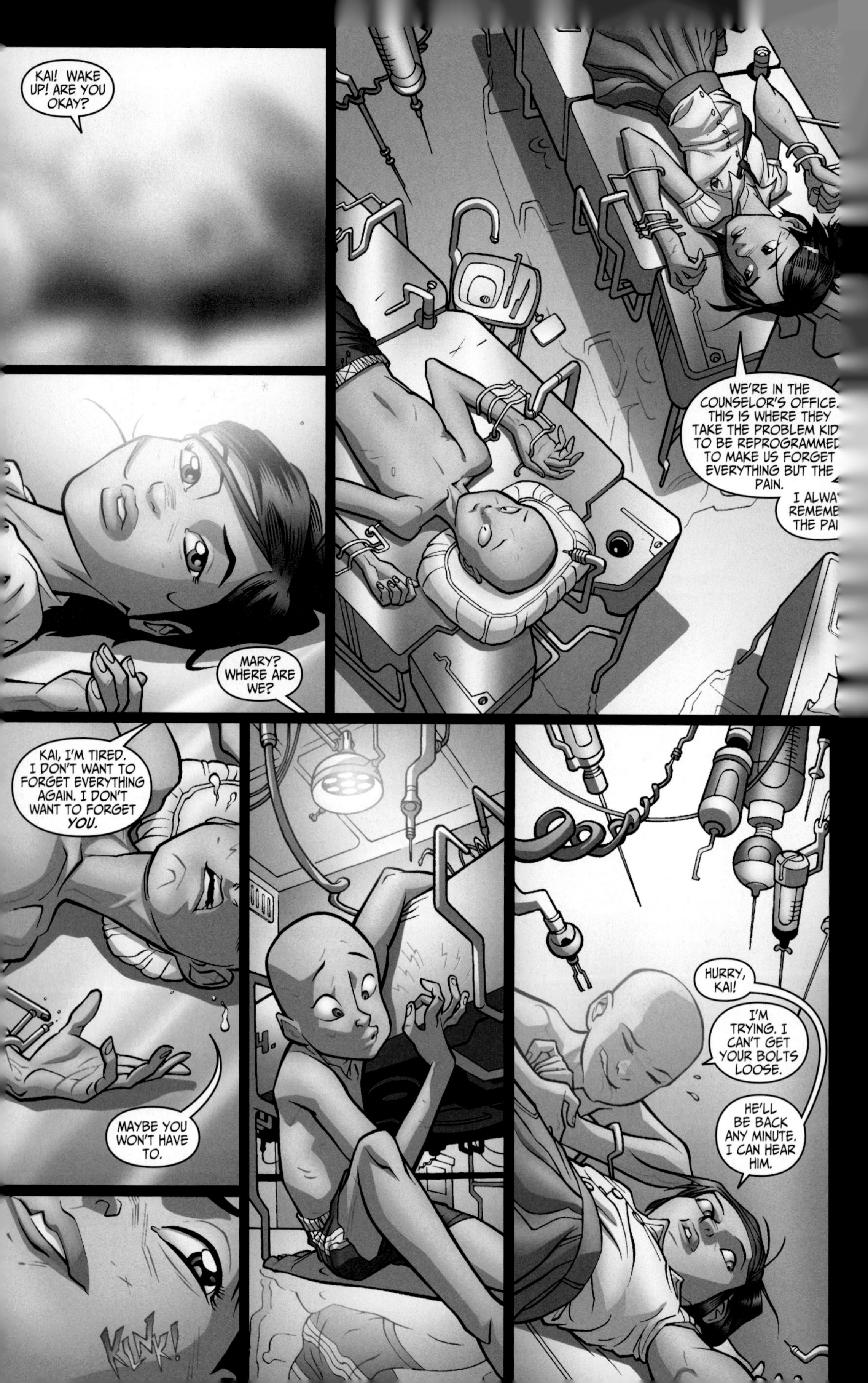
KAI! WAKE UP! ARE YOU OKAY?
MARY? WHERE ARE WE?
WE'RE IN THE COUNSELOR'S OFFICE. THIS IS WHERE THEY TAKE THE PROBLEM KID TO BE REPROGRAMMED TO MAKE US FORGET EVERYTHING BUT THE PAIN.
KAI, I'M TIRED. I DON'T WANT TO FORGET EVERYTHING AGAIN. I DON'T WANT TO FORGET *YOU*.
MAYBE YOU WON'T HAVE TO.
KLINK!
HURRY, KAI!
I'M TRYING. I CAN'T GET YOUR BOLTS LOOSE.
HE'LL BE BACK ANY MINUTE. I CAN HEAR HIM.

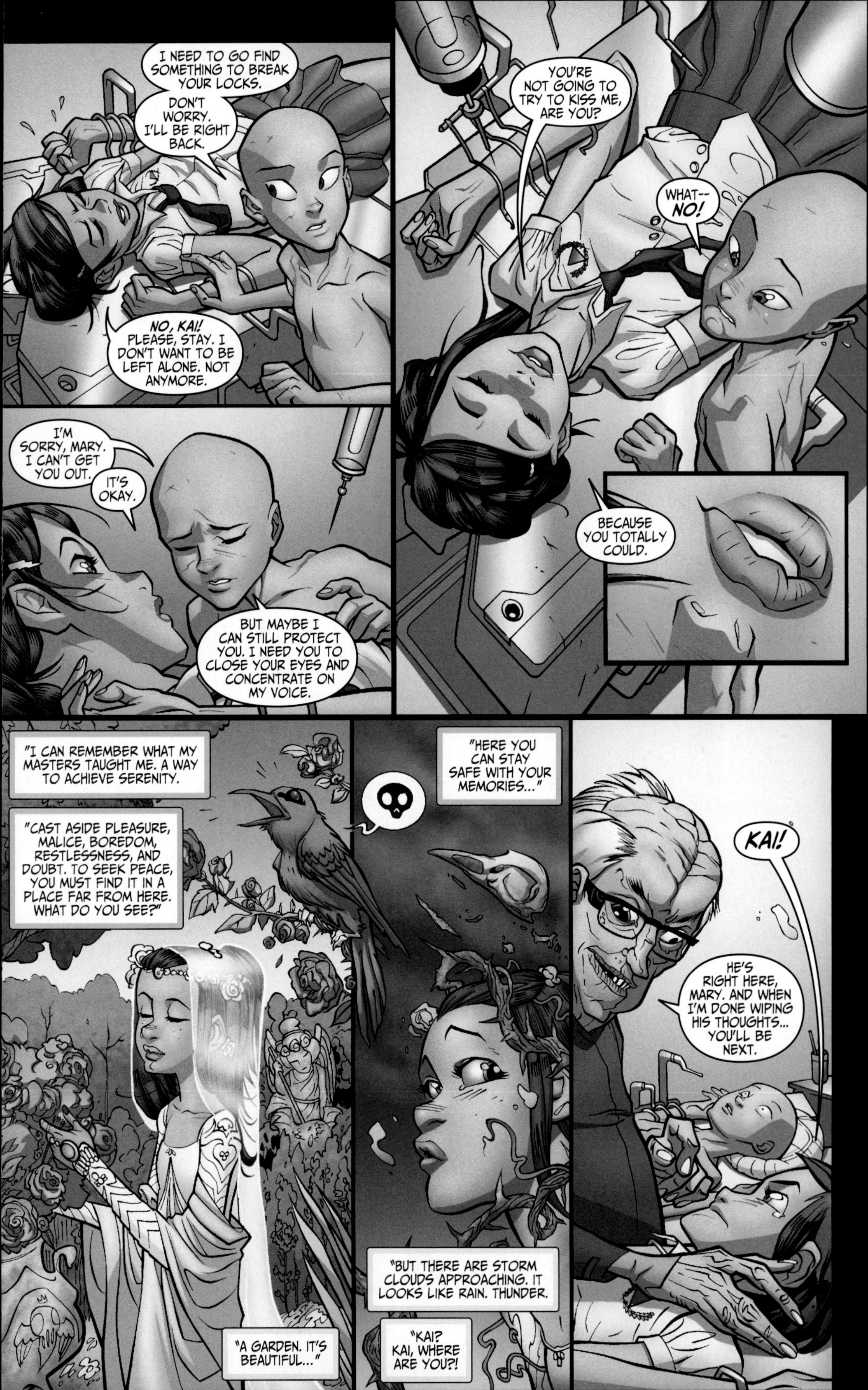
I NEED TO GO FIND SOMETHING TO BREAK YOUR LOCKS.
DON'T WORRY. I'LL BE RIGHT BACK.
NO, KAI! PLEASE, STAY. I DON'T WANT TO BE LEFT ALONE. NOT ANYMORE.
YOU'RE NOT GOING TO TRY TO KISS ME, ARE YOU?
WHAT-- NO!
I'M SORRY, MARY. I CAN'T GET YOU OUT.
IT'S OKAY.
BUT MAYBE I CAN STILL PROTECT YOU. I NEED YOU TO CLOSE YOUR EYES AND CONCENTRATE ON MY VOICE.
BECAUSE YOU TOTALLY COULD.
"I CAN REMEMBER WHAT MY MASTERS TAUGHT ME. A WAY TO ACHIEVE SERENITY.
"CAST ASIDE PLEASURE, MALICE, BOREDOM, RESTLESSNESS, AND DOUBT. TO SEEK PEACE, YOU MUST FIND IT IN A PLACE FAR FROM HERE. WHAT DO YOU SEE?"
"A GARDEN. IT'S BEAUTIFUL..."
"HERE YOU CAN STAY SAFE WITH YOUR MEMORIES..."
"BUT THERE ARE STORM CLOUDS APPROACHING. IT LOOKS LIKE RAIN. THUNDER.
"KAI? KAI, WHERE ARE YOU?!
KAI!
HE'S RIGHT HERE, MARY. AND WHEN I'M DONE WIPING HIS THOUGHTS... YOU'LL BE NEXT.

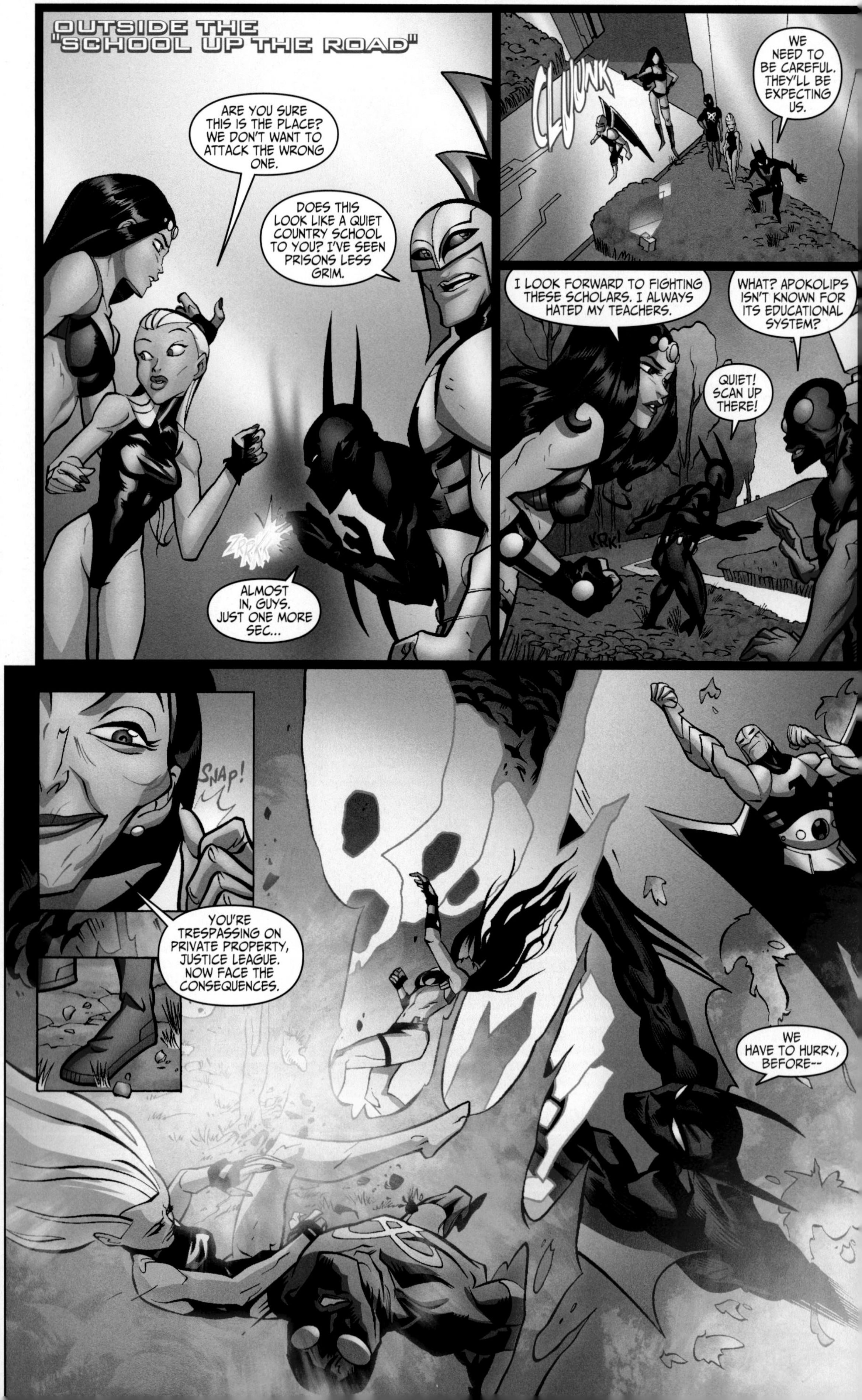
OUTSIDE THE "SCHOOL UP THE ROAD"
ARE YOU SURE THIS IS THE PLACE? WE DON'T WANT TO ATTACK THE WRONG ONE.
DOES THIS LOOK LIKE A QUIET COUNTRY SCHOOL TO YOU? I'VE SEEN PRISONS LESS GRIM.
ZRRKK
ALMOST IN, GUYS. JUST ONE MORE SEC...
CLUUNK
WE NEED TO BE CAREFUL. THEY'LL BE EXPECTING US.
I LOOK FORWARD TO FIGHTING THESE SCHOLARS. I ALWAYS HATED MY TEACHERS.
WHAT? APOKOLIPS ISN'T KNOWN FOR ITS EDUCATIONAL SYSTEM?
QUIET! SCAN UP THERE!
KRK!
SNAP!
YOU'RE TRESPASSING ON PRIVATE PROPERTY, JUSTICE LEAGUE. NOW FACE THE CONSEQUENCES.
WE HAVE TO HURRY, BEFORE--

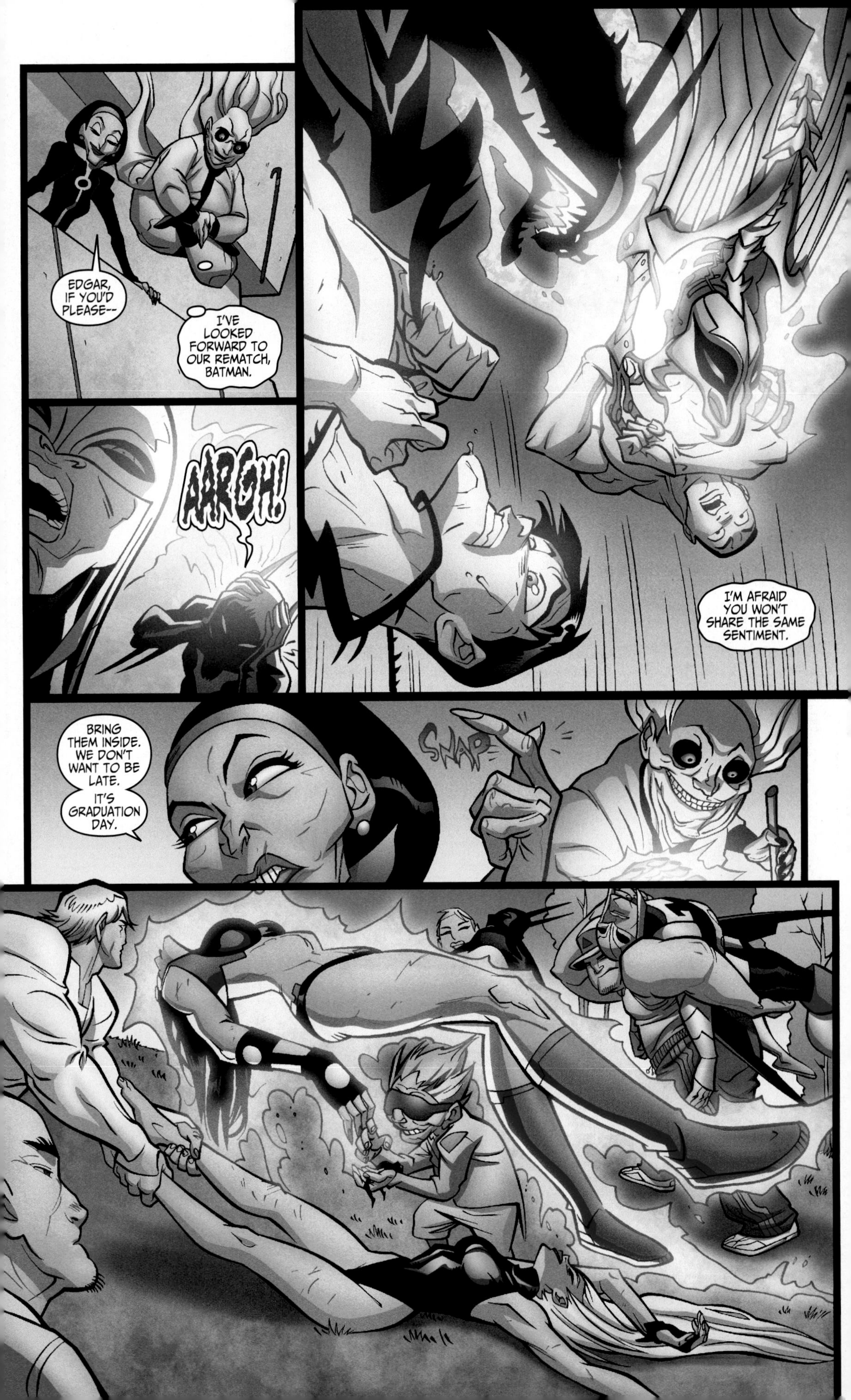
EDGAR, IF YOU'D PLEASE--
I'VE LOOKED FORWARD TO OUR REMATCH, BATMAN.
AARGH!
I'M AFRAID YOU WON'T SHARE THE SAME SENTIMENT.
BRING THEM INSIDE. WE DON'T WANT TO BE LATE.
IT'S GRADUATION DAY.
SNAP

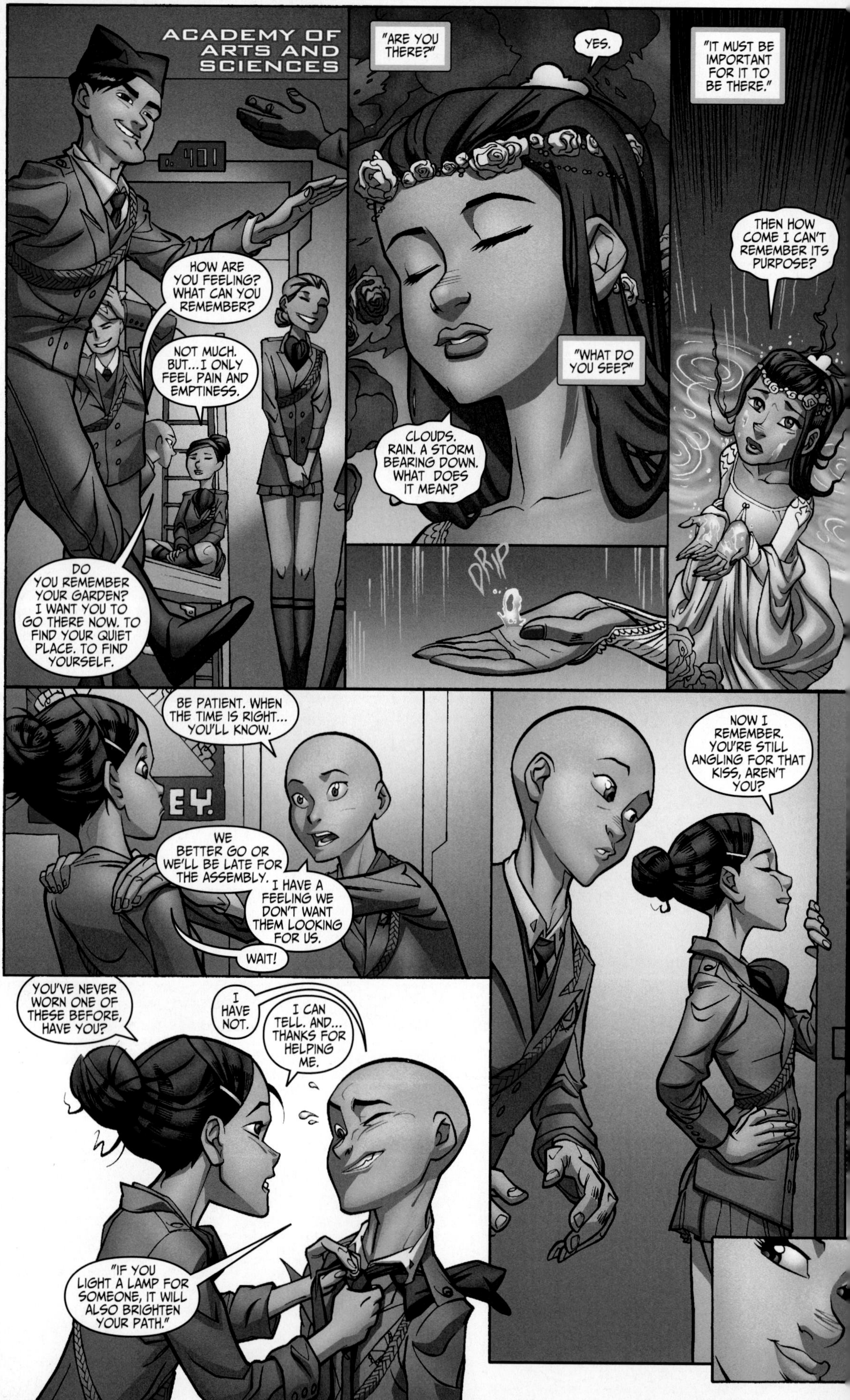
ACADEMY OF ARTS AND SCIENCES
401
HOW ARE YOU FEELING? WHAT CAN YOU REMEMBER?
NOT MUCH. BUT...I ONLY FEEL PAIN AND EMPTINESS.
DO YOU REMEMBER YOUR GARDEN? I WANT YOU TO GO THERE NOW. TO FIND YOUR QUIET PLACE. TO FIND YOURSELF.
"ARE YOU THERE?"
YES.
"WHAT DO YOU SEE?"
CLOUDS. RAIN. A STORM BEARING DOWN. WHAT DOES IT MEAN?
DRIP
"IT MUST BE IMPORTANT FOR IT TO BE THERE."
THEN HOW COME I CAN'T REMEMBER ITS PURPOSE?
BE PATIENT. WHEN THE TIME IS RIGHT... YOU'LL KNOW.
WE BETTER GO OR WE'LL BE LATE FOR THE ASSEMBLY.
I HAVE A FEELING WE DON'T WANT THEM LOOKING FOR US.
WAIT!
YOU'VE NEVER WORN ONE OF THESE BEFORE, HAVE YOU?
I HAVE NOT.
I CAN TELL. AND... THANKS FOR HELPING ME.
"IF YOU LIGHT A LAMP FOR SOMEONE, IT WILL ALSO BRIGHTEN YOUR PATH."
NOW I REMEMBER. YOU'RE STILL ANGLING FOR THAT KISS, AREN'T YOU?

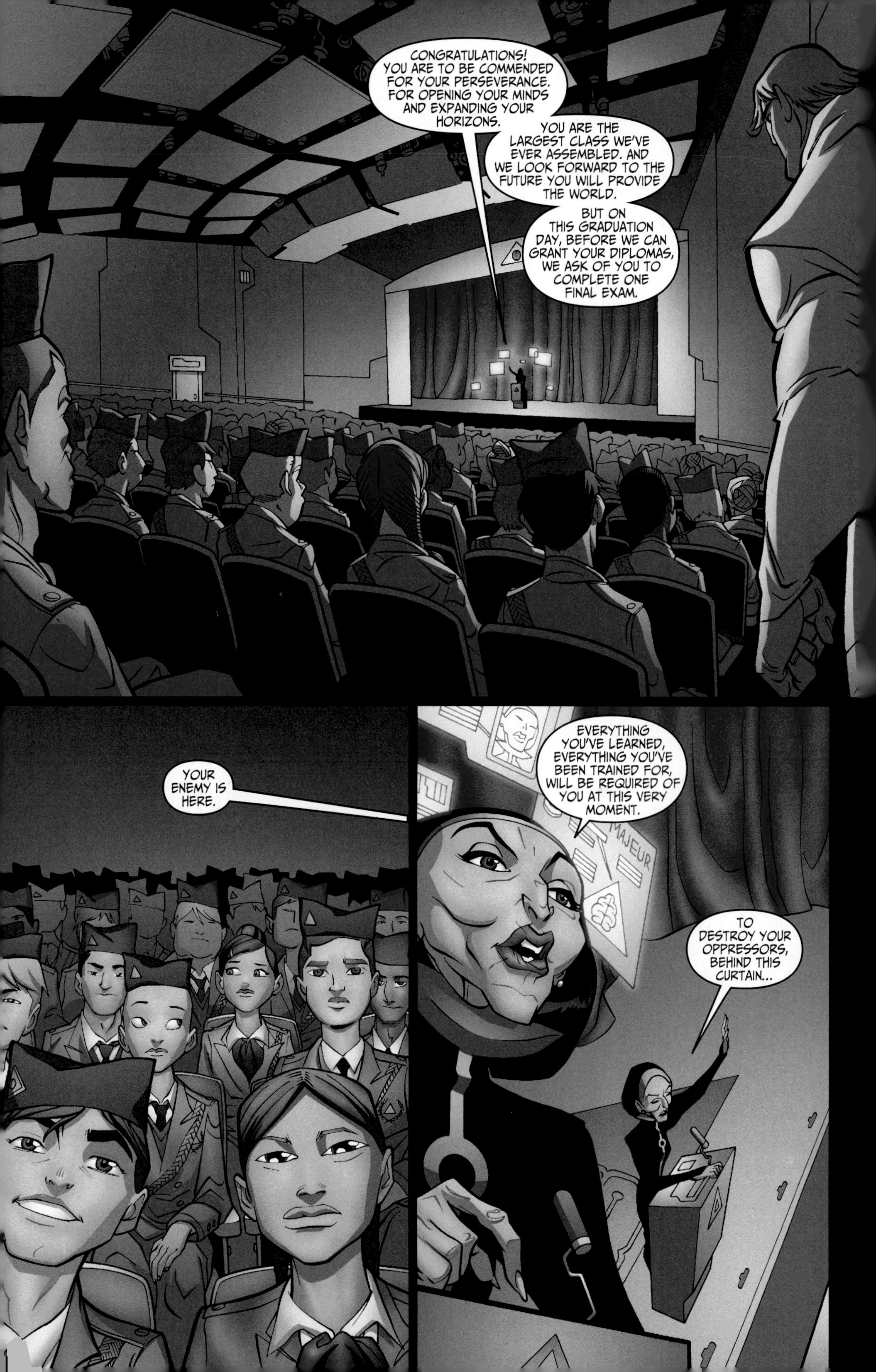
CONGRATULATIONS! YOU ARE TO BE COMMENDED FOR YOUR PERSEVERANCE. FOR OPENING YOUR MINDS AND EXPANDING YOUR HORIZONS.
YOU ARE THE LARGEST CLASS WE'VE EVER ASSEMBLED. AND WE LOOK FORWARD TO THE FUTURE YOU WILL PROVIDE THE WORLD.
BUT ON THIS GRADUATION DAY, BEFORE WE CAN GRANT YOUR DIPLOMAS, WE ASK OF YOU TO COMPLETE ONE FINAL EXAM.
YOUR ENEMY IS HERE.
EVERYTHING YOU'VE LEARNED, EVERYTHING YOU'VE BEEN TRAINED FOR, WILL BE REQUIRED OF YOU AT THIS VERY MOMENT.
MAJEUR
TO DESTROY YOUR OPPRESSORS, BEHIND THIS CURTAIN...

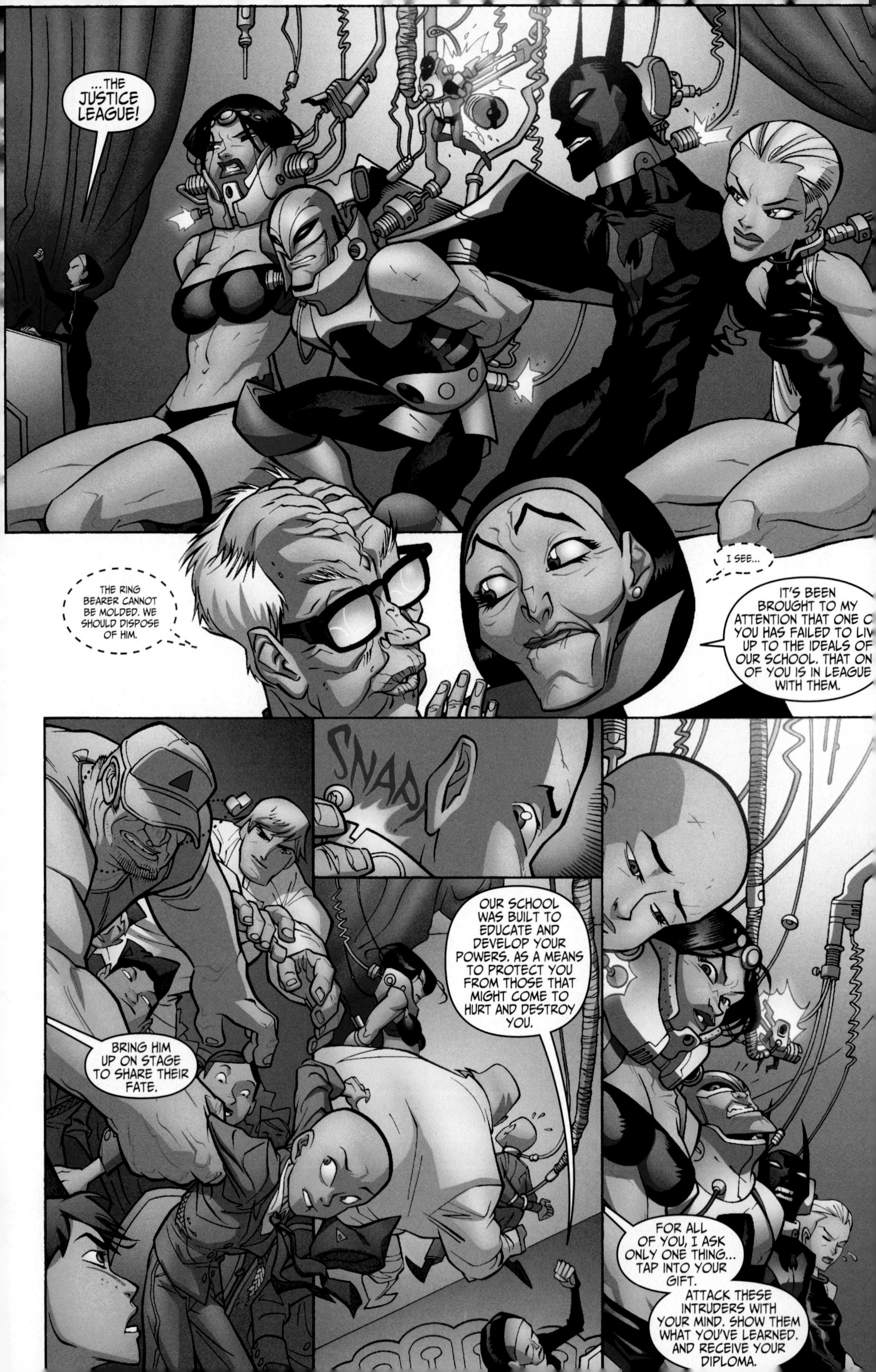
...THE JUSTICE LEAGUE!
THE RING BEARER CANNOT BE MOLDED. WE SHOULD DISPOSE OF HIM.
I SEE...
IT'S BEEN BROUGHT TO MY ATTENTION THAT ONE O YOU HAS FAILED TO LIV UP TO THE IDEALS OF OUR SCHOOL. THAT ON OF YOU IS IN LEAGUE WITH THEM.
BRING HIM UP ON STAGE TO SHARE THEIR FATE.
SNAP!
OUR SCHOOL WAS BUILT TO EDUCATE AND DEVELOP YOUR POWERS. AS A MEANS TO PROTECT YOU FROM THOSE THAT MIGHT COME TO HURT AND DESTROY YOU.
FOR ALL OF YOU, I ASK ONLY ONE THING... TAP INTO YOUR GIFT.
ATTACK THESE INTRUDERS WITH YOUR MIND. SHOW THEM WHAT YOU'VE LEARNED. AND RECEIVE YOUR DIPLOMA.

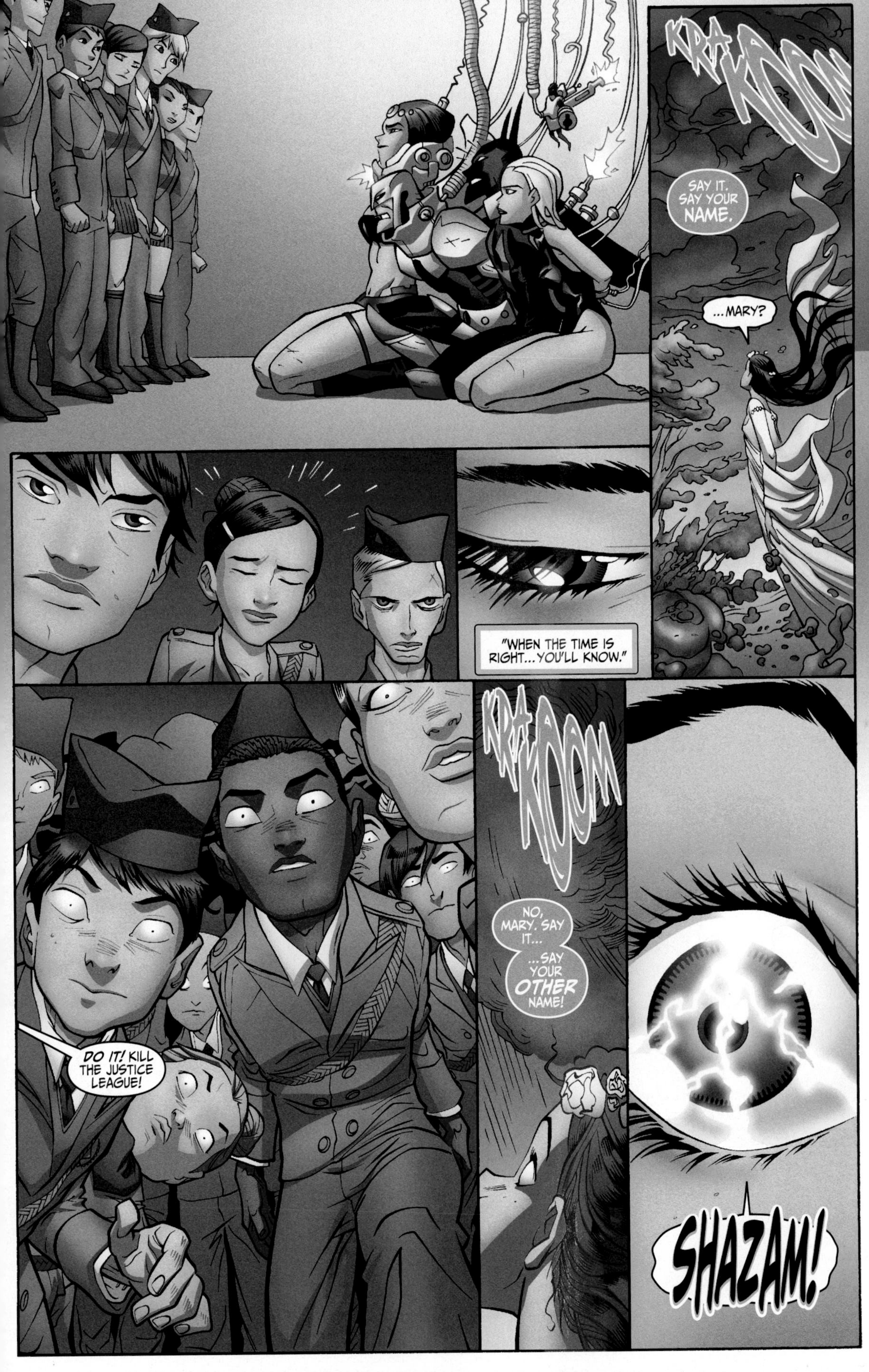
KRA KOOOM
SAY IT. SAY YOUR NAME.
...MARY?
"WHEN THE TIME IS RIGHT... YOU'LL KNOW."
DO IT! KILL THE JUSTICE LEAGUE!
KRA KOOOM
NO, MARY. SAY IT...
...SAY YOUR OTHER NAME!
SHAZAM!

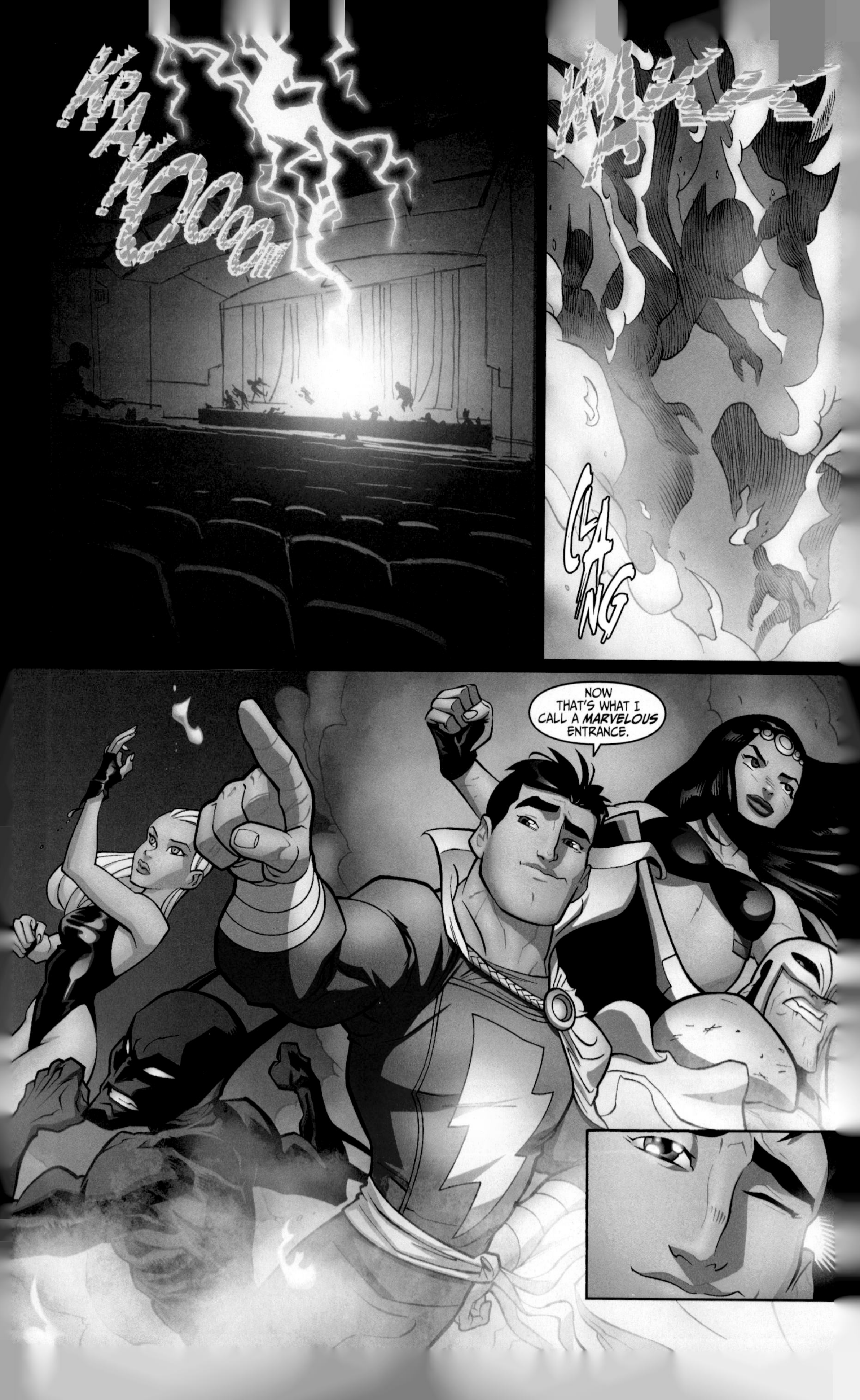
KRA! KOOOOM!
CLANG
NOW THAT'S WHAT I CALL A *MARVELOUS* ENTRANCE.

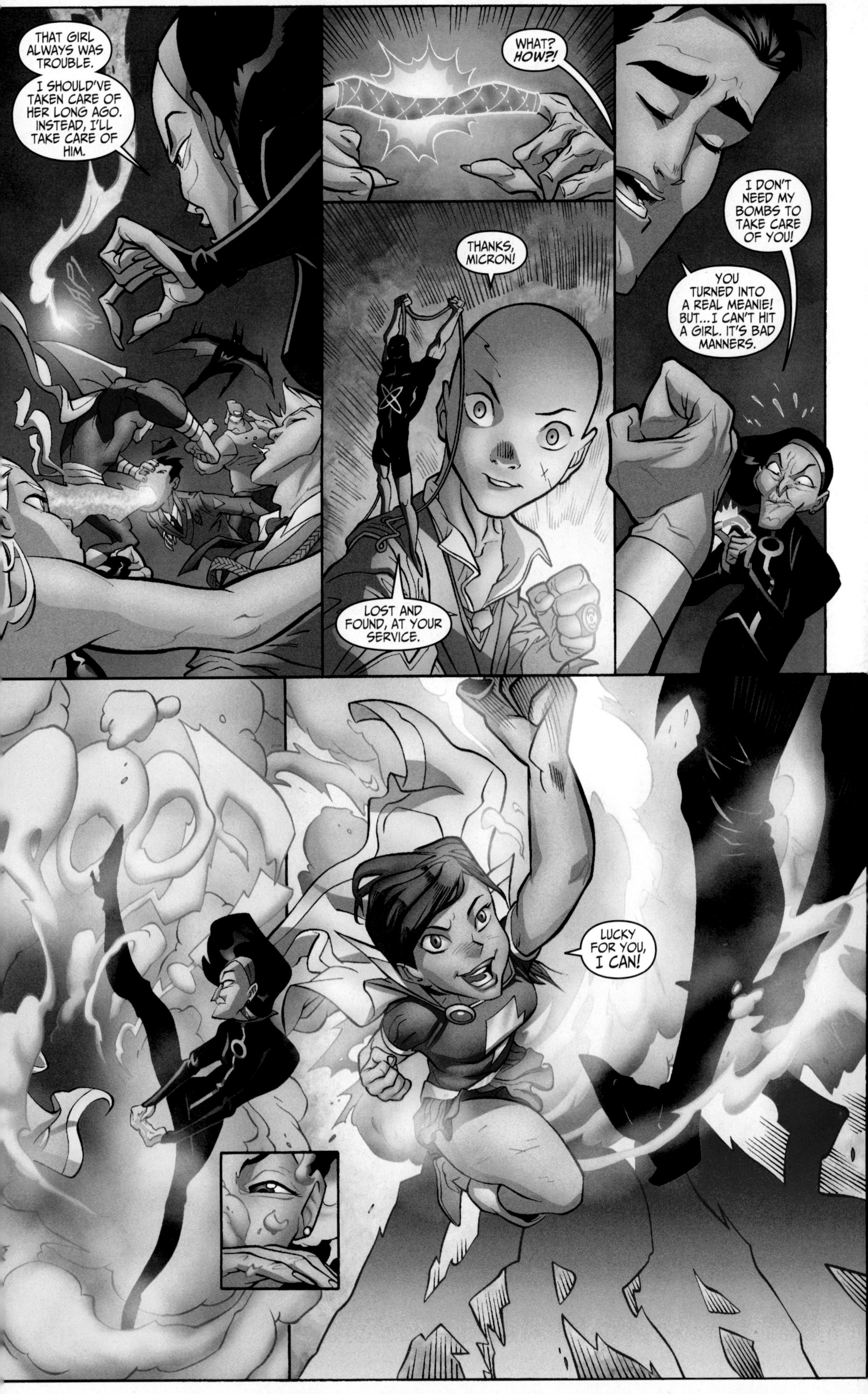
THAT GIRL ALWAYS WAS TROUBLE.
I SHOULD'VE TAKEN CARE OF HER LONG AGO. INSTEAD, I'LL TAKE CARE OF HIM.
WHAT? HOW?!
THANKS, MICRON!
LOST AND FOUND, AT YOUR SERVICE.
I DON'T NEED MY BOMBS TO TAKE CARE OF YOU!
YOU TURNED INTO A REAL MEANIE! BUT... I CAN'T HIT A GIRL. IT'S BAD MANNERS.
LUCKY FOR YOU, I CAN!

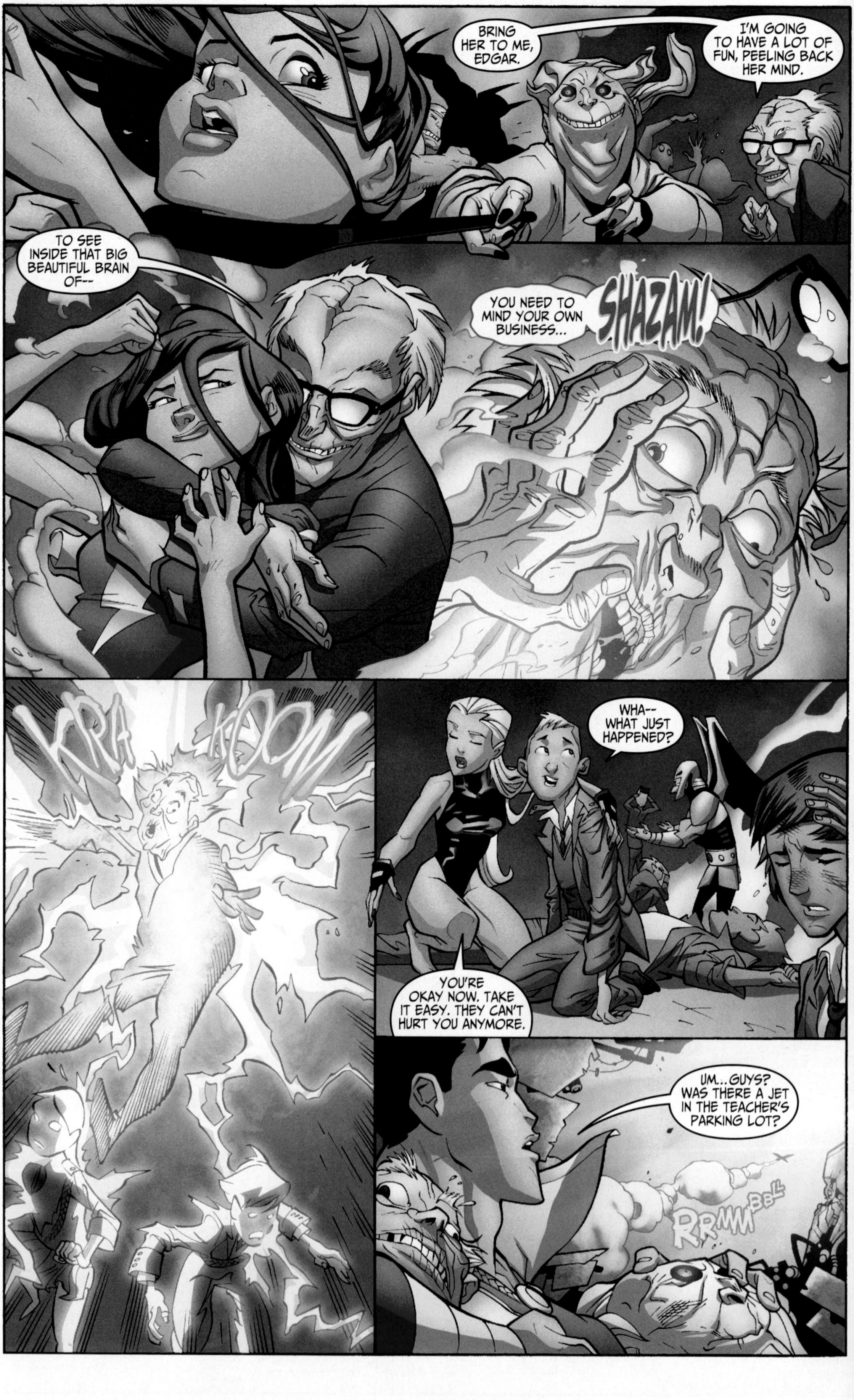
BRING HER TO ME, EDGAR.
I'M GOING TO HAVE A LOT OF FUN, PEELING BACK HER MIND.
TO SEE INSIDE THAT BIG BEAUTIFUL BRAIN OF--
YOU NEED TO MIND YOUR OWN BUSINESS...
SHAZAM!
KRA KOOOM
WHA-- WHAT JUST HAPPENED?
YOU'RE OKAY NOW. TAKE IT EASY. THEY CAN'T HURT YOU ANYMORE.
UM...GUYS? WAS THERE A JET IN THE TEACHER'S PARKING LOT?
RRMMMBBLL

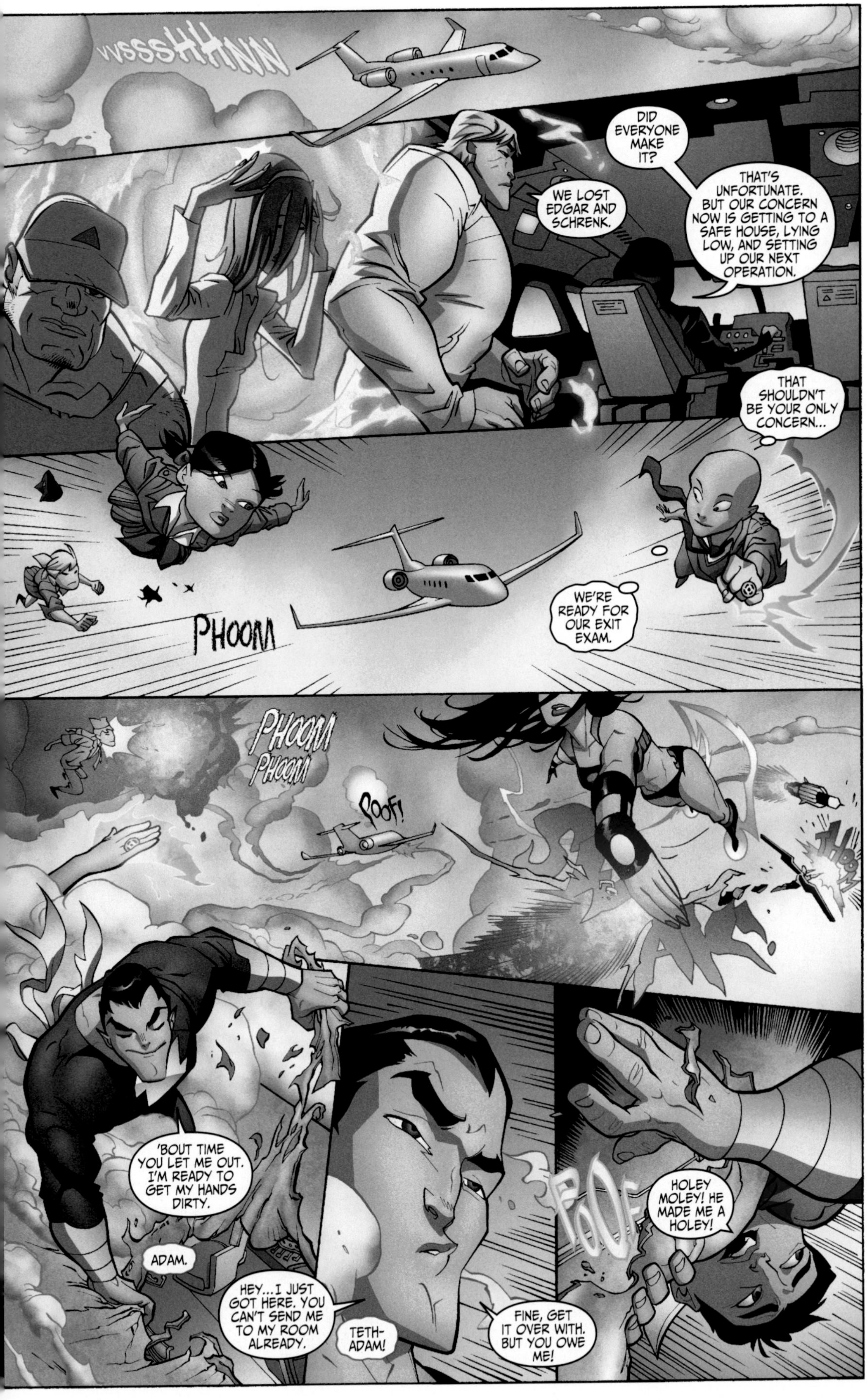
VVSSSHHHNN
DID EVERYONE MAKE IT?
WE LOST EDGAR AND SCHRENK.
THAT'S UNFORTUNATE. BUT OUR CONCERN NOW IS GETTING TO A SAFE HOUSE, LYING LOW, AND SETTING UP OUR NEXT OPERATION.
THAT SHOULDN'T BE YOUR ONLY CONCERN...
WE'RE READY FOR OUR EXIT EXAM.
PHOOM
PHOOM
PHOOM
POOF!
'BOUT TIME YOU LET ME OUT. I'M READY TO GET MY HANDS DIRTY.
ADAM.
HEY... I JUST GOT HERE. YOU CAN'T SEND ME TO MY ROOM ALREADY.
TETH-ADAM!
FINE, GET IT OVER WITH. BUT YOU OWE ME!
POOF
HOLEY MOLEY! HE MADE ME A HOLEY!

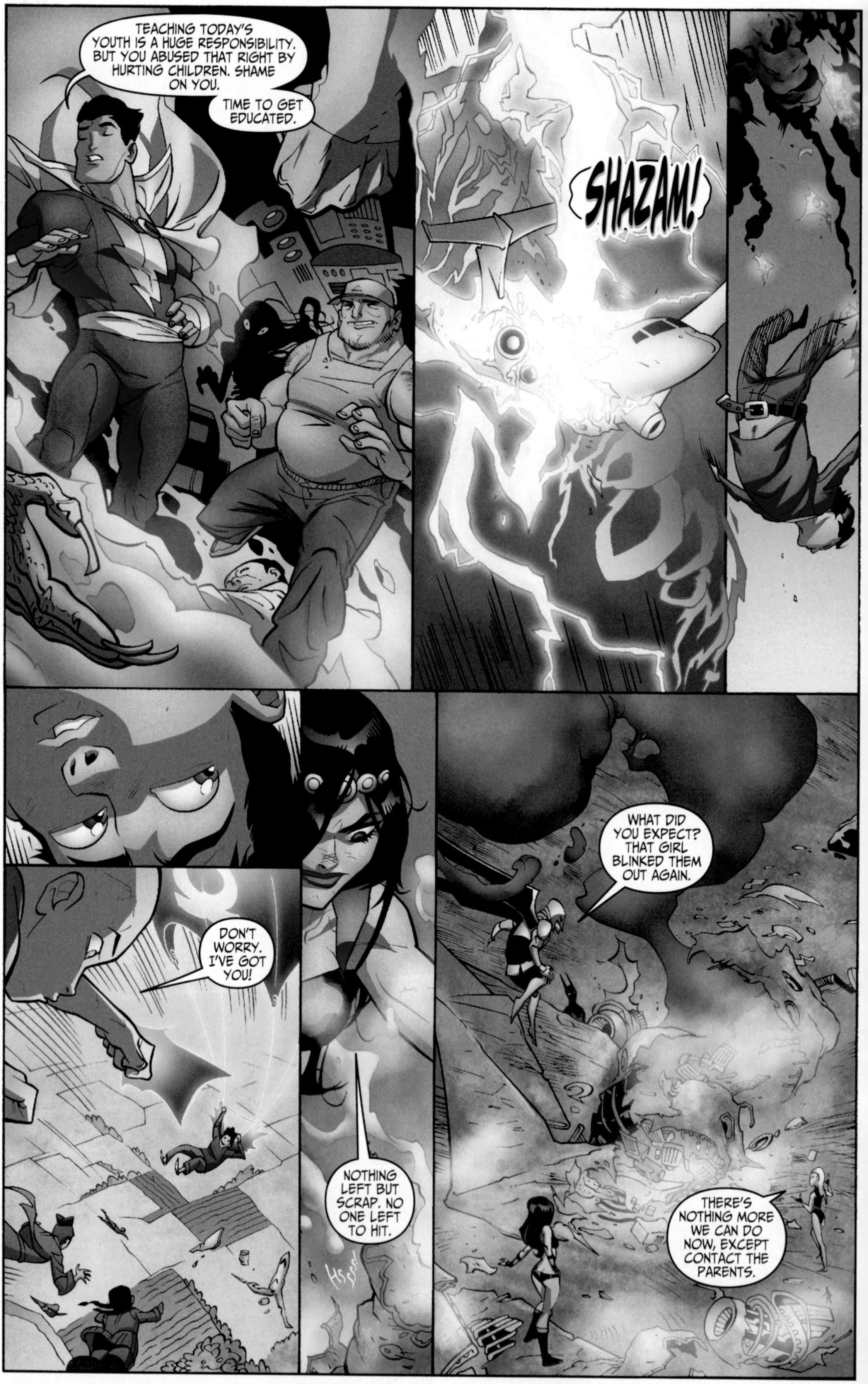
TEACHING TODAY'S YOUTH IS A HUGE RESPONSIBILITY. BUT YOU ABUSED THAT RIGHT BY HURTING CHILDREN. SHAME ON YOU.
TIME TO GET EDUCATED.
SHAZAM!
DON'T WORRY. I'VE GOT YOU!
NOTHING LEFT BUT SCRAP. NO ONE LEFT TO HIT.
HSSSS!
WHAT DID YOU EXPECT? THAT GIRL BLINKED THEM OUT AGAIN.
THERE'S NOTHING MORE WE CAN DO NOW, EXCEPT CONTACT THE PARENTS.

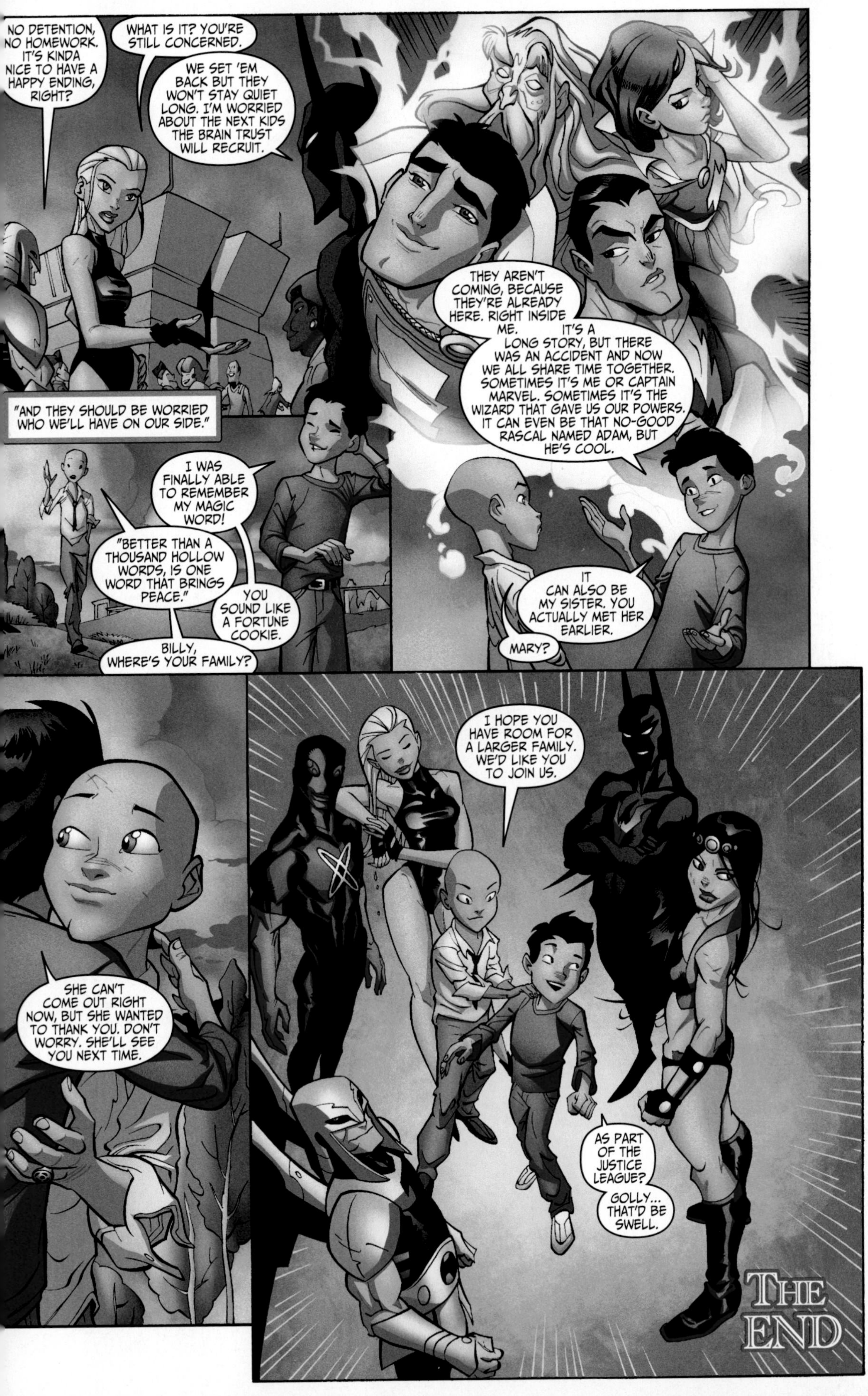
NO DETENTION, NO HOMEWORK. IT'S KINDA NICE TO HAVE A HAPPY ENDING, RIGHT?
WHAT IS IT? YOU'RE STILL CONCERNED.
WE SET 'EM BACK BUT THEY WON'T STAY QUIET LONG. I'M WORRIED ABOUT THE NEXT KIDS THE BRAIN TRUST WILL RECRUIT.
"AND THEY SHOULD BE WORRIED WHO WE'LL HAVE ON OUR SIDE."
I WAS FINALLY ABLE TO REMEMBER MY MAGIC WORD!
"BETTER THAN A THOUSAND HOLLOW WORDS, IS ONE WORD THAT BRINGS PEACE."
YOU SOUND LIKE A FORTUNE COOKIE.
BILLY, WHERE'S YOUR FAMILY?
THEY AREN'T COMING, BECAUSE THEY'RE ALREADY HERE. RIGHT INSIDE ME.
IT'S A LONG STORY, BUT THERE WAS AN ACCIDENT AND NOW WE ALL SHARE TIME TOGETHER. SOMETIMES IT'S ME OR CAPTAIN MARVEL. SOMETIMES IT'S THE WIZARD THAT GAVE US OUR POWERS. IT CAN EVEN BE THAT NO-GOOD RASCAL NAMED ADAM, BUT HE'S COOL.
IT CAN ALSO BE MY SISTER. YOU ACTUALLY MET HER EARLIER.
MARY?
SHE CAN'T COME OUT RIGHT NOW, BUT SHE WANTED TO THANK YOU. DON'T WORRY. SHE'LL SEE YOU NEXT TIME.
I HOPE YOU HAVE ROOM FOR A LARGER FAMILY. WE'D LIKE YOU TO JOIN US.
AS PART OF THE JUSTICE LEAGUE?
GOLLY... THAT'D BE SWELL.
THE END

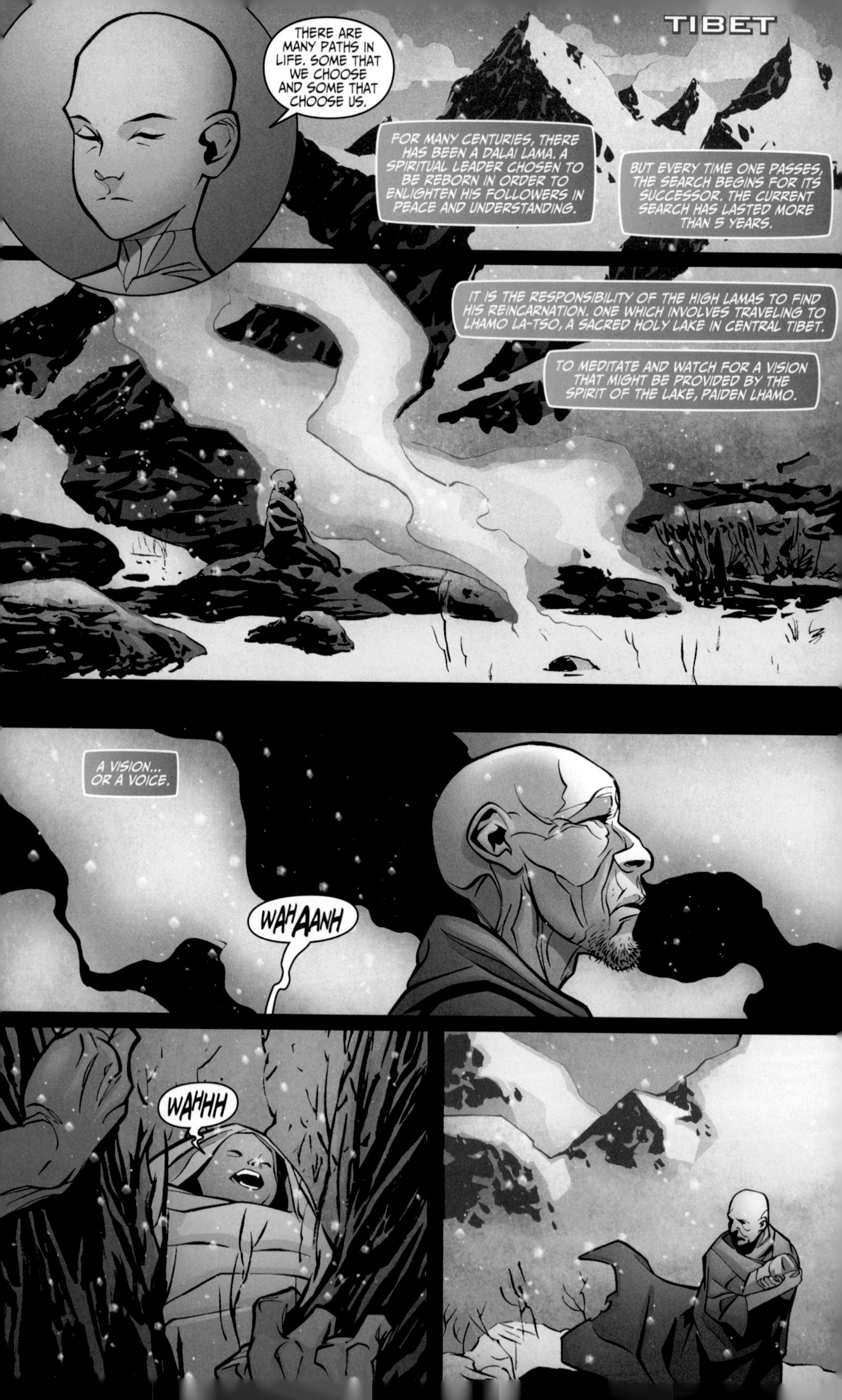
TIBET
THERE ARE MANY PATHS IN LIFE. SOME THAT WE CHOOSE AND SOME THAT CHOOSE US.
FOR MANY CENTURIES, THERE HAS BEEN A DALAI LAMA. A SPIRITUAL LEADER CHOSEN TO BE REBORN IN ORDER TO ENLIGHTEN HIS FOLLOWERS IN PEACE AND UNDERSTANDING.
BUT EVERY TIME ONE PASSES, THE SEARCH BEGINS FOR ITS SUCCESSOR. THE CURRENT SEARCH HAS LASTED MORE THAN 5 YEARS.
IT IS THE RESPONSIBILITY OF THE HIGH LAMAS TO FIND HIS REINCARNATION. ONE WHICH INVOLVES TRAVELING TO LHAMO LA-TSO, A SACRED HOLY LAKE IN CENTRAL TIBET.
TO MEDITATE AND WATCH FOR A VISION THAT MIGHT BE PROVIDED BY THE SPIRIT OF THE LAKE, PAIDEN LHAMO.
A VISION... OR A VOICE.
WAHAANH
WAHHH

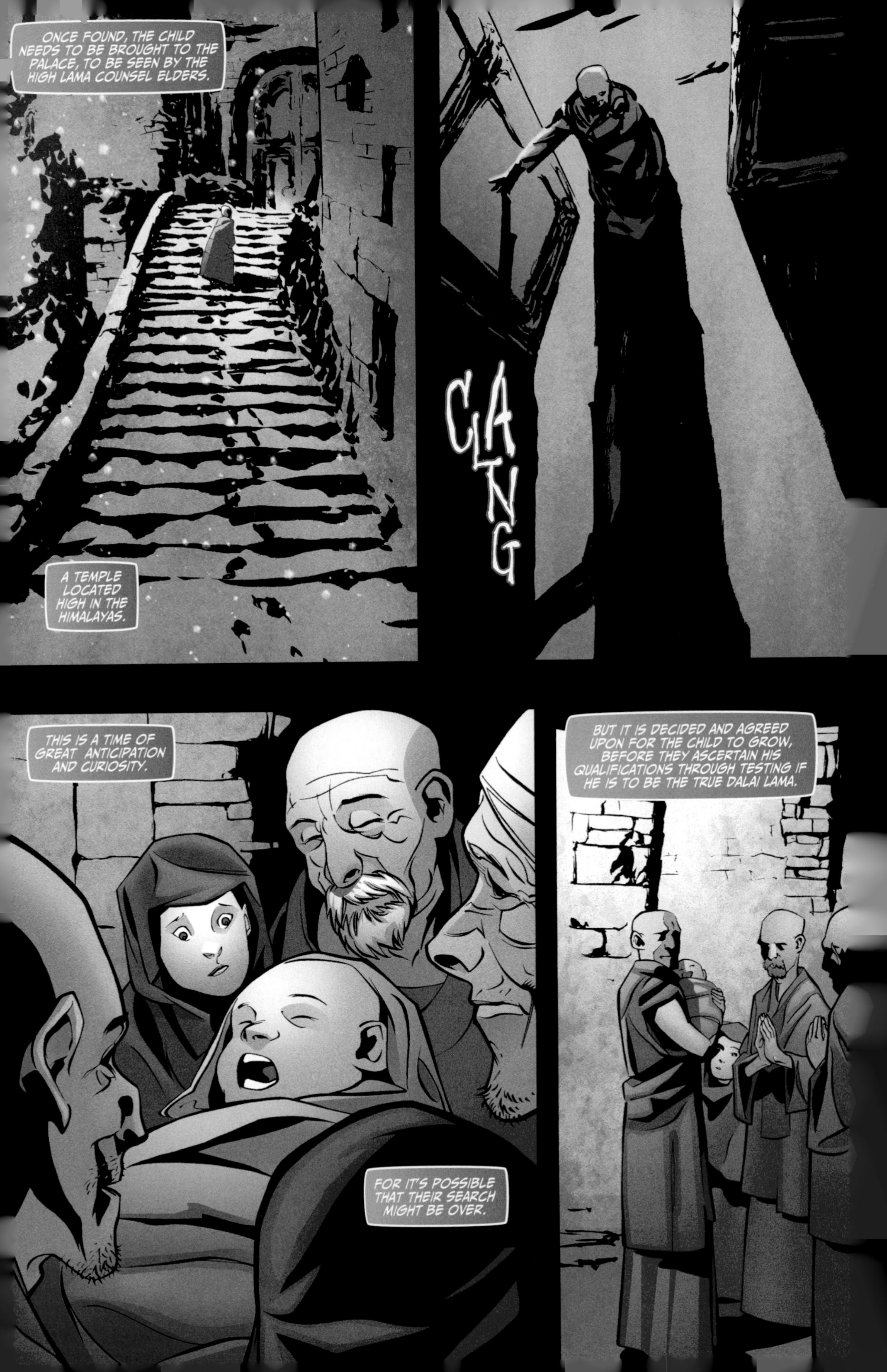

ONCE FOUND, THE CHILD NEEDS TO BE BROUGHT TO THE PALACE, TO BE SEEN BY THE HIGH LAMA COUNSEL ELDERS.
A TEMPLE LOCATED HIGH IN THE HIMALAYAS.
CLANG
THIS IS A TIME OF GREAT ANTICIPATION AND CURIOSITY.
FOR IT'S POSSIBLE THAT THEIR SEARCH MIGHT BE OVER.
BUT IT IS DECIDED AND AGREED UPON FOR THE CHILD TO GROW, BEFORE THEY ASCERTAIN HIS QUALIFICATIONS THROUGH TESTING IF HE IS TO BE THE TRUE DALAI LAMA.

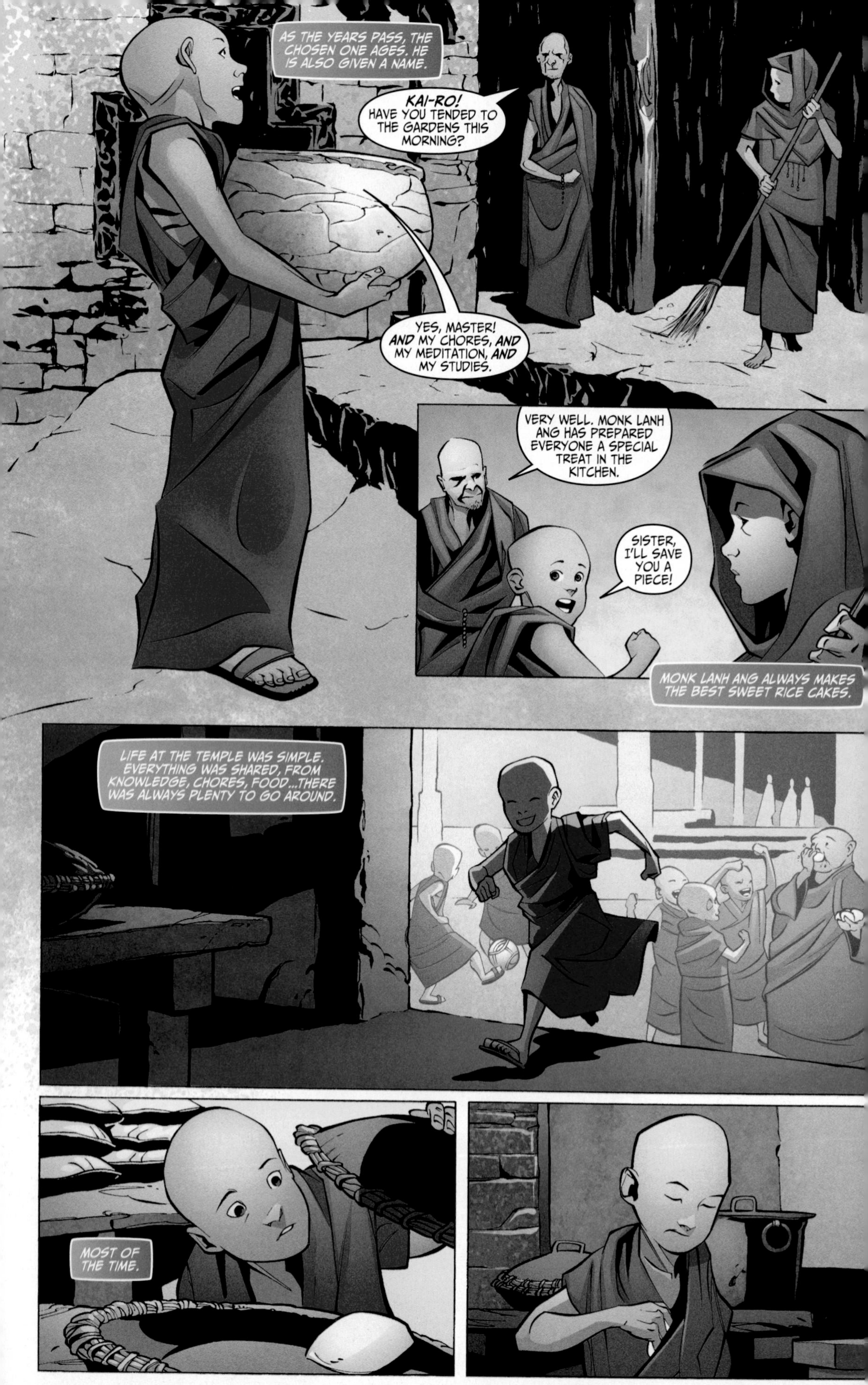

AS THE YEARS PASS, THE CHOSEN ONE AGES. HE IS ALSO GIVEN A NAME.
KAI-RO! HAVE YOU TENDED TO THE GARDENS THIS MORNING?
YES, MASTER! AND MY CHORES, AND MY MEDITATION, AND MY STUDIES.
VERY WELL. MONK LANH ANG HAS PREPARED EVERYONE A SPECIAL TREAT IN THE KITCHEN.
SISTER, I'LL SAVE YOU A PIECE!
MONK LANH ANG ALWAYS MAKES THE BEST SWEET RICE CAKES.
LIFE AT THE TEMPLE WAS SIMPLE. EVERYTHING WAS SHARED, FROM KNOWLEDGE, CHORES, FOOD...THERE WAS ALWAYS PLENTY TO GO AROUND.
MOST OF THE TIME.

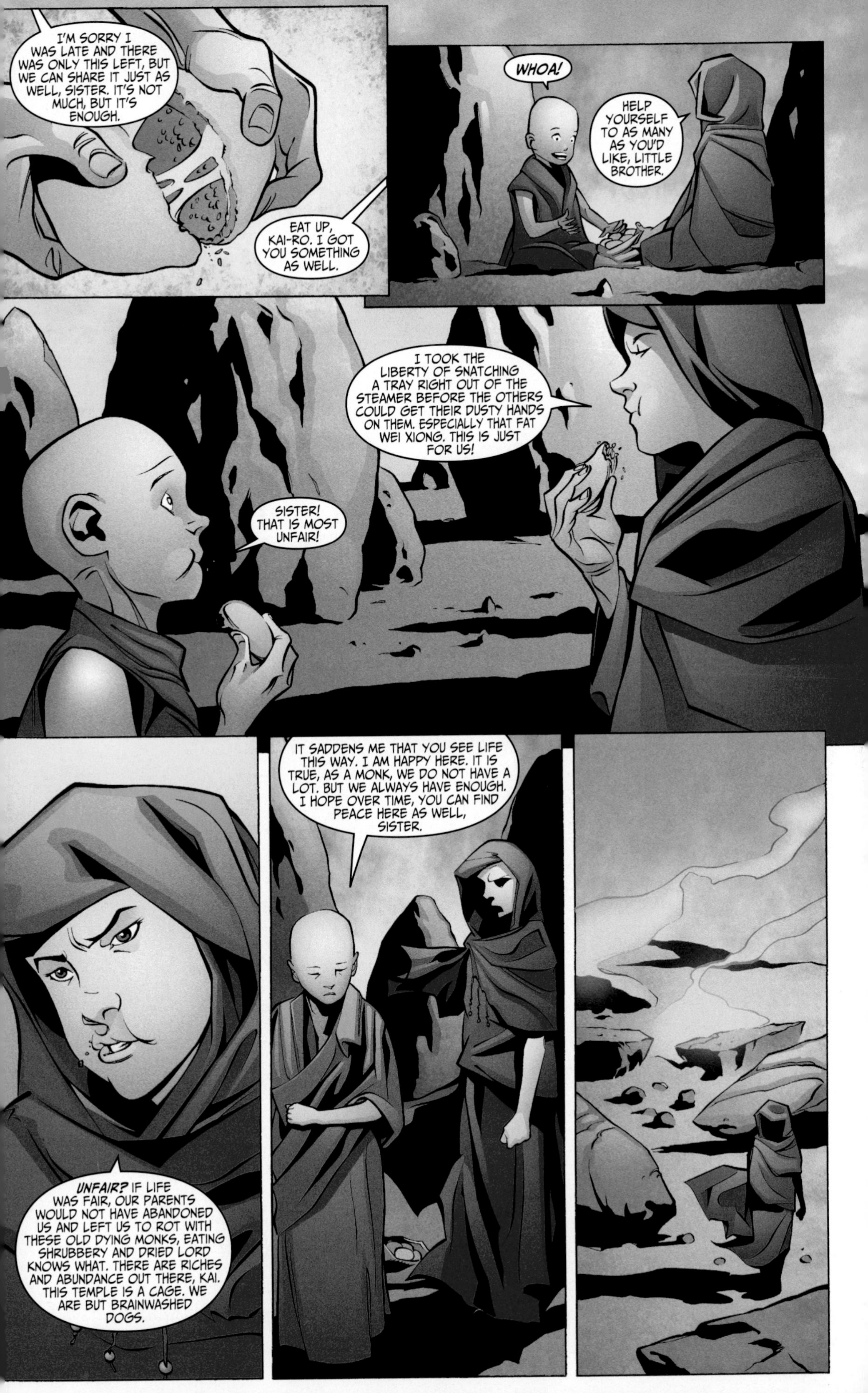

I'M SORRY I WAS LATE AND THERE WAS ONLY THIS LEFT, BUT WE CAN SHARE IT JUST AS WELL, SISTER. IT'S NOT MUCH, BUT IT'S ENOUGH.
EAT UP, KAI-RO. I GOT YOU SOMETHING AS WELL.
WHOA!
HELP YOURSELF TO AS MANY AS YOU'D LIKE, LITTLE BROTHER.
I TOOK THE LIBERTY OF SNATCHING A TRAY RIGHT OUT OF THE STEAMER BEFORE THE OTHERS COULD GET THEIR DUSTY HANDS ON THEM. ESPECIALLY THAT FAT WEI XIONG. THIS IS JUST FOR US!
SISTER! THAT IS MOST UNFAIR!
UNFAIR? IF LIFE WAS FAIR, OUR PARENTS WOULD NOT HAVE ABANDONED US AND LEFT US TO ROT WITH THESE OLD DYING MONKS, EATING SHRUBBERY AND DRIED LORD KNOWS WHAT. THERE ARE RICHES AND ABUNDANCE OUT THERE, KAI. THIS TEMPLE IS A CAGE. WE ARE BUT BRAINWASHED DOGS.
IT SADDENS ME THAT YOU SEE LIFE THIS WAY. I AM HAPPY HERE. IT IS TRUE, AS A MONK, WE DO NOT HAVE A LOT. BUT WE ALWAYS HAVE ENOUGH. I HOPE OVER TIME, YOU CAN FIND PEACE HERE AS WELL, SISTER.

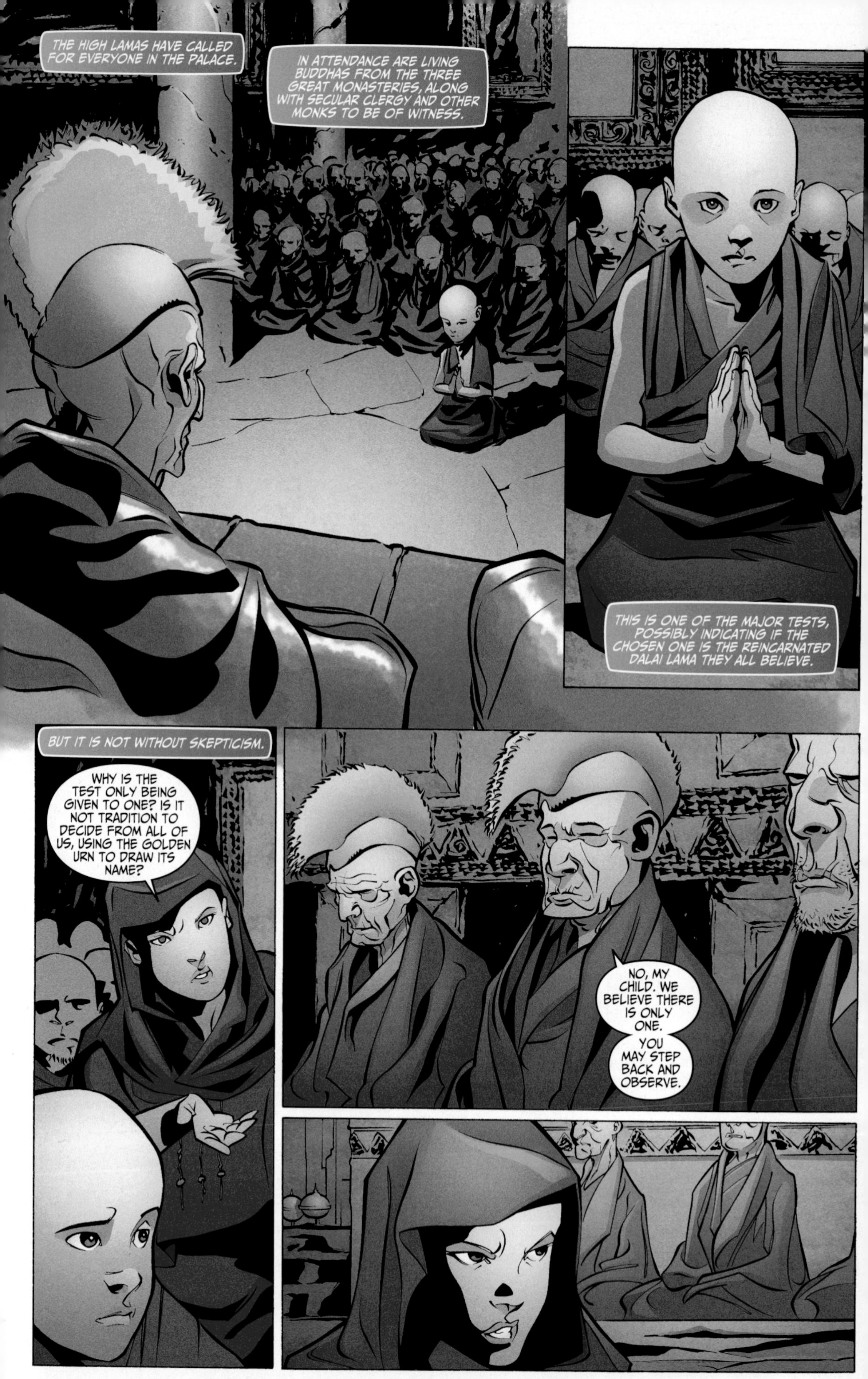
THE HIGH LAMAS HAVE CALLED FOR EVERYONE IN THE PALACE.
IN ATTENDANCE ARE LIVING BUDDHAS FROM THE THREE GREAT MONASTERIES, ALONG WITH SECULAR CLERGY AND OTHER MONKS TO BE OF WITNESS.
THIS IS ONE OF THE MAJOR TESTS, POSSIBLY INDICATING IF THE CHOSEN ONE IS THE REINCARNATED DALAI LAMA THEY ALL BELIEVE.
BUT IT IS NOT WITHOUT SKEPTICISM.
WHY IS THE TEST ONLY BEING GIVEN TO ONE? IS IT NOT TRADITION TO DECIDE FROM ALL OF US, USING THE GOLDEN URN TO DRAW ITS NAME?
NO, MY CHILD. WE BELIEVE THERE IS ONLY ONE.
YOU MAY STEP BACK AND OBSERVE.

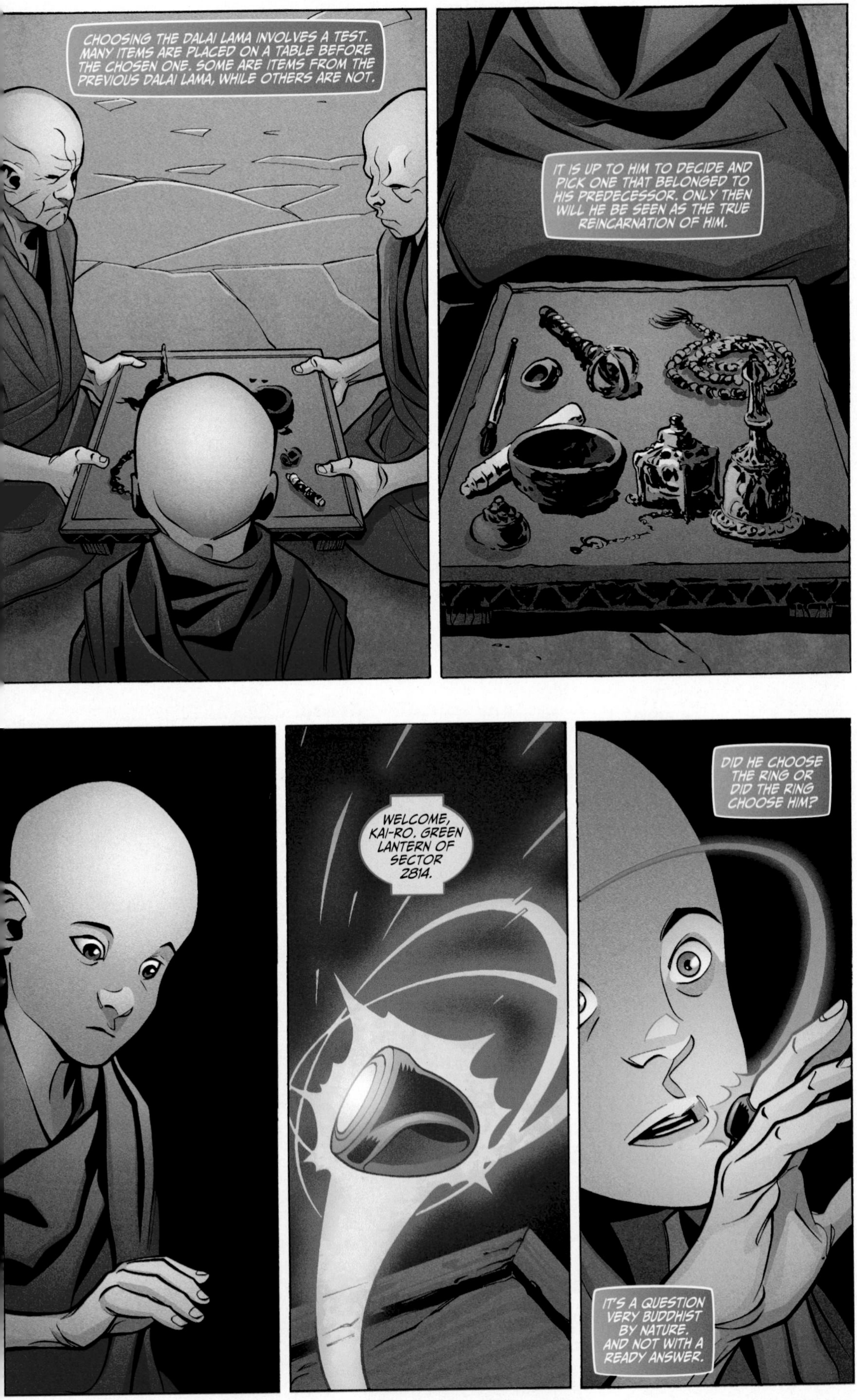
CHOOSING THE DALAI LAMA INVOLVES A TEST. MANY ITEMS ARE PLACED ON A TABLE BEFORE THE CHOSEN ONE. SOME ARE ITEMS FROM THE PREVIOUS DALAI LAMA, WHILE OTHERS ARE NOT.
IT IS UP TO HIM TO DECIDE AND PICK ONE THAT BELONGED TO HIS PREDECESSOR. ONLY THEN WILL HE BE SEEN AS THE TRUE REINCARNATION OF HIM.
WELCOME, KAI-RO. GREEN LANTERN OF SECTOR 2814.
DID HE CHOOSE THE RING OR DID THE RING CHOOSE HIM?
IT'S A QUESTION VERY BUDDHIST BY NATURE. AND NOT WITH A READY ANSWER.

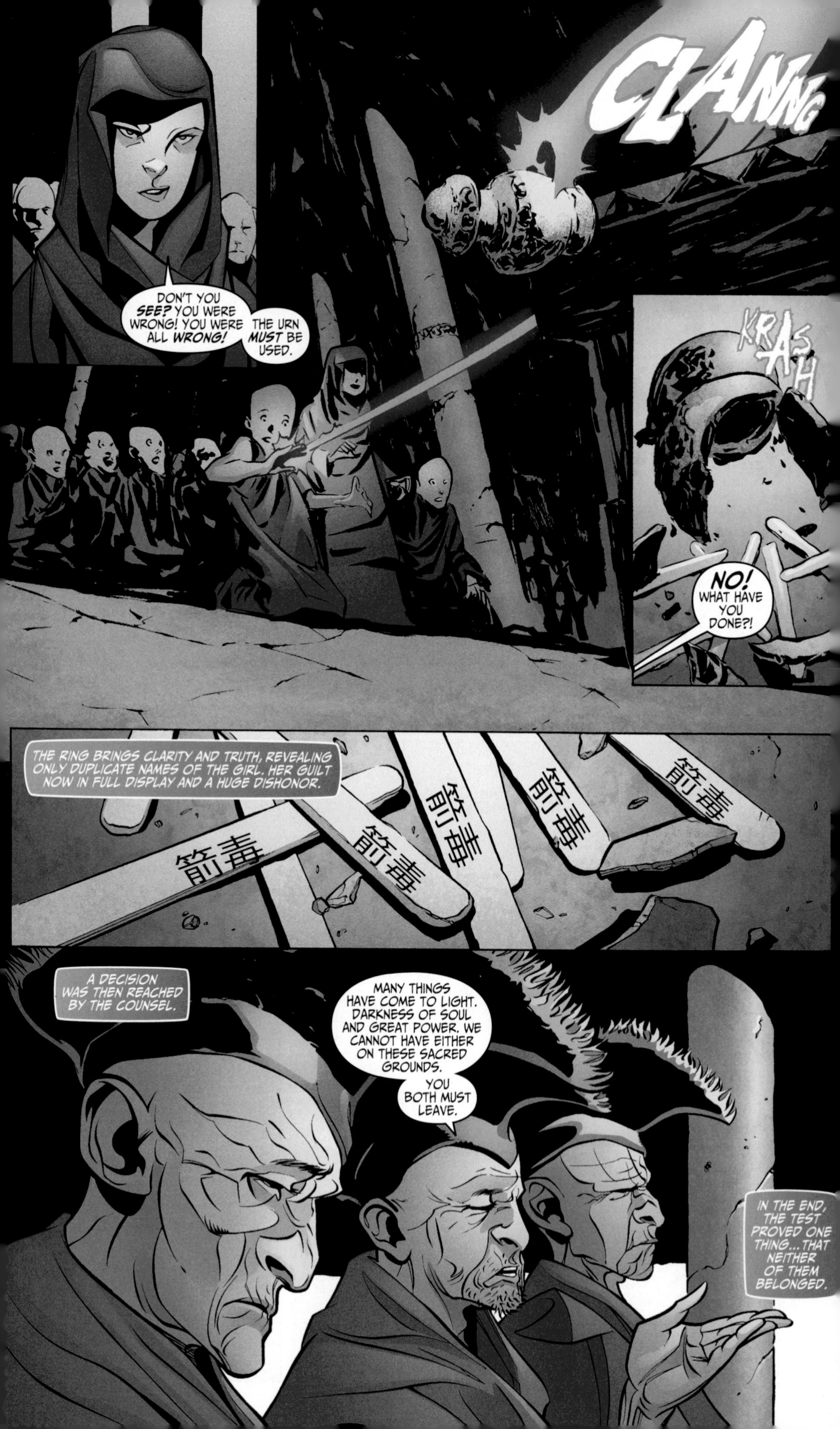
CLANNG
DON'T YOU SEE? YOU WERE WRONG! YOU WERE ALL WRONG!
THE URN MUST BE USED.
KRASH
NO! WHAT HAVE YOU DONE?!
THE RING BRINGS CLARITY AND TRUTH, REVEALING ONLY DUPLICATE NAMES OF THE GIRL. HER GUILT NOW IN FULL DISPLAY AND A HUGE DISHONOR.
箭毒
箭毒
箭毒
箭毒
箭毒
A DECISION WAS THEN REACHED BY THE COUNSEL.
MANY THINGS HAVE COME TO LIGHT. DARKNESS OF SOUL AND GREAT POWER. WE CANNOT HAVE EITHER ON THESE SACRED GROUNDS.
YOU BOTH MUST LEAVE.
IN THE END, THE TEST PROVED ONE THING...THAT NEITHER OF THEM BELONGED.

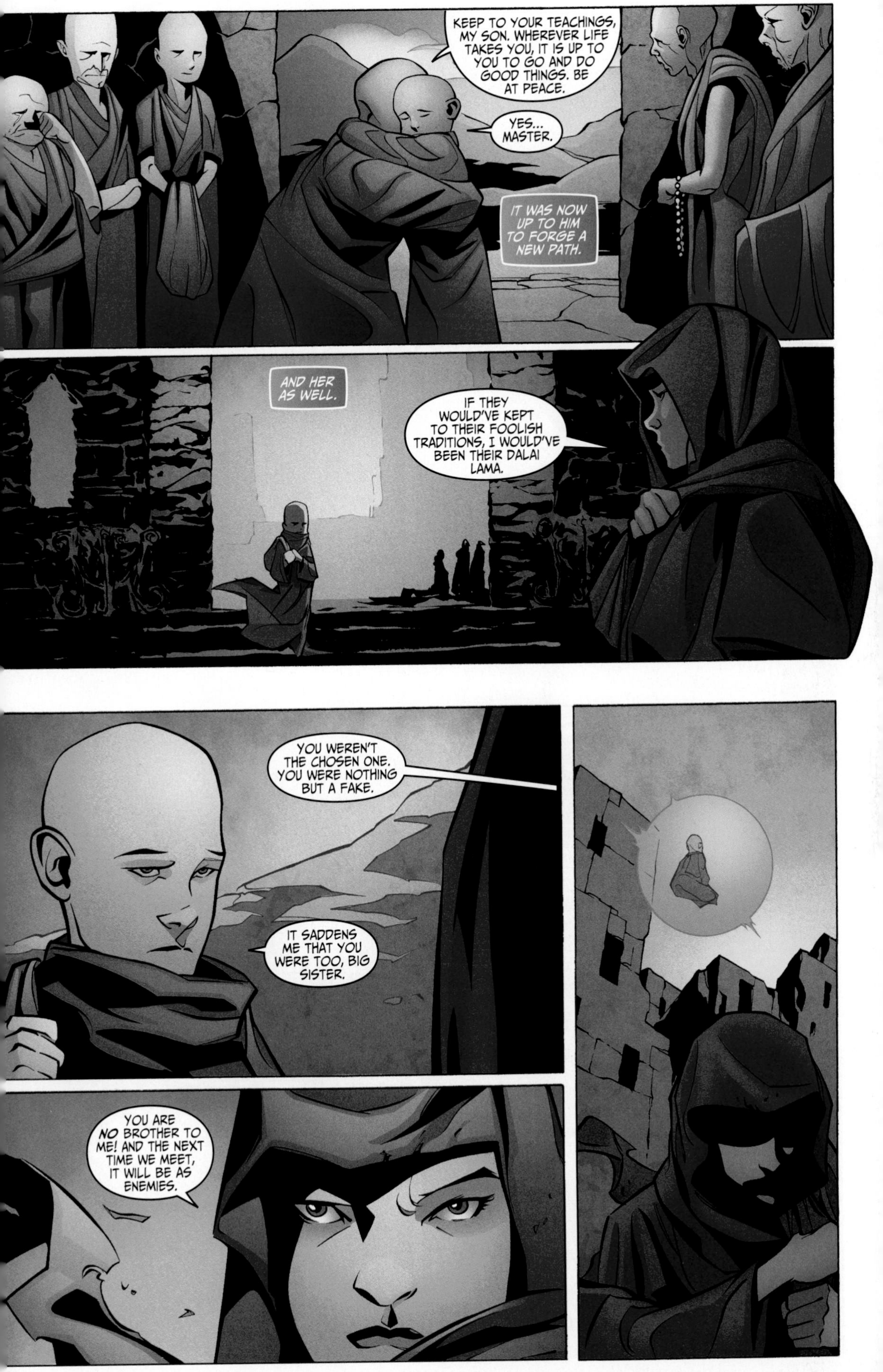
KEEP TO YOUR TEACHINGS, MY SON. WHEREVER LIFE TAKES YOU, IT IS UP TO YOU TO GO AND DO GOOD THINGS. BE AT PEACE.
YES... MASTER.
IT WAS NOW UP TO HIM TO FORGE A NEW PATH.
AND HER AS WELL.
IF THEY WOULD'VE KEPT TO THEIR FOOLISH TRADITIONS, I WOULD'VE BEEN THEIR DALAI LAMA.
YOU WEREN'T THE CHOSEN ONE. YOU WERE NOTHING BUT A FAKE.
IT SADDENS ME THAT YOU WERE TOO, BIG SISTER.
YOU ARE NO BROTHER TO ME! AND THE NEXT TIME WE MEET, IT WILL BE AS ENEMIES.

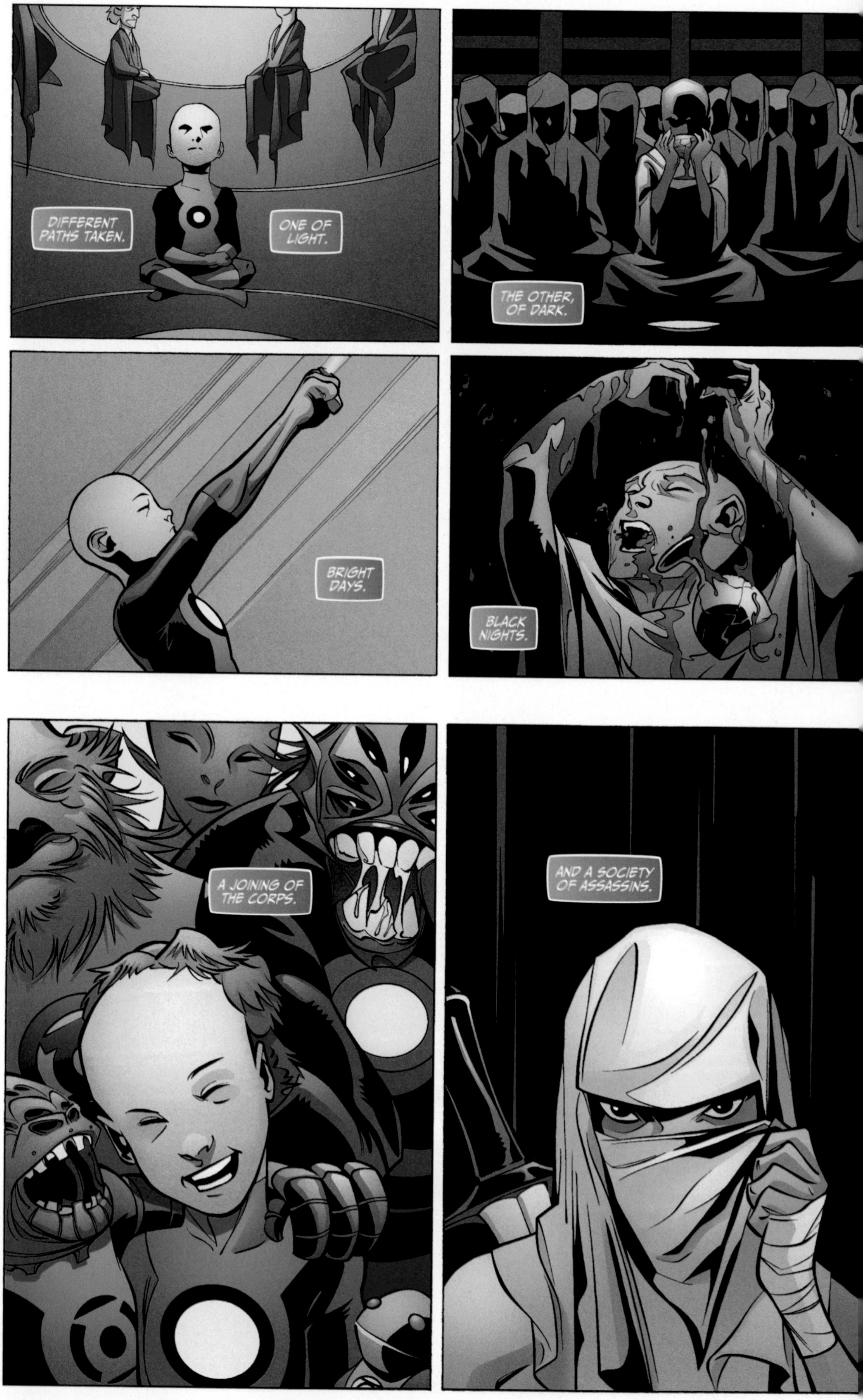
DIFFERENT PATHS TAKEN.
ONE OF LIGHT.
THE OTHER, OF DARK.
BRIGHT DAYS.
BLACK NIGHTS.
A JOINING OF THE CORPS.
AND A SOCIETY OF ASSASSINS.

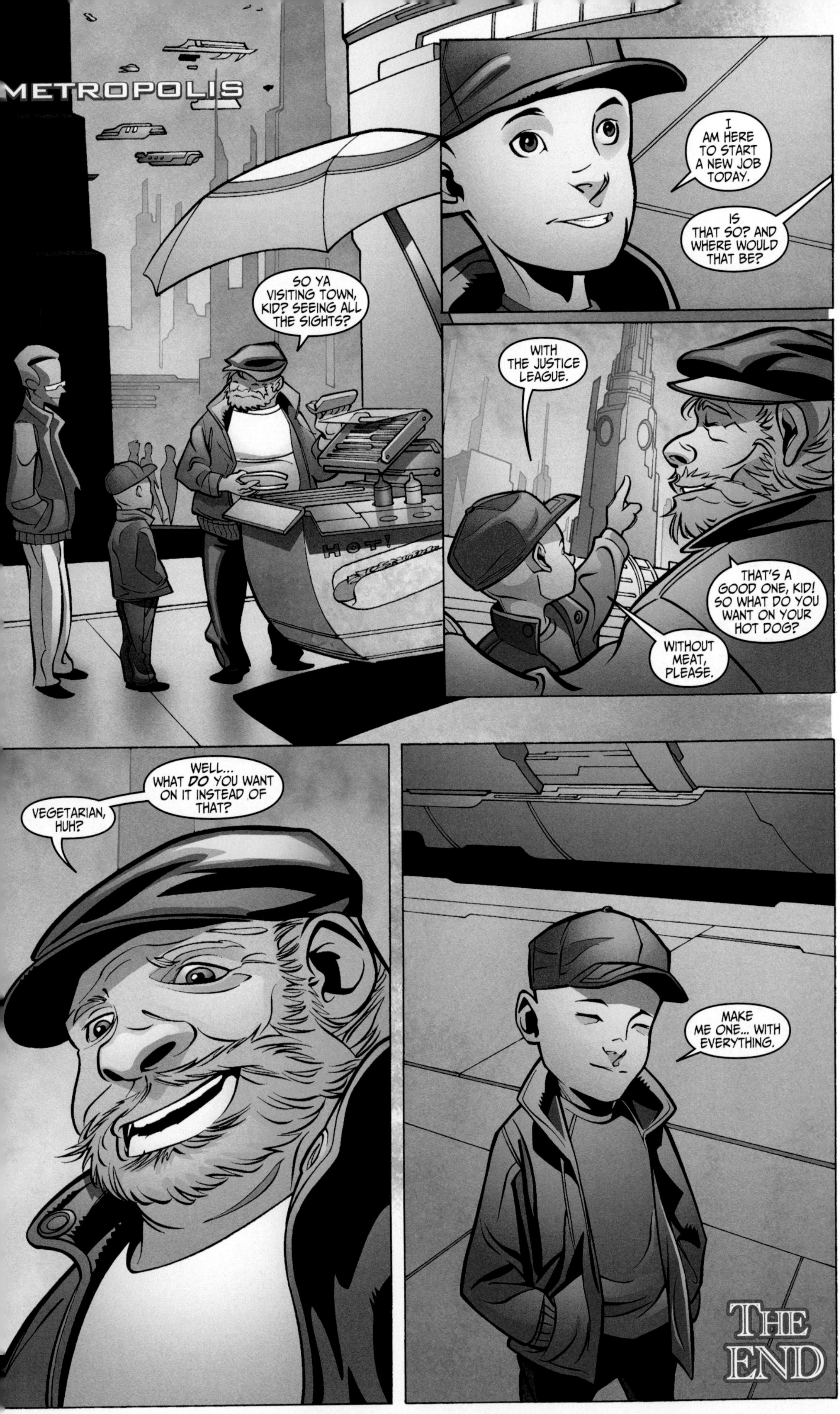
METROPOLIS
SO YA VISITING TOWN, KID? SEEING ALL THE SIGHTS?
HOT!
I AM HERE TO START A NEW JOB TODAY.
IS THAT SO? AND WHERE WOULD THAT BE?
WITH THE JUSTICE LEAGUE.
THAT'S A GOOD ONE, KID! SO WHAT DO YOU WANT ON YOUR HOT DOG?
WITHOUT MEAT, PLEASE.
VEGETARIAN, HUH?
WELL... WHAT DO YOU WANT ON IT INSTEAD OF THAT?
MAKE ME ONE... WITH EVERYTHING.
THE END

JUSTICE LEAGUE
BEYOND

SUPERMAN BEYOND

WRITTEN BY
JT KRUL

PENCILS BY
HOWARD PORTER

INKS BY
LIVESAY

COLORS BY
CARRIE STRACHAN

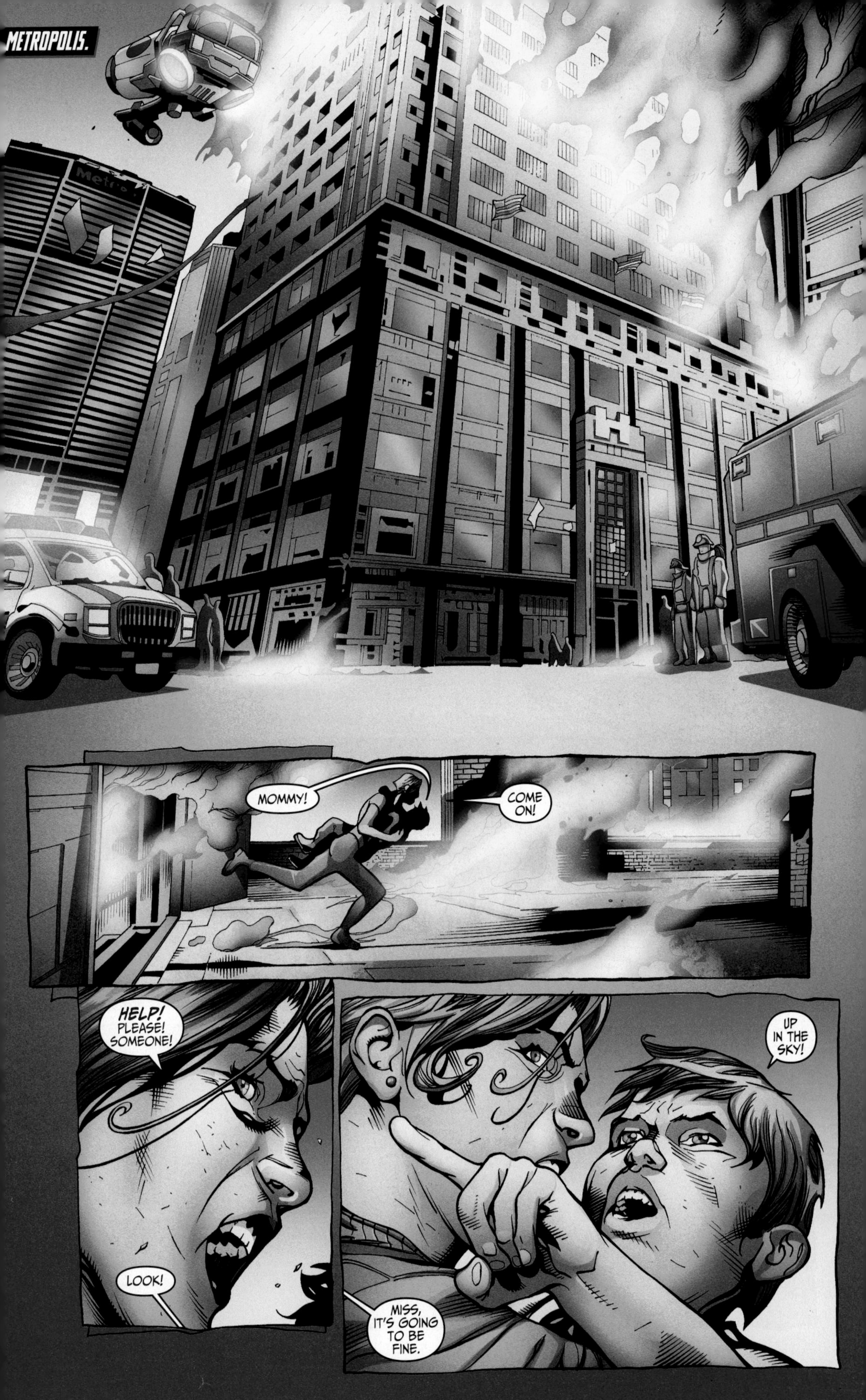
METROPOLIS.
MOMMY!
COME ON!
HELP! PLEASE! SOMEONE!
LOOK!
UP IN THE SKY!
MISS, IT'S GOING TO BE FINE.

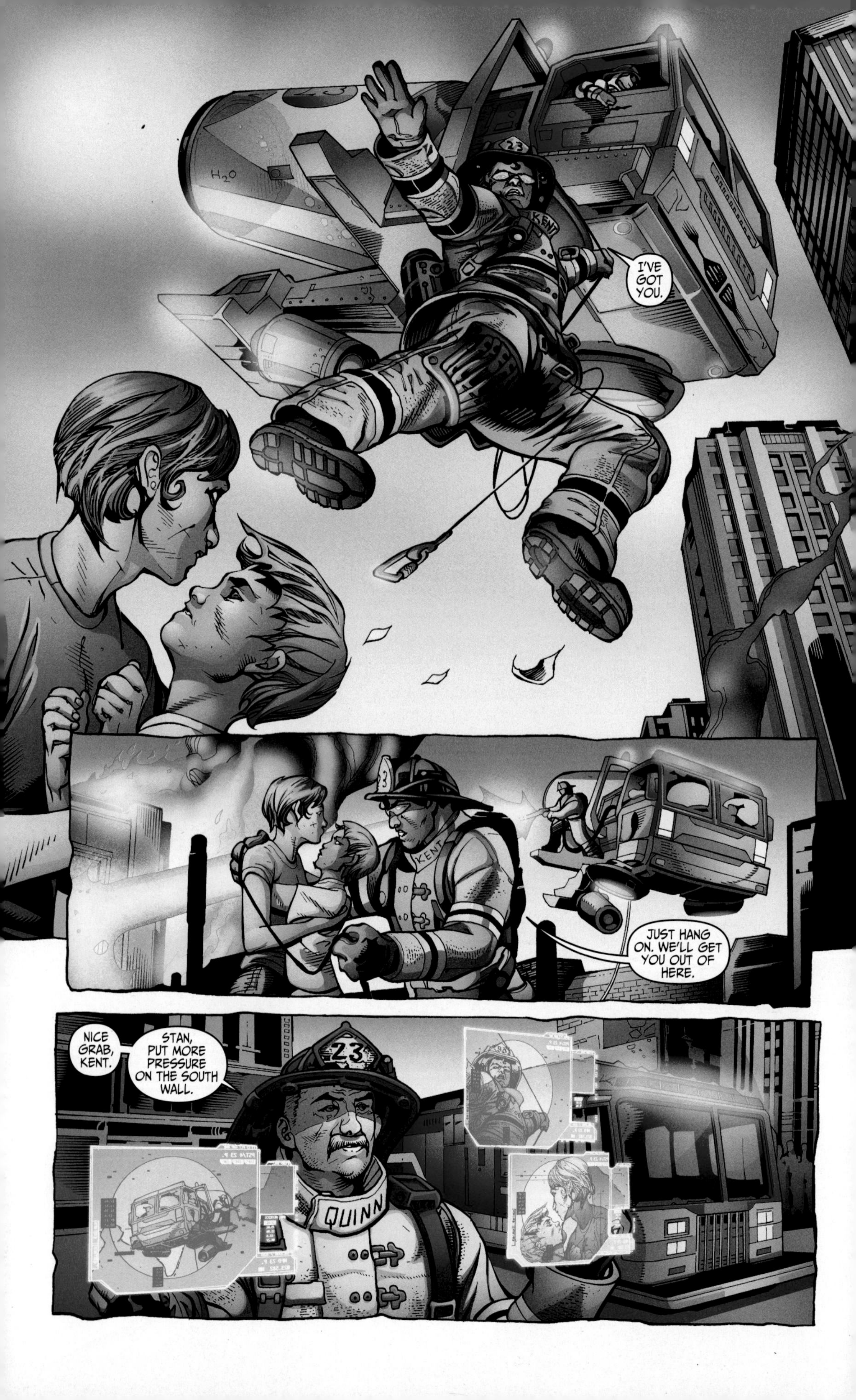
I'VE GOT YOU.
JUST HANG ON. WE'LL GET YOU OUT OF HERE.
NICE GRAB, KENT.
STAN, PUT MORE PRESSURE ON THE SOUTH WALL.

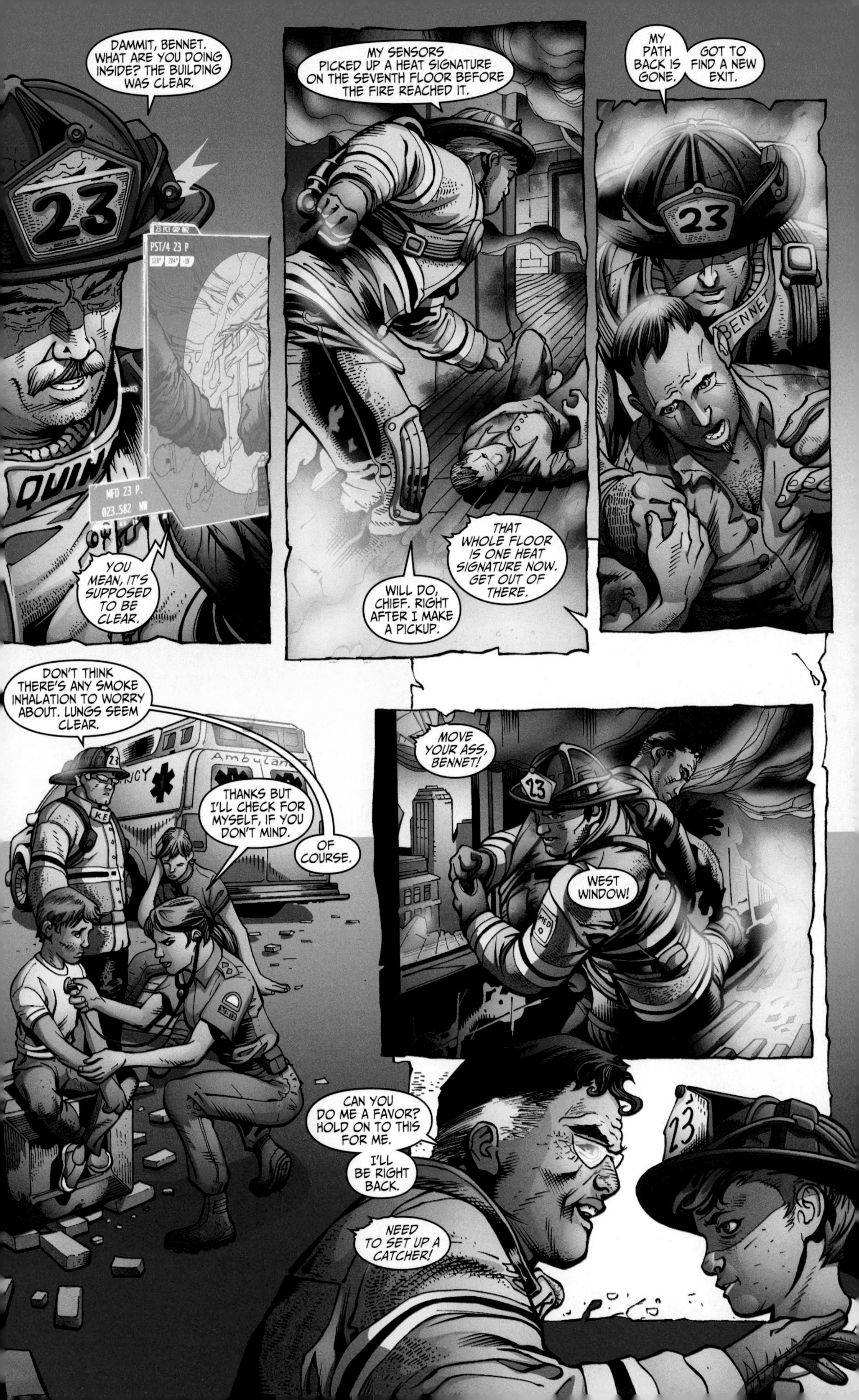

DAMMIT, BENNET. WHAT ARE YOU DOING INSIDE? THE BUILDING WAS CLEAR.
PST/4 23 P
MFD 23 P.
023.582 NW
YOU MEAN, IT'S SUPPOSED TO BE CLEAR.
MY SENSORS PICKED UP A HEAT SIGNATURE ON THE SEVENTH FLOOR BEFORE THE FIRE REACHED IT.
THAT WHOLE FLOOR IS ONE HEAT SIGNATURE NOW. GET OUT OF THERE.
WILL DO, CHIEF. RIGHT AFTER I MAKE A PICKUP.
MY PATH BACK IS GONE.
GOT TO FIND A NEW EXIT.
BENNET
DON'T THINK THERE'S ANY SMOKE INHALATION TO WORRY ABOUT. LUNGS SEEM CLEAR.
THANKS BUT I'LL CHECK FOR MYSELF, IF YOU DON'T MIND.
OF COURSE.
MOVE YOUR ASS, BENNET!
WEST WINDOW!
CAN YOU DO ME A FAVOR? HOLD ON TO THIS FOR ME.
I'LL BE RIGHT BACK.
NEED TO SET UP A CATCHER!

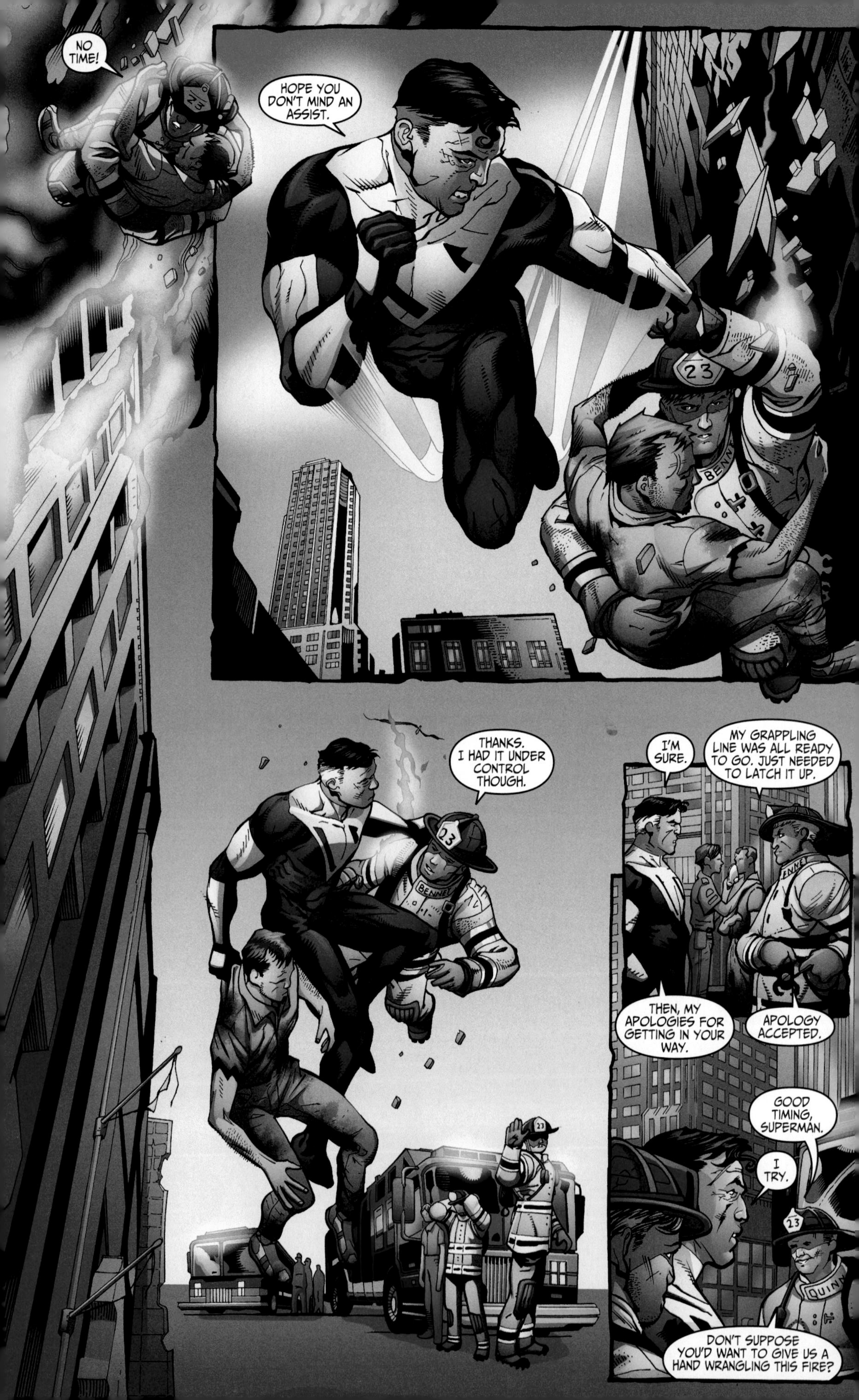
NO TIME!
HOPE YOU DON'T MIND AN ASSIST.
THANKS. I HAD IT UNDER CONTROL THOUGH.
I'M SURE.
MY GRAPPLING LINE WAS ALL READY TO GO. JUST NEEDED TO LATCH IT UP.
THEN, MY APOLOGIES FOR GETTING IN YOUR WAY.
APOLOGY ACCEPTED.
GOOD TIMING, SUPERMAN.
I TRY.
DON'T SUPPOSE YOU'D WANT TO GIVE US A HAND WRANGLING THIS FIRE?

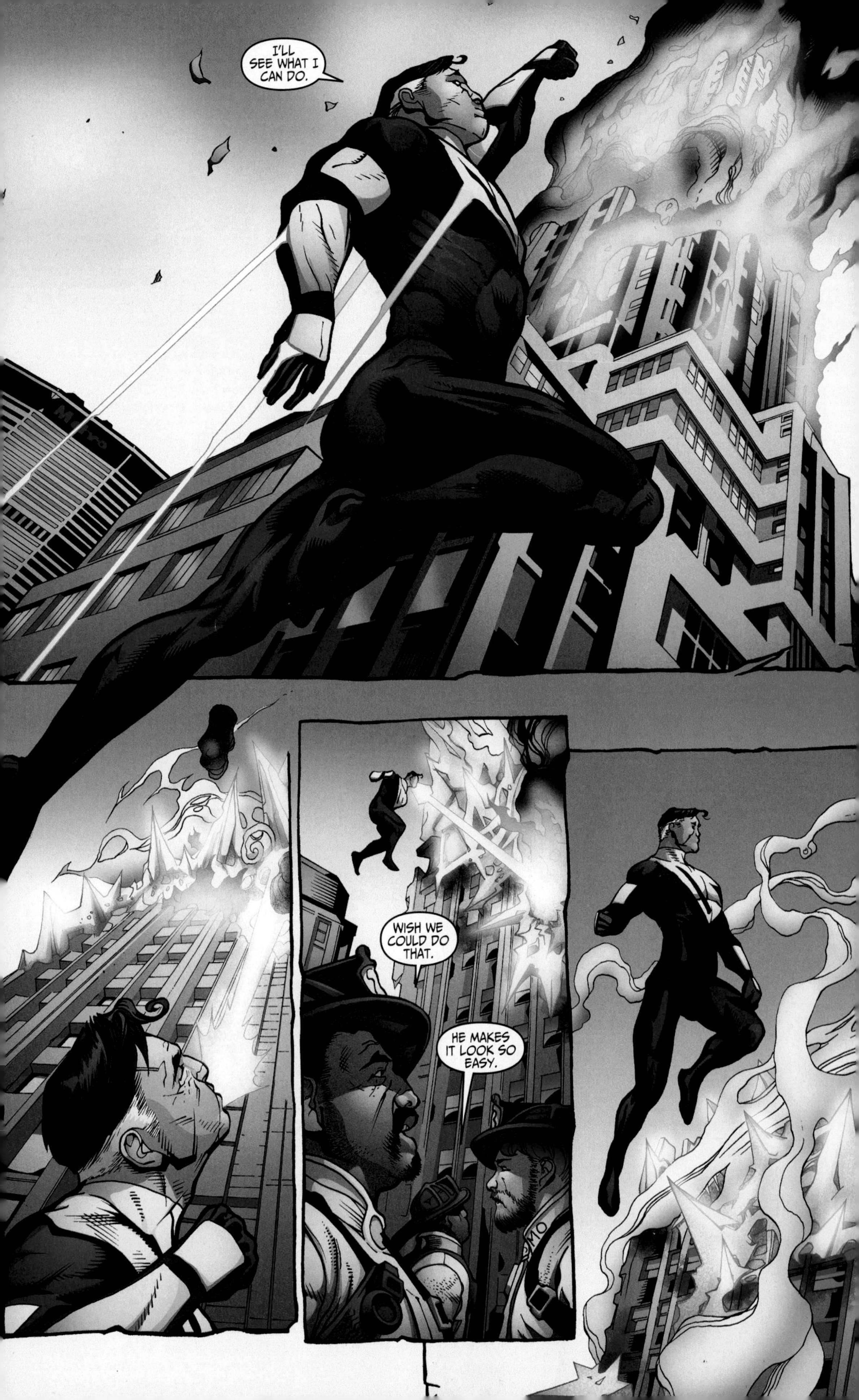
I'LL SEE WHAT I CAN DO.
WISH WE COULD DO THAT.
HE MAKES IT LOOK SO EASY.

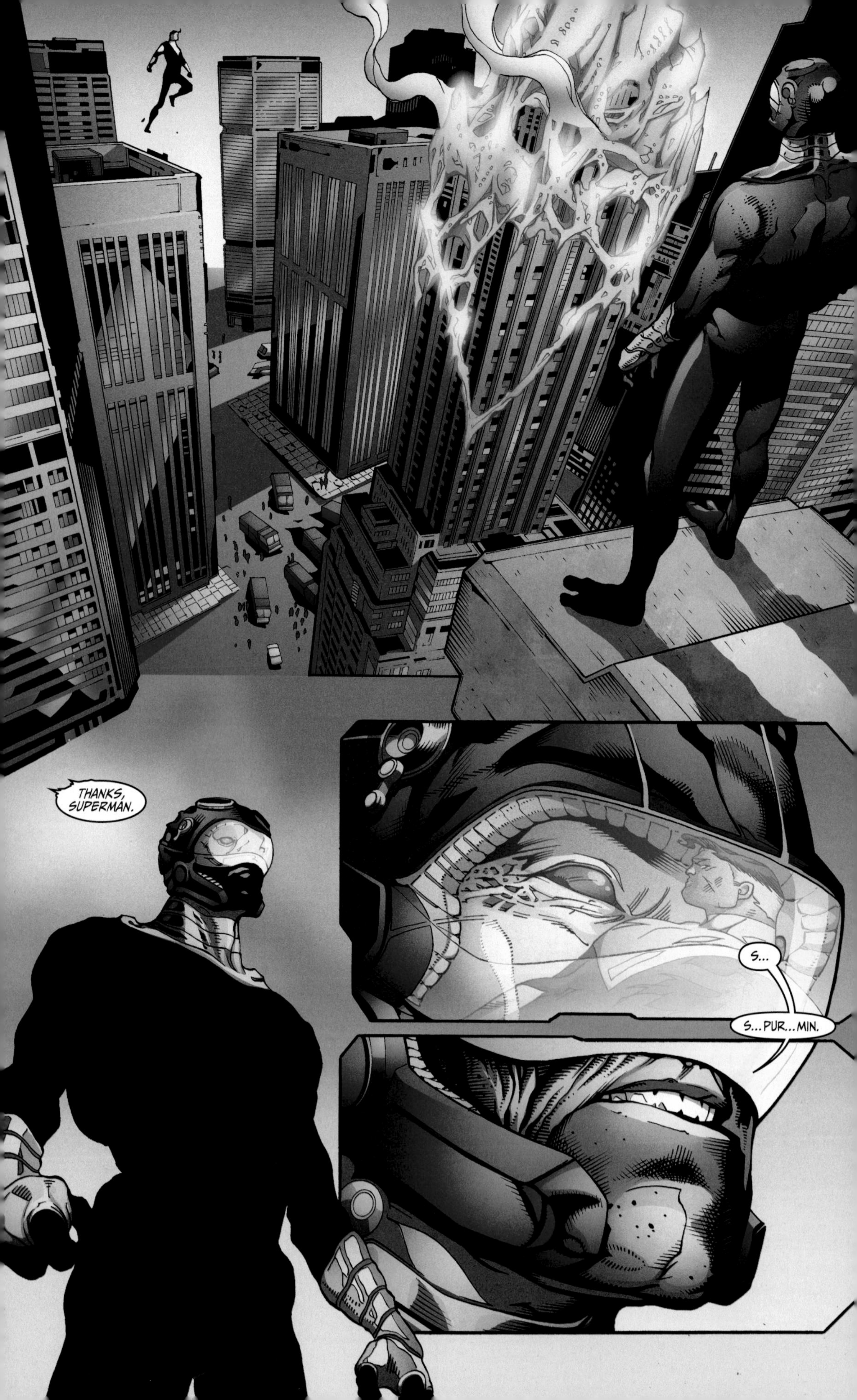
THANKS, SUPERMAN.
S...
S...PUR...MIN.

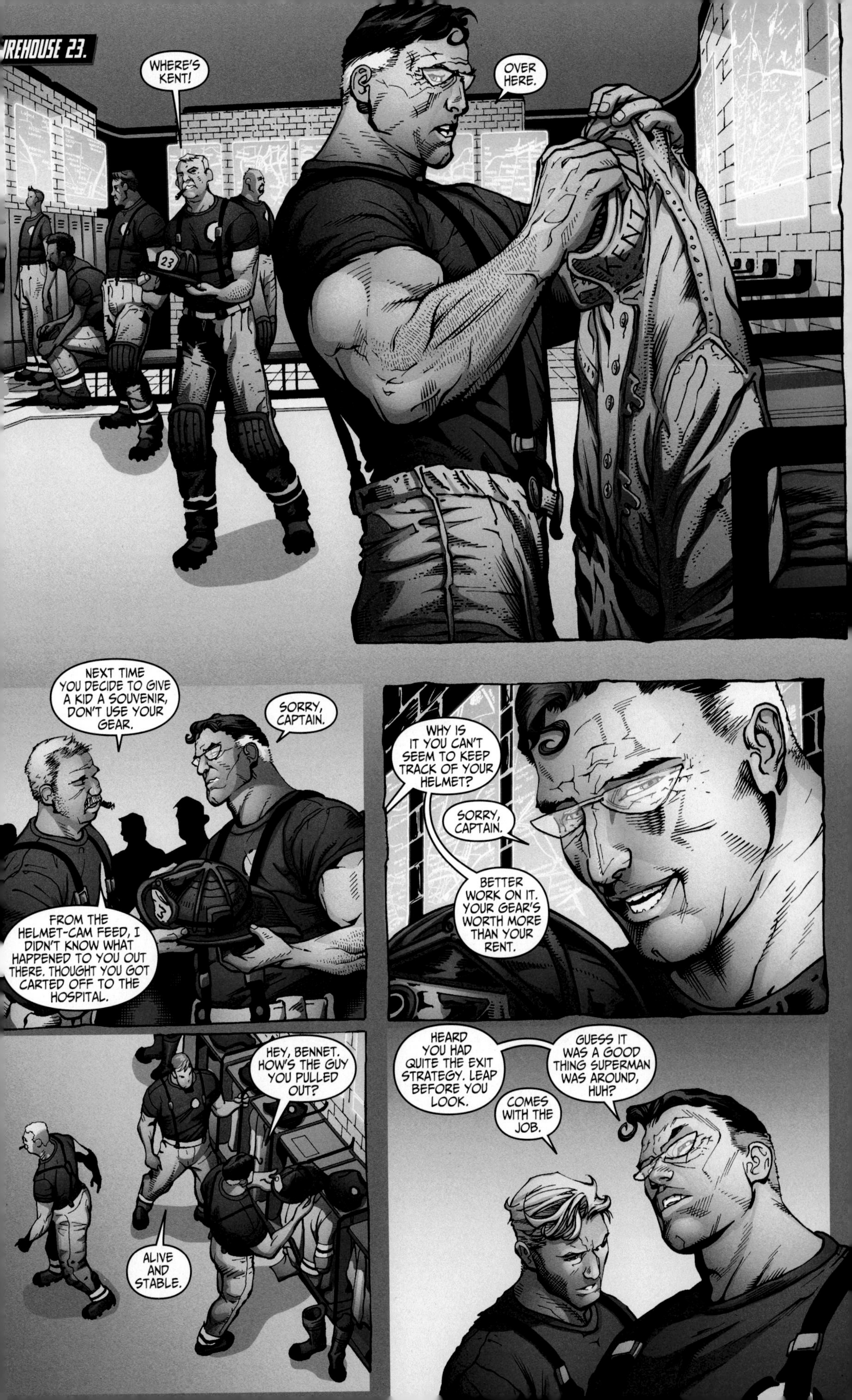

REHOUSE 23.
WHERE'S KENT!
OVER HERE.
NEXT TIME YOU DECIDE TO GIVE A KID A SOUVENIR, DON'T USE YOUR GEAR.
SORRY, CAPTAIN.
FROM THE HELMET-CAM FEED, I DIDN'T KNOW WHAT HAPPENED TO YOU OUT THERE. THOUGHT YOU GOT CARTED OFF TO THE HOSPITAL.
WHY IS IT YOU CAN'T SEEM TO KEEP TRACK OF YOUR HELMET?
SORRY, CAPTAIN.
BETTER WORK ON IT. YOUR GEAR'S WORTH MORE THAN YOUR RENT.
HEY, BENNET. HOW'S THE GUY YOU PULLED OUT?
ALIVE AND STABLE.
HEARD YOU HAD QUITE THE EXIT STRATEGY. LEAP BEFORE YOU LOOK.
COMES WITH THE JOB.
GUESS IT WAS A GOOD THING SUPERMAN WAS AROUND, HUH?

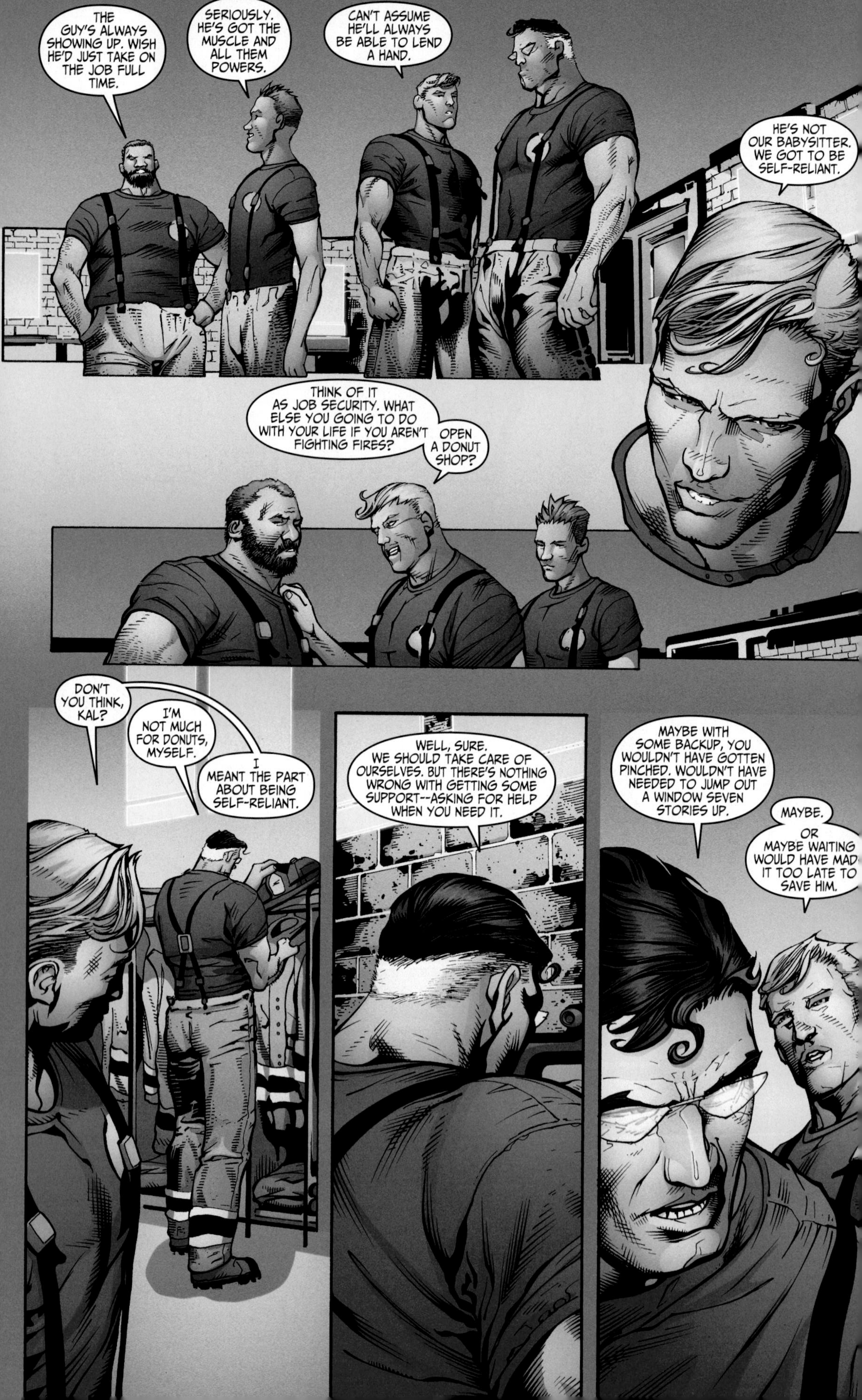
THE GUY'S ALWAYS SHOWING UP. WISH HE'D JUST TAKE ON THE JOB FULL TIME.
SERIOUSLY. HE'S GOT THE MUSCLE AND ALL THEM POWERS.
CAN'T ASSUME HE'LL ALWAYS BE ABLE TO LEND A HAND.
HE'S NOT OUR BABYSITTER. WE GOT TO BE SELF-RELIANT.
THINK OF IT AS JOB SECURITY. WHAT ELSE YOU GOING TO DO WITH YOUR LIFE IF YOU AREN'T FIGHTING FIRES?
OPEN A DONUT SHOP?
DON'T YOU THINK, KAL?
I'M NOT MUCH FOR DONUTS, MYSELF.
I MEANT THE PART ABOUT BEING SELF-RELIANT.
WELL, SURE. WE SHOULD TAKE CARE OF OURSELVES. BUT THERE'S NOTHING WRONG WITH GETTING SOME SUPPORT--ASKING FOR HELP WHEN YOU NEED IT.
MAYBE WITH SOME BACKUP, YOU WOULDN'T HAVE GOTTEN PINCHED. WOULDN'T HAVE NEEDED TO JUMP OUT A WINDOW SEVEN STORIES UP.
MAYBE.
OR MAYBE WAITING WOULD HAVE MAD IT TOO LATE TO SAVE HIM.

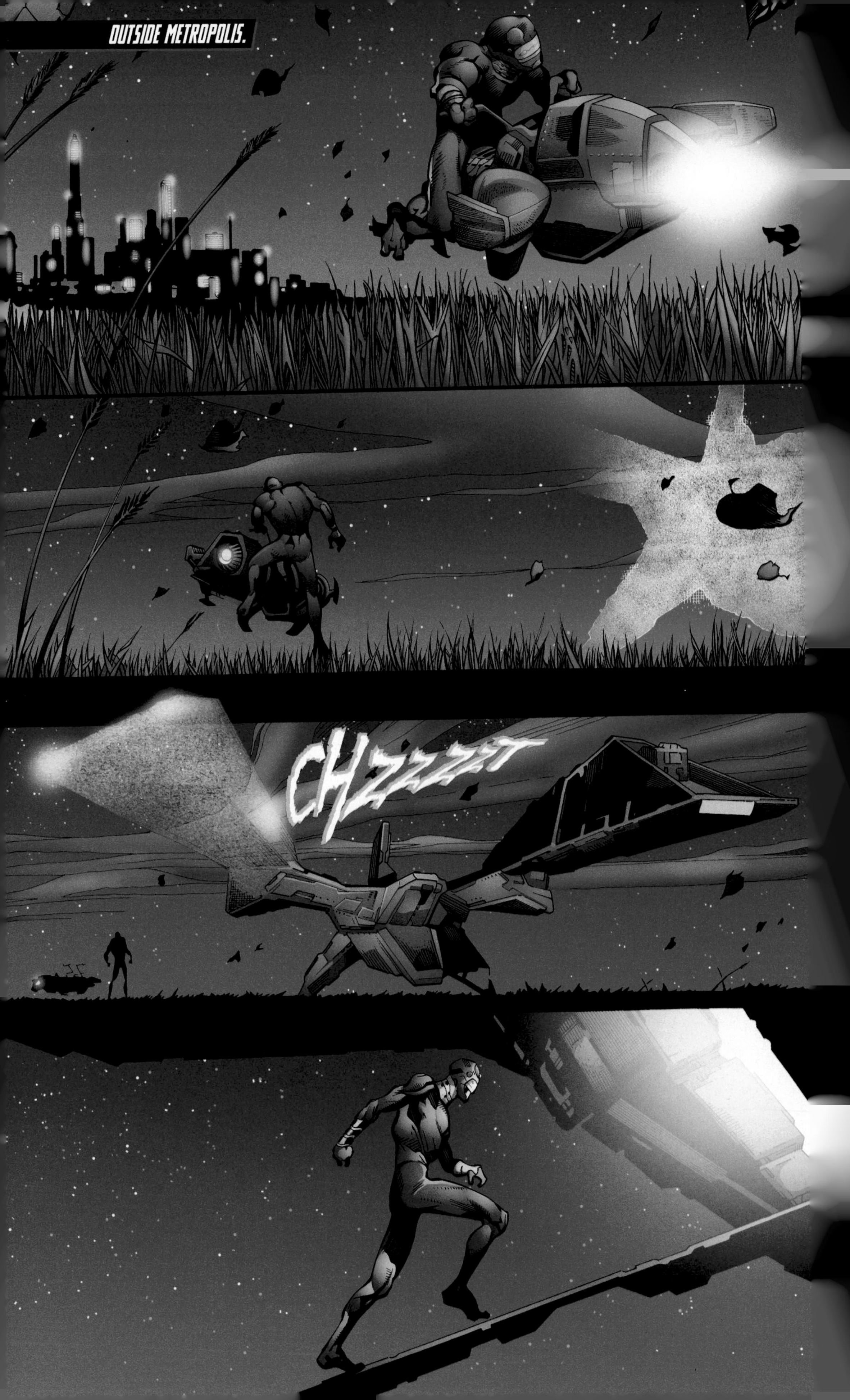
OUTSIDE METROPOLIS.
CHZZZZT

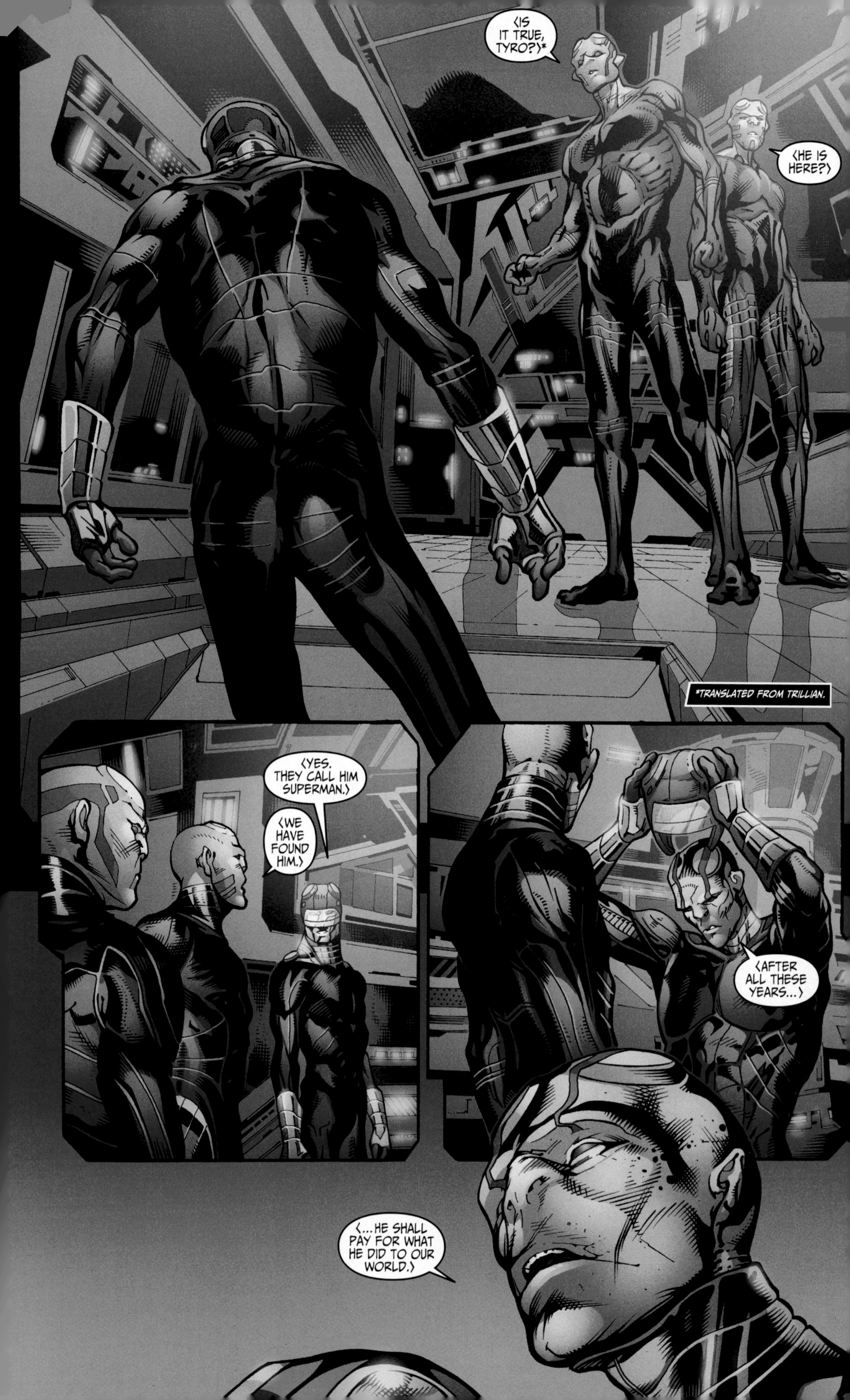
‹IS IT TRUE, TYRO?›*
‹HE IS HERE?›
*TRANSLATED FROM TRILLIAN.
‹YES. THEY CALL HIM SUPERMAN.›
‹WE HAVE FOUND HIM.›
‹AFTER ALL THESE YEARS...›
‹...HE SHALL PAY FOR WHAT HE DID TO OUR WORLD.›

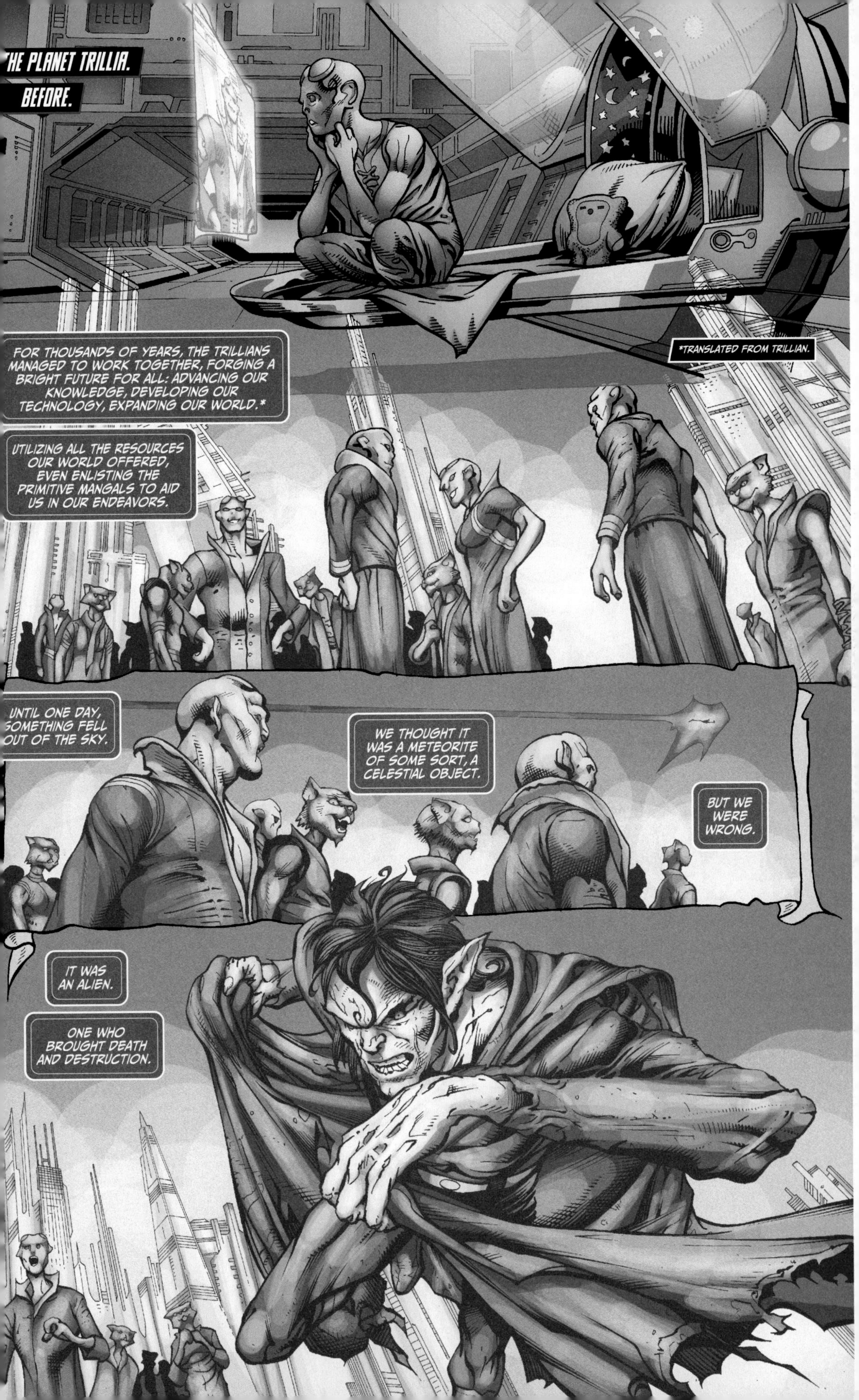
THE PLANET TRILLIA.
BEFORE.
FOR THOUSANDS OF YEARS, THE TRILLIANS MANAGED TO WORK TOGETHER, FORGING A BRIGHT FUTURE FOR ALL: ADVANCING OUR KNOWLEDGE, DEVELOPING OUR TECHNOLOGY, EXPANDING OUR WORLD.*
*TRANSLATED FROM TRILLIAN.
UTILIZING ALL THE RESOURCES OUR WORLD OFFERED, EVEN ENLISTING THE PRIMITIVE MANGALS TO AID US IN OUR ENDEAVORS.
UNTIL ONE DAY, SOMETHING FELL OUT OF THE SKY.
WE THOUGHT IT WAS A METEORITE OF SOME SORT, A CELESTIAL OBJECT.
BUT WE WERE WRONG.
IT WAS AN ALIEN.
ONE WHO BROUGHT DEATH AND DESTRUCTION.

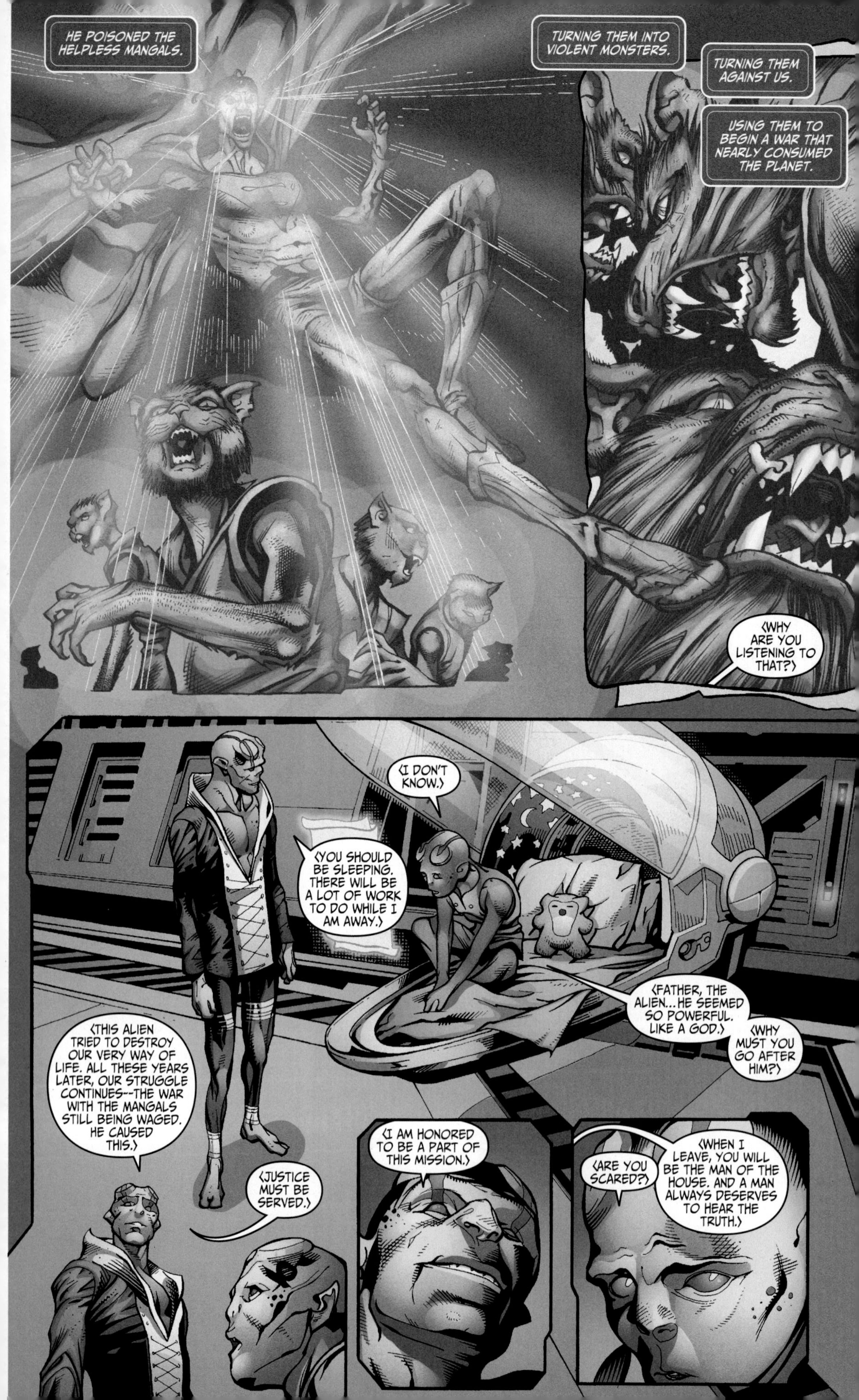
HE POISONED THE HELPLESS MANGALS.
TURNING THEM INTO VIOLENT MONSTERS.
TURNING THEM AGAINST US.
USING THEM TO BEGIN A WAR THAT NEARLY CONSUMED THE PLANET.
‹WHY ARE YOU LISTENING TO THAT?›
‹I DON'T KNOW.›
‹YOU SHOULD BE SLEEPING. THERE WILL BE A LOT OF WORK TO DO WHILE I AM AWAY.›
‹FATHER, THE ALIEN... HE SEEMED SO POWERFUL. LIKE A GOD.›
‹WHY MUST YOU GO AFTER HIM?›
‹THIS ALIEN TRIED TO DESTROY OUR VERY WAY OF LIFE. ALL THESE YEARS LATER, OUR STRUGGLE CONTINUES--THE WAR WITH THE MANGALS STILL BEING WAGED. HE CAUSED THIS.›
‹JUSTICE MUST BE SERVED.›
‹I AM HONORED TO BE A PART OF THIS MISSION.›
‹ARE YOU SCARED?›
‹WHEN I LEAVE, YOU WILL BE THE MAN OF THE HOUSE. AND A MAN ALWAYS DESERVES TO HEAR THE TRUTH.›

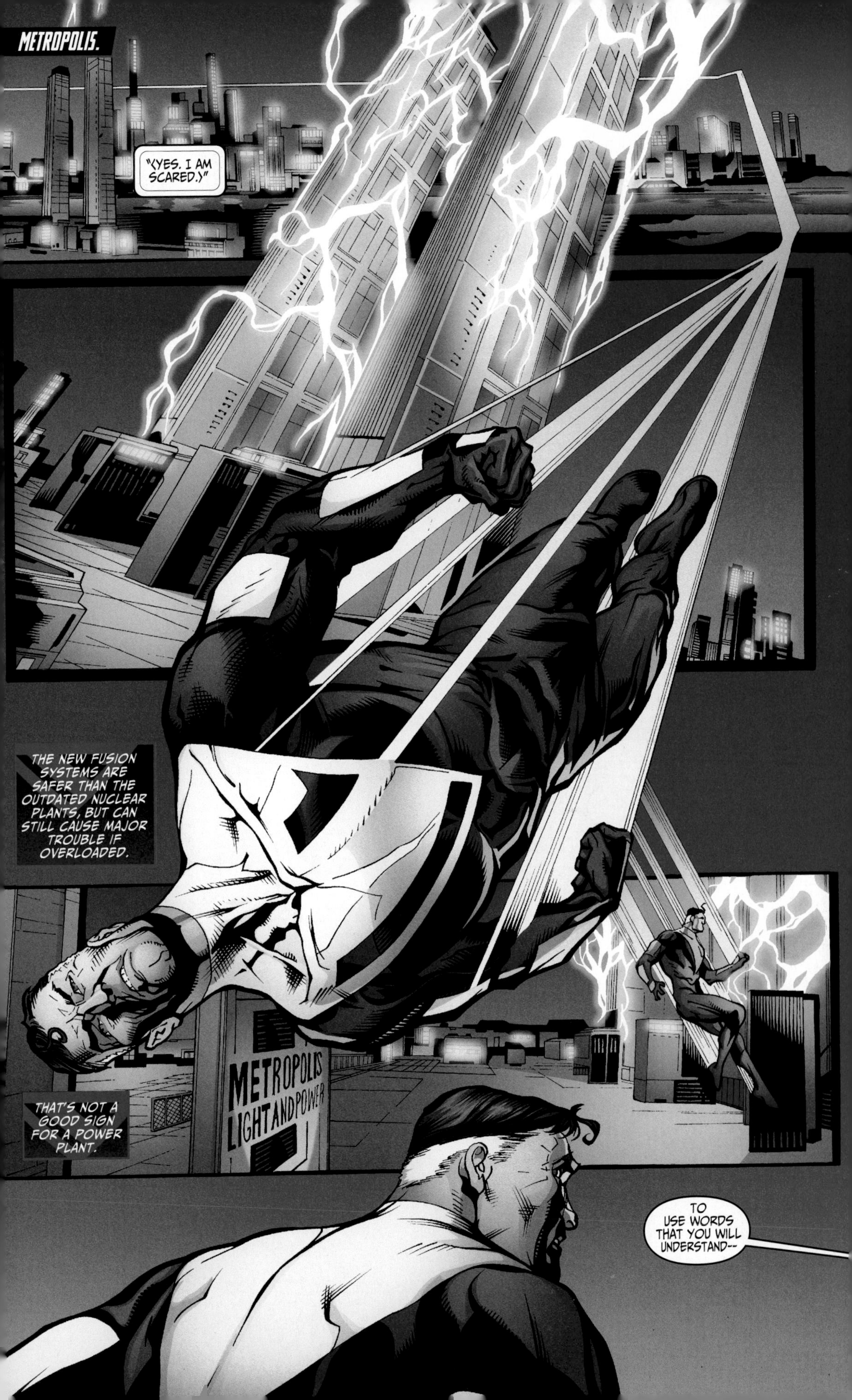
METROPOLIS.
"‹YES. I AM SCARED.›"
THE NEW FUSION SYSTEMS ARE SAFER THAN THE OUTDATED NUCLEAR PLANTS, BUT CAN STILL CAUSE MAJOR TROUBLE IF OVERLOADED.
METROPOLIS LIGHT AND POWER
THAT'S NOT A GOOD SIGN FOR A POWER PLANT.
TO USE WORDS THAT YOU WILL UNDERSTAND--

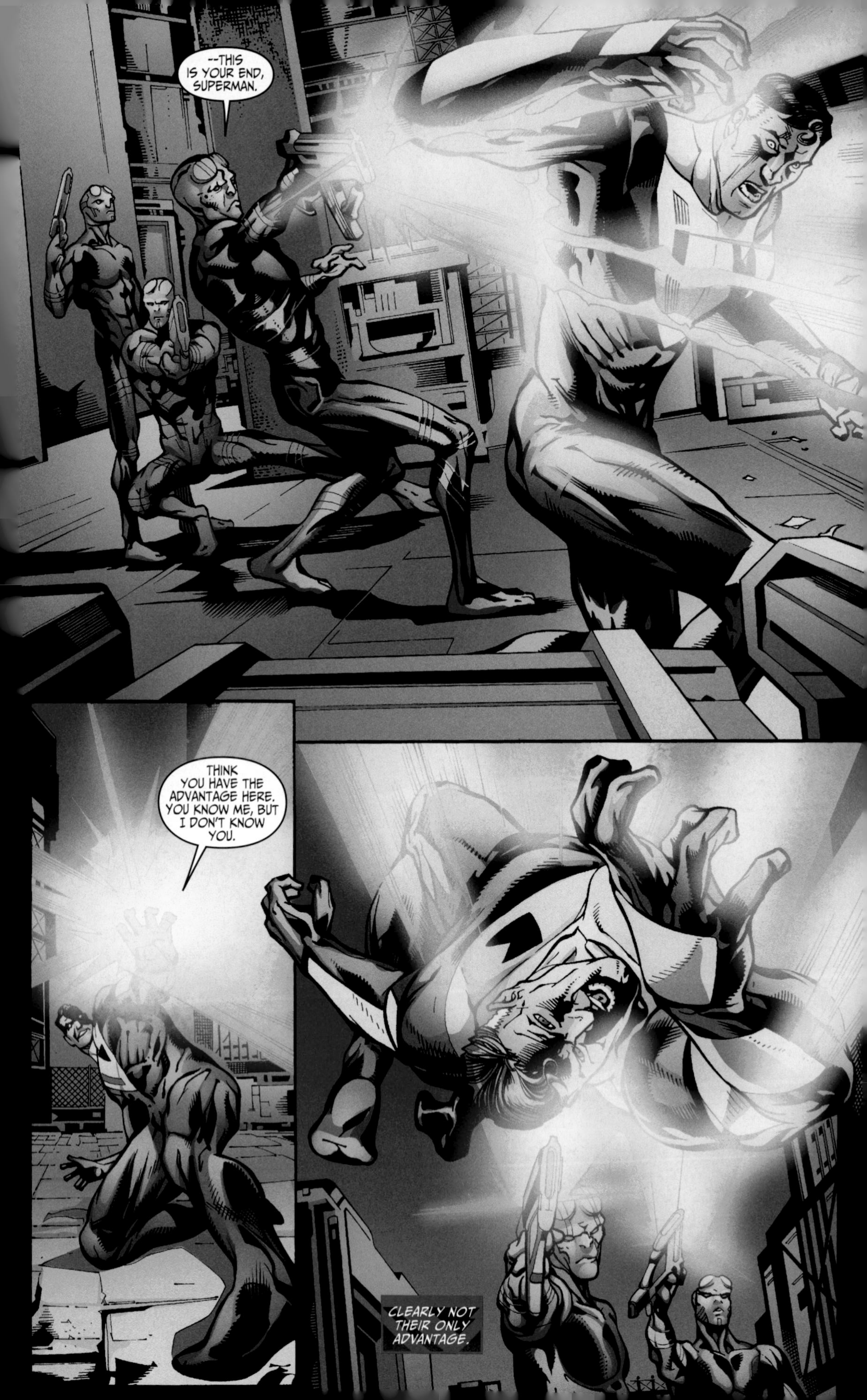
--THIS IS YOUR END, SUPERMAN.
THINK YOU HAVE THE ADVANTAGE HERE. YOU KNOW ME, BUT I DON'T KNOW YOU.
CLEARLY NOT THEIR ONLY ADVANTAGE.

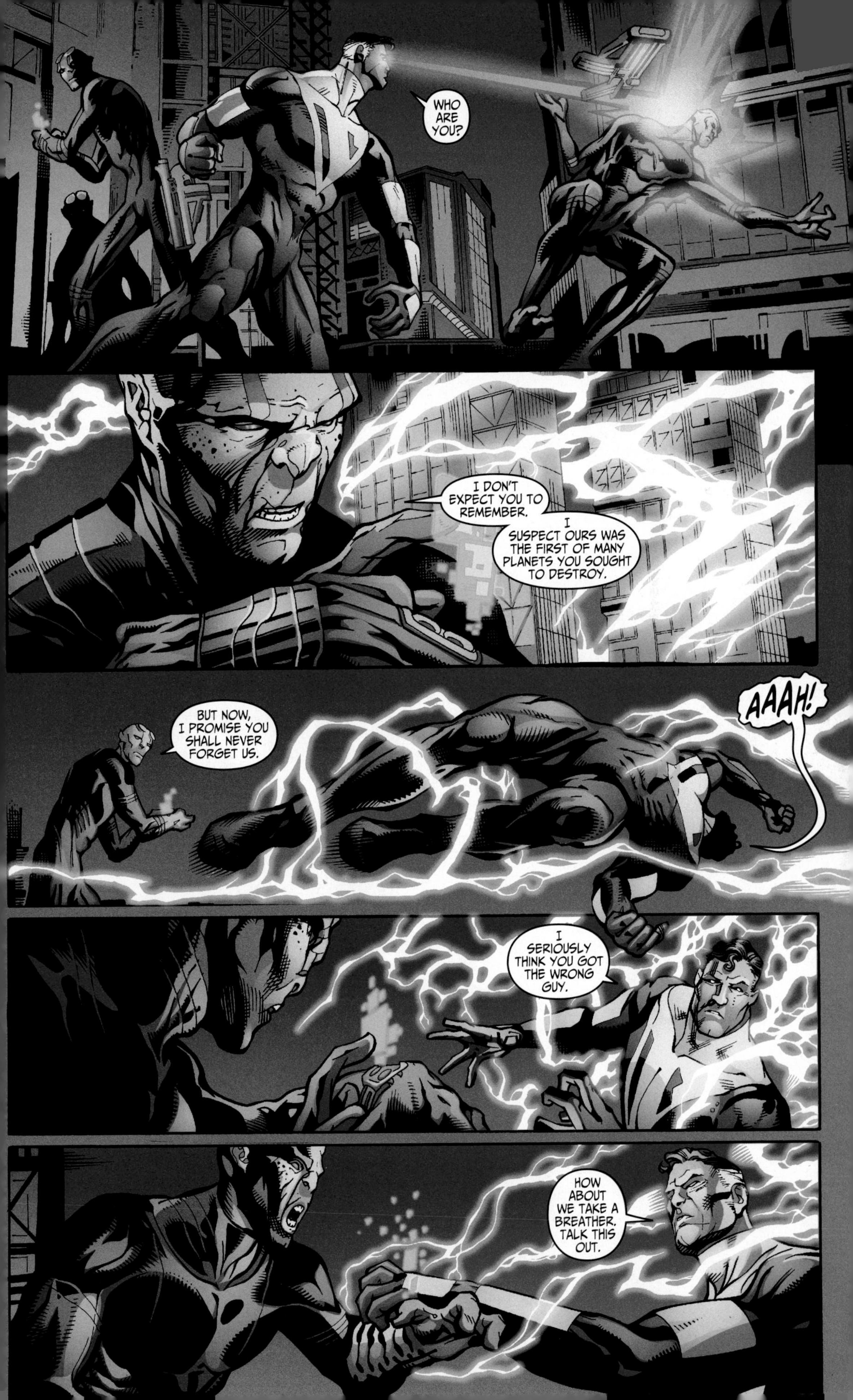
WHO ARE YOU?
I DON'T EXPECT YOU TO REMEMBER.
I SUSPECT OURS WAS THE FIRST OF MANY PLANETS YOU SOUGHT TO DESTROY.
BUT NOW, I PROMISE YOU SHALL NEVER FORGET US.
AAAH!
I SERIOUSLY THINK YOU GOT THE WRONG GUY.
HOW ABOUT WE TAKE A BREATHER. TALK THIS OUT.

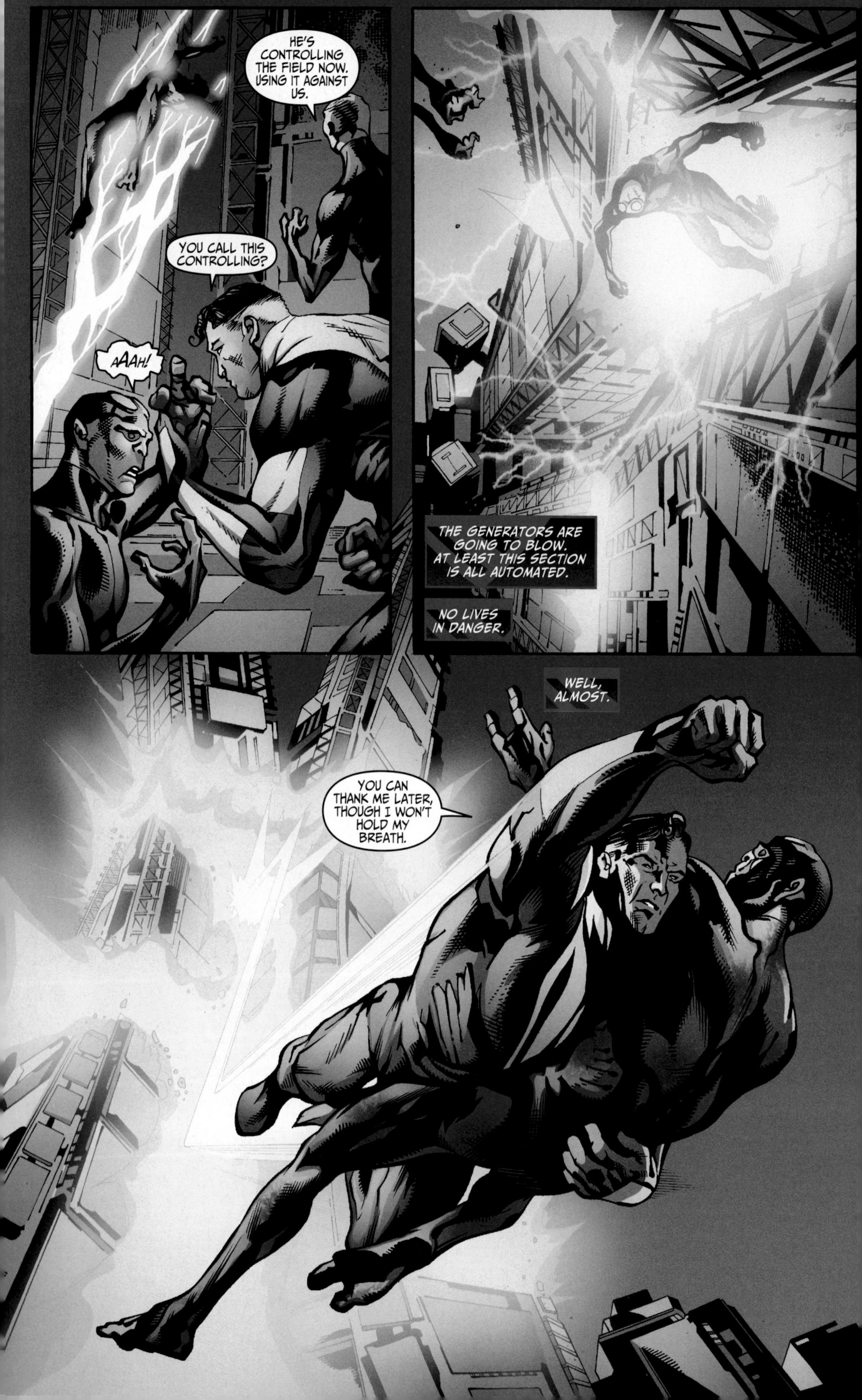
HE'S CONTROLLING THE FIELD NOW. USING IT AGAINST US.
YOU CALL THIS CONTROLLING?
AAAH!
THE GENERATORS ARE GOING TO BLOW. AT LEAST THIS SECTION IS ALL AUTOMATED.
NO LIVES IN DANGER.
WELL, ALMOST.
YOU CAN THANK ME LATER, THOUGH I WON'T HOLD MY BREATH.

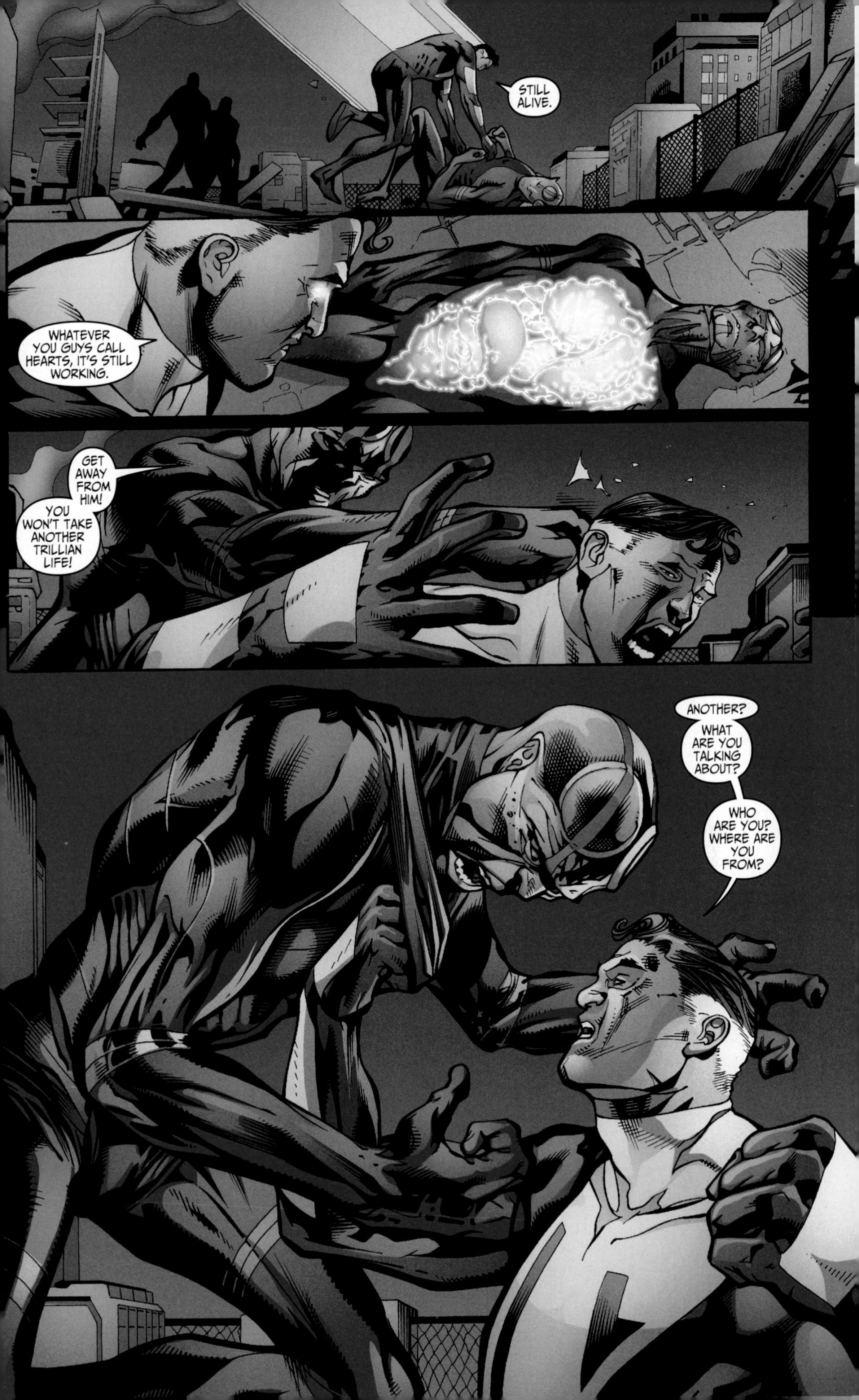
STILL ALIVE.
WHATEVER YOU GUYS CALL HEARTS, IT'S STILL WORKING.
GET AWAY FROM HIM!
YOU WON'T TAKE ANOTHER TRILLIAN LIFE!
ANOTHER? WHAT ARE YOU TALKING ABOUT?
WHO ARE YOU? WHERE ARE YOU FROM?

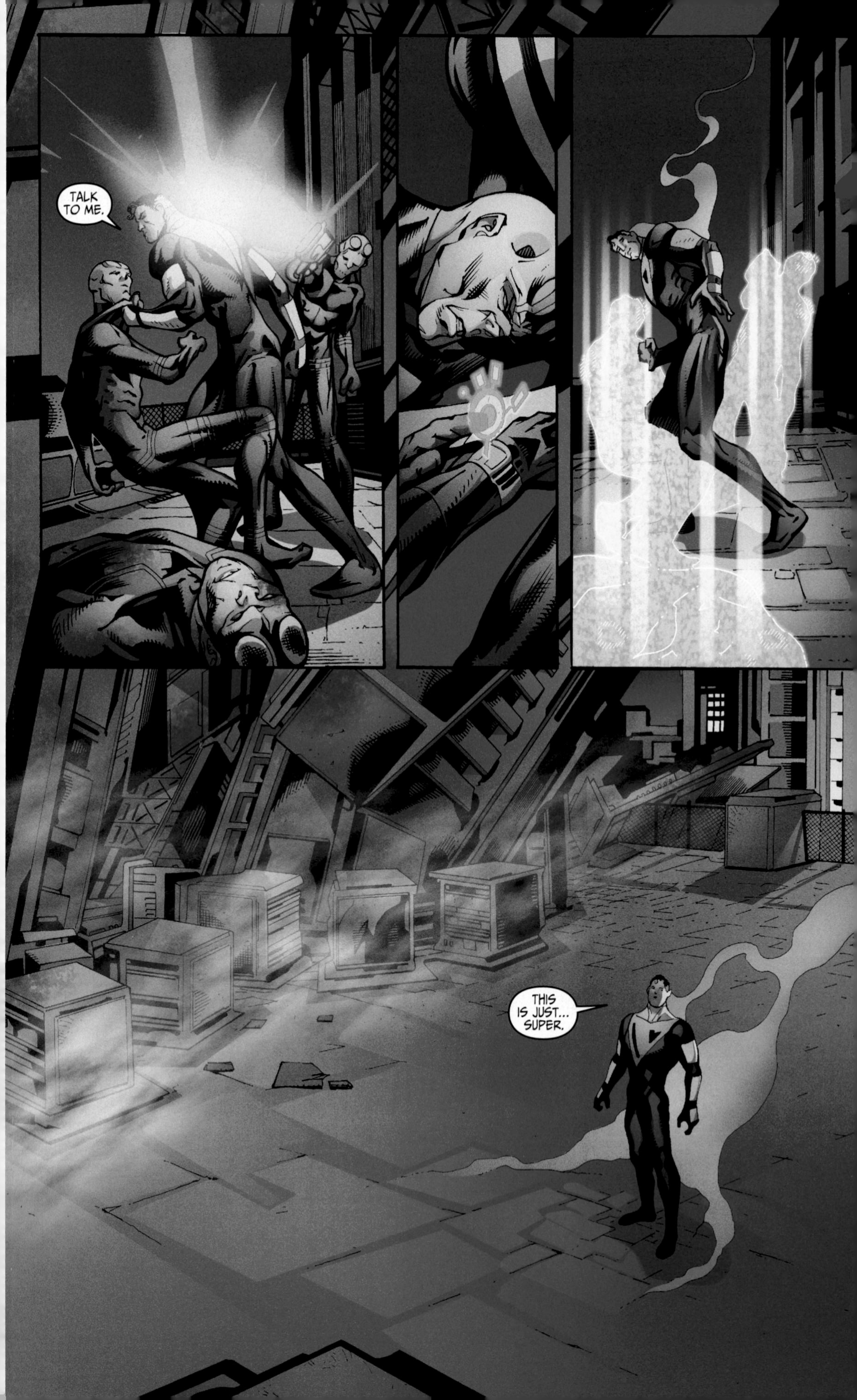
TALK TO ME.
THIS IS JUST... SUPER.

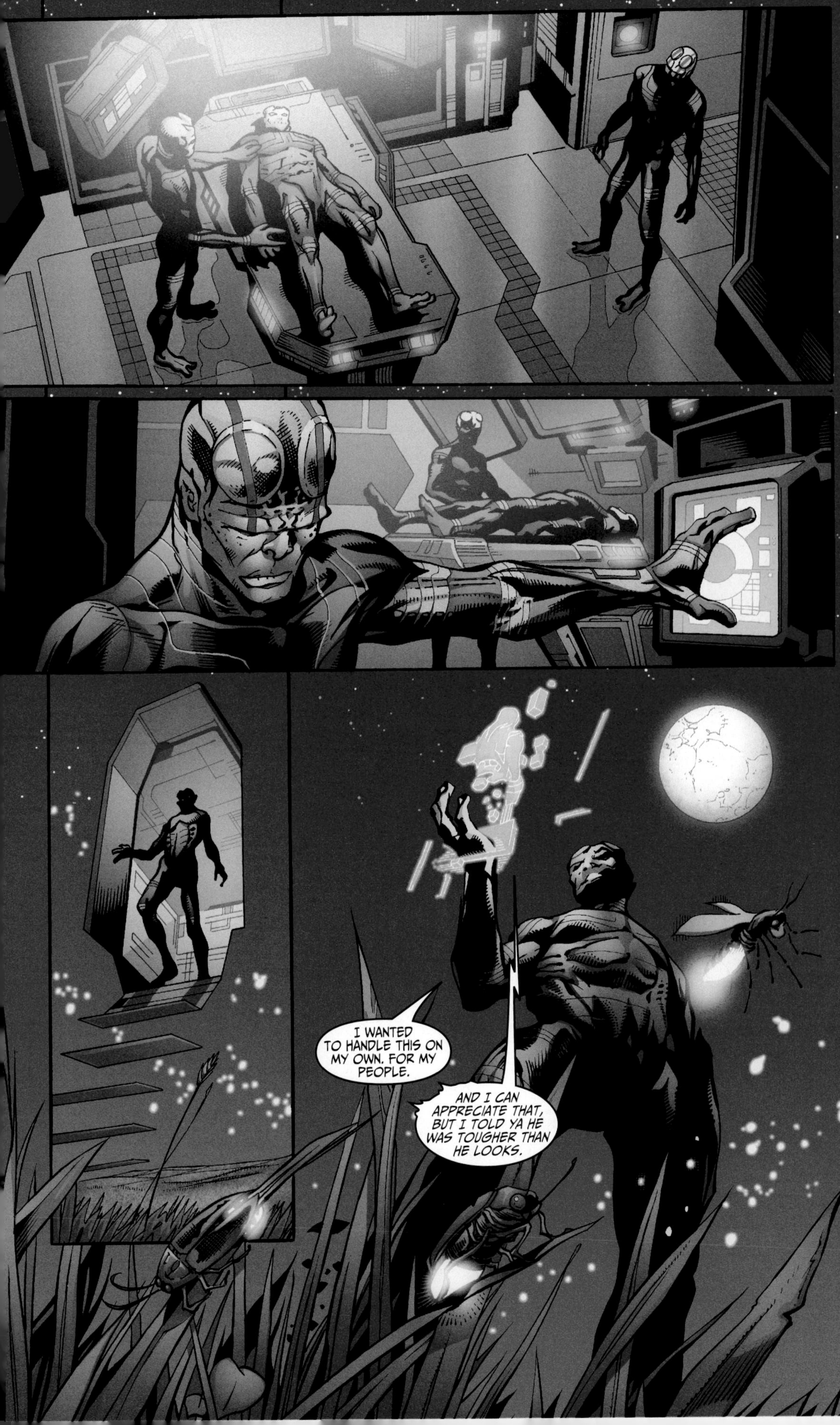
I WANTED TO HANDLE THIS ON MY OWN. FOR MY PEOPLE.
AND I CAN APPRECIATE THAT, BUT I TOLD YA HE WAS TOUGHER THAN HE LOOKS.

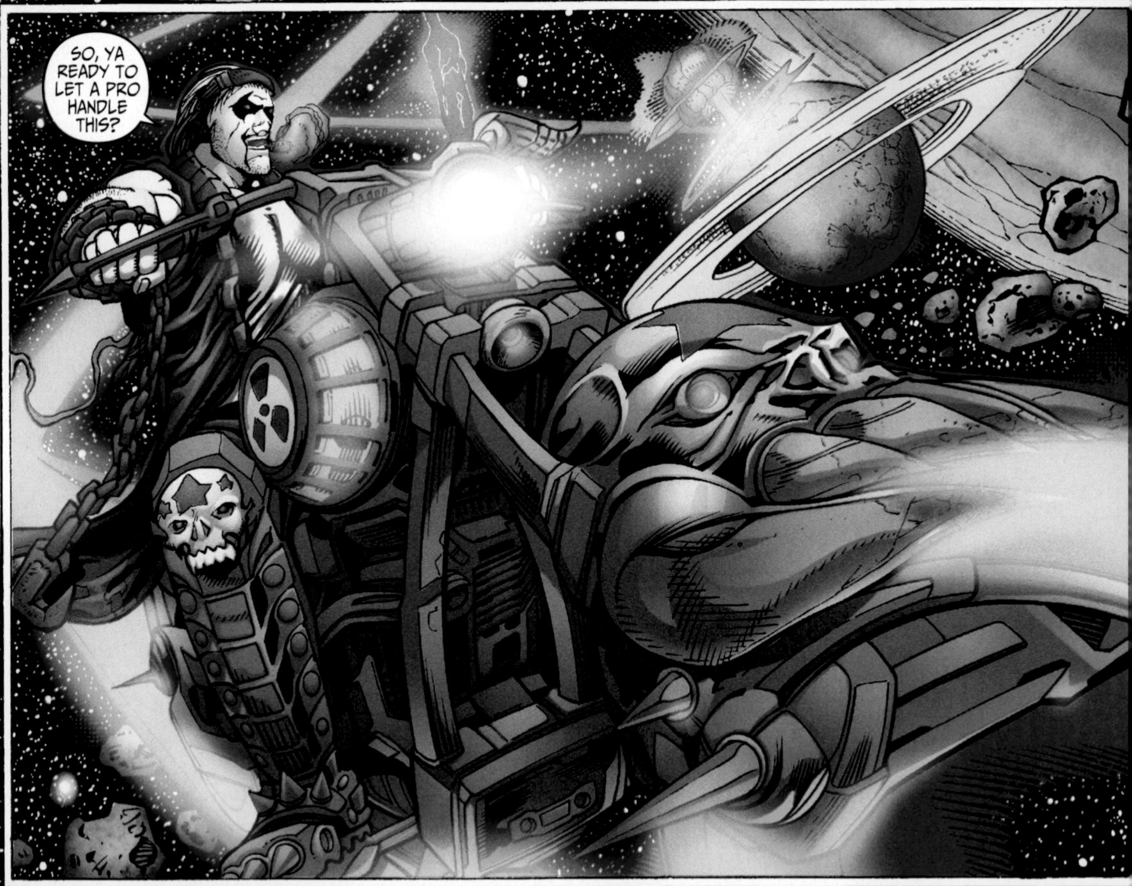
SO, YA READY TO LET A PRO HANDLE THIS?

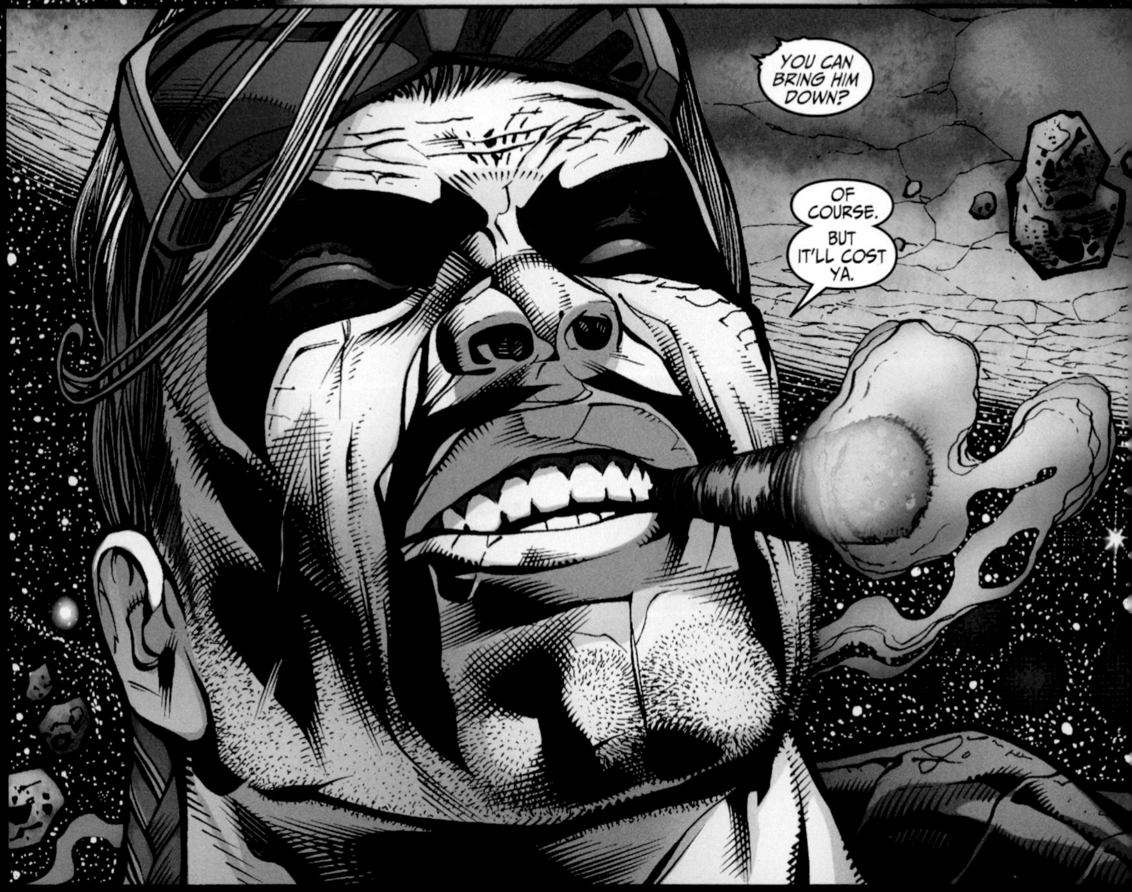
YOU CAN BRING HIM DOWN?
OF COURSE.
BUT IT'LL COST YA.

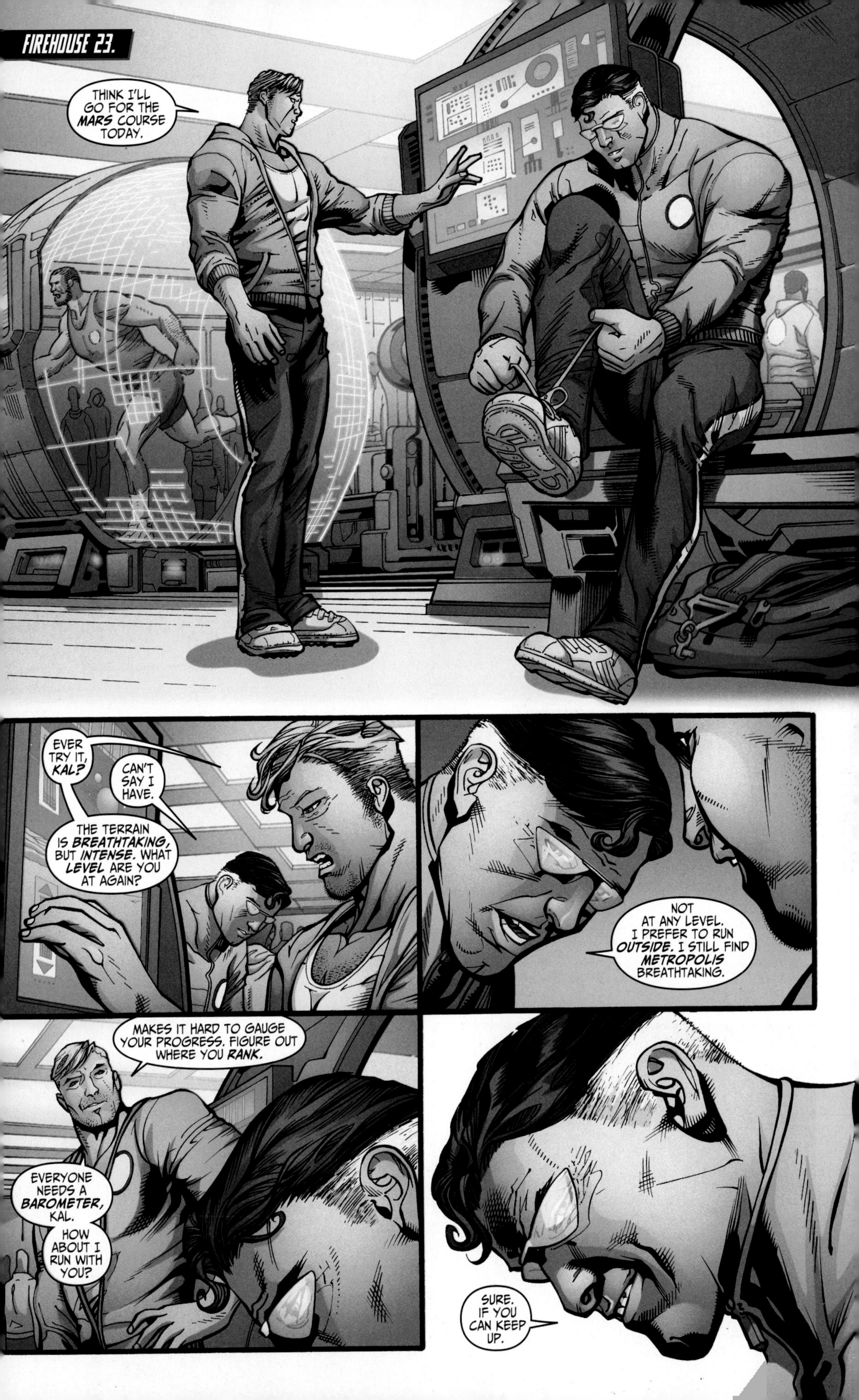
FIREHOUSE 23.
THINK I'LL GO FOR THE MARS COURSE TODAY.
EVER TRY IT, KAL?
CAN'T SAY I HAVE.
THE TERRAIN IS BREATHTAKING, BUT INTENSE. WHAT LEVEL ARE YOU AT AGAIN?
NOT AT ANY LEVEL. I PREFER TO RUN OUTSIDE. I STILL FIND METROPOLIS BREATHTAKING.
MAKES IT HARD TO GAUGE YOUR PROGRESS. FIGURE OUT WHERE YOU RANK.
EVERYONE NEEDS A BAROMETER, KAL.
HOW ABOUT I RUN WITH YOU?
SURE. IF YOU CAN KEEP UP.

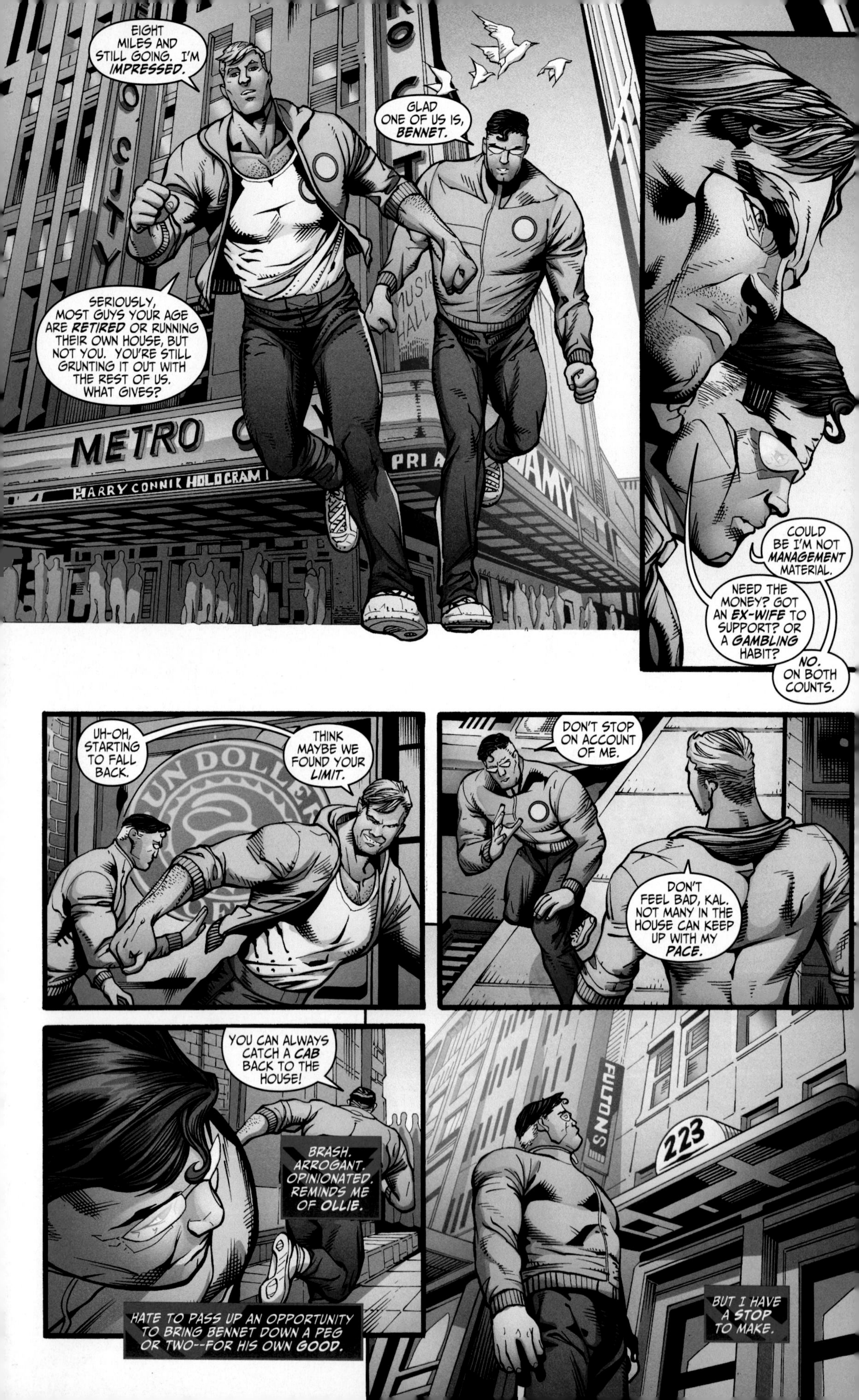
EIGHT MILES AND STILL GOING. I'M IMPRESSED.
GLAD ONE OF US IS, BENNET.
SERIOUSLY, MOST GUYS YOUR AGE ARE RETIRED OR RUNNING THEIR OWN HOUSE, BUT NOT YOU. YOU'RE STILL GRUNTING IT OUT WITH THE REST OF US. WHAT GIVES?
METRO
HARRY CONNIK HOLOGRAM
COULD BE I'M NOT MANAGEMENT MATERIAL.
NEED THE MONEY? GOT AN EX-WIFE TO SUPPORT? OR A GAMBLING HABIT?
NO. ON BOTH COUNTS.
UH-OH, STARTING TO FALL BACK.
THINK MAYBE WE FOUND YOUR LIMIT.
DON'T STOP ON ACCOUNT OF ME.
DON'T FEEL BAD, KAL. NOT MANY IN THE HOUSE CAN KEEP UP WITH MY PACE.
YOU CAN ALWAYS CATCH A CAB BACK TO THE HOUSE!
BRASH. ARROGANT. OPINIONATED. REMINDS ME OF OLLIE.
HATE TO PASS UP AN OPPORTUNITY TO BRING BENNET DOWN A PEG OR TWO--FOR HIS OWN GOOD.
FULTON'S
223
BUT I HAVE A STOP TO MAKE.

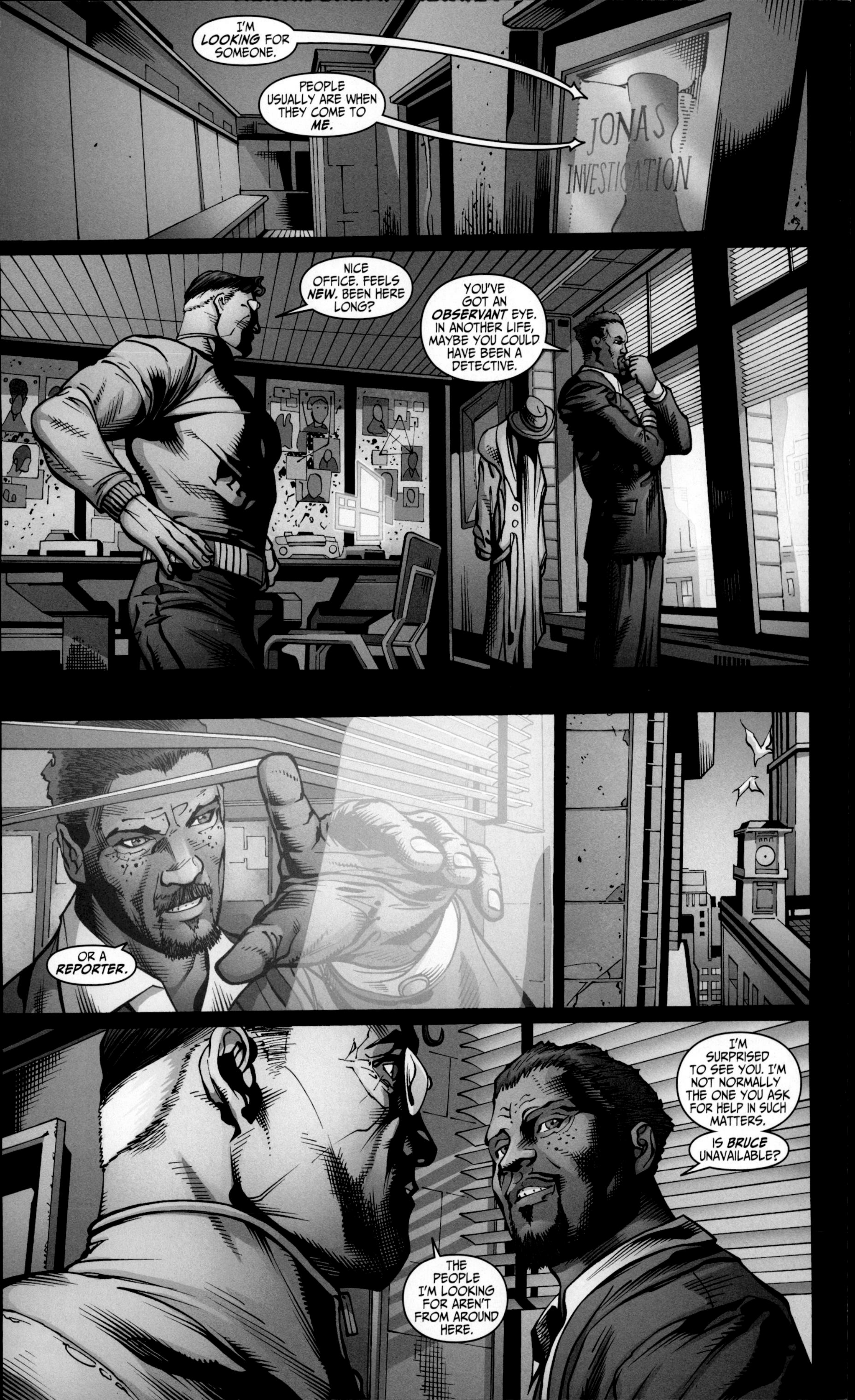
I'M LOOKING FOR SOMEONE.
PEOPLE USUALLY ARE WHEN THEY COME TO ME.
JONAS INVESTIGATION
NICE OFFICE. FEELS NEW. BEEN HERE LONG?
YOU'VE GOT AN OBSERVANT EYE. IN ANOTHER LIFE, MAYBE YOU COULD HAVE BEEN A DETECTIVE.
OR A REPORTER.
I'M SURPRISED TO SEE YOU. I'M NOT NORMALLY THE ONE YOU ASK FOR HELP IN SUCH MATTERS.
IS BRUCE UNAVAILABLE?
THE PEOPLE I'M LOOKING FOR AREN'T FROM AROUND HERE.

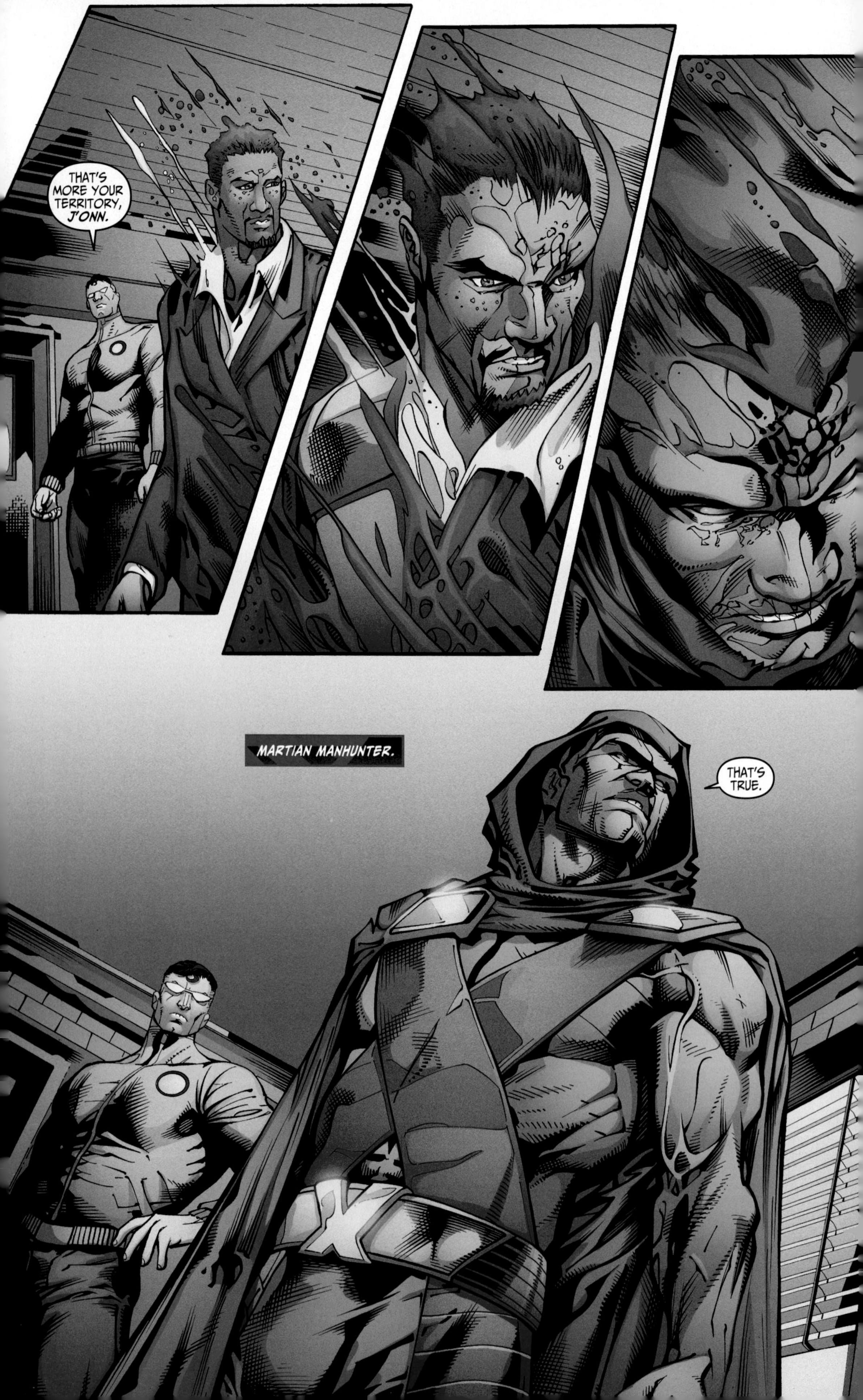
THAT'S MORE YOUR TERRITORY, J'ONN.
MARTIAN MANHUNTER.
THAT'S TRUE.

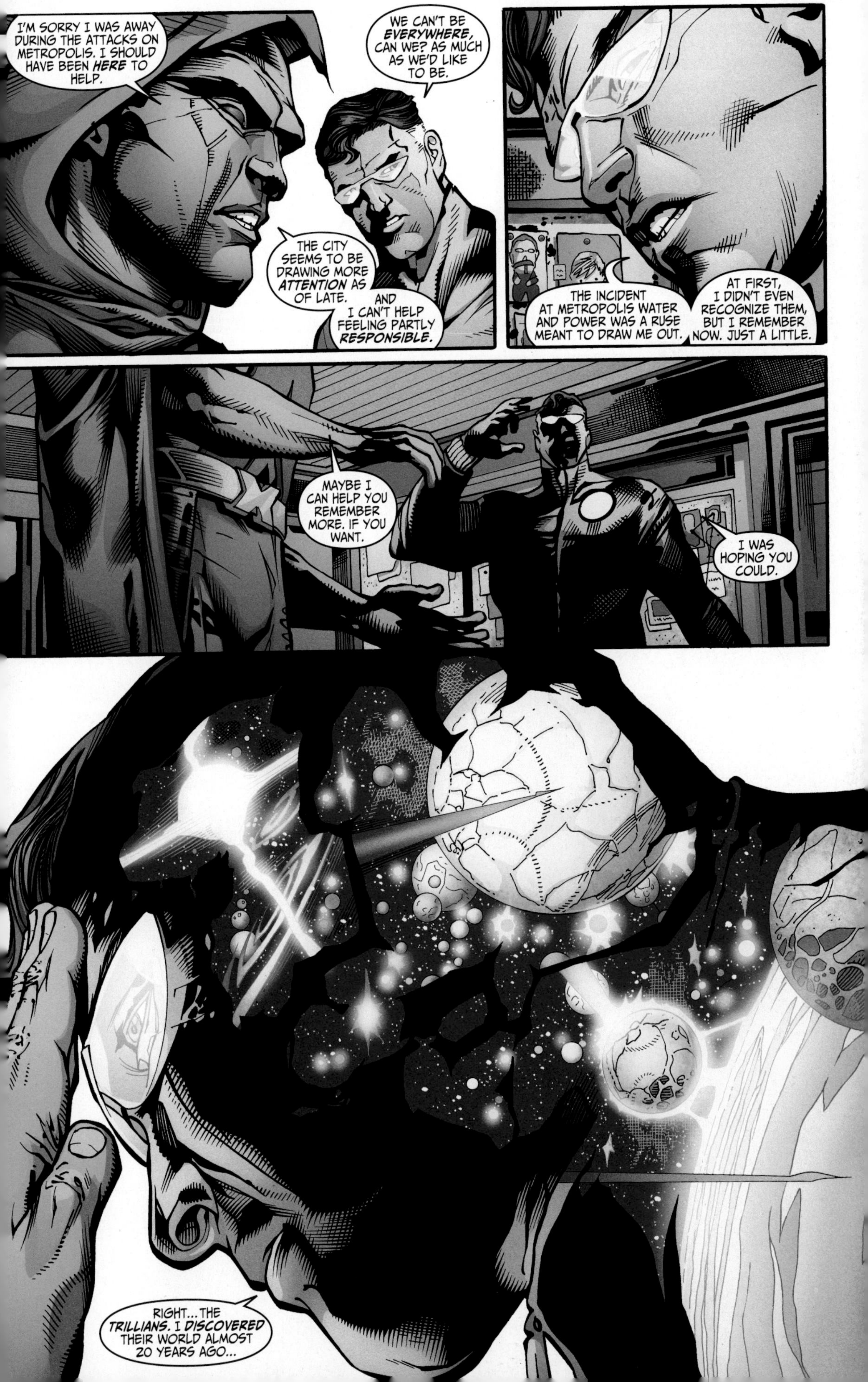
I'M SORRY I WAS AWAY DURING THE ATTACKS ON METROPOLIS. I SHOULD HAVE BEEN *HERE* TO HELP.
WE CAN'T BE *EVERYWHERE*, CAN WE? AS MUCH AS WE'D LIKE TO BE.
THE CITY SEEMS TO BE DRAWING MORE *ATTENTION* AS OF LATE.
AND I CAN'T HELP FEELING PARTLY *RESPONSIBLE*.
THE INCIDENT AT METROPOLIS WATER AND POWER WAS A RUSE MEANT TO DRAW ME OUT.
AT FIRST, I DIDN'T EVEN RECOGNIZE THEM, BUT I REMEMBER NOW. JUST A LITTLE.
MAYBE I CAN HELP YOU REMEMBER MORE. IF YOU WANT.
I WAS HOPING YOU COULD.
RIGHT... THE *TRILLIANS*. I *DISCOVERED* THEIR WORLD ALMOST 20 YEARS AGO...

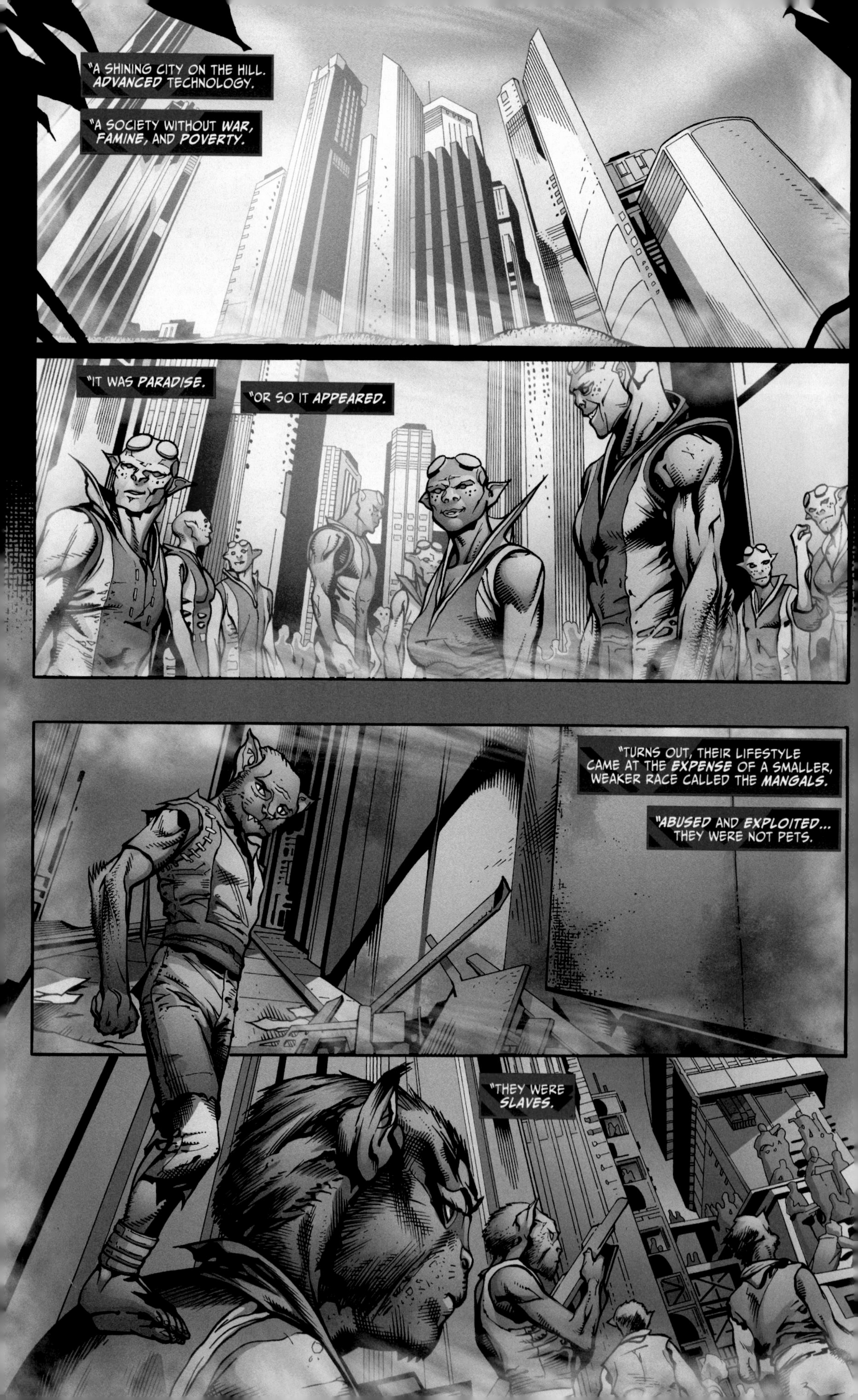
"A SHINING CITY ON THE HILL. *ADVANCED* TECHNOLOGY.
"A SOCIETY WITHOUT *WAR, FAMINE,* AND *POVERTY.*
"IT WAS *PARADISE.*
"OR SO IT *APPEARED.*
"TURNS OUT, THEIR LIFESTYLE CAME AT THE *EXPENSE* OF A SMALLER, WEAKER RACE CALLED THE *MANGALS.*
"*ABUSED* AND *EXPLOITED*... THEY WERE NOT PETS.
"THEY WERE *SLAVES.*

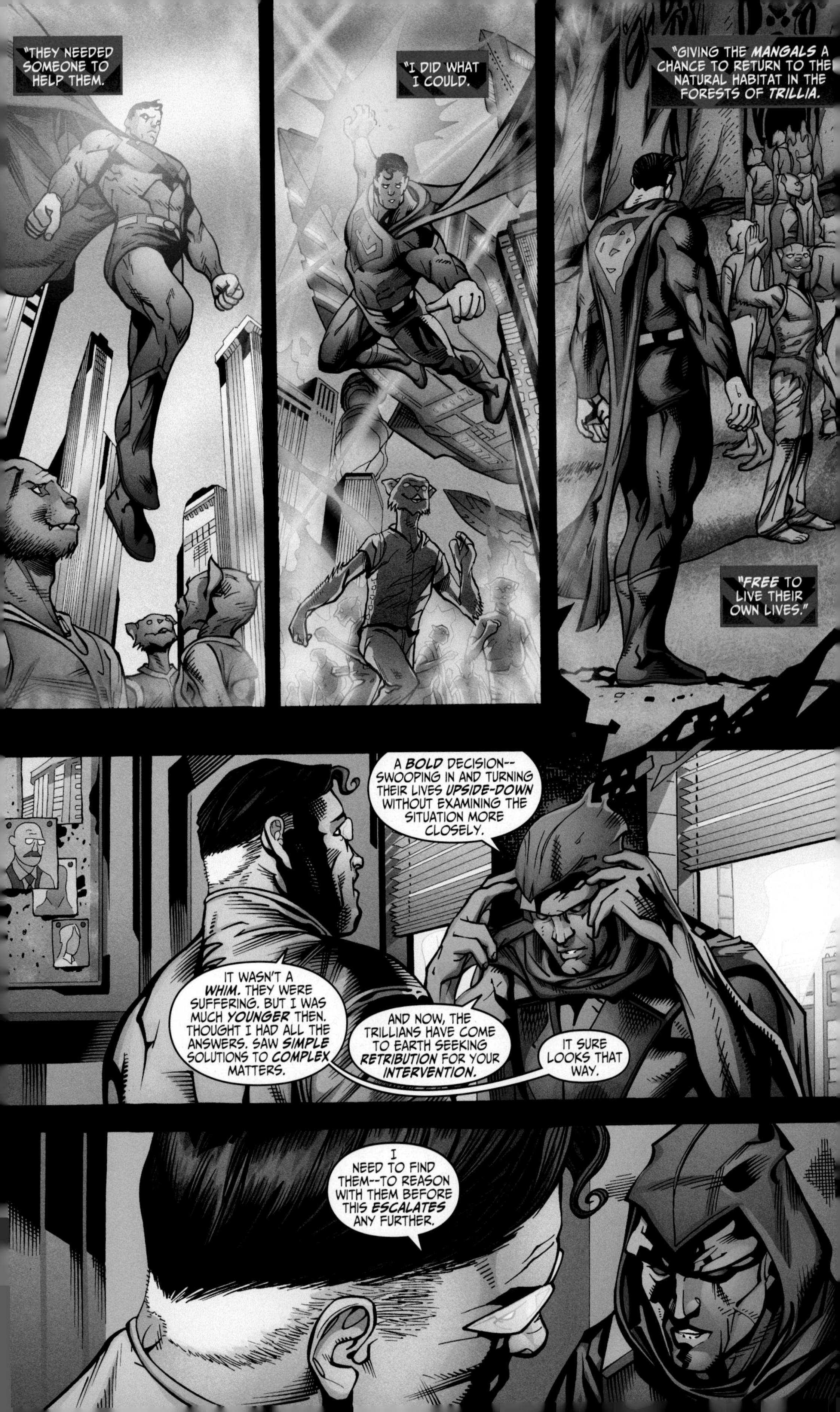
"THEY NEEDED SOMEONE TO HELP THEM.
"I DID WHAT I COULD.
"GIVING THE MANGALS A CHANCE TO RETURN TO THE NATURAL HABITAT IN THE FORESTS OF TRILLIA.
"FREE TO LIVE THEIR OWN LIVES."
A BOLD DECISION--SWOOPING IN AND TURNING THEIR LIVES UPSIDE-DOWN WITHOUT EXAMINING THE SITUATION MORE CLOSELY.
IT WASN'T A WHIM. THEY WERE SUFFERING. BUT I WAS MUCH YOUNGER THEN. THOUGHT I HAD ALL THE ANSWERS. SAW SIMPLE SOLUTIONS TO COMPLEX MATTERS.
AND NOW, THE TRILLIANS HAVE COME TO EARTH SEEKING RETRIBUTION FOR YOUR INTERVENTION.
IT SURE LOOKS THAT WAY.
I NEED TO FIND THEM--TO REASON WITH THEM BEFORE THIS ESCALATES ANY FURTHER.

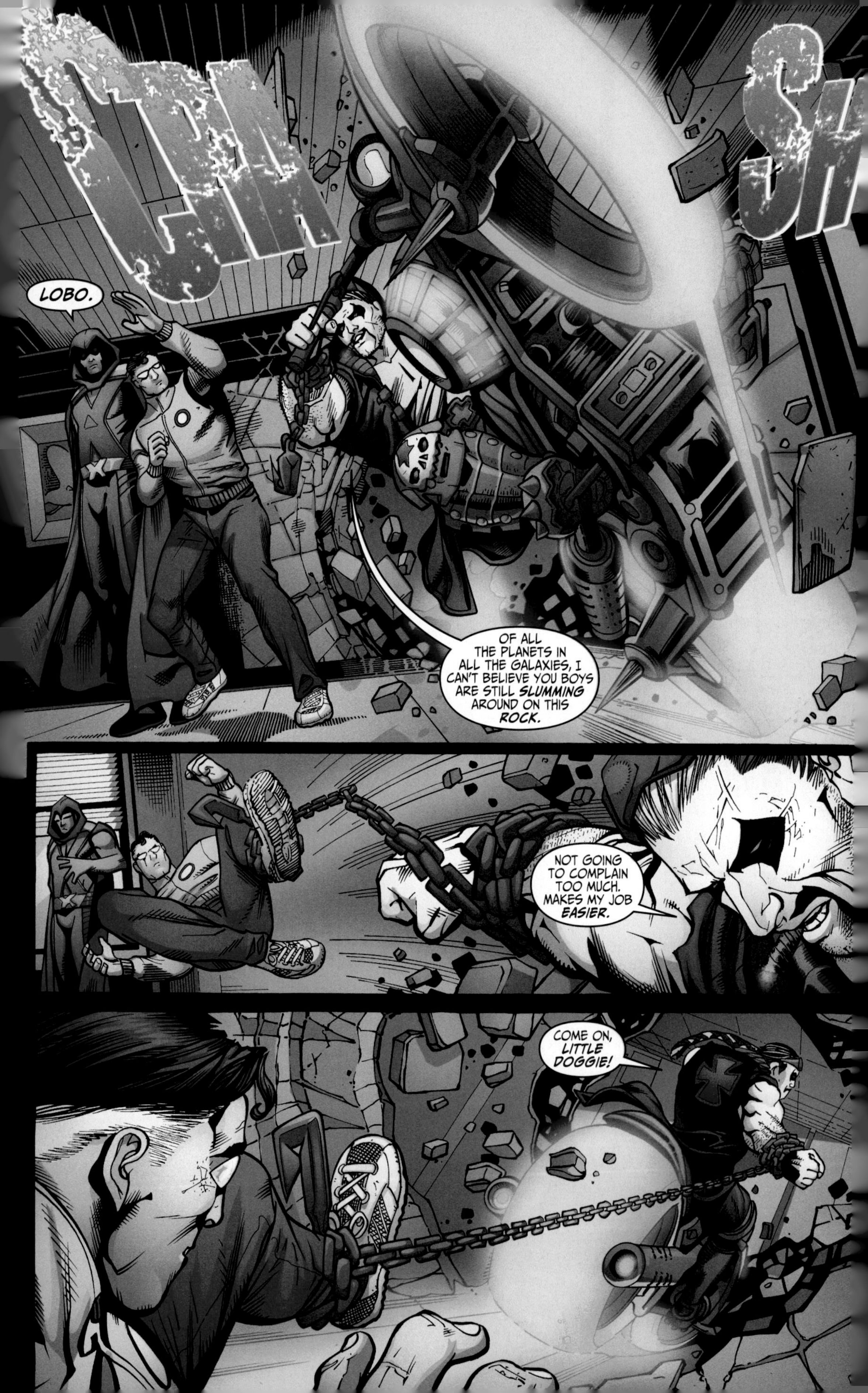

LOBO.
OF ALL THE PLANETS IN ALL THE GALAXIES, I CAN'T BELIEVE YOU BOYS ARE STILL SLUMMING AROUND ON THIS ROCK.
NOT GOING TO COMPLAIN TOO MUCH. MAKES MY JOB EASIER.
COME ON, LITTLE DOGGIE!

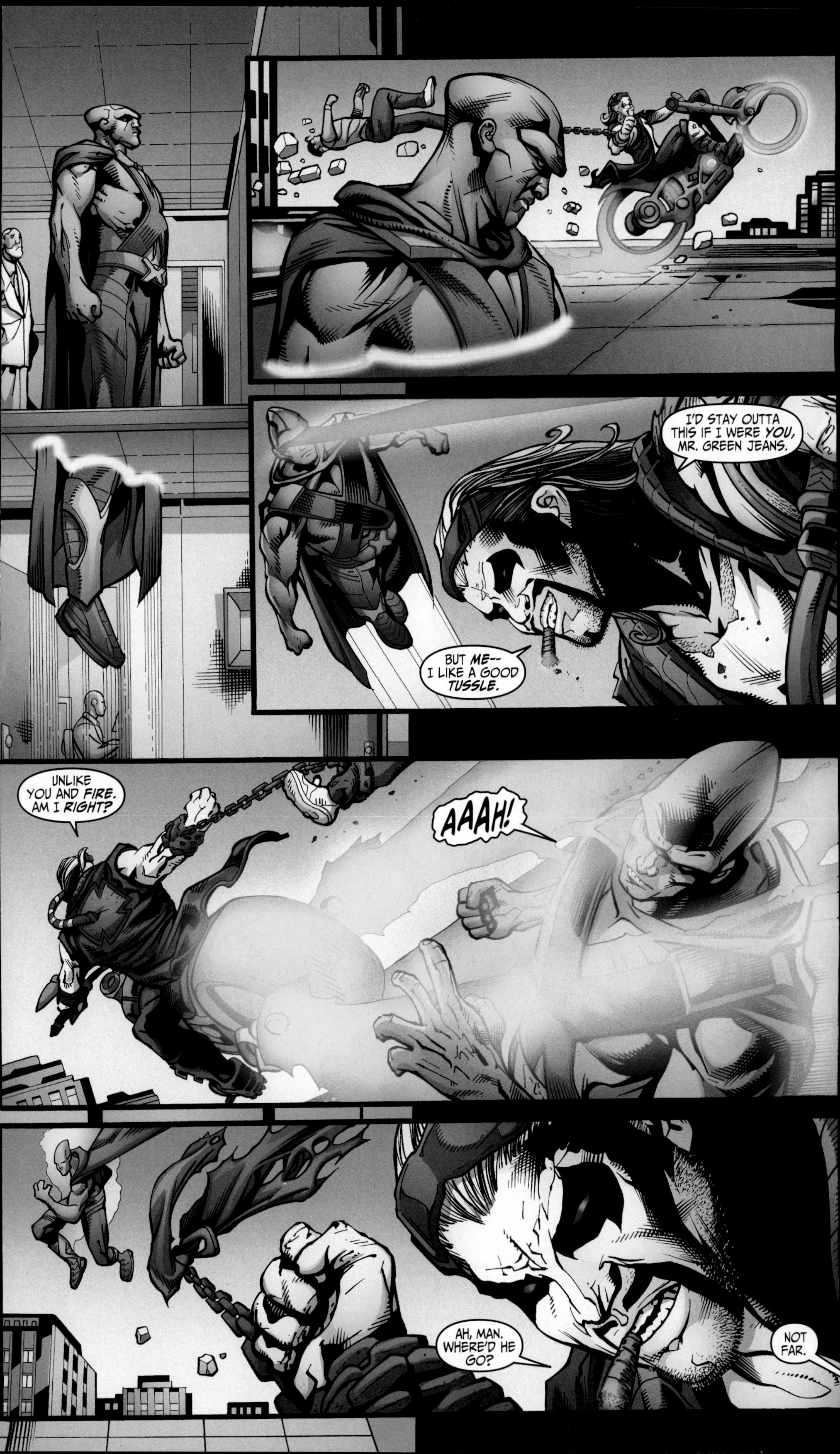
I'D STAY OUTTA THIS IF I WERE YOU, MR. GREEN JEANS.
BUT ME-- I LIKE A GOOD TUSSLE.
UNLIKE YOU AND FIRE. AM I RIGHT?
AAAH!
AH, MAN. WHERE'D HE GO?
NOT FAR.

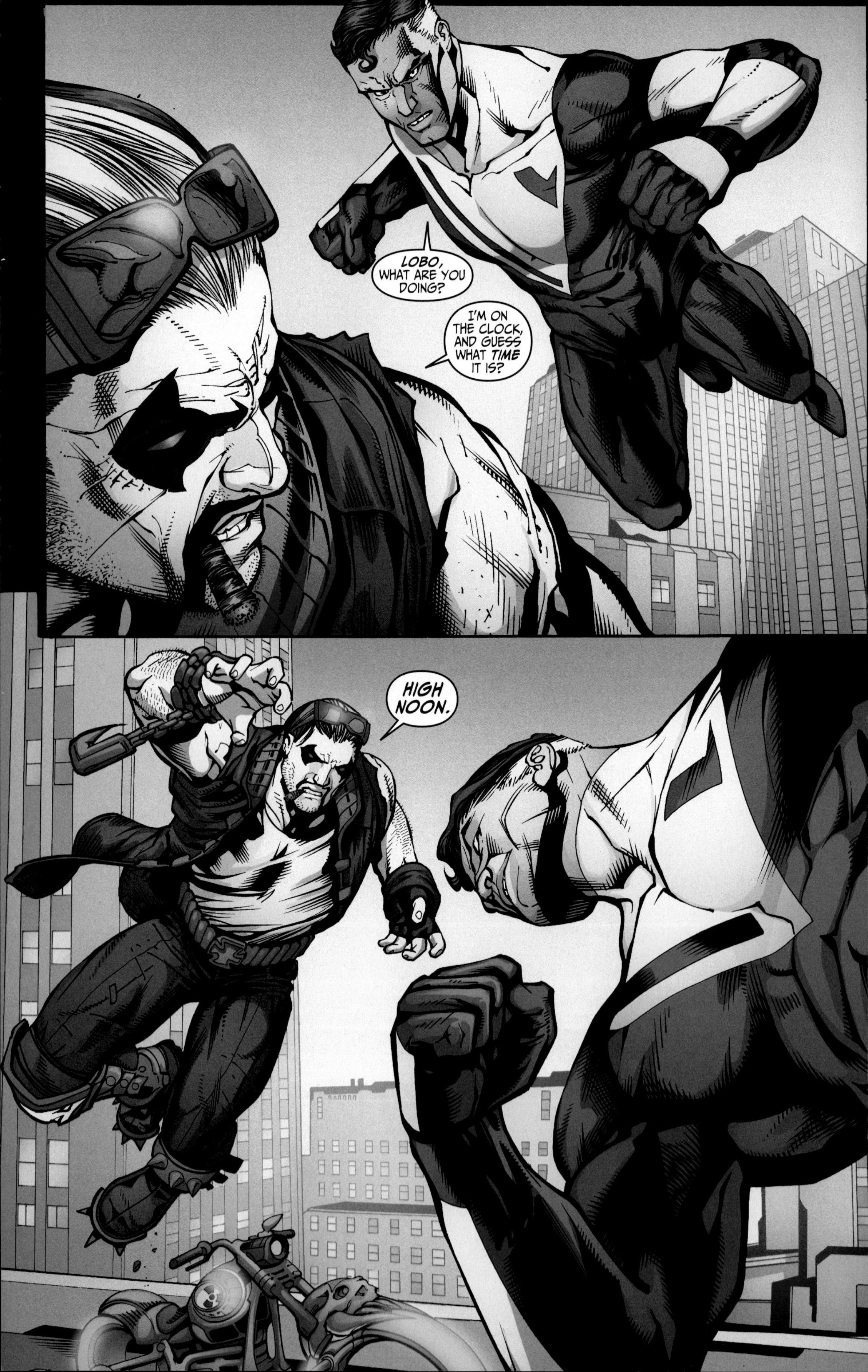

LOBO, WHAT ARE YOU DOING?
I'M ON THE CLOCK, AND GUESS WHAT TIME IT IS?
HIGH NOON.

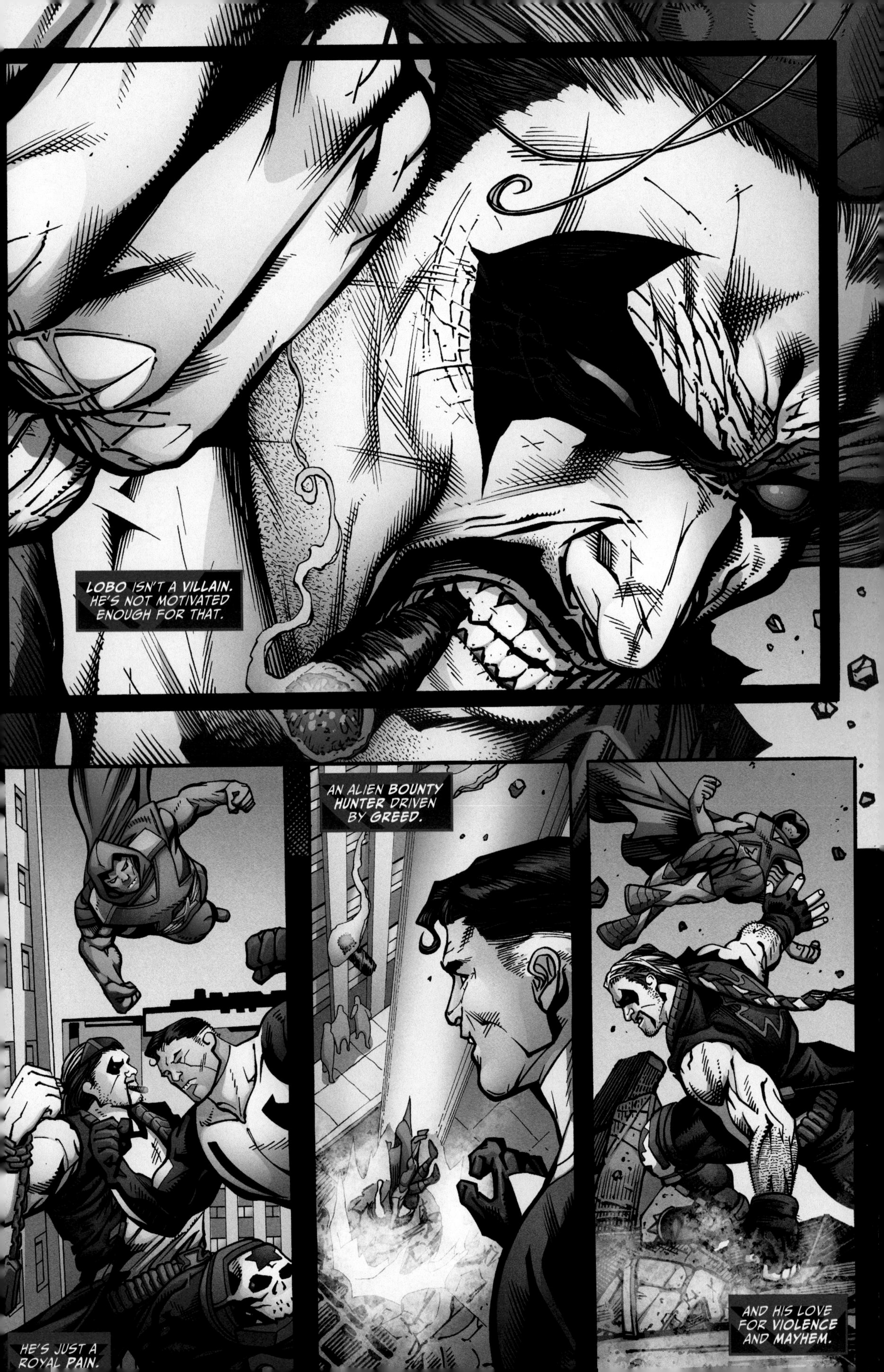
LOBO ISN'T A VILLAIN. HE'S NOT MOTIVATED ENOUGH FOR THAT.
HE'S JUST A ROYAL PAIN.
AN ALIEN BOUNTY HUNTER DRIVEN BY GREED.
AND HIS LOVE FOR VIOLENCE AND MAYHEM.

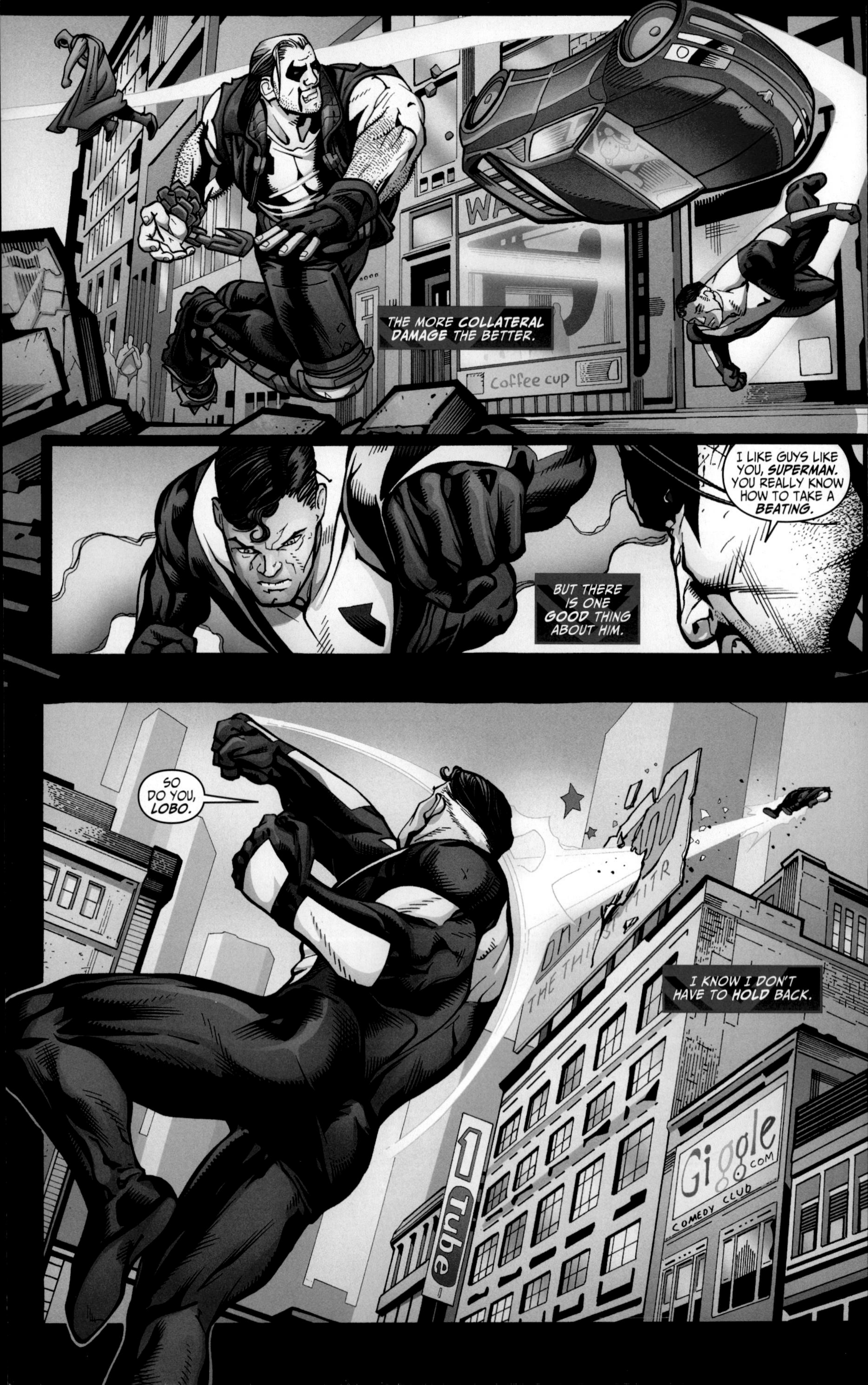
THE MORE COLLATERAL DAMAGE THE BETTER.
Coffee cup
I LIKE GUYS LIKE YOU, SUPERMAN. YOU REALLY KNOW HOW TO TAKE A BEATING.
BUT THERE IS ONE GOOD THING ABOUT HIM.
SO DO YOU, LOBO.
I KNOW I DON'T HAVE TO HOLD BACK.
Tube
Giggle.com
COMEDY CLUB

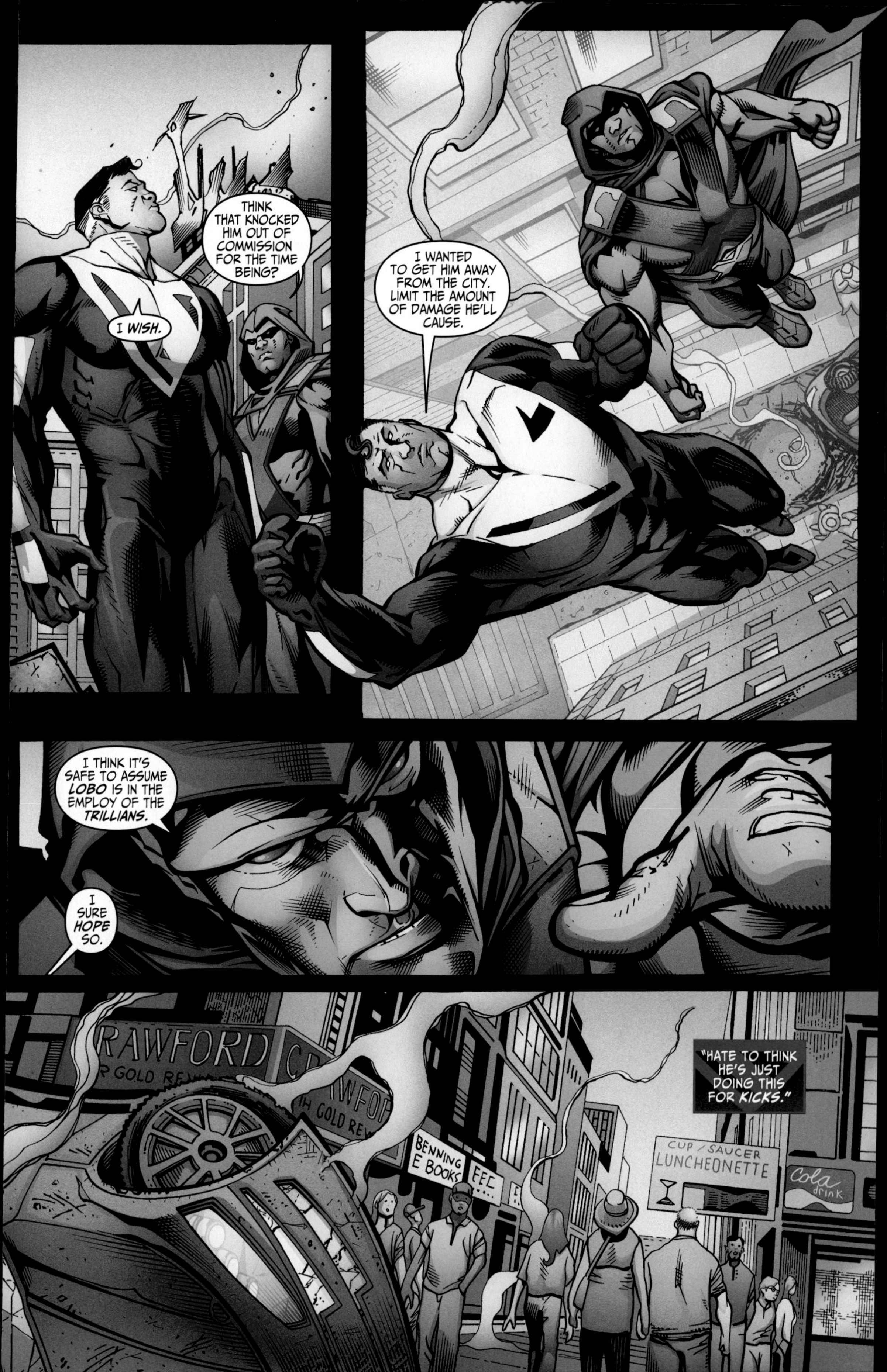
THINK THAT KNOCKED HIM OUT OF COMMISSION FOR THE TIME BEING?
I WISH.
I WANTED TO GET HIM AWAY FROM THE CITY. LIMIT THE AMOUNT OF DAMAGE HE'LL CAUSE.
I THINK IT'S SAFE TO ASSUME LOBO IS IN THE EMPLOY OF THE TRILLIANS.
I SURE HOPE SO.
RAWFORD
R GOLD REV
IH GOLD REV
BENNING E BOOKS
F.F.C.
CUP / SAUCER LUNCHEONETTE
Cola drink
"HATE TO THINK HE'S JUST DOING THIS FOR KICKS."

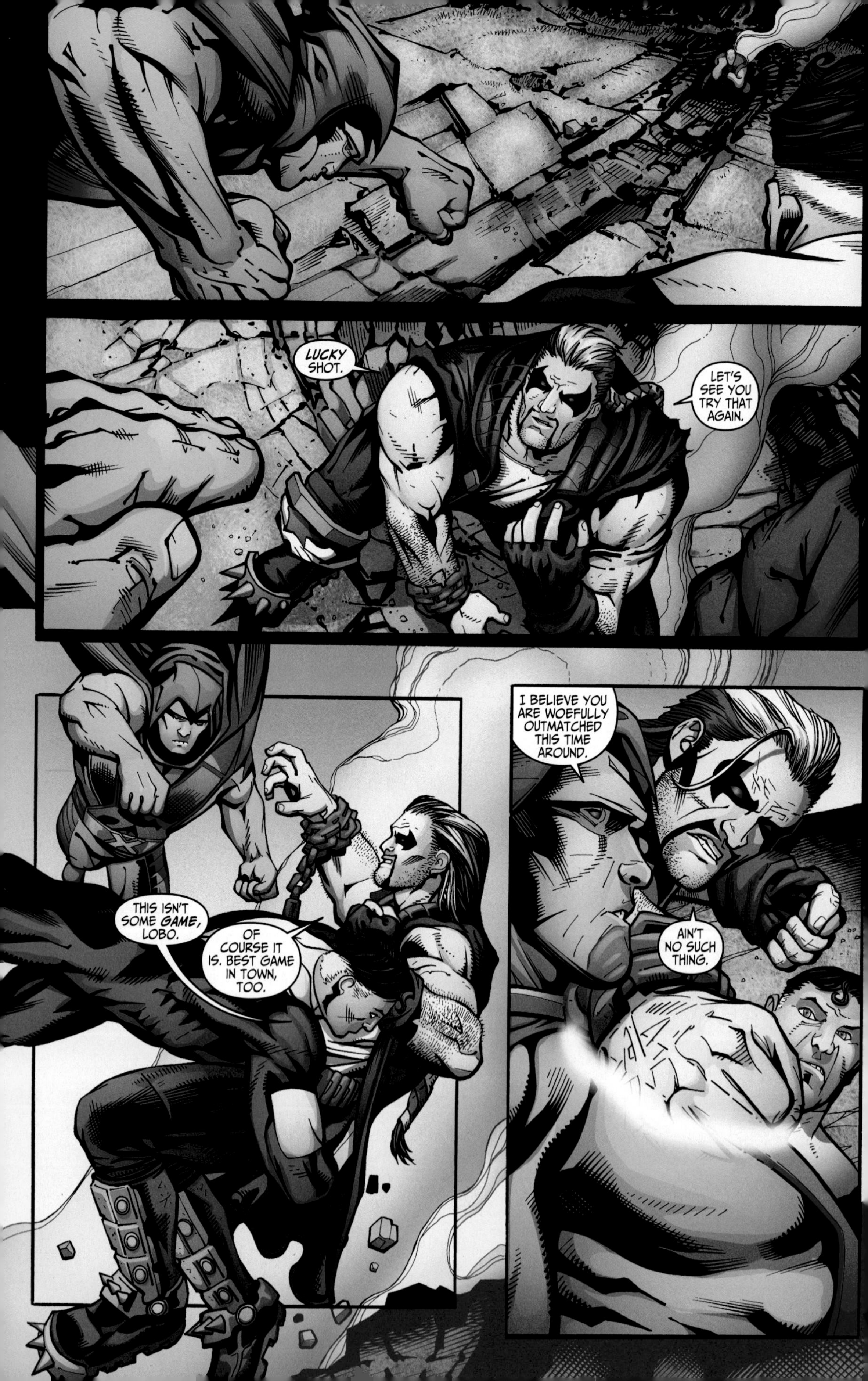
LUCKY SHOT.
LET'S SEE YOU TRY THAT AGAIN.
THIS ISN'T SOME GAME, LOBO.
OF COURSE IT IS. BEST GAME IN TOWN, TOO.
I BELIEVE YOU ARE WOEFULLY OUTMATCHED THIS TIME AROUND.
AIN'T NO SUCH THING.

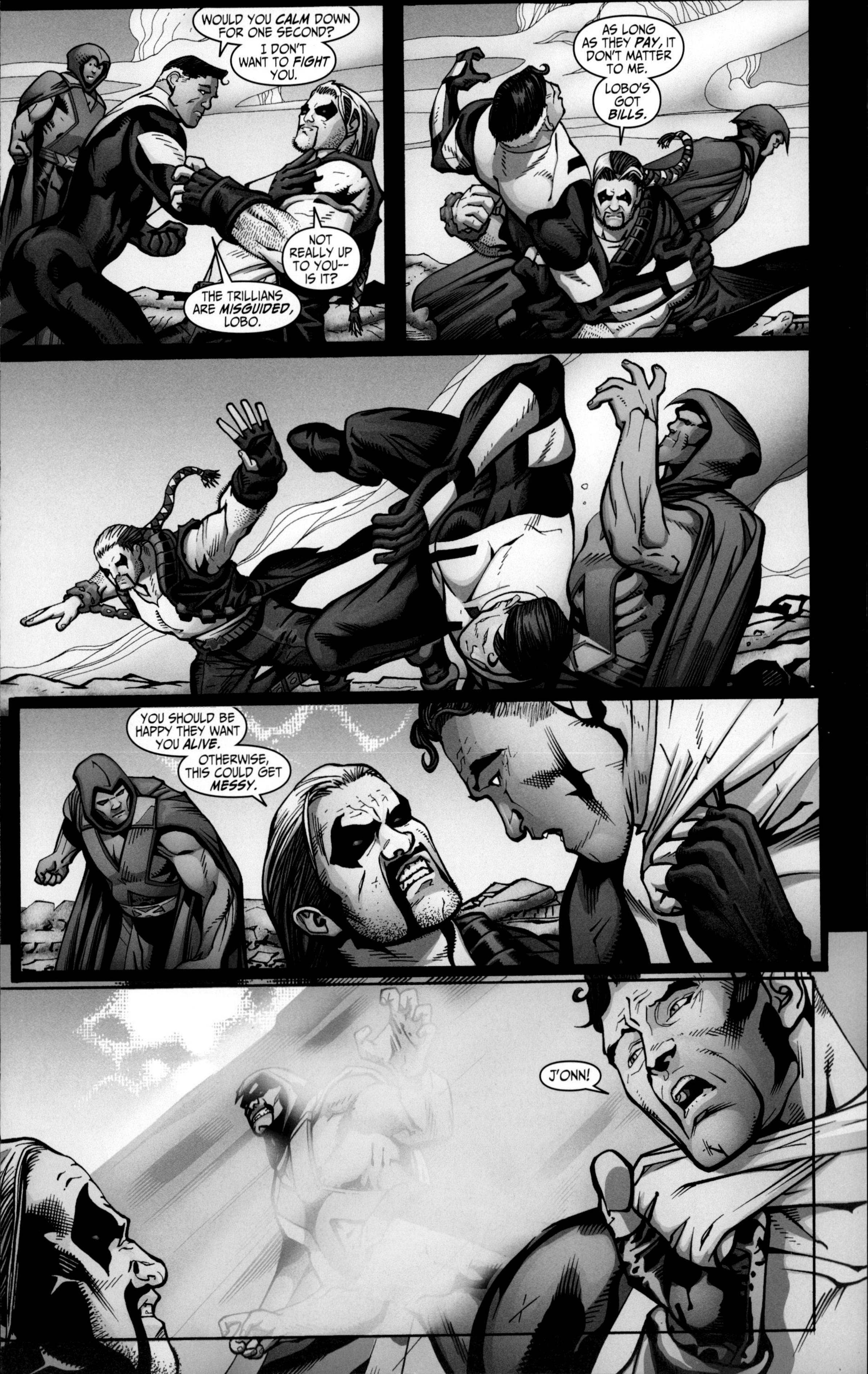
WOULD YOU CALM DOWN FOR ONE SECOND?
I DON'T WANT TO FIGHT YOU.
THE TRILLIANS ARE MISGUIDED, LOBO.
NOT REALLY UP TO YOU-- IS IT?
AS LONG AS THEY PAY, IT DON'T MATTER TO ME.
LOBO'S GOT BILLS.
YOU SHOULD BE HAPPY THEY WANT YOU ALIVE.
OTHERWISE, THIS COULD GET MESSY.
J'ONN!

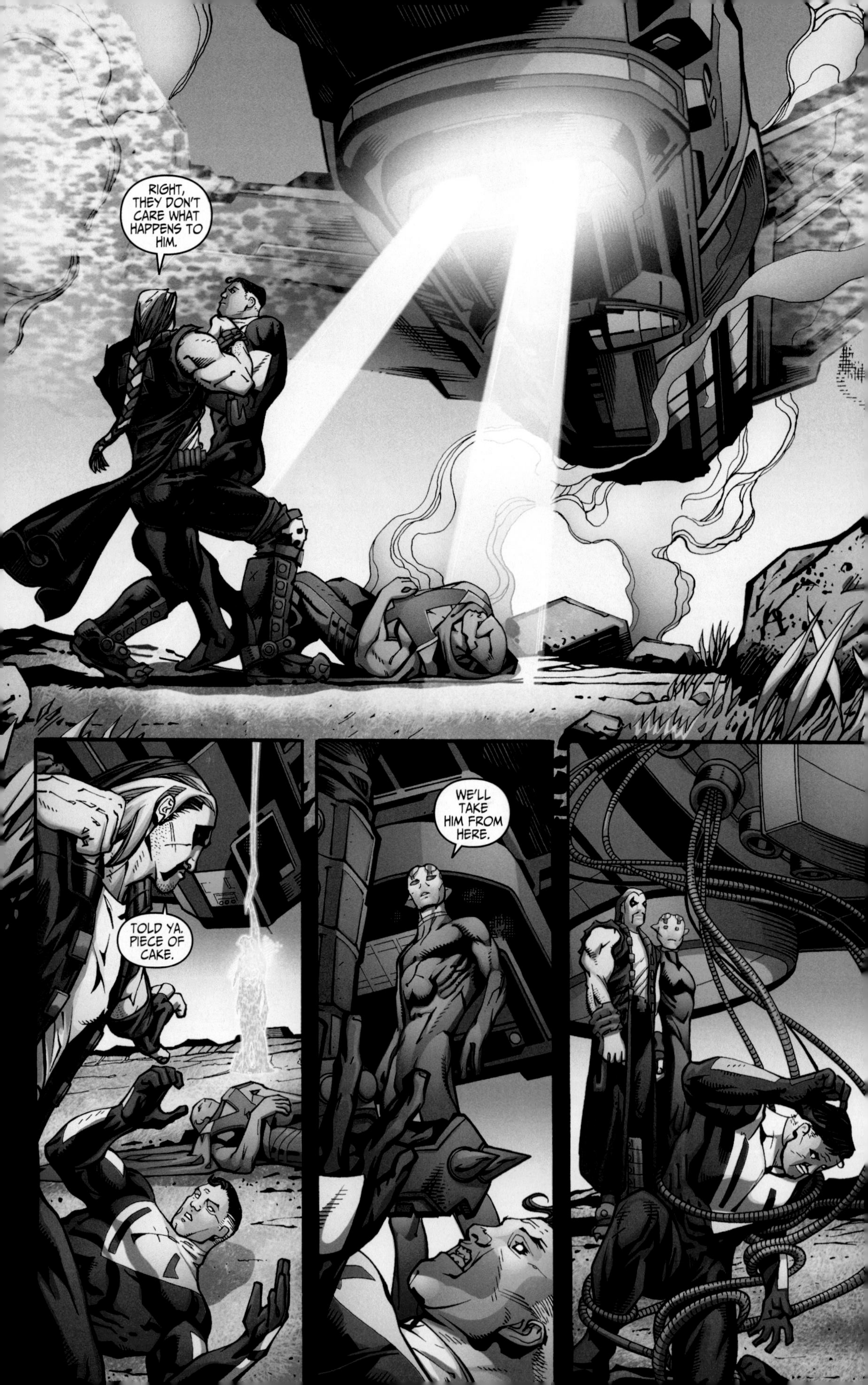
RIGHT, THEY DON'T CARE WHAT HAPPENS TO HIM.
TOLD YA. PIECE OF CAKE.
WE'LL TAKE HIM FROM HERE.

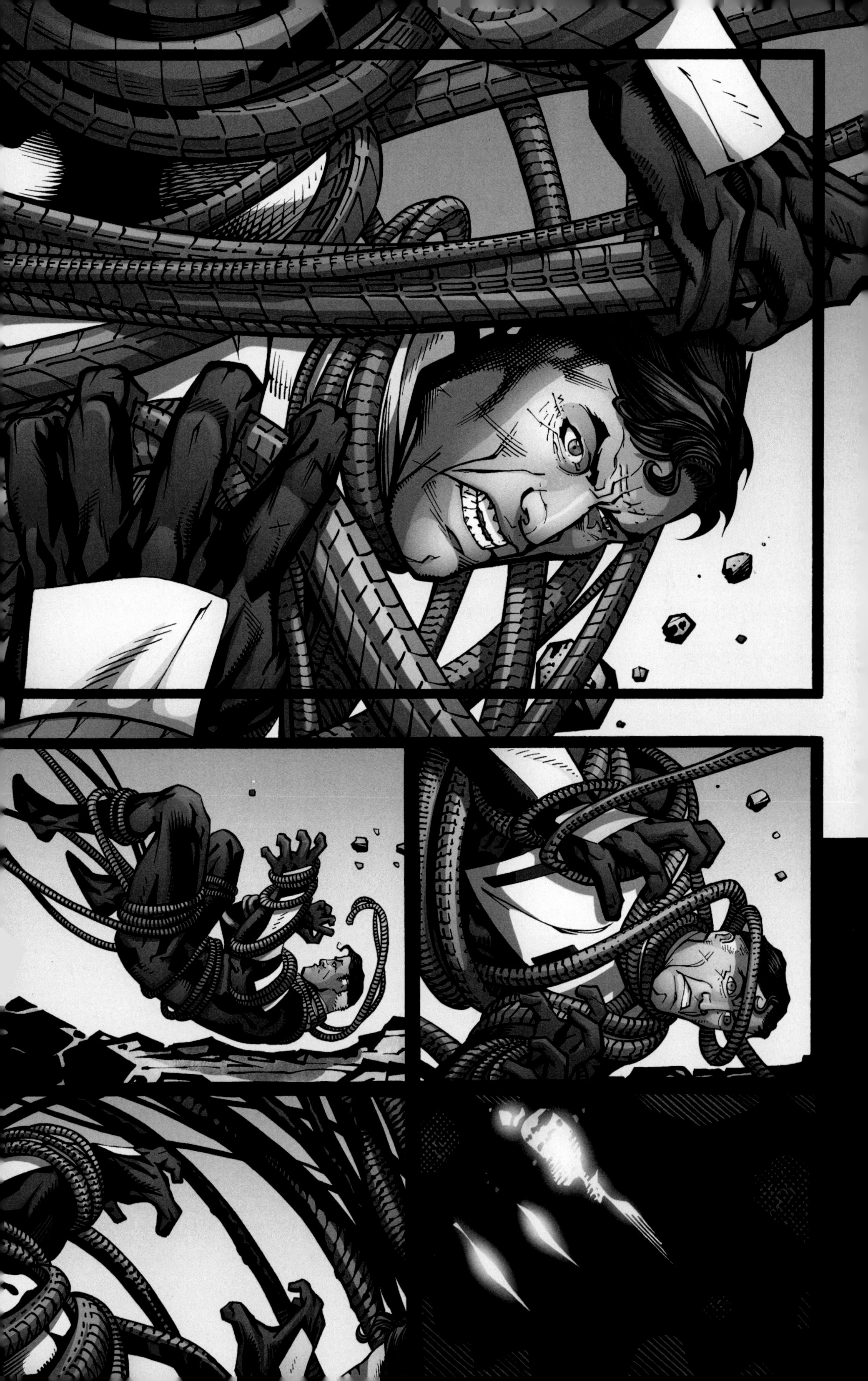

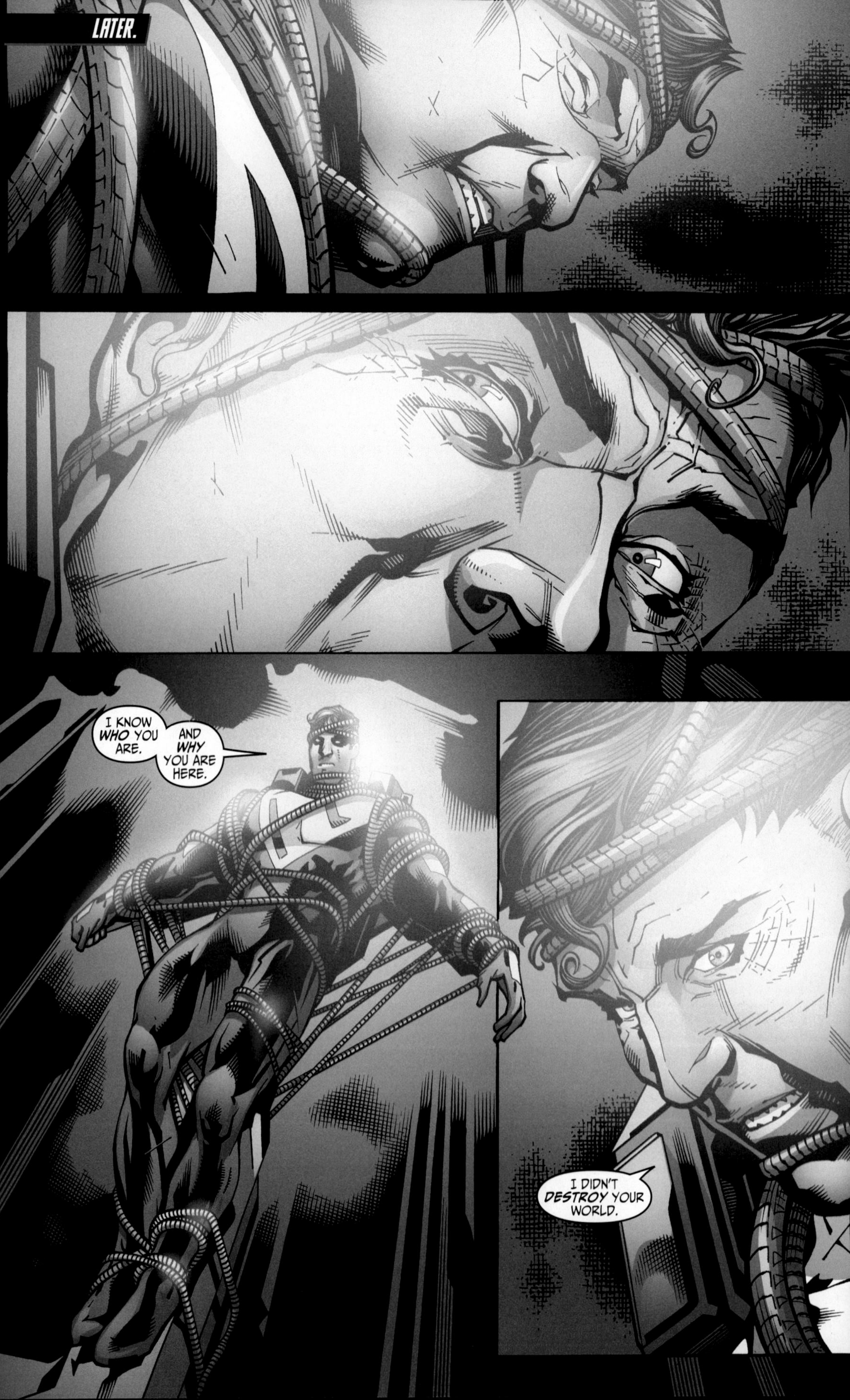
LATER.
I KNOW WHO YOU ARE.
AND WHY YOU ARE HERE.
I DIDN'T DESTROY YOUR WORLD.

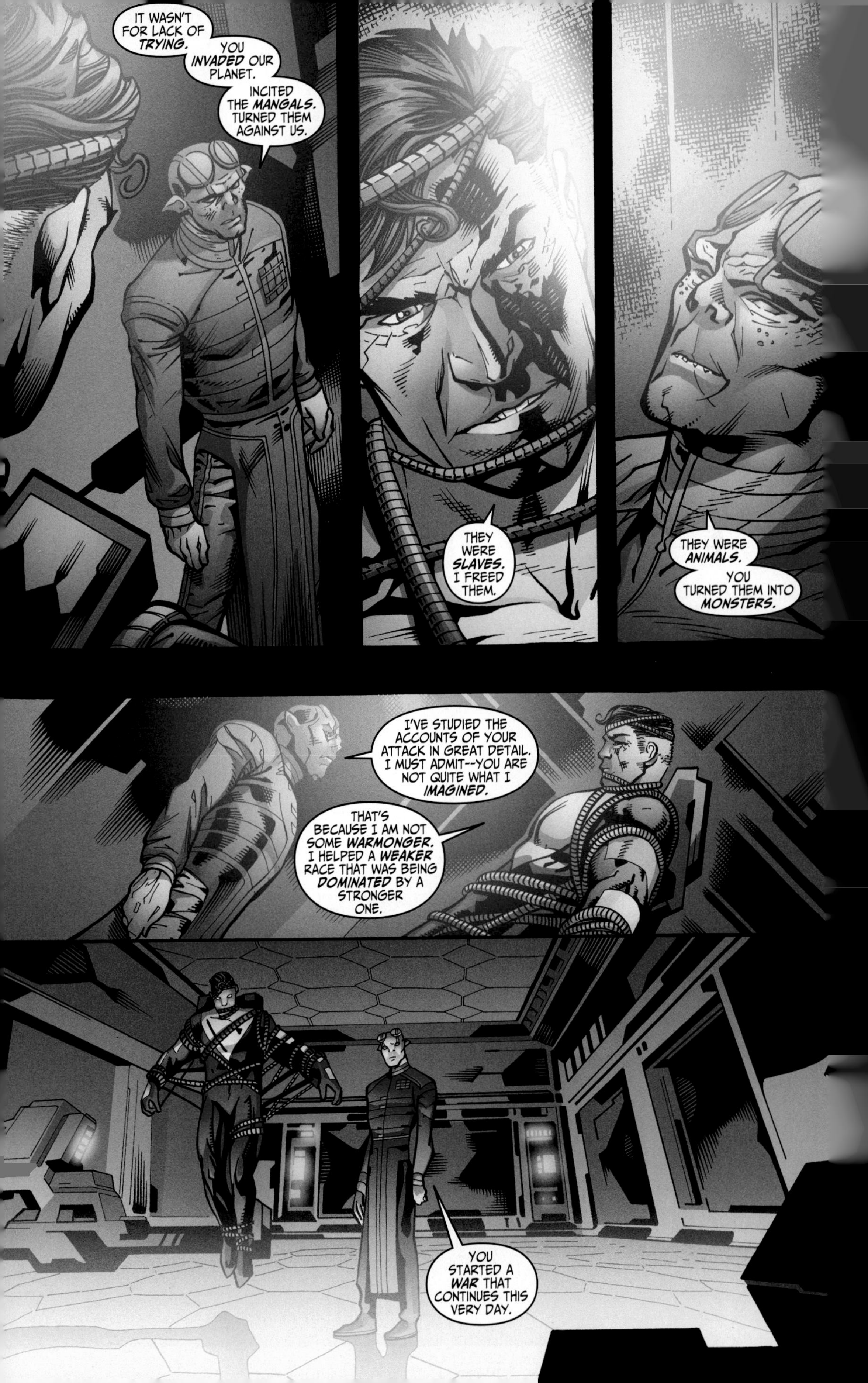
IT WASN'T FOR LACK OF TRYING.
YOU INVADED OUR PLANET.
INCITED THE MANGALS. TURNED THEM AGAINST US.
THEY WERE SLAVES. I FREED THEM.
THEY WERE ANIMALS.
YOU TURNED THEM INTO MONSTERS.
I'VE STUDIED THE ACCOUNTS OF YOUR ATTACK IN GREAT DETAIL. I MUST ADMIT--YOU ARE NOT QUITE WHAT I IMAGINED.
THAT'S BECAUSE I AM NOT SOME WARMONGER. I HELPED A WEAKER RACE THAT WAS BEING DOMINATED BY A STRONGER ONE.
YOU STARTED A WAR THAT CONTINUES THIS VERY DAY.

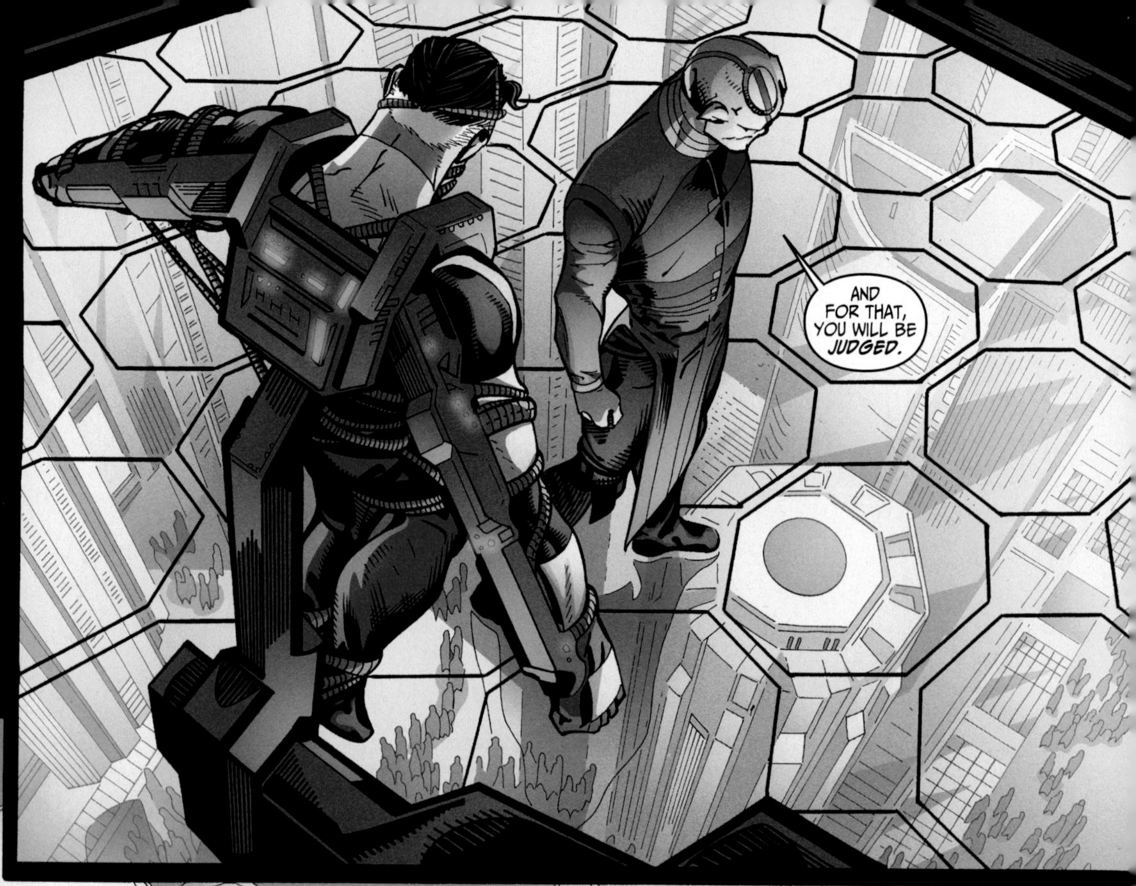
AND FOR THAT, YOU WILL BE JUDGED.

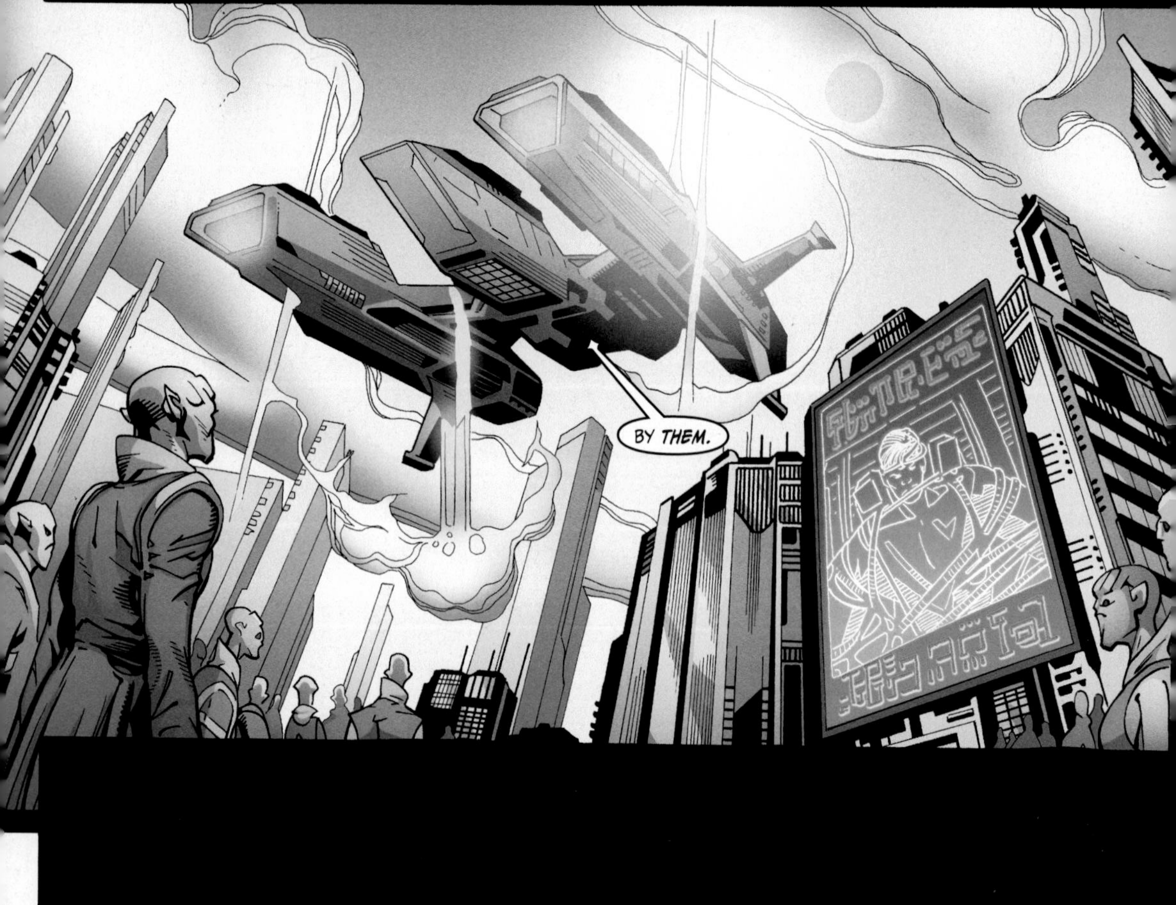
BY THEM.

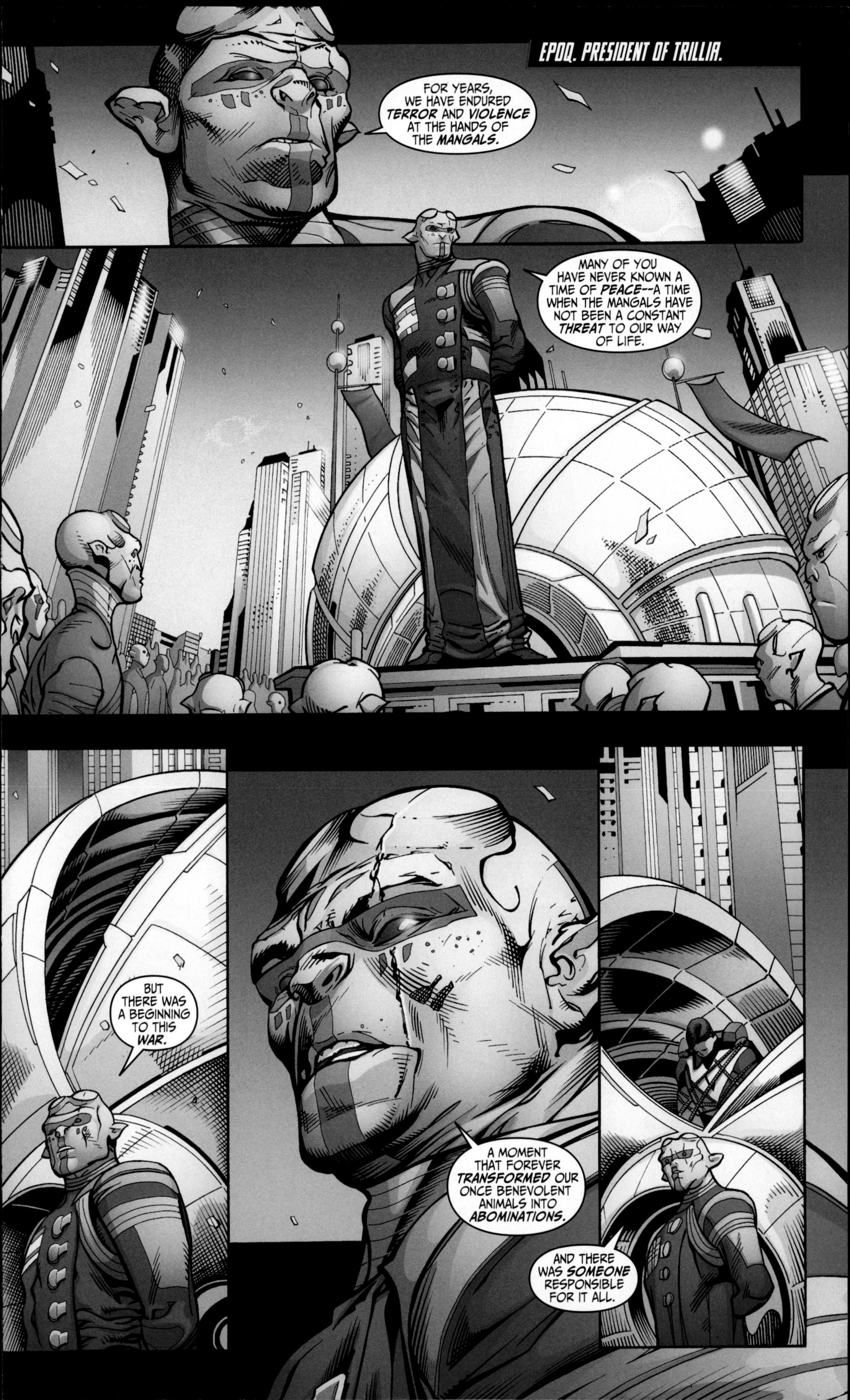
EPOQ. PRESIDENT OF TRILLIA.
FOR YEARS, WE HAVE ENDURED TERROR AND VIOLENCE AT THE HANDS OF THE MANGALS.
MANY OF YOU HAVE NEVER KNOWN A TIME OF PEACE--A TIME WHEN THE MANGALS HAVE NOT BEEN A CONSTANT THREAT TO OUR WAY OF LIFE.
BUT THERE WAS A BEGINNING TO THIS WAR.
A MOMENT THAT FOREVER TRANSFORMED OUR ONCE BENEVOLENT ANIMALS INTO ABOMINATIONS.
AND THERE WAS SOMEONE RESPONSIBLE FOR IT ALL.

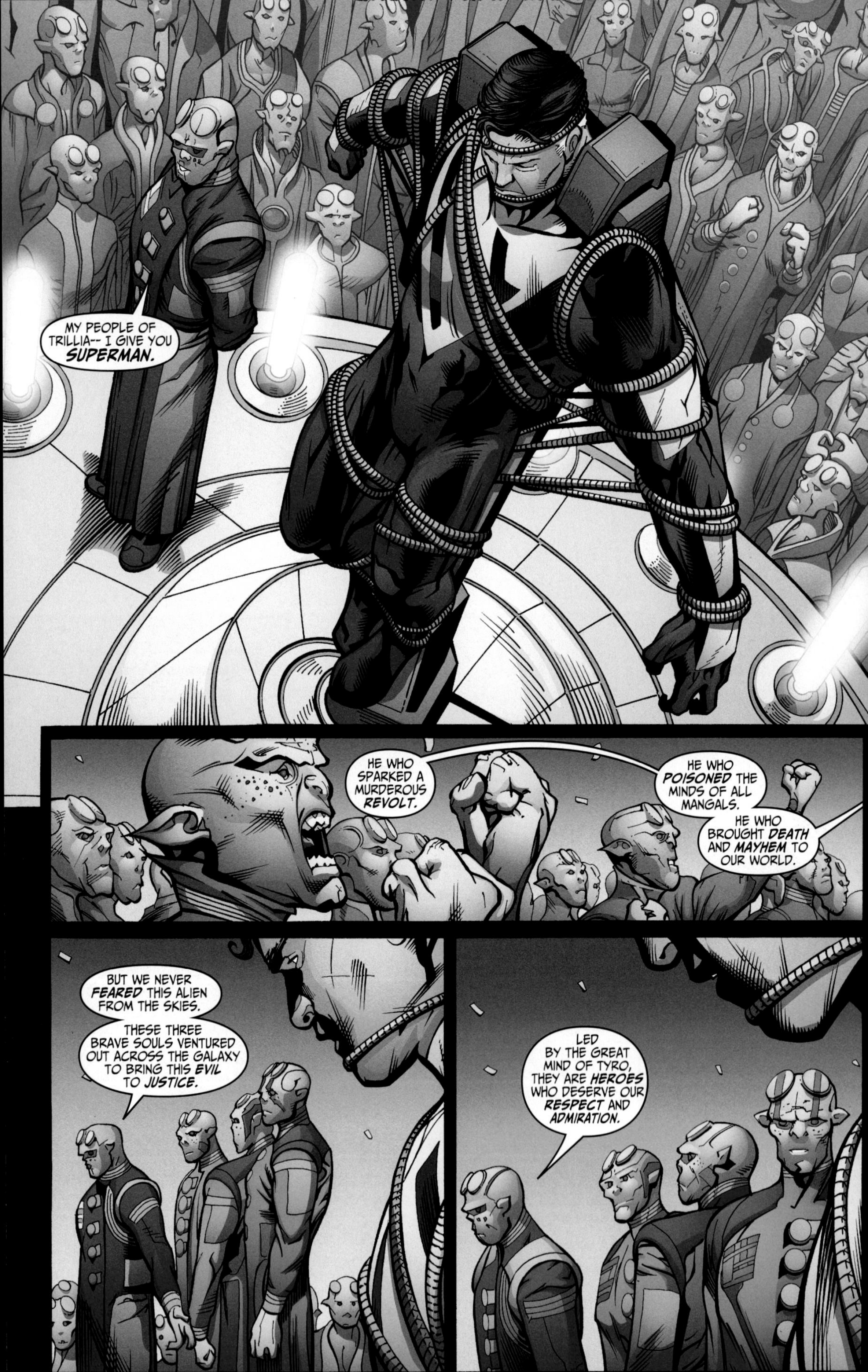
MY PEOPLE OF TRILLIA-- I GIVE YOU SUPERMAN.
HE WHO SPARKED A MURDEROUS REVOLT.
HE WHO POISONED THE MINDS OF ALL MANGALS.
HE WHO BROUGHT DEATH AND MAYHEM TO OUR WORLD.
BUT WE NEVER FEARED THIS ALIEN FROM THE SKIES.
THESE THREE BRAVE SOULS VENTURED OUT ACROSS THE GALAXY TO BRING THIS EVIL TO JUSTICE.
LED BY THE GREAT MIND OF TYRO, THEY ARE HEROES WHO DESERVE OUR RESPECT AND ADMIRATION.

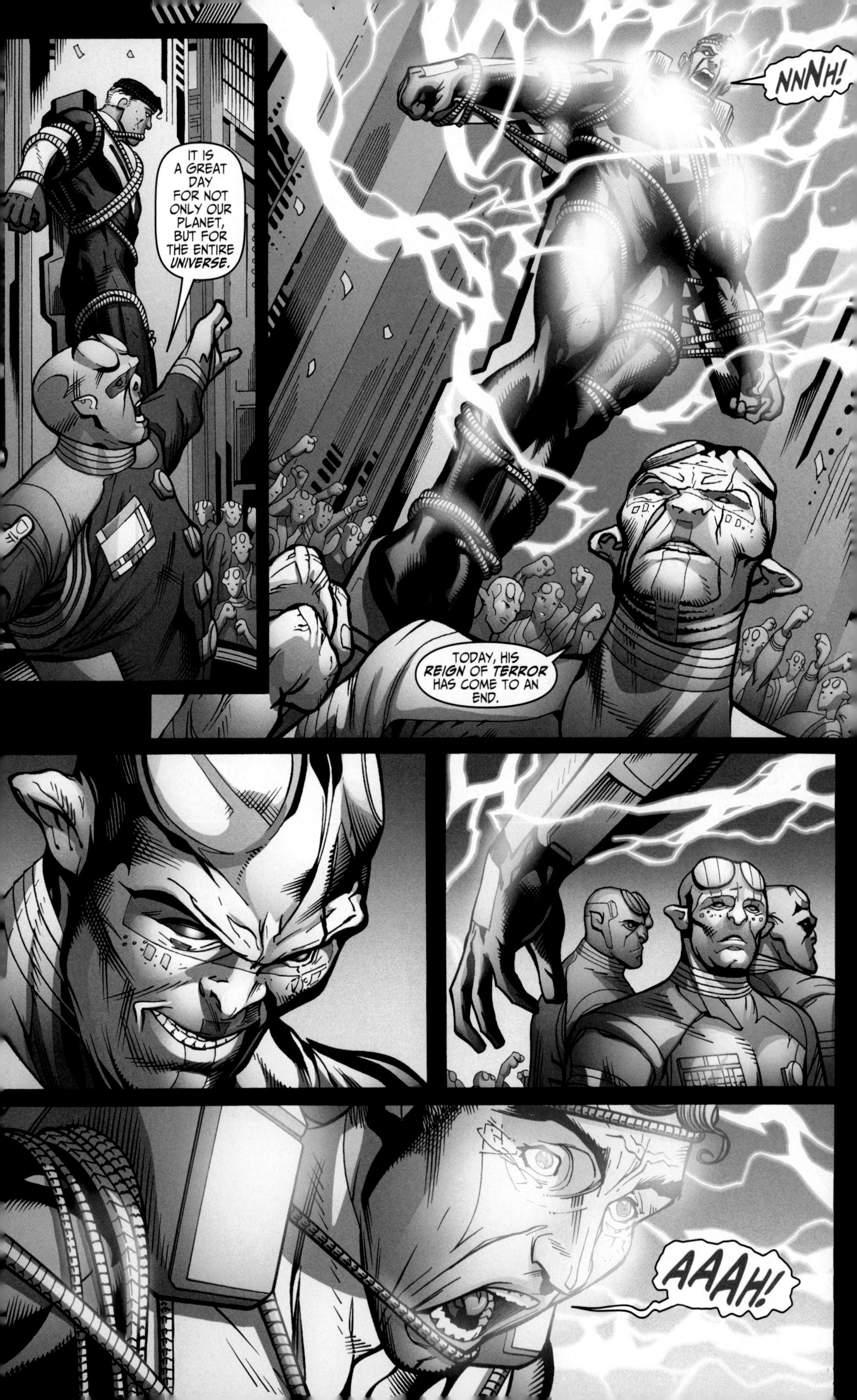
IT IS A GREAT DAY FOR NOT ONLY OUR PLANET, BUT FOR THE ENTIRE UNIVERSE.
NNNH!
TODAY, HIS REIGN OF TERROR HAS COME TO AN END.
AAAH!

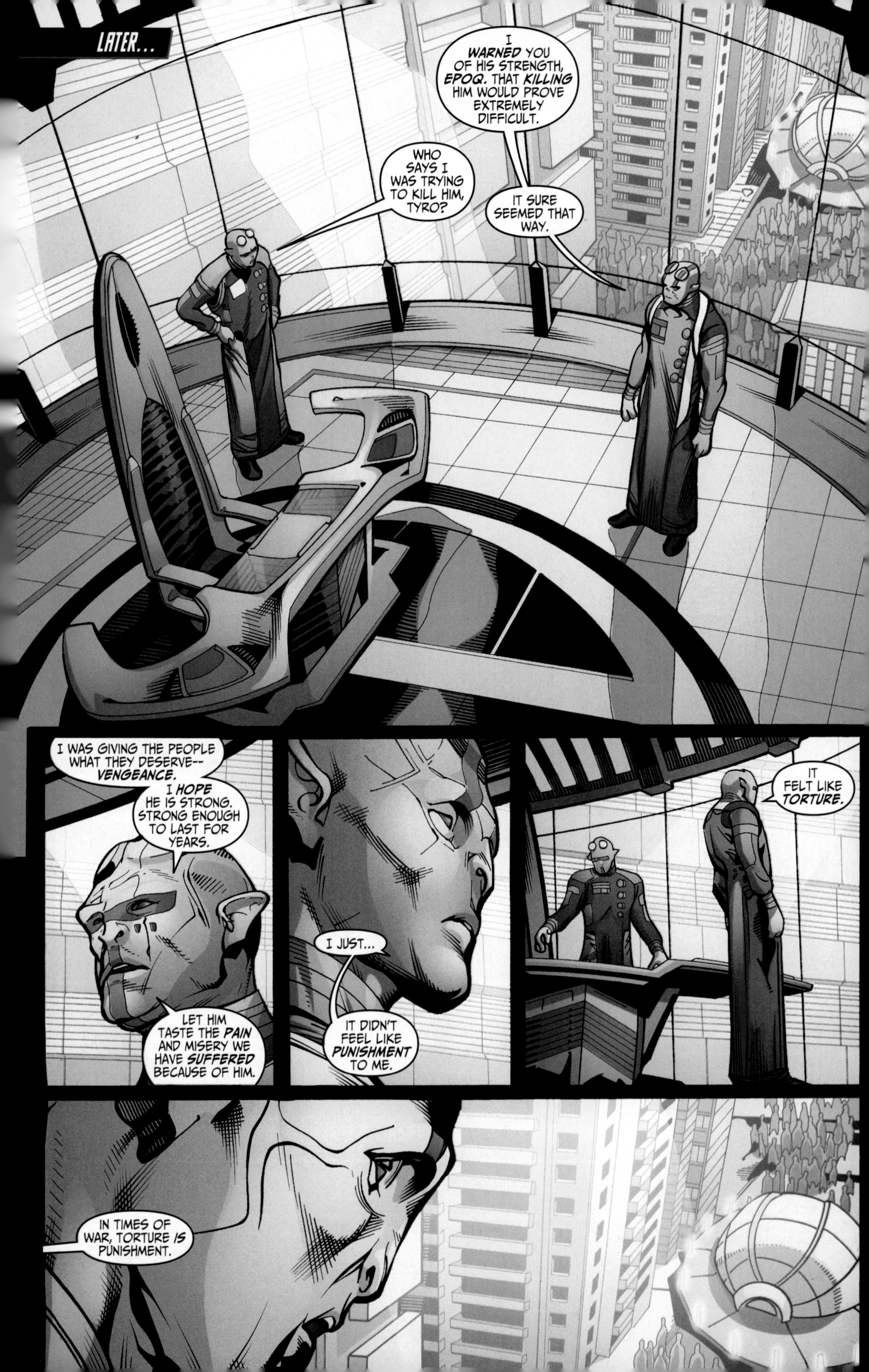
LATER...
I WARNED YOU OF HIS STRENGTH, EPOQ. THAT KILLING HIM WOULD PROVE EXTREMELY DIFFICULT.
WHO SAYS I WAS TRYING TO KILL HIM, TYRO?
IT SURE SEEMED THAT WAY.
I WAS GIVING THE PEOPLE WHAT THEY DESERVE-- VENGEANCE.
I HOPE HE IS STRONG. STRONG ENOUGH TO LAST FOR YEARS.
LET HIM TASTE THE PAIN AND MISERY WE HAVE SUFFERED BECAUSE OF HIM.
I JUST...
IT DIDN'T FEEL LIKE PUNISHMENT TO ME.
IT FELT LIKE TORTURE.
IN TIMES OF WAR, TORTURE IS PUNISHMENT.

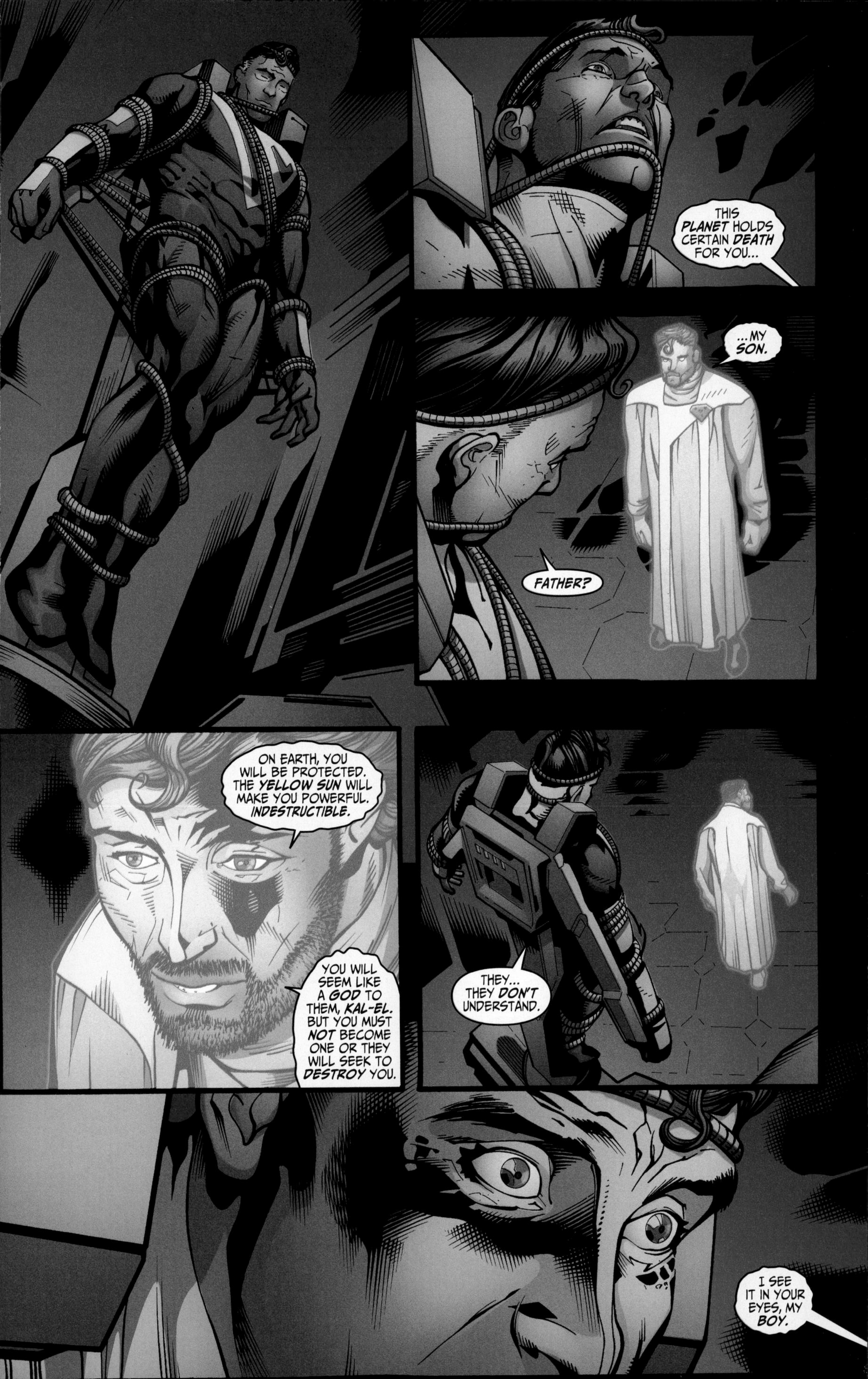
THIS PLANET HOLDS CERTAIN DEATH FOR YOU...
...MY SON.
FATHER?
ON EARTH, YOU WILL BE PROTECTED. THE YELLOW SUN WILL MAKE YOU POWERFUL. INDESTRUCTIBLE.
YOU WILL SEEM LIKE A GOD TO THEM, KAL-EL. BUT YOU MUST NOT BECOME ONE OR THEY WILL SEEK TO DESTROY YOU.
THEY... THEY DON'T UNDERSTAND.
I SEE IT IN YOUR EYES, MY BOY.

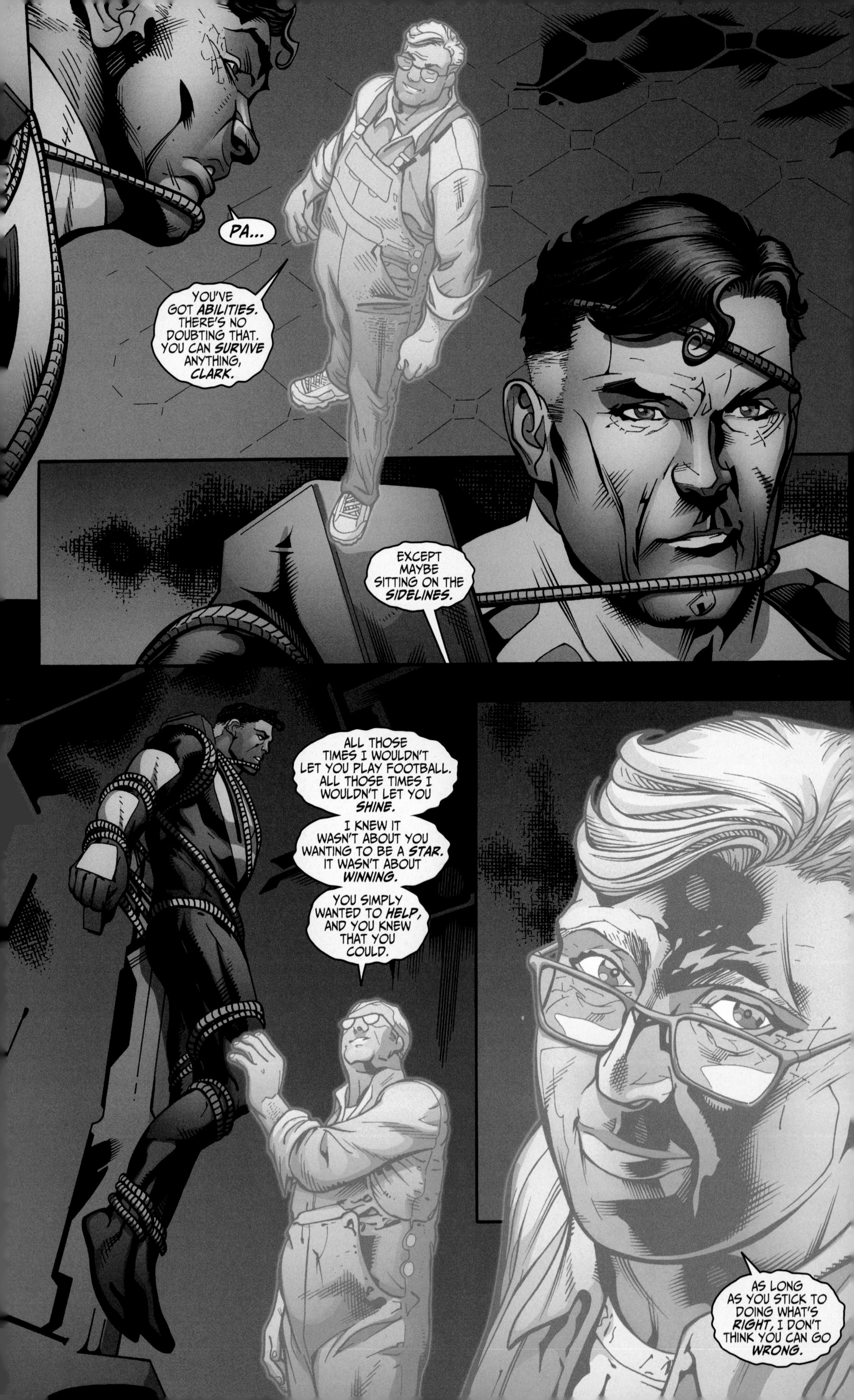
PA...
YOU'VE GOT ABILITIES. THERE'S NO DOUBTING THAT. YOU CAN SURVIVE ANYTHING, CLARK.
EXCEPT MAYBE SITTING ON THE SIDELINES.
ALL THOSE TIMES I WOULDN'T LET YOU PLAY FOOTBALL. ALL THOSE TIMES I WOULDN'T LET YOU SHINE.
I KNEW IT WASN'T ABOUT YOU WANTING TO BE A STAR. IT WASN'T ABOUT WINNING.
YOU SIMPLY WANTED TO HELP, AND YOU KNEW THAT YOU COULD.
AS LONG AS YOU STICK TO DOING WHAT'S RIGHT, I DON'T THINK YOU CAN GO WRONG.

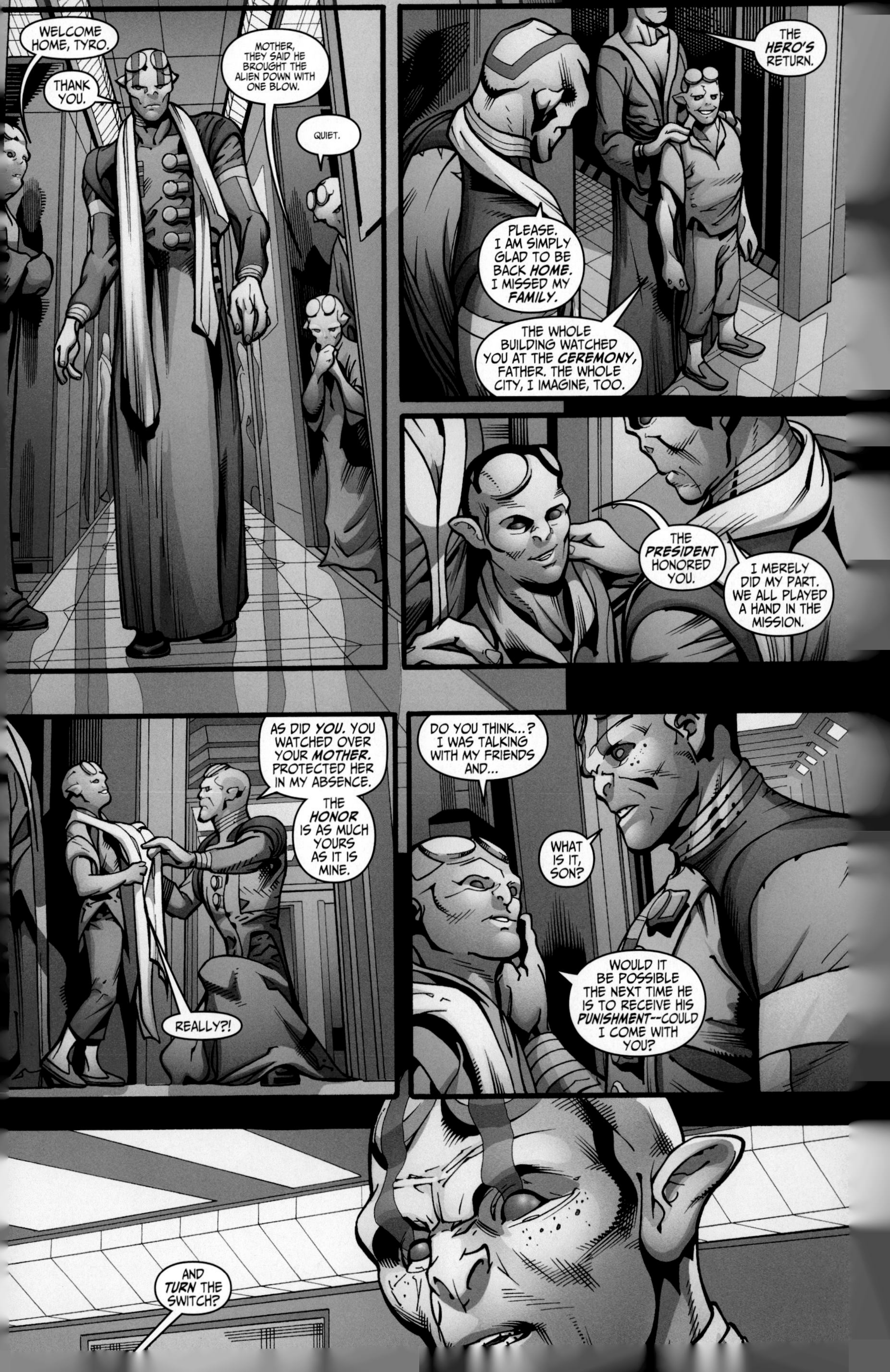
WELCOME HOME, TYRO.
THANK YOU.
MOTHER, THEY SAID HE BROUGHT THE ALIEN DOWN WITH ONE BLOW.
QUIET.
THE HERO'S RETURN.
PLEASE. I AM SIMPLY GLAD TO BE BACK HOME. I MISSED MY FAMILY.
THE WHOLE BUILDING WATCHED YOU AT THE CEREMONY, FATHER. THE WHOLE CITY, I IMAGINE, TOO.
THE PRESIDENT HONORED YOU.
I MERELY DID MY PART. WE ALL PLAYED A HAND IN THE MISSION.
AS DID YOU. YOU WATCHED OVER YOUR MOTHER. PROTECTED HER IN MY ABSENCE.
THE HONOR IS AS MUCH YOURS AS IT IS MINE.
REALLY?!
DO YOU THINK...? I WAS TALKING WITH MY FRIENDS AND...
WHAT IS IT, SON?
WOULD IT BE POSSIBLE THE NEXT TIME HE IS TO RECEIVE HIS PUNISHMENT--COULD I COME WITH YOU?
AND TURN THE SWITCH?

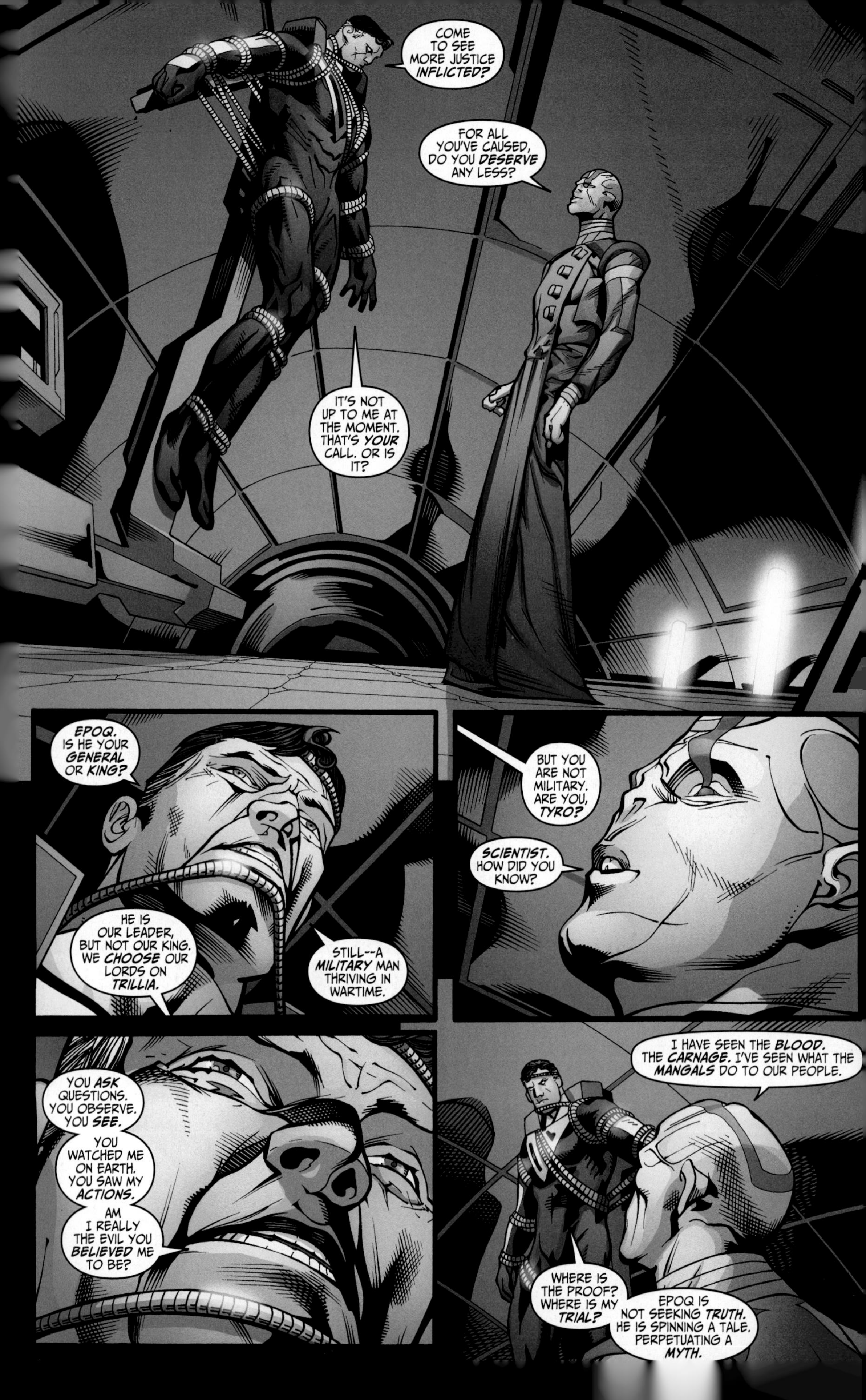
COME TO SEE MORE JUSTICE *INFLICTED?*
FOR ALL YOU'VE CAUSED, DO YOU *DESERVE* ANY LESS?
IT'S NOT UP TO ME AT THE MOMENT. THAT'S *YOUR* CALL. OR IS IT?
EPOQ. IS HE YOUR *GENERAL* OR *KING?*
HE IS OUR LEADER, BUT NOT OUR KING. WE *CHOOSE* OUR LORDS ON *TRILLIA.*
STILL--A *MILITARY* MAN THRIVING IN WARTIME.
BUT YOU ARE NOT MILITARY. ARE YOU, *TYRO?*
SCIENTIST. HOW DID YOU KNOW?
YOU *ASK* QUESTIONS. YOU OBSERVE. YOU *SEE.*
YOU WATCHED ME ON EARTH. YOU SAW MY *ACTIONS.*
AM I REALLY THE EVIL YOU *BELIEVED* ME TO BE?
I HAVE SEEN THE *BLOOD.* THE *CARNAGE.* I'VE SEEN WHAT THE *MANGALS* DO TO OUR PEOPLE.
WHERE IS THE PROOF? WHERE IS MY *TRIAL?*
EPOQ IS NOT SEEKING *TRUTH.* HE IS SPINNING A TALE. PERPETUATING A *MYTH.*

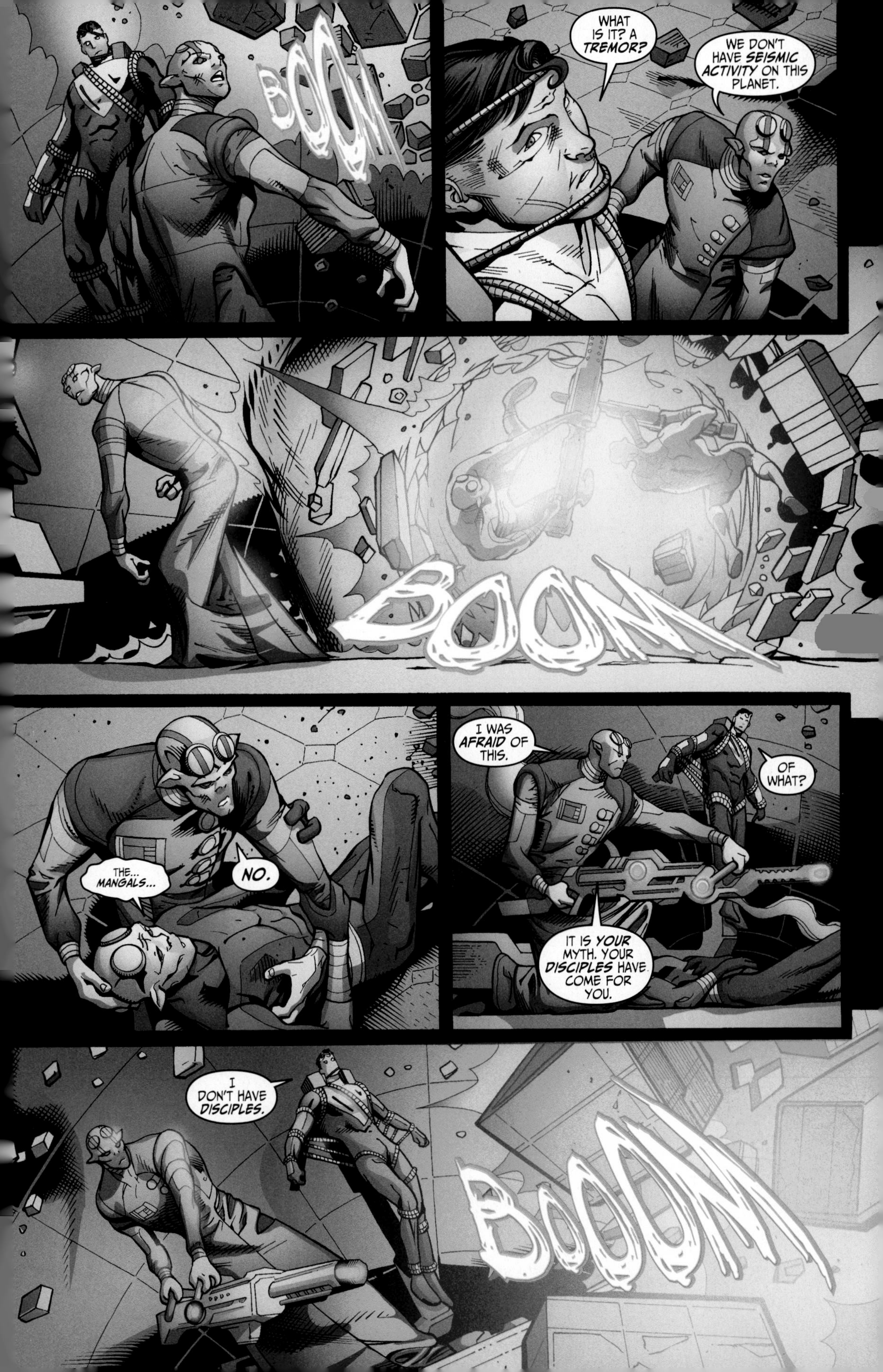
BOOOM
WHAT IS IT? A TREMOR?
WE DON'T HAVE SEISMIC ACTIVITY ON THIS PLANET.
BOOM
THE... MANGALS...
NO.
I WAS AFRAID OF THIS.
OF WHAT?
IT IS YOUR MYTH. YOUR DISCIPLES HAVE COME FOR YOU.
I DON'T HAVE DISCIPLES.
BOOOM

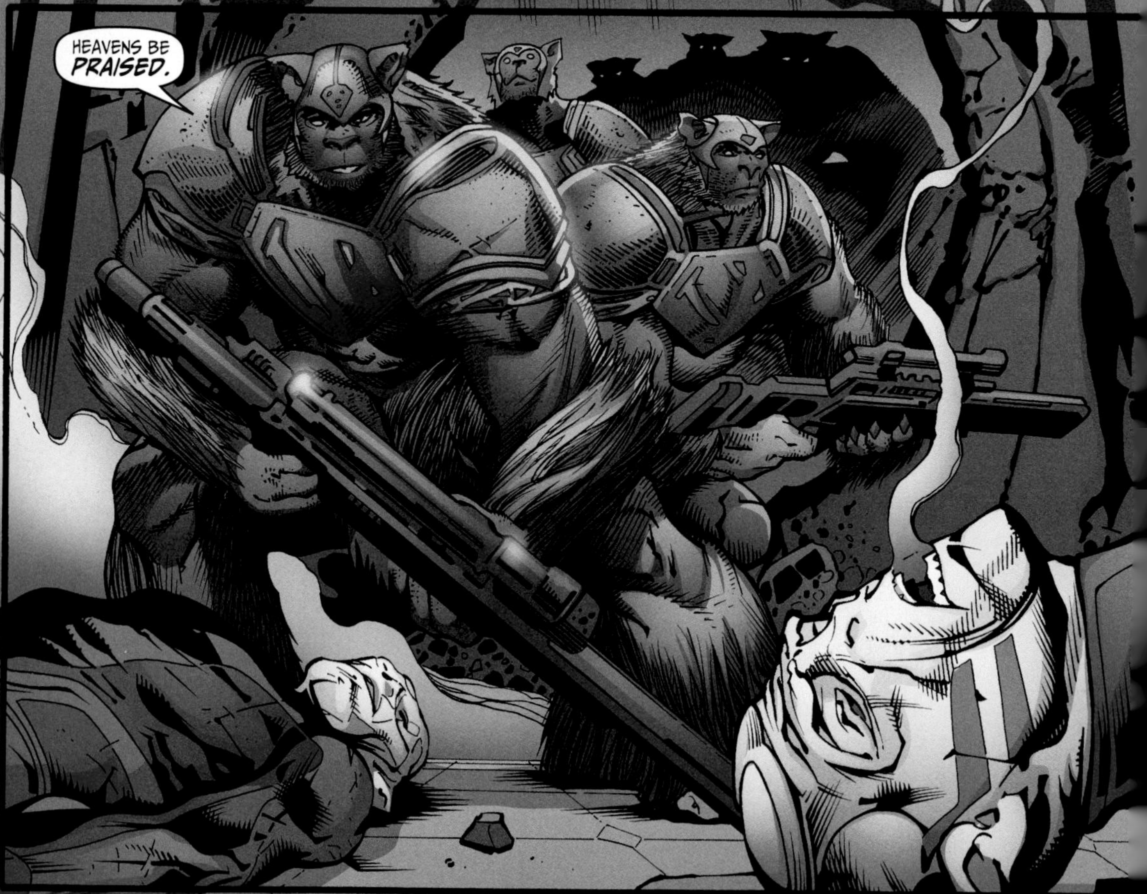
HEAVENS BE PRAISED.

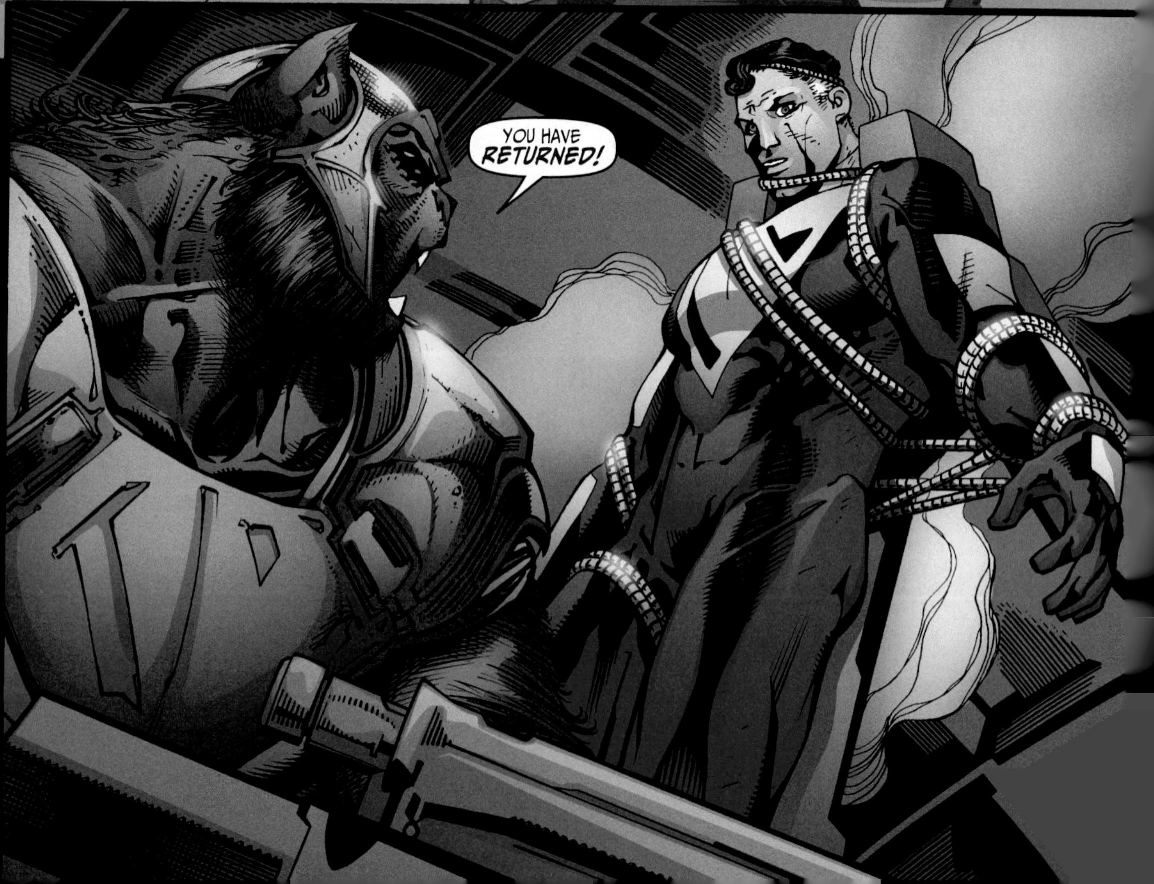
YOU HAVE RETURNED!

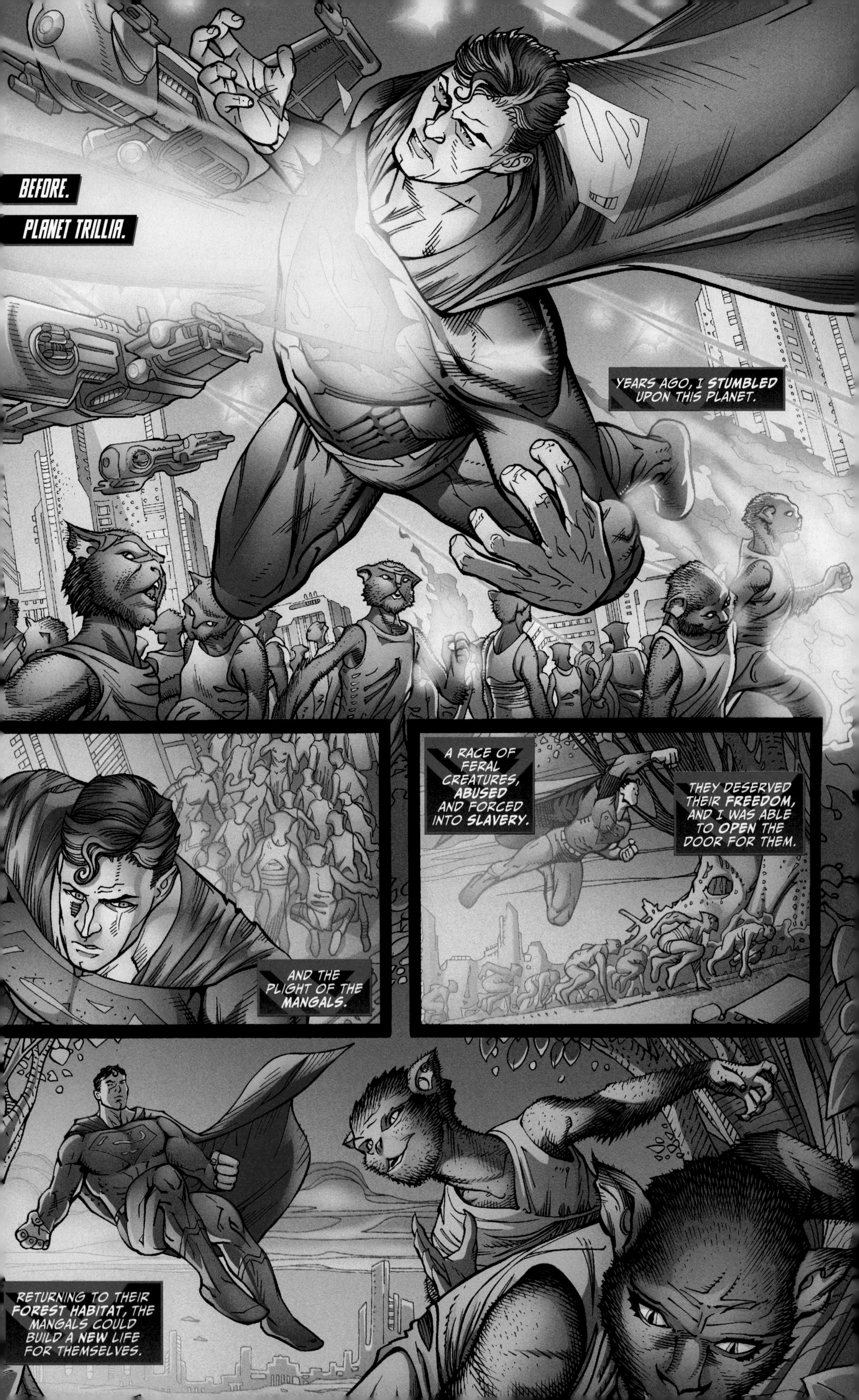
BEFORE.
PLANET TRILLIA.
YEARS AGO, I STUMBLED UPON THIS PLANET.
AND THE PLIGHT OF THE MANGALS.
A RACE OF FERAL CREATURES, ABUSED AND FORCED INTO SLAVERY.
THEY DESERVED THEIR FREEDOM, AND I WAS ABLE TO OPEN THE DOOR FOR THEM.
RETURNING TO THEIR FOREST HABITAT, THE MANGALS COULD BUILD A NEW LIFE FOR THEMSELVES.

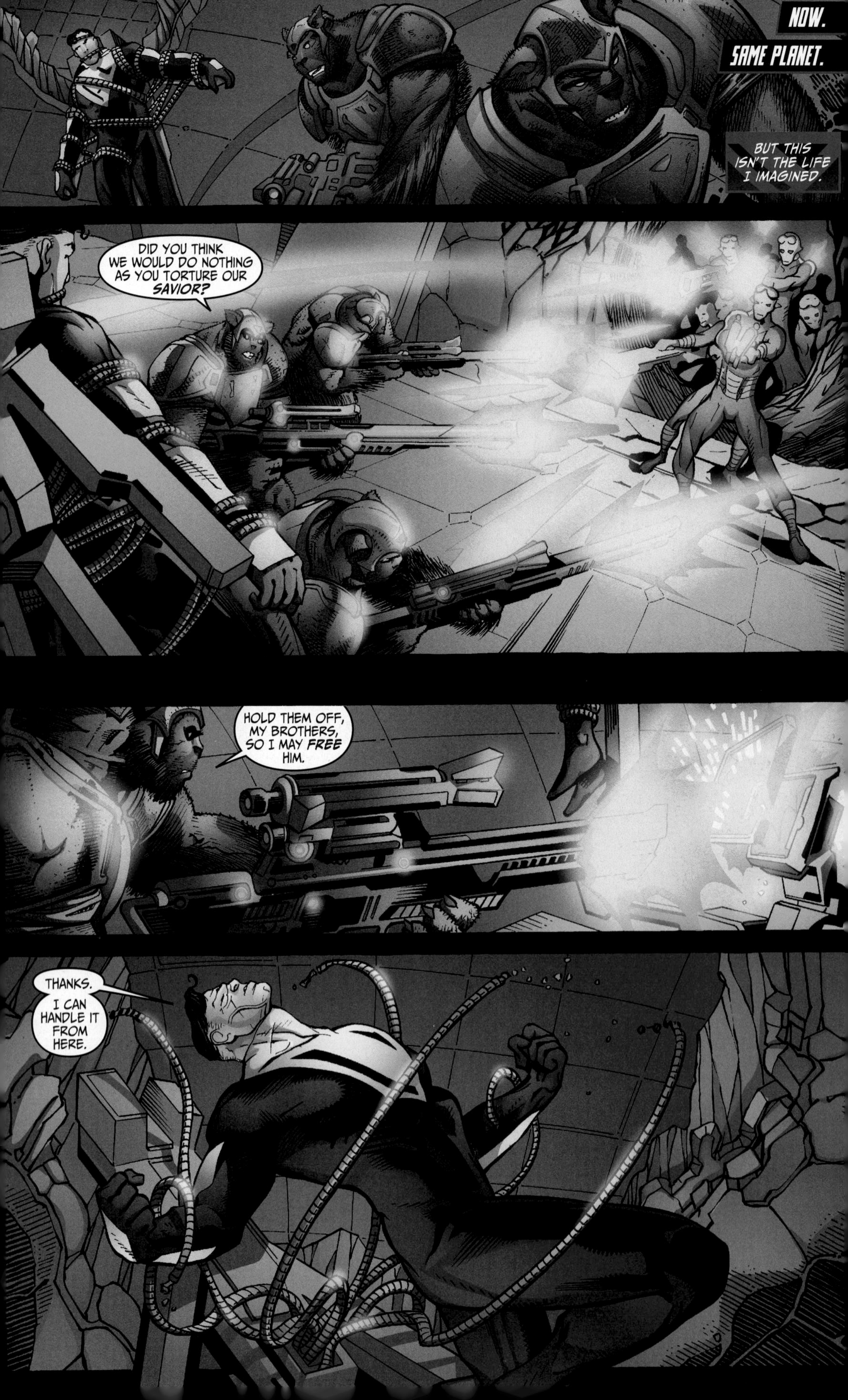
NOW.
SAME PLANET.
BUT THIS ISN'T THE LIFE I IMAGINED.
DID YOU THINK WE WOULD DO NOTHING AS YOU TORTURE OUR SAVIOR?
HOLD THEM OFF, MY BROTHERS, SO I MAY FREE HIM.
THANKS. I CAN HANDLE IT FROM HERE.

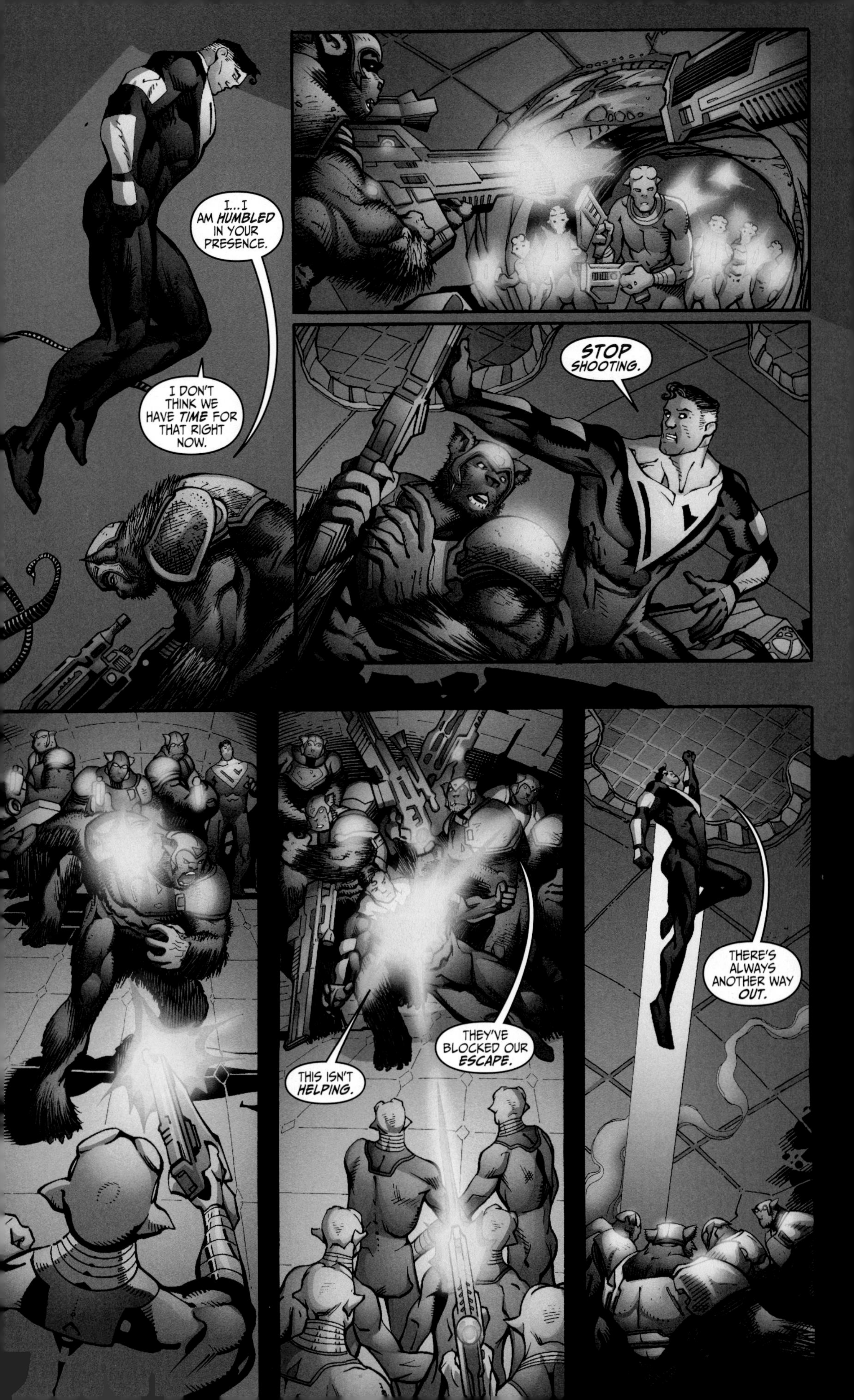
I...I AM HUMBLED IN YOUR PRESENCE.
I DON'T THINK WE HAVE TIME FOR THAT RIGHT NOW.
STOP SHOOTING.
THEY'VE BLOCKED OUR ESCAPE.
THIS ISN'T HELPING.
THERE'S ALWAYS ANOTHER WAY OUT.

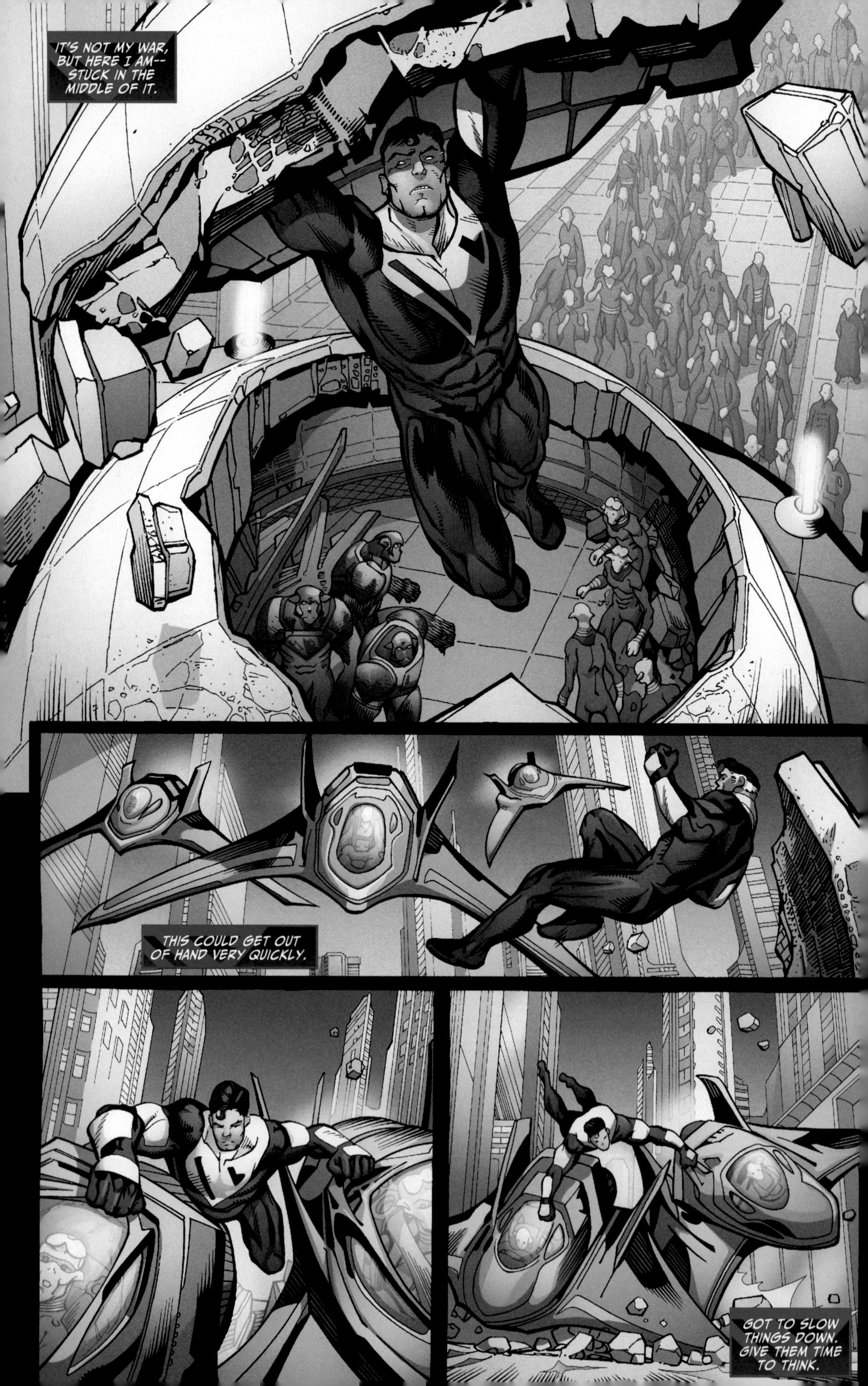
IT'S NOT MY WAR, BUT HERE I AM-- STUCK IN THE MIDDLE OF IT.
THIS COULD GET OUT OF HAND VERY QUICKLY.
GOT TO SLOW THINGS DOWN. GIVE THEM TIME TO THINK.

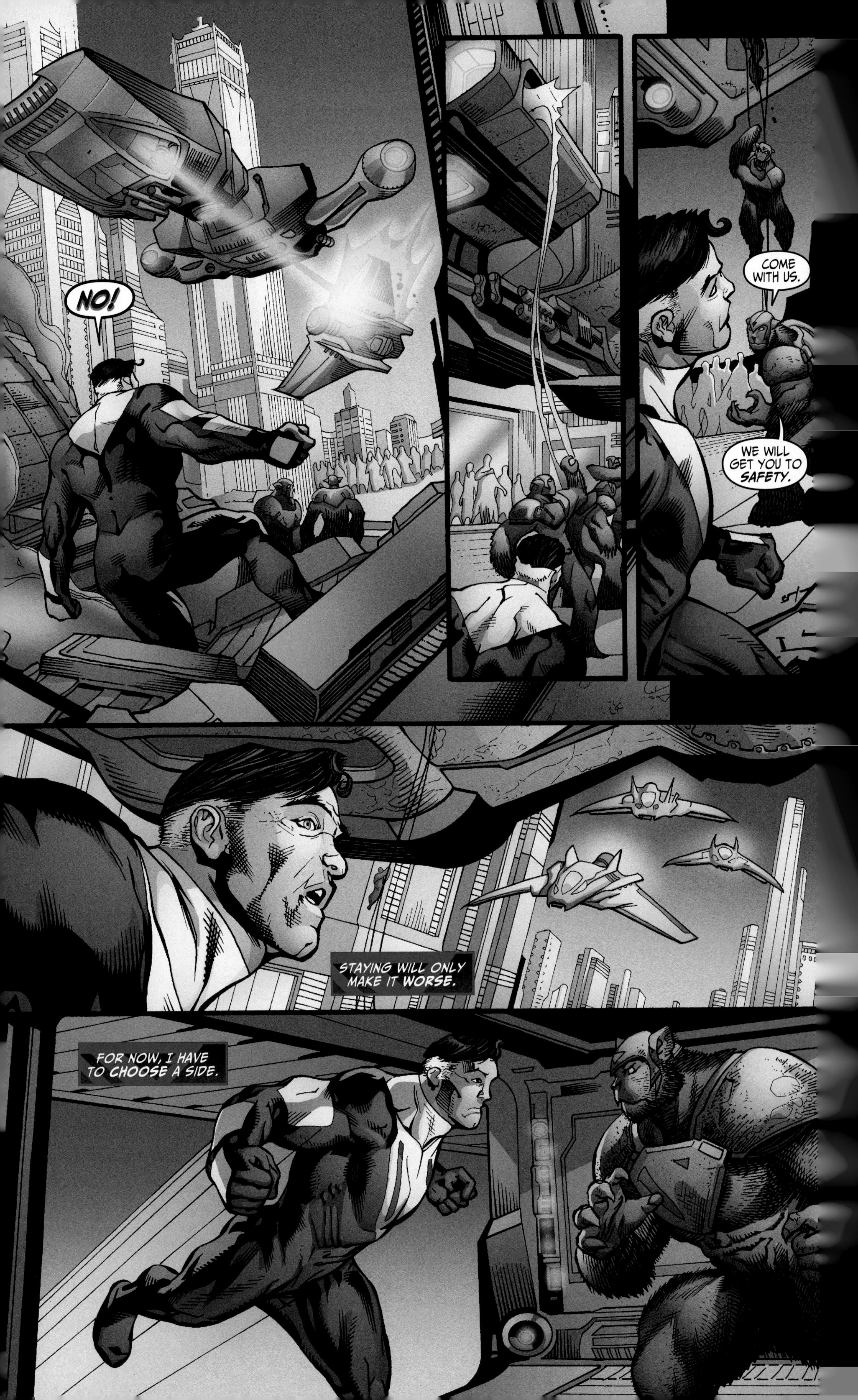
NO!
COME WITH US.
WE WILL GET YOU TO SAFETY.
STAYING WILL ONLY MAKE IT WORSE.
FOR NOW, I HAVE TO CHOOSE A SIDE.

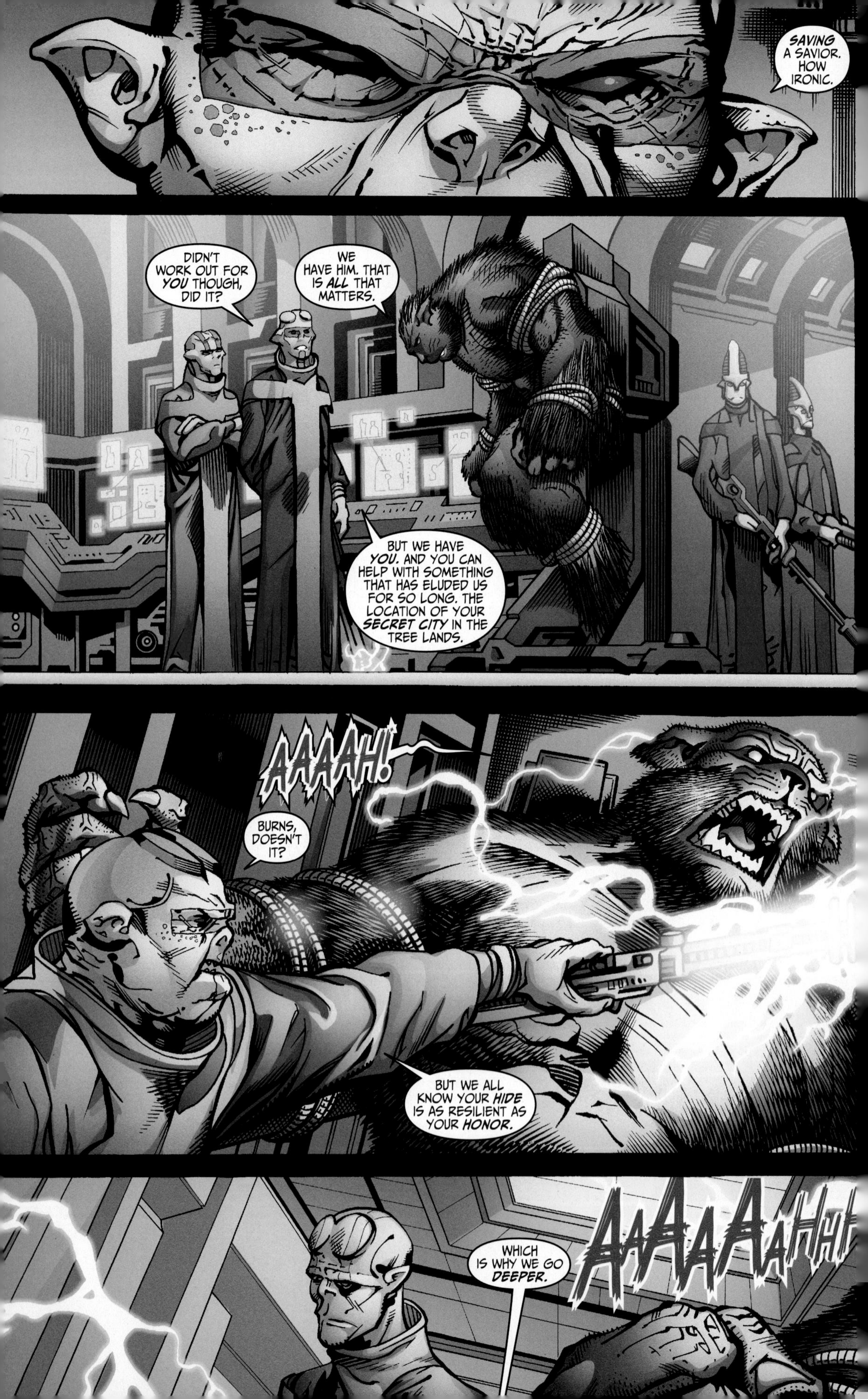

SAVING A SAVIOR. HOW IRONIC.
DIDN'T WORK OUT FOR YOU THOUGH, DID IT?
WE HAVE HIM. THAT IS ALL THAT MATTERS.
BUT WE HAVE YOU. AND YOU CAN HELP WITH SOMETHING THAT HAS ELUDED US FOR SO LONG. THE LOCATION OF YOUR SECRET CITY IN THE TREE LANDS.
AAAAH!
BURNS, DOESN'T IT?
BUT WE ALL KNOW YOUR HIDE IS AS RESILIENT AS YOUR HONOR.
WHICH IS WHY WE GO DEEPER.
AAAAAAHH!

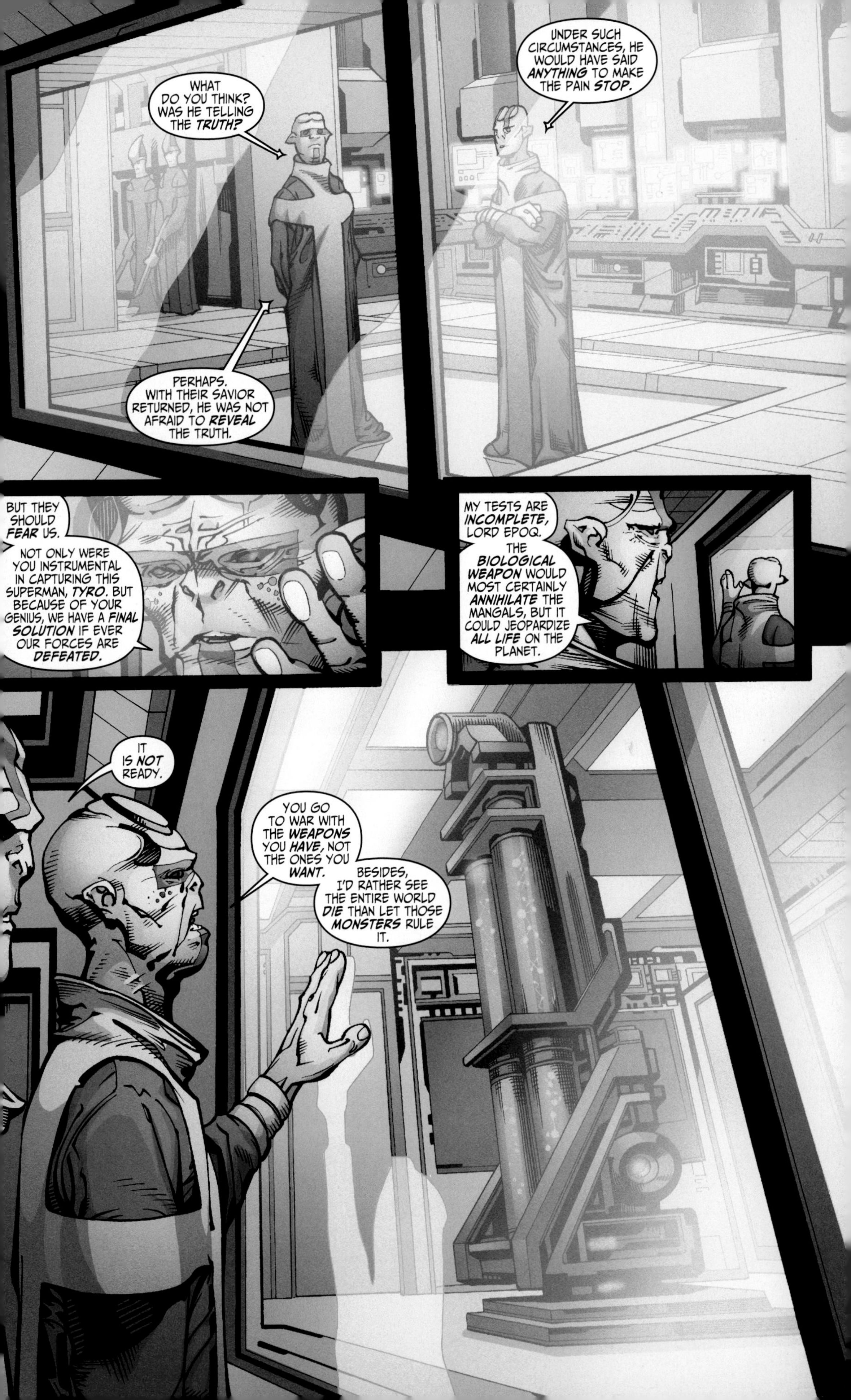
WHAT DO YOU THINK? WAS HE TELLING THE *TRUTH?*
UNDER SUCH CIRCUMSTANCES, HE WOULD HAVE SAID *ANYTHING* TO MAKE THE PAIN *STOP.*
PERHAPS. WITH THEIR SAVIOR RETURNED, HE WAS NOT AFRAID TO *REVEAL* THE TRUTH.
BUT THEY SHOULD *FEAR* US.
NOT ONLY WERE YOU INSTRUMENTAL IN CAPTURING THIS SUPERMAN, *TYRO.* BUT BECAUSE OF YOUR GENIUS, WE HAVE A *FINAL SOLUTION* IF EVER OUR FORCES ARE *DEFEATED.*
MY TESTS ARE *INCOMPLETE,* LORD EPOQ.
THE *BIOLOGICAL WEAPON* WOULD MOST CERTAINLY *ANNIHILATE* THE MANGALS, BUT IT COULD JEOPARDIZE *ALL LIFE* ON THE PLANET.
IT IS *NOT* READY.
YOU GO TO WAR WITH THE *WEAPONS* YOU *HAVE,* NOT THE ONES YOU *WANT.*
BESIDES, I'D RATHER SEE THE ENTIRE WORLD *DIE* THAN LET THOSE *MONSTERS* RULE IT.

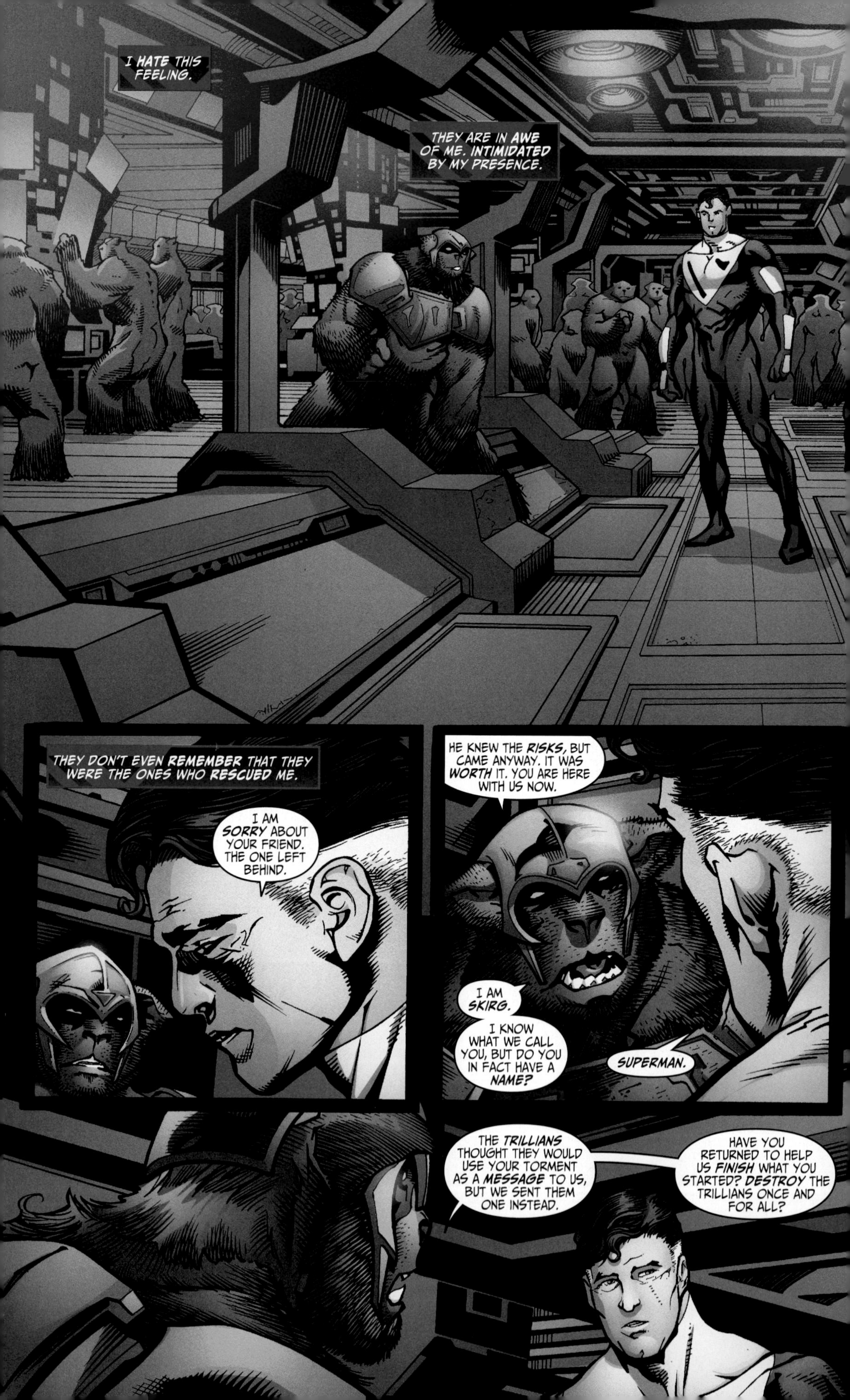
I HATE THIS FEELING.
THEY ARE IN AWE OF ME. INTIMIDATED BY MY PRESENCE.
THEY DON'T EVEN REMEMBER THAT THEY WERE THE ONES WHO RESCUED ME.
I AM SORRY ABOUT YOUR FRIEND. THE ONE LEFT BEHIND.
HE KNEW THE RISKS, BUT CAME ANYWAY. IT WAS WORTH IT. YOU ARE HERE WITH US NOW.
I AM SKIRG.
I KNOW WHAT WE CALL YOU, BUT DO YOU IN FACT HAVE A NAME?
SUPERMAN.
THE TRILLIANS THOUGHT THEY WOULD USE YOUR TORMENT AS A MESSAGE TO US, BUT WE SENT THEM ONE INSTEAD.
HAVE YOU RETURNED TO HELP US FINISH WHAT YOU STARTED? DESTROY THE TRILLIANS ONCE AND FOR ALL?

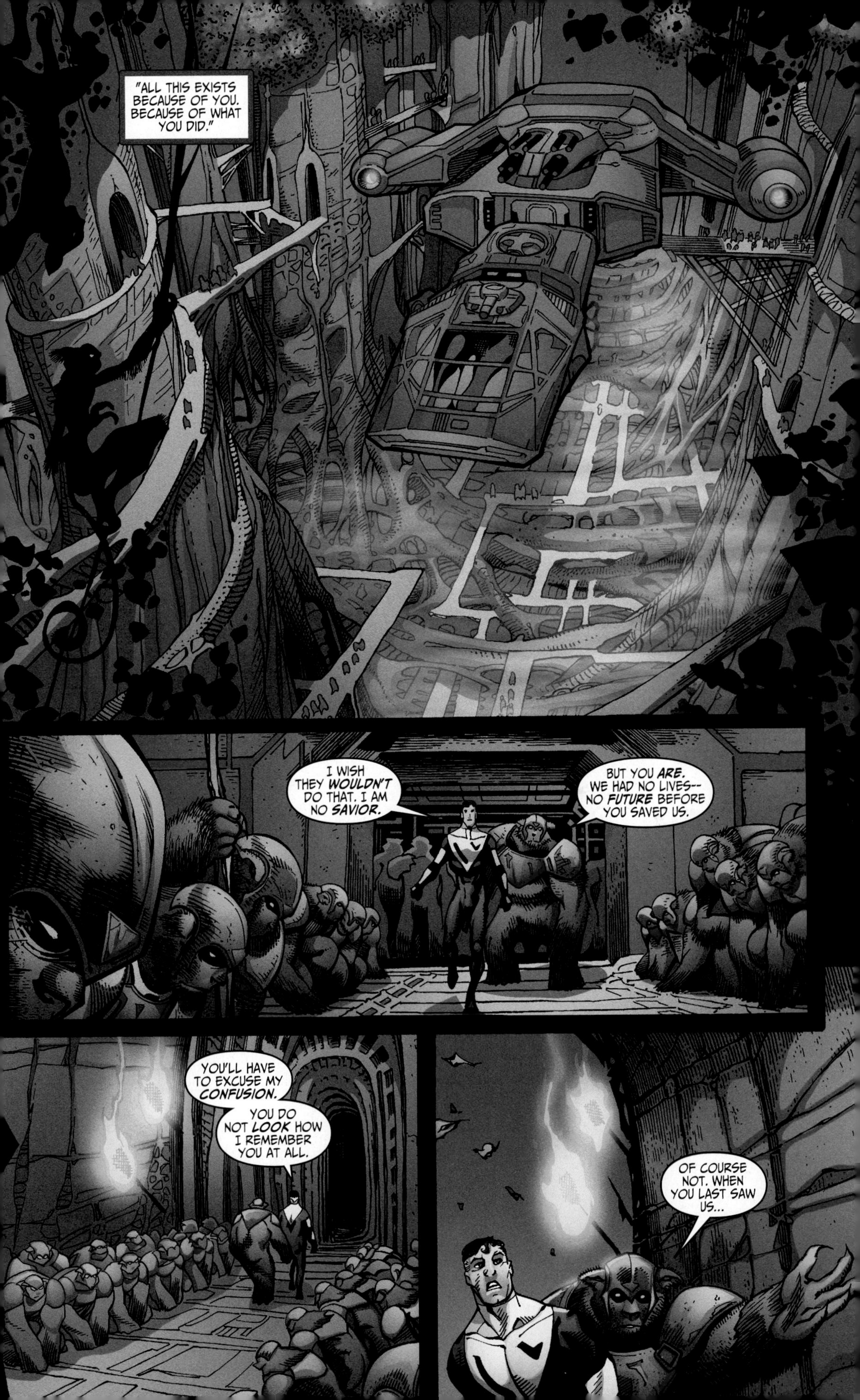
"ALL THIS EXISTS BECAUSE OF YOU. BECAUSE OF WHAT YOU DID."
I WISH THEY WOULDN'T DO THAT. I AM NO SAVIOR.
BUT YOU ARE. WE HAD NO LIVES-- NO FUTURE BEFORE YOU SAVED US.
YOU'LL HAVE TO EXCUSE MY CONFUSION.
YOU DO NOT LOOK HOW I REMEMBER YOU AT ALL.
OF COURSE NOT. WHEN YOU LAST SAW US...

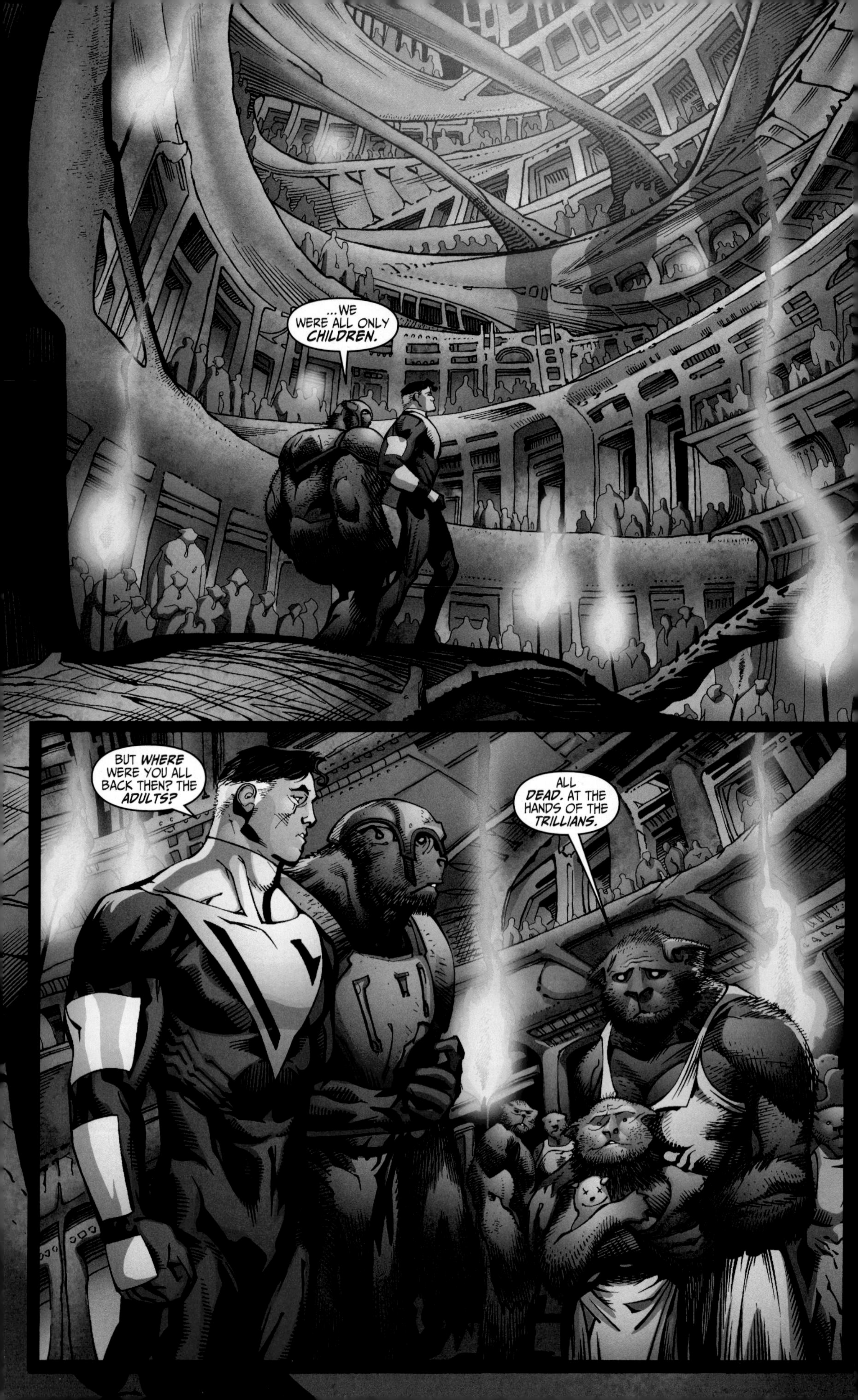
...WE WERE ALL ONLY CHILDREN.
BUT WHERE WERE YOU ALL BACK THEN? THE ADULTS?
ALL DEAD. AT THE HANDS OF THE TRILLIANS.

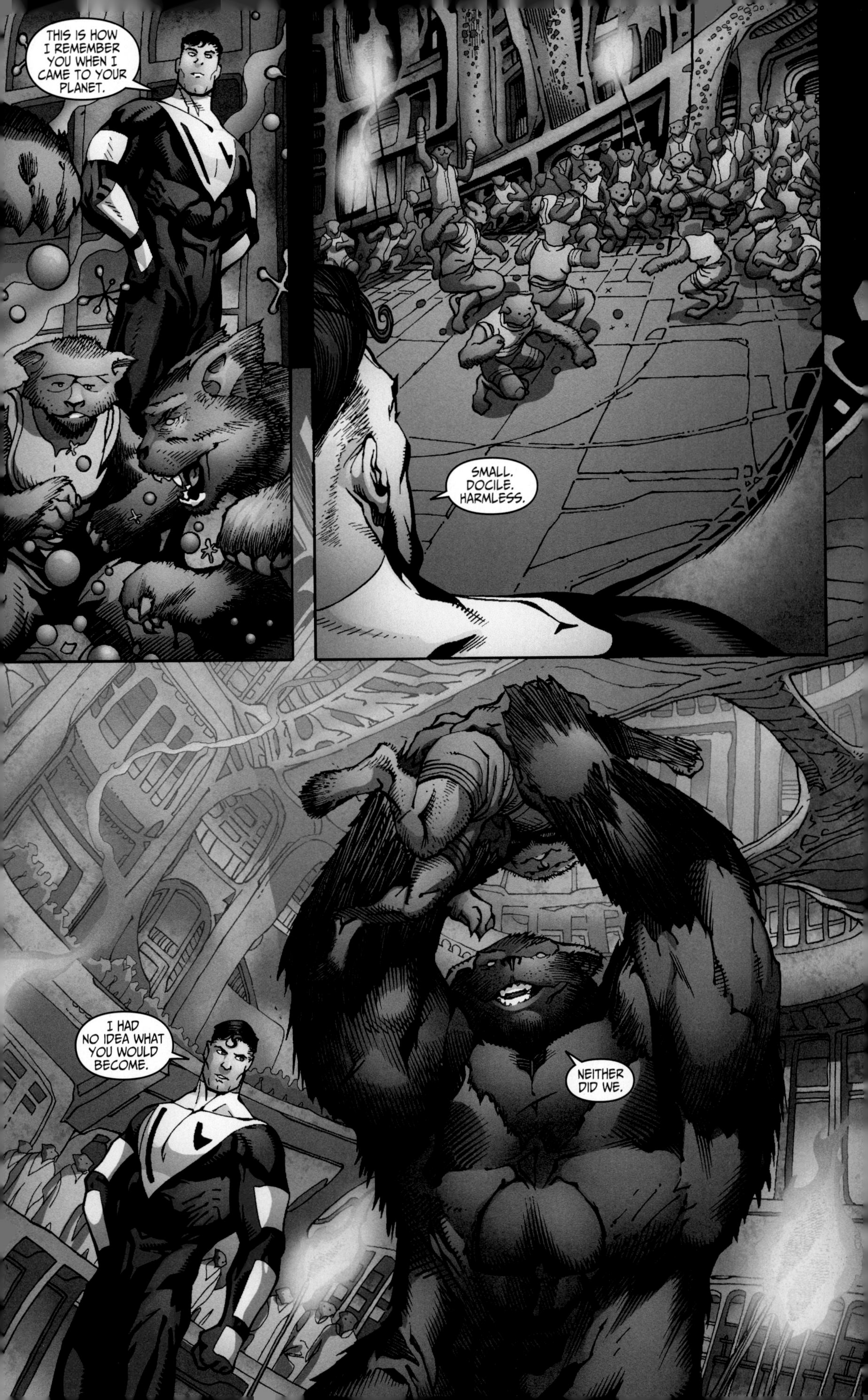
THIS IS HOW I REMEMBER YOU WHEN I CAME TO YOUR PLANET.
SMALL. DOCILE. HARMLESS.
I HAD NO IDEA WHAT YOU WOULD BECOME.
NEITHER DID WE.

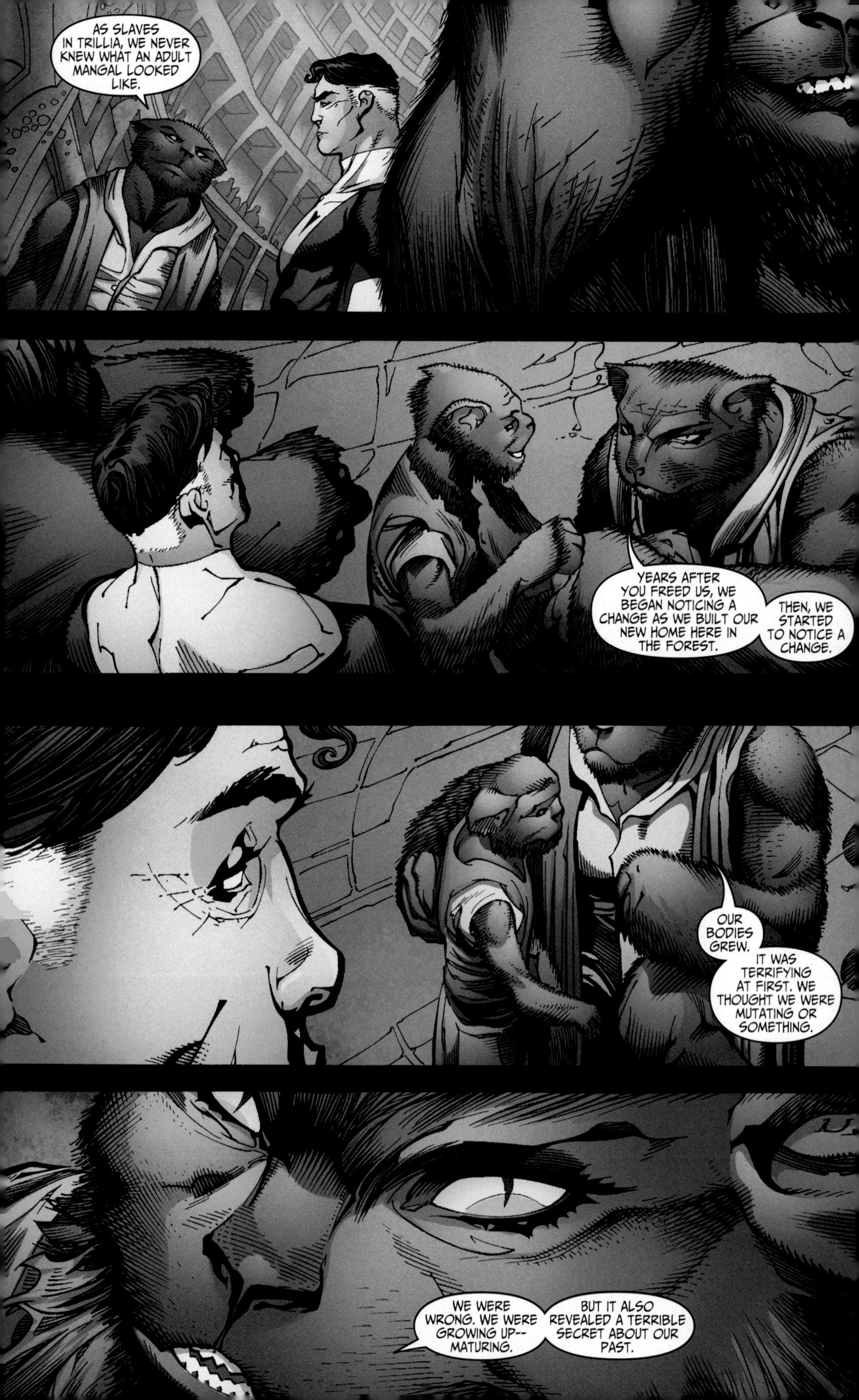
AS SLAVES IN TRILLIA, WE NEVER KNEW WHAT AN ADULT MANGAL LOOKED LIKE.
YEARS AFTER YOU FREED US, WE BEGAN NOTICING A CHANGE AS WE BUILT OUR NEW HOME HERE IN THE FOREST.
THEN, WE STARTED TO NOTICE A CHANGE.
OUR BODIES GREW.
IT WAS TERRIFYING AT FIRST. WE THOUGHT WE WERE MUTATING OR SOMETHING.
WE WERE WRONG. WE WERE GROWING UP-- MATURING.
BUT IT ALSO REVEALED A TERRIBLE SECRET ABOUT OUR PAST.

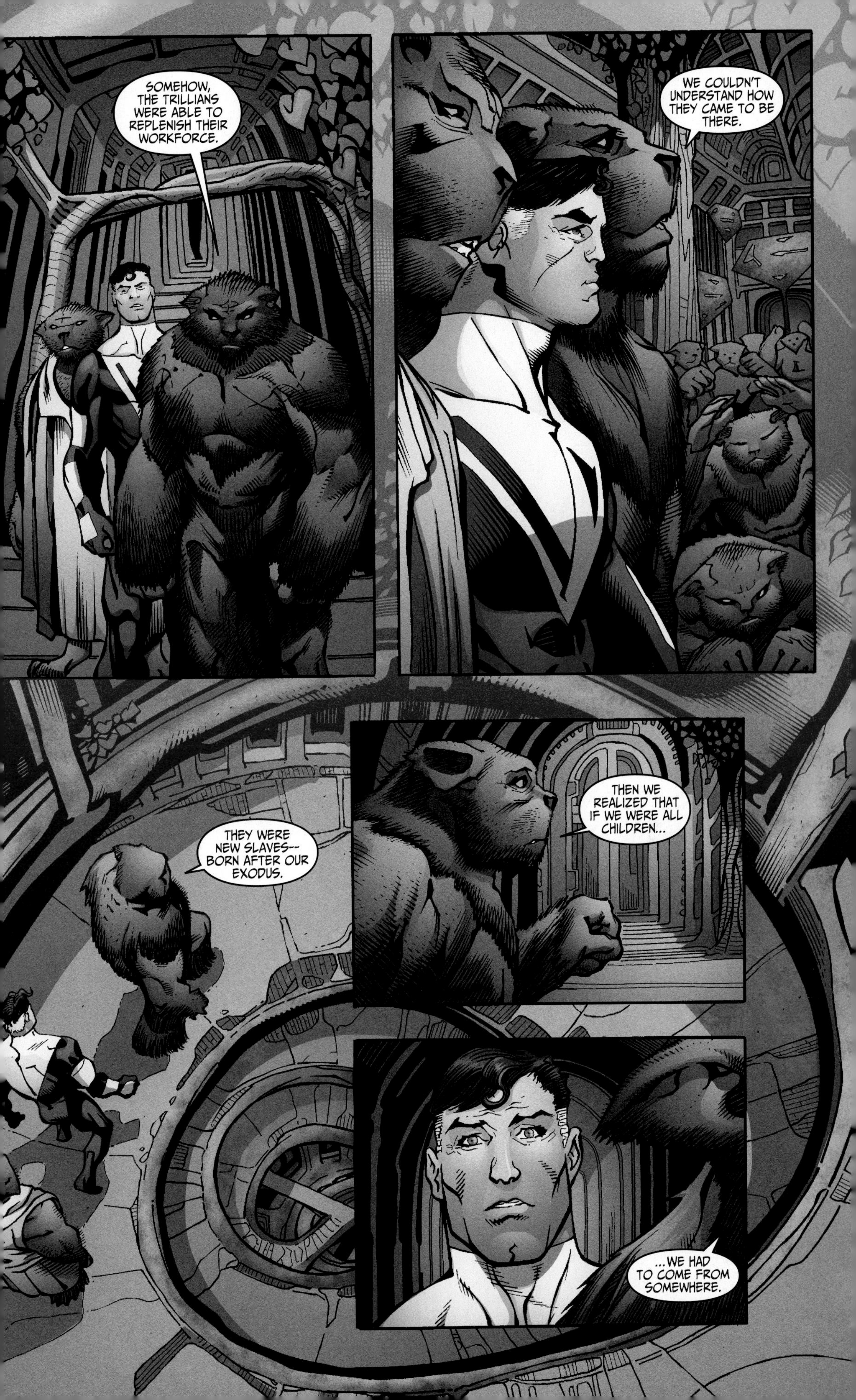
SOMEHOW, THE TRILLIANS WERE ABLE TO REPLENISH THEIR WORKFORCE.
WE COULDN'T UNDERSTAND HOW THEY CAME TO BE THERE.
THEY WERE NEW SLAVES-- BORN AFTER OUR EXODUS.
THEN WE REALIZED THAT IF WE WERE ALL CHILDREN...
...WE HAD TO COME FROM SOMEWHERE.

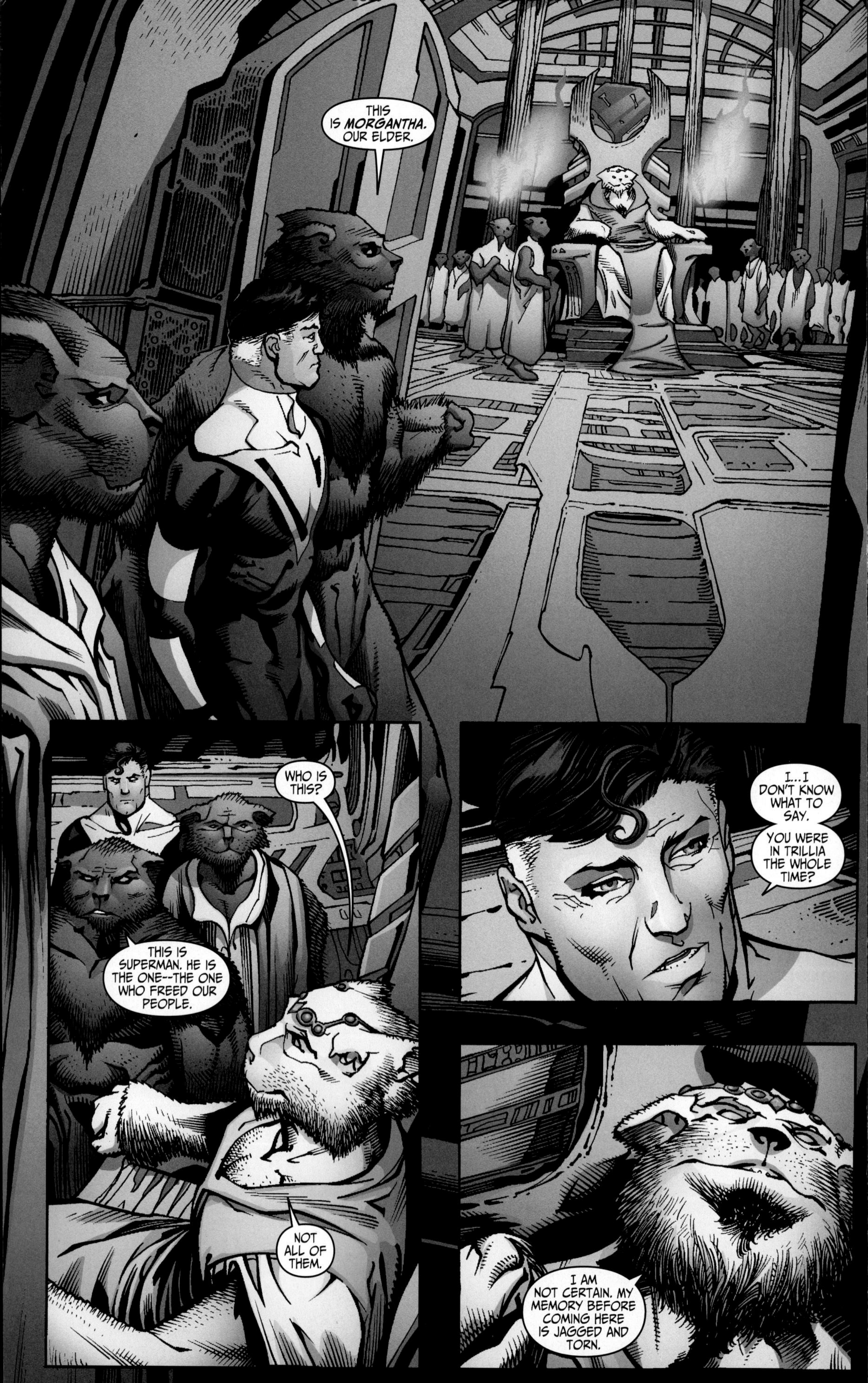
THIS IS MORGANTHA. OUR ELDER.
WHO IS THIS?
THIS IS SUPERMAN. HE IS THE ONE--THE ONE WHO FREED OUR PEOPLE.
NOT ALL OF THEM.
I...I DON'T KNOW WHAT TO SAY.
YOU WERE IN TRILLIA THE WHOLE TIME?
I AM NOT CERTAIN. MY MEMORY BEFORE COMING HERE IS JAGGED AND TORN.

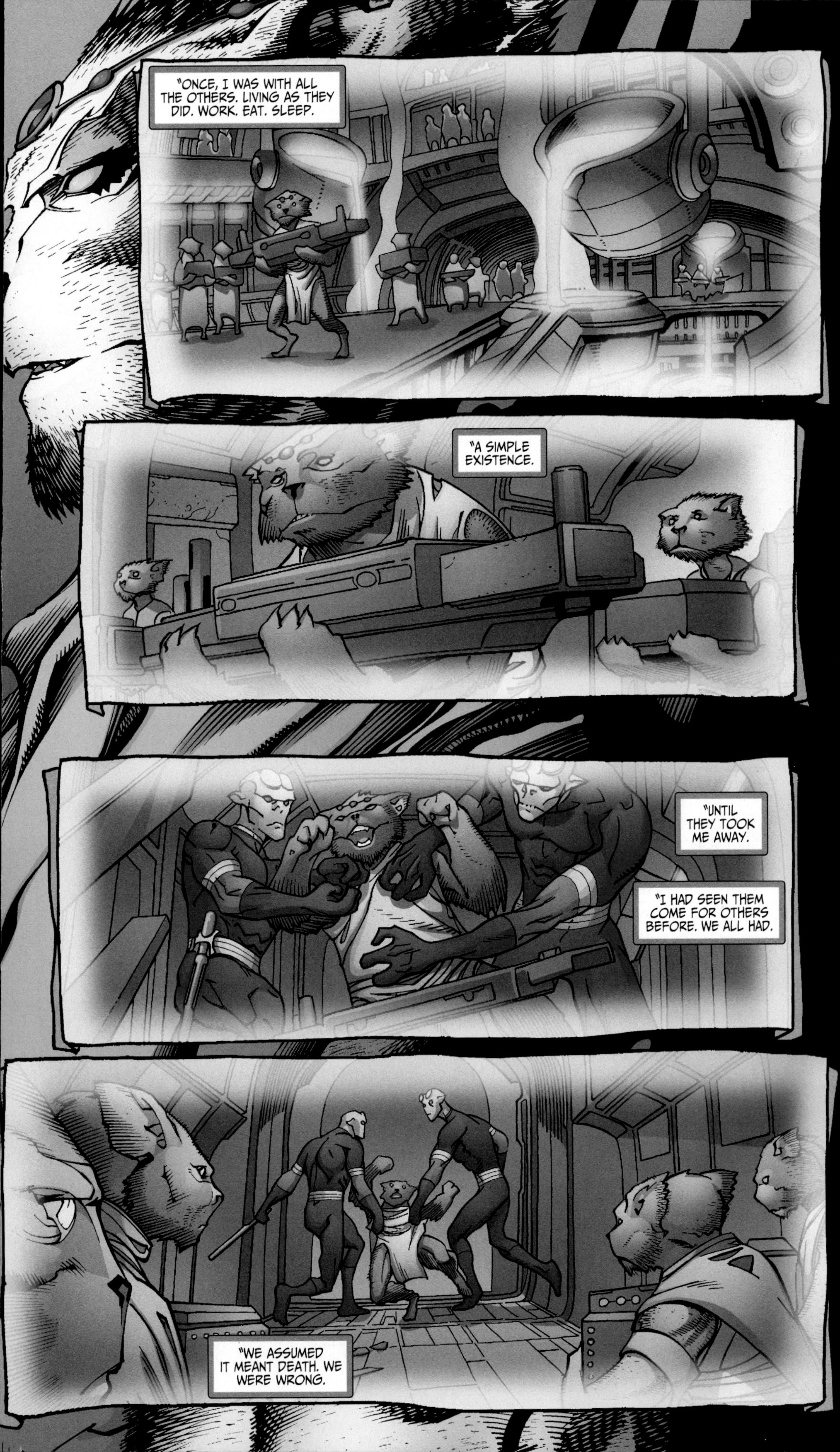
"ONCE, I WAS WITH ALL THE OTHERS. LIVING AS THEY DID. WORK. EAT. SLEEP.
"A SIMPLE EXISTENCE.
"UNTIL THEY TOOK ME AWAY.
"I HAD SEEN THEM COME FOR OTHERS BEFORE. WE ALL HAD.
"WE ASSUMED IT MEANT DEATH. WE WERE WRONG.

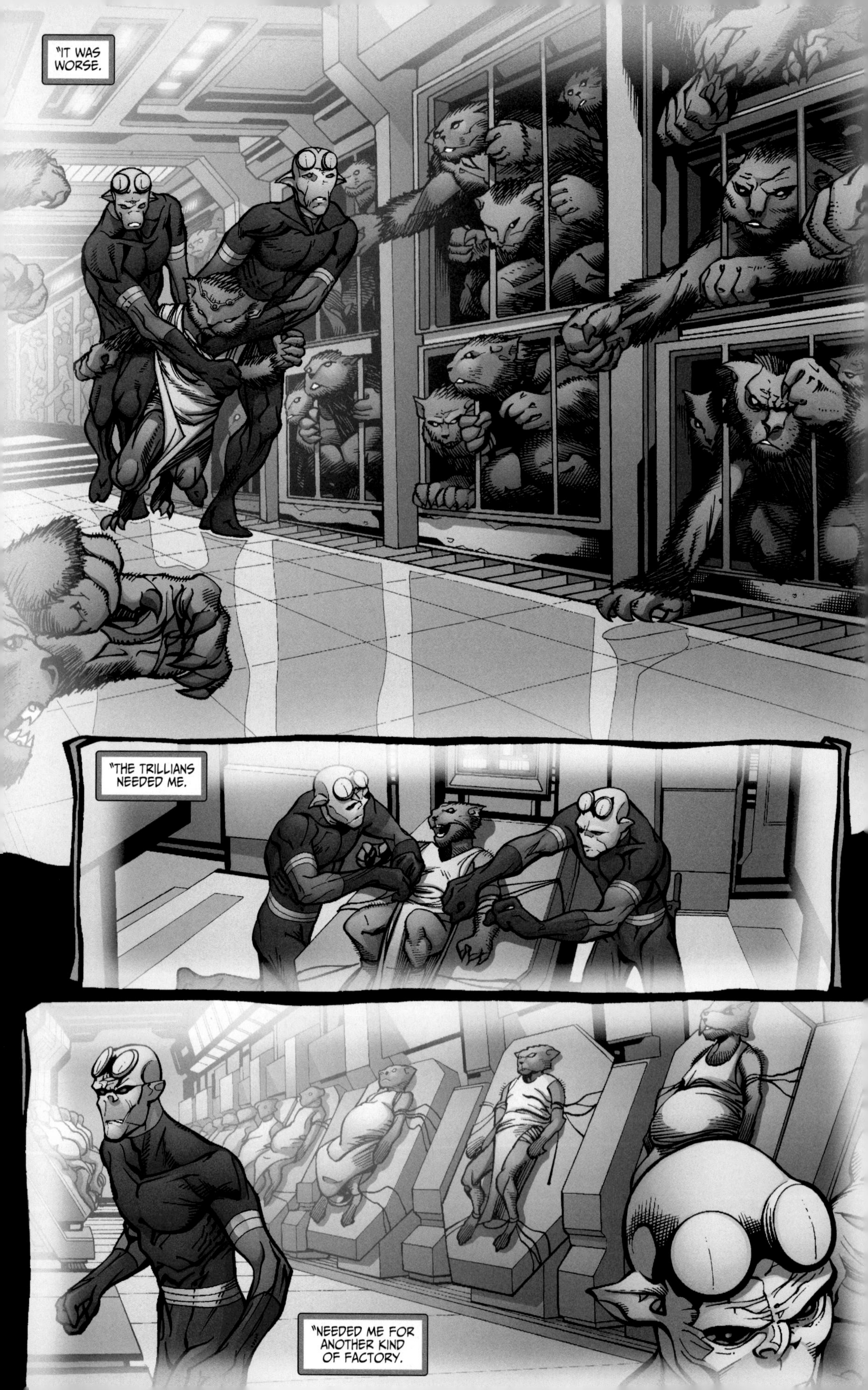
"IT WAS WORSE.
"THE TRILLIANS NEEDED ME.
"NEEDED ME FOR ANOTHER KIND OF FACTORY.

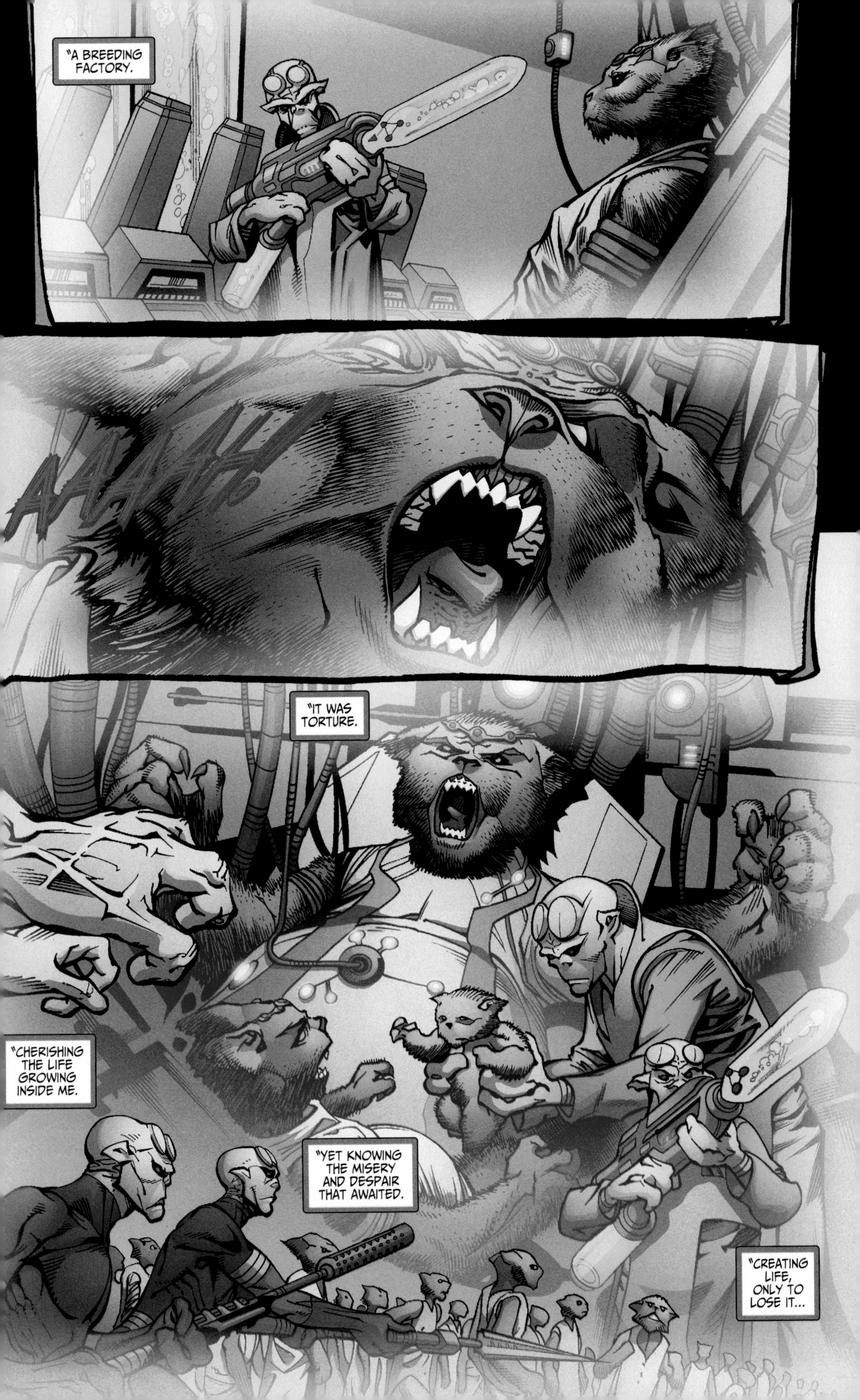
"A BREEDING FACTORY.
AAAAH!
"IT WAS TORTURE.
"CHERISHING THE LIFE GROWING INSIDE ME.
"YET KNOWING THE MISERY AND DESPAIR THAT AWAITED.
"CREATING LIFE, ONLY TO LOSE IT...

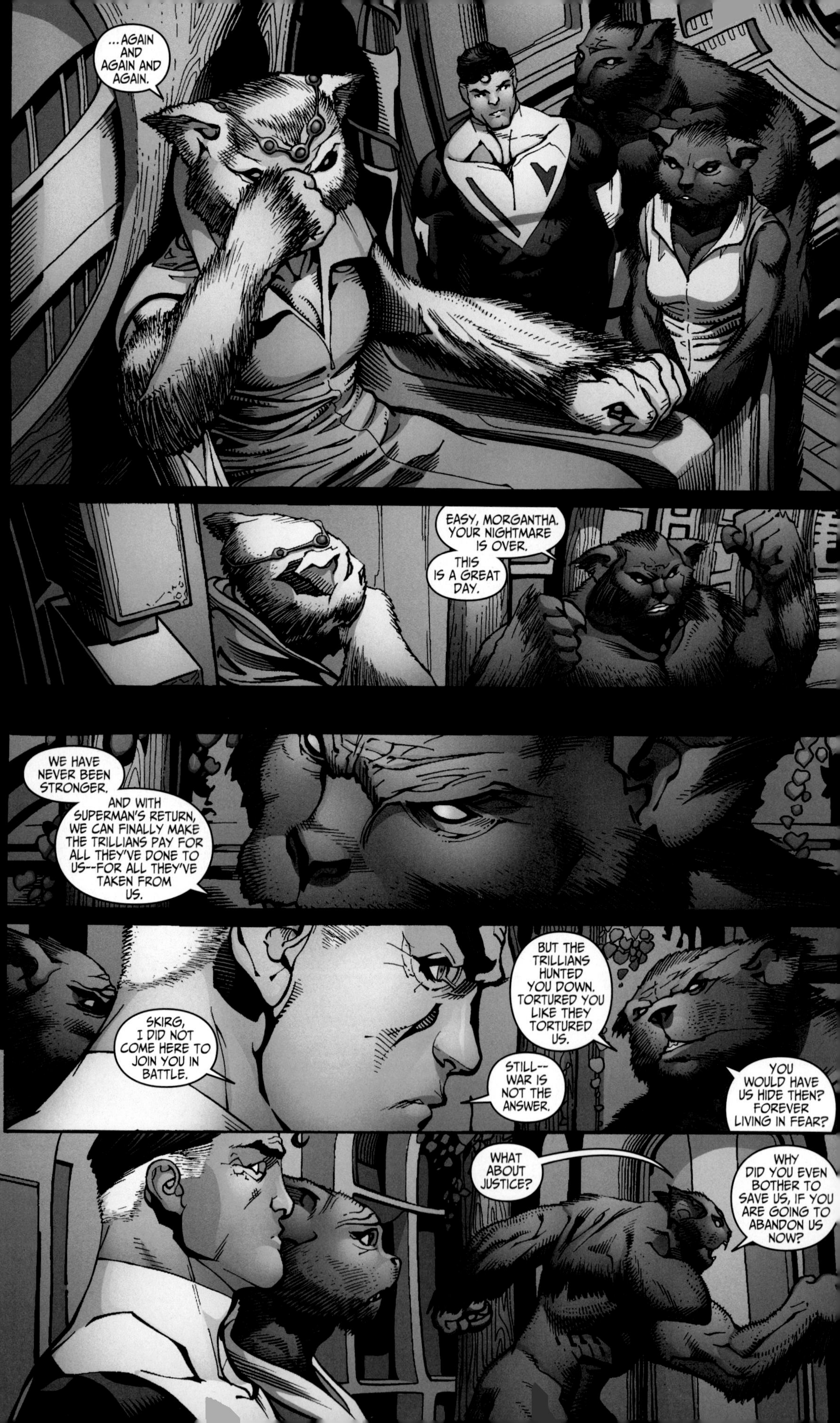
...AGAIN AND AGAIN AND AGAIN.
EASY, MORGANTHA. YOUR NIGHTMARE IS OVER.
THIS IS A GREAT DAY.
WE HAVE NEVER BEEN STRONGER.
AND WITH SUPERMAN'S RETURN, WE CAN FINALLY MAKE THE TRILLIANS PAY FOR ALL THEY'VE DONE TO US--FOR ALL THEY'VE TAKEN FROM US.
SKIRG, I DID NOT COME HERE TO JOIN YOU IN BATTLE.
BUT THE TRILLIANS HUNTED YOU DOWN. TORTURED YOU LIKE THEY TORTURED US.
STILL-- WAR IS NOT THE ANSWER.
YOU WOULD HAVE US HIDE THEN? FOREVER LIVING IN FEAR?
WHAT ABOUT JUSTICE?
WHY DID YOU EVEN BOTHER TO SAVE US, IF YOU ARE GOING TO ABANDON US NOW?

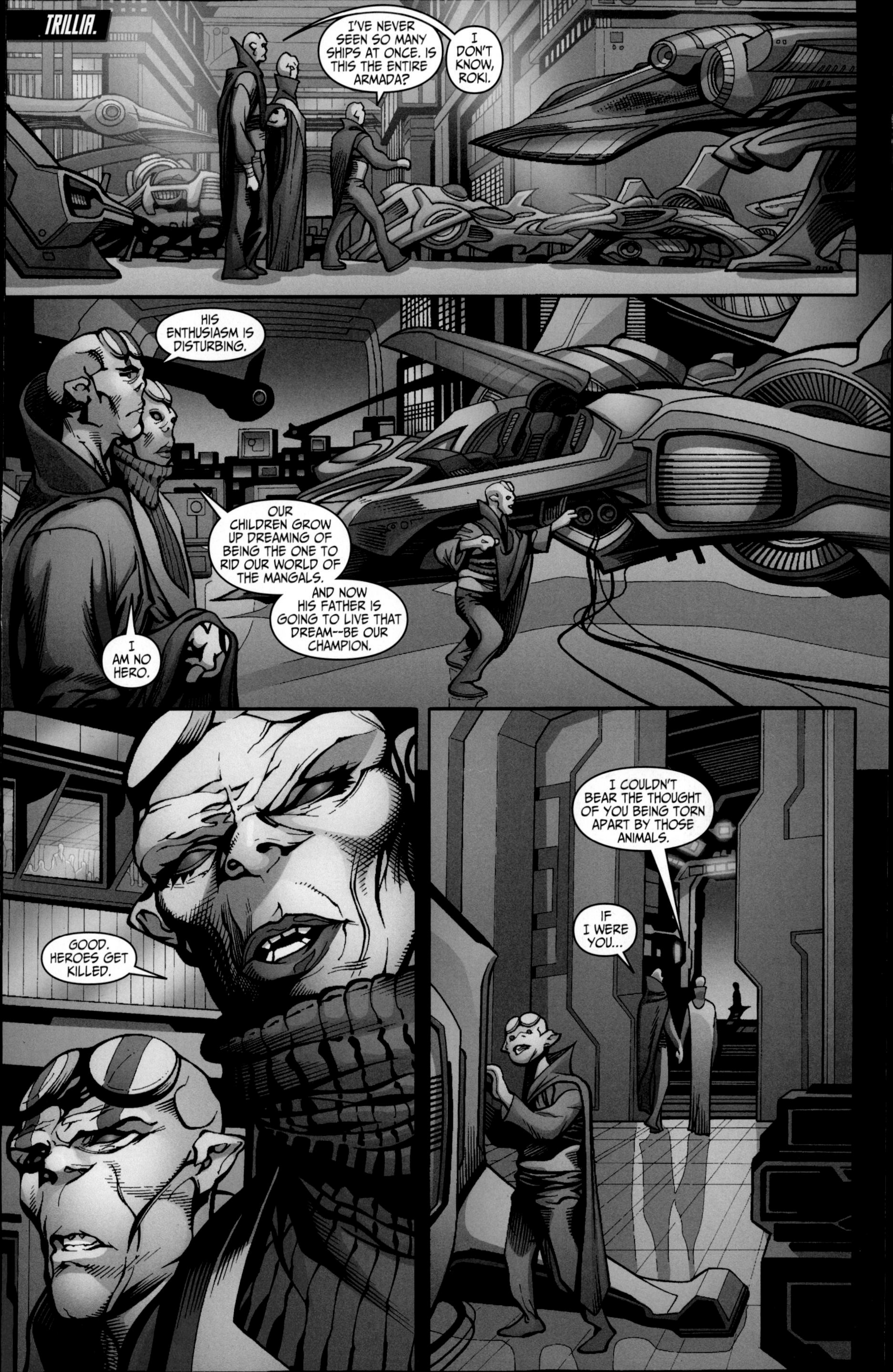
TRILLIA.
I'VE NEVER SEEN SO MANY SHIPS AT ONCE. IS THIS THE ENTIRE ARMADA?
I DON'T KNOW, ROKI.
HIS ENTHUSIASM IS DISTURBING.
OUR CHILDREN GROW UP DREAMING OF BEING THE ONE TO RID OUR WORLD OF THE MANGALS.
AND NOW HIS FATHER IS GOING TO LIVE THAT DREAM--BE OUR CHAMPION.
I AM NO HERO.
GOOD. HEROES GET KILLED.
I COULDN'T BEAR THE THOUGHT OF YOU BEING TORN APART BY THOSE ANIMALS.
IF I WERE YOU...

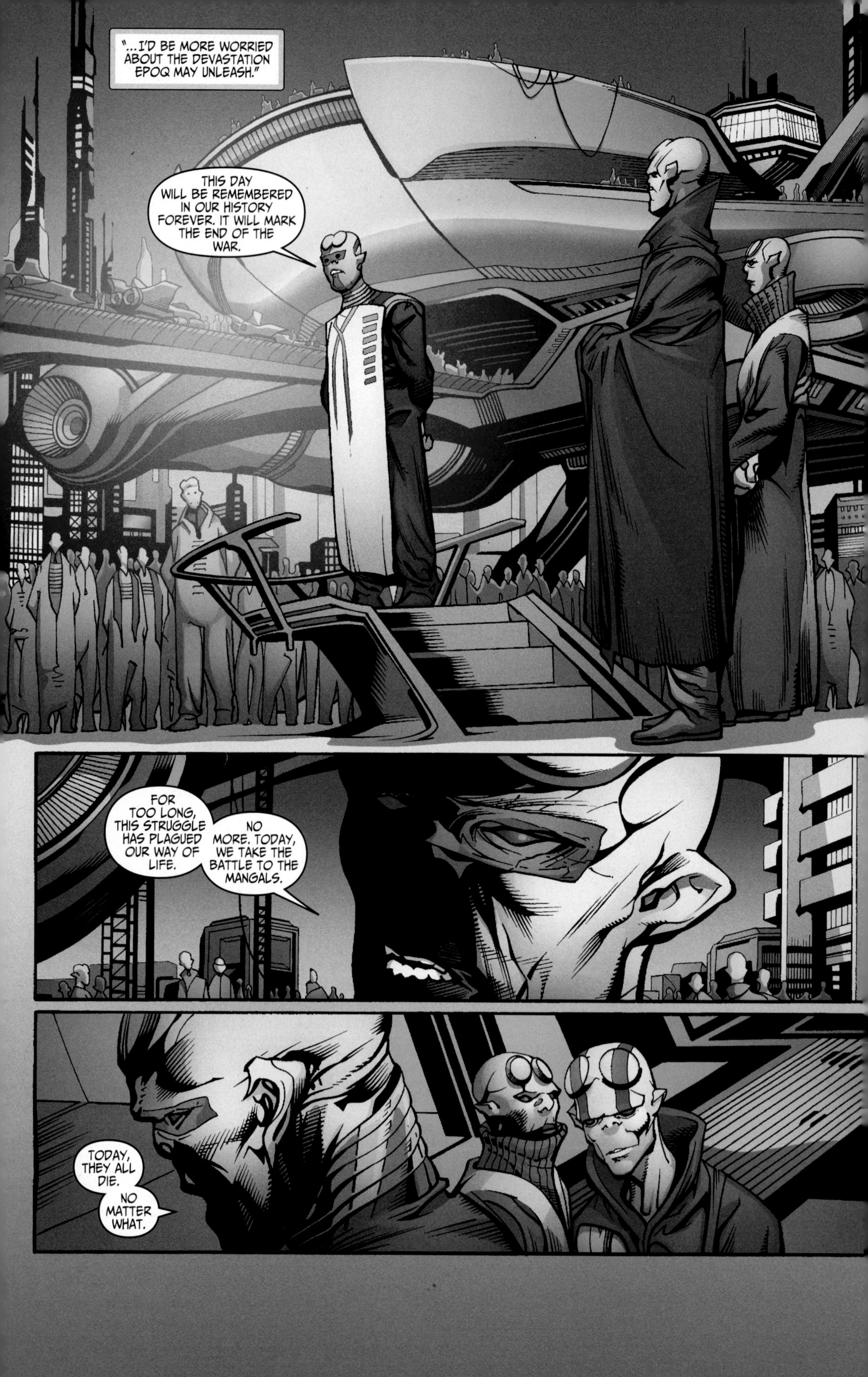
"...I'D BE MORE WORRIED ABOUT THE DEVASTATION EPOQ MAY UNLEASH."
THIS DAY WILL BE REMEMBERED IN OUR HISTORY FOREVER. IT WILL MARK THE END OF THE WAR.
FOR TOO LONG, THIS STRUGGLE HAS PLAGUED OUR WAY OF LIFE.
NO MORE. TODAY, WE TAKE THE BATTLE TO THE MANGALS.
TODAY, THEY ALL DIE.
NO MATTER WHAT.

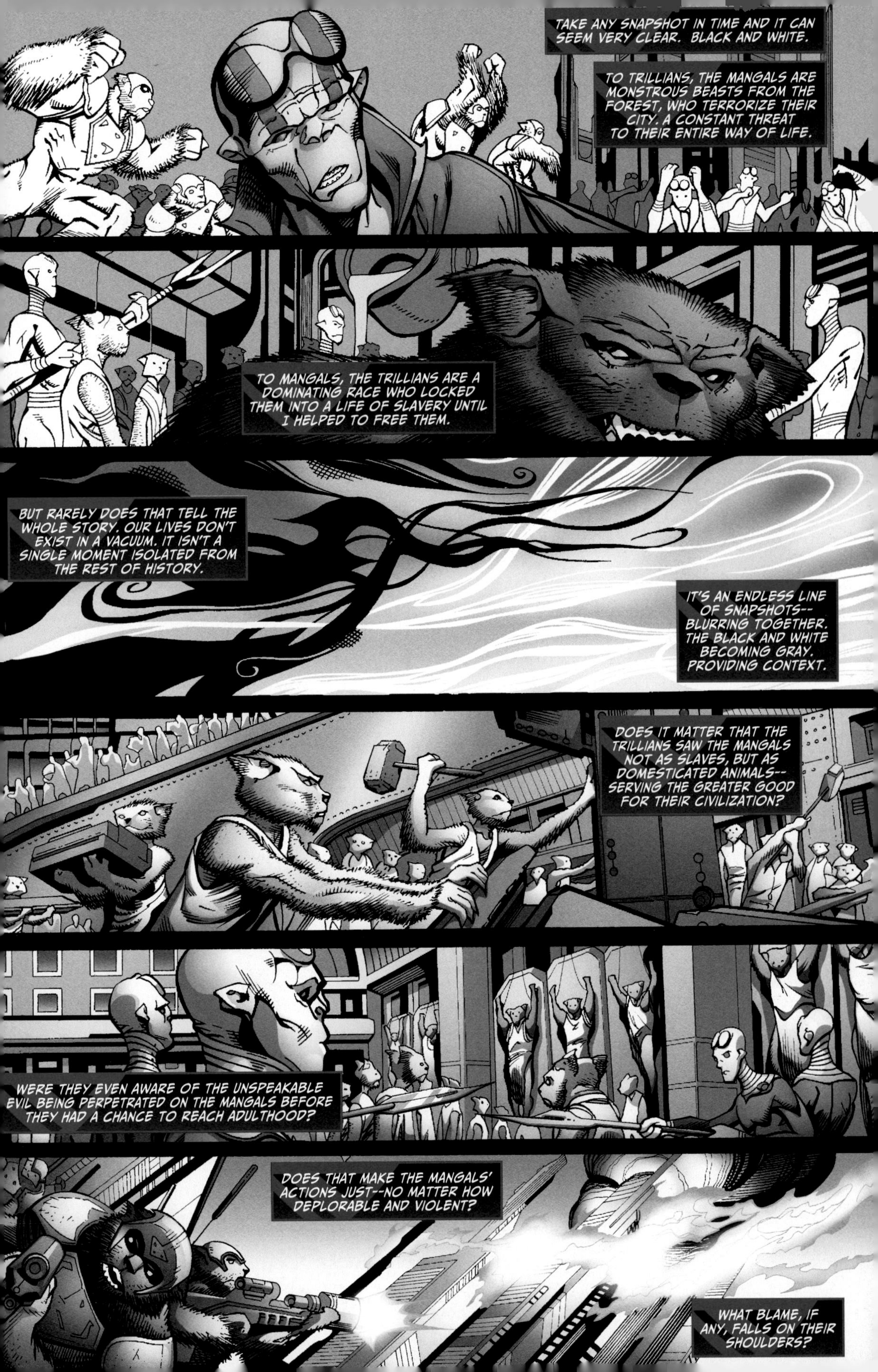

TAKE ANY SNAPSHOT IN TIME AND IT CAN SEEM VERY CLEAR. BLACK AND WHITE.
TO TRILLIANS, THE MANGALS ARE MONSTROUS BEASTS FROM THE FOREST, WHO TERRORIZE THEIR CITY. A CONSTANT THREAT TO THEIR ENTIRE WAY OF LIFE.
TO MANGALS, THE TRILLIANS ARE A DOMINATING RACE WHO LOCKED THEM INTO A LIFE OF SLAVERY UNTIL I HELPED TO FREE THEM.
BUT RARELY DOES THAT TELL THE WHOLE STORY. OUR LIVES DON'T EXIST IN A VACUUM. IT ISN'T A SINGLE MOMENT ISOLATED FROM THE REST OF HISTORY.
IT'S AN ENDLESS LINE OF SNAPSHOTS-- BLURRING TOGETHER. THE BLACK AND WHITE BECOMING GRAY. PROVIDING CONTEXT.
DOES IT MATTER THAT THE TRILLIANS SAW THE MANGALS NOT AS SLAVES, BUT AS DOMESTICATED ANIMALS-- SERVING THE GREATER GOOD FOR THEIR CIVILIZATION?
WERE THEY EVEN AWARE OF THE UNSPEAKABLE EVIL BEING PERPETRATED ON THE MANGALS BEFORE THEY HAD A CHANCE TO REACH ADULTHOOD?
DOES THAT MAKE THE MANGALS' ACTIONS JUST--NO MATTER HOW DEPLORABLE AND VIOLENT?
WHAT BLAME, IF ANY, FALLS ON THEIR SHOULDERS?

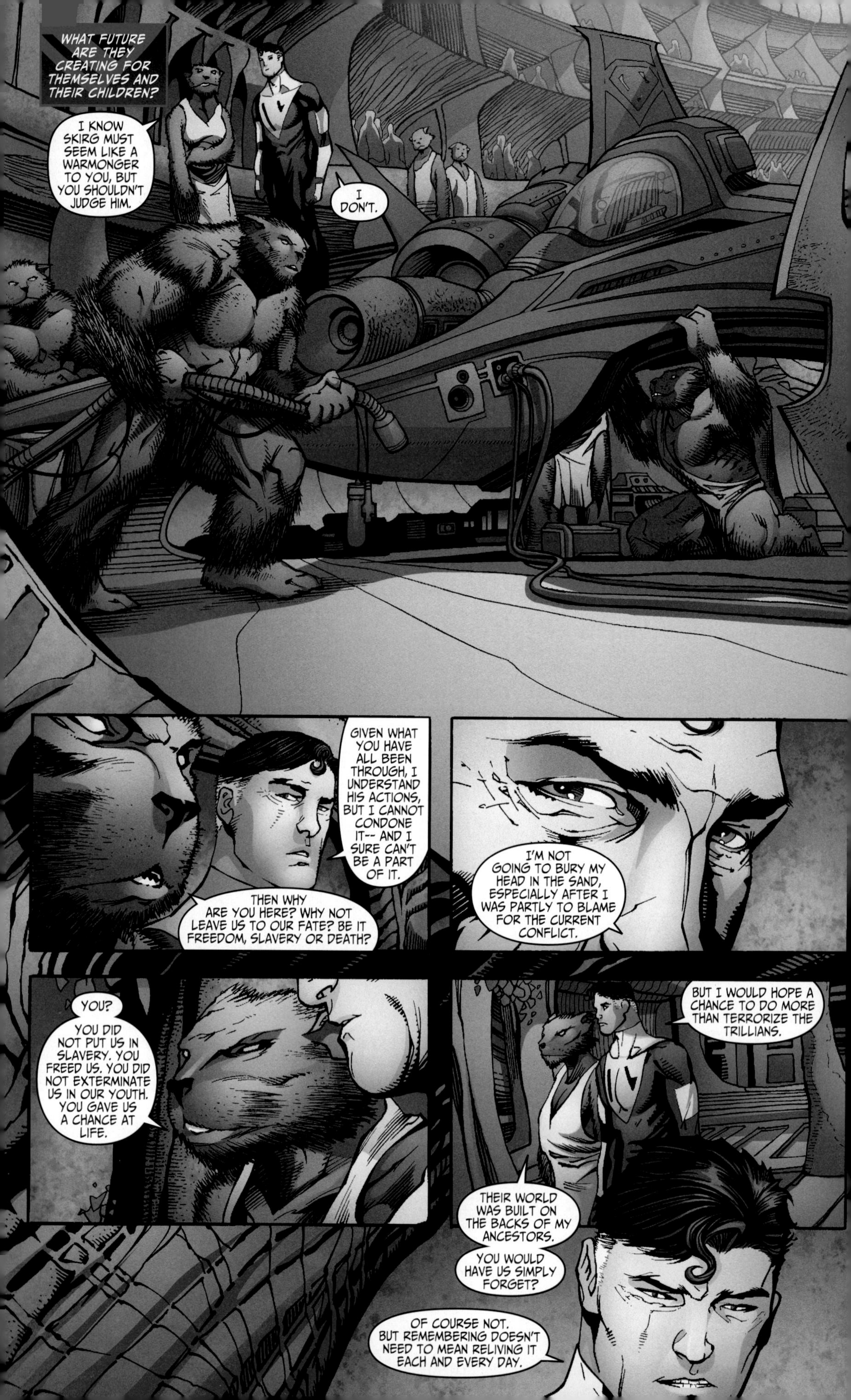
WHAT FUTURE ARE THEY CREATING FOR THEMSELVES AND THEIR CHILDREN?
I KNOW SKIRG MUST SEEM LIKE A WARMONGER TO YOU, BUT YOU SHOULDN'T JUDGE HIM.
I DON'T.
GIVEN WHAT YOU HAVE ALL BEEN THROUGH, I UNDERSTAND HIS ACTIONS, BUT I CANNOT CONDONE IT-- AND I SURE CAN'T BE A PART OF IT.
THEN WHY ARE YOU HERE? WHY NOT LEAVE US TO OUR FATE? BE IT FREEDOM, SLAVERY OR DEATH?
I'M NOT GOING TO BURY MY HEAD IN THE SAND, ESPECIALLY AFTER I WAS PARTLY TO BLAME FOR THE CURRENT CONFLICT.
YOU?
YOU DID NOT PUT US IN SLAVERY. YOU FREED US. YOU DID NOT EXTERMINATE US IN OUR YOUTH. YOU GAVE US A CHANCE AT LIFE.
BUT I WOULD HOPE A CHANCE TO DO MORE THAN TERRORIZE THE TRILLIANS.
THEIR WORLD WAS BUILT ON THE BACKS OF MY ANCESTORS.
YOU WOULD HAVE US SIMPLY FORGET?
OF COURSE NOT. BUT REMEMBERING DOESN'T NEED TO MEAN RELIVING IT EACH AND EVERY DAY.

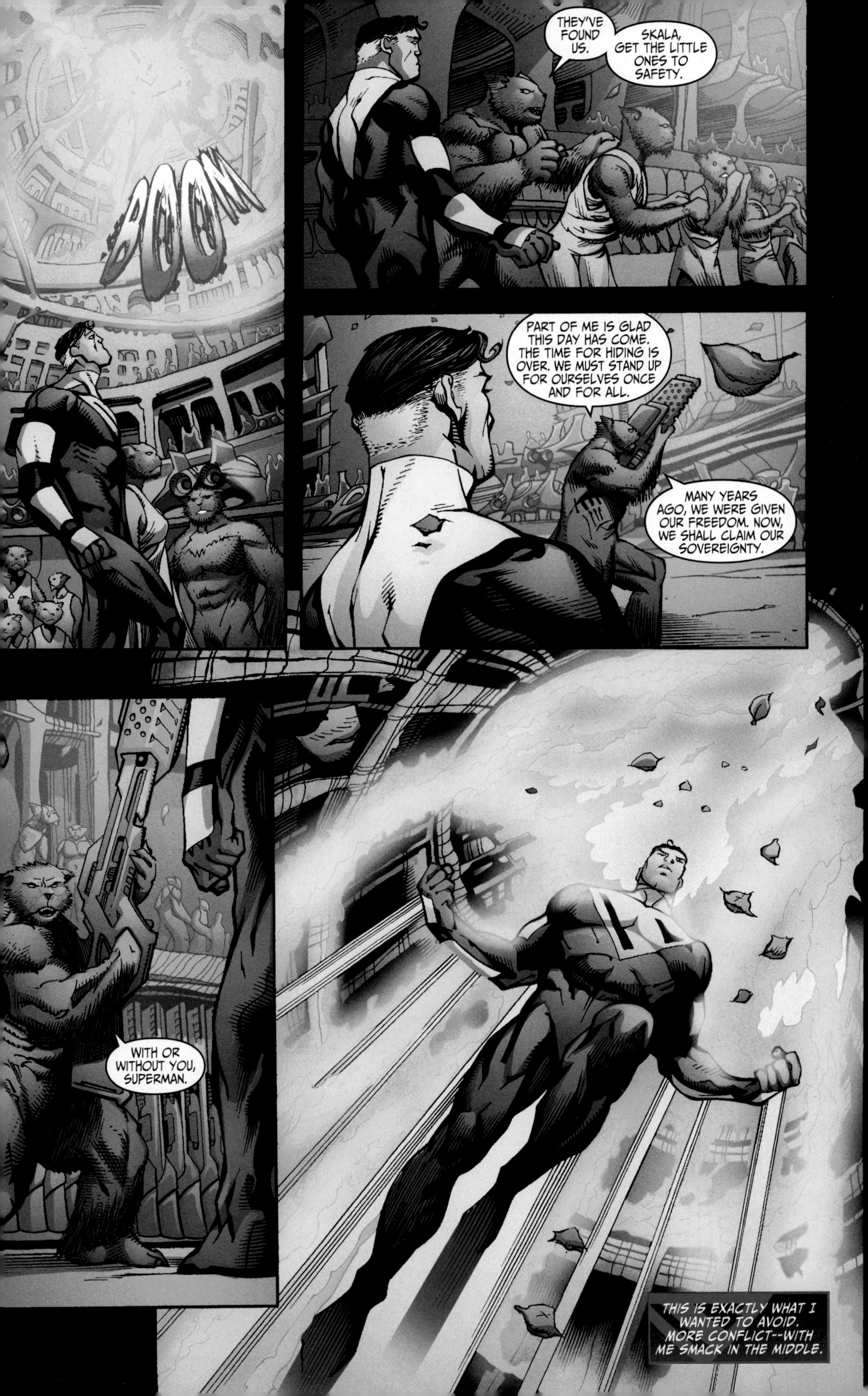
BOOM
THEY'VE FOUND US.
SKALA, GET THE LITTLE ONES TO SAFETY.
PART OF ME IS GLAD THIS DAY HAS COME. THE TIME FOR HIDING IS OVER. WE MUST STAND UP FOR OURSELVES ONCE AND FOR ALL.
MANY YEARS AGO, WE WERE GIVEN OUR FREEDOM. NOW, WE SHALL CLAIM OUR SOVEREIGNTY.
WITH OR WITHOUT YOU, SUPERMAN.
THIS IS EXACTLY WHAT I WANTED TO AVOID. MORE CONFLICT--WITH ME SMACK IN THE MIDDLE.

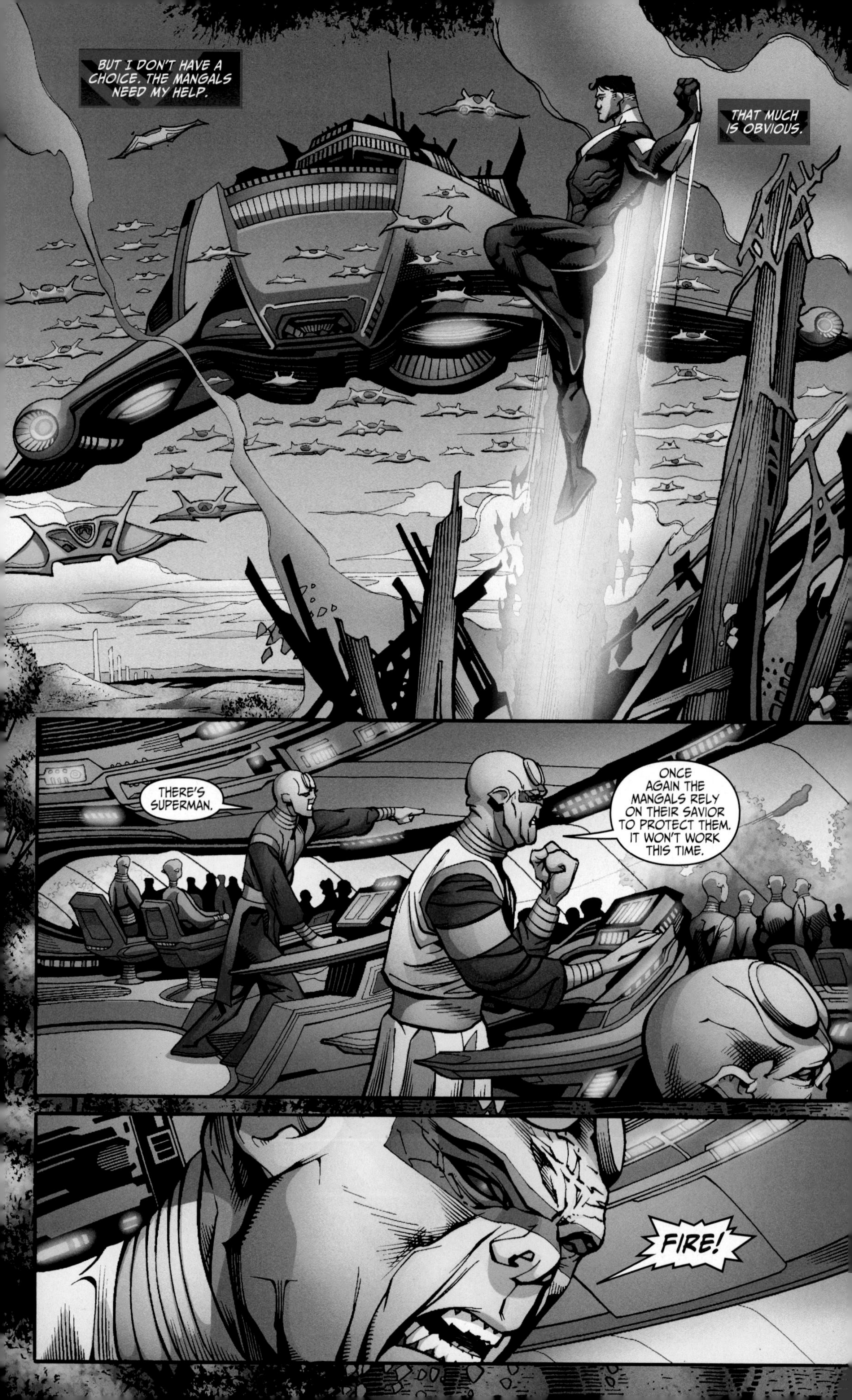
BUT I DON'T HAVE A CHOICE. THE MANGALS NEED MY HELP.
THAT MUCH IS OBVIOUS.
THERE'S SUPERMAN.
ONCE AGAIN THE MANGALS RELY ON THEIR SAVIOR TO PROTECT THEM. IT WON'T WORK THIS TIME.
FIRE!

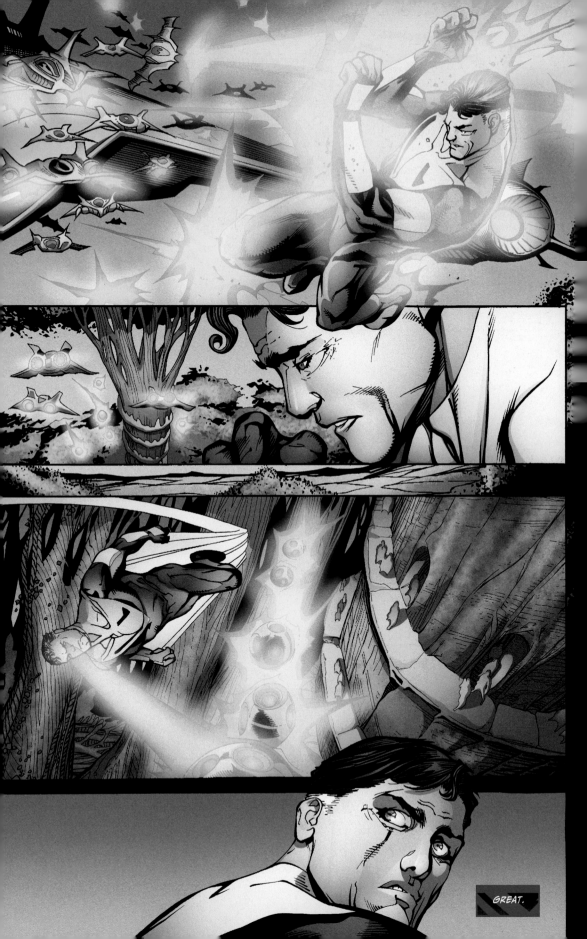

GREAT.

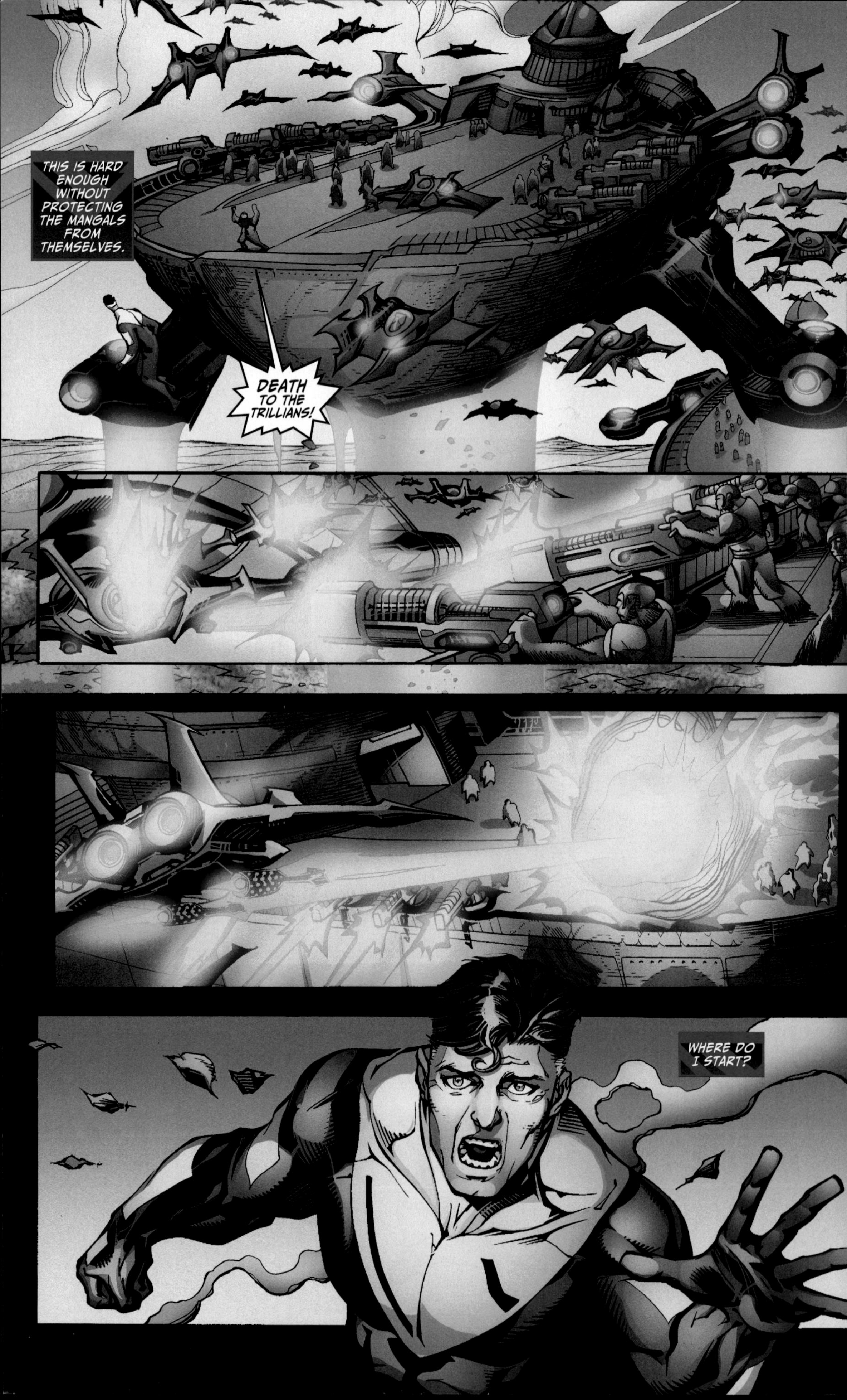
THIS IS HARD ENOUGH WITHOUT PROTECTING THE MANGALS FROM THEMSELVES.
DEATH TO THE TRILLIANS!
WHERE DO I START?

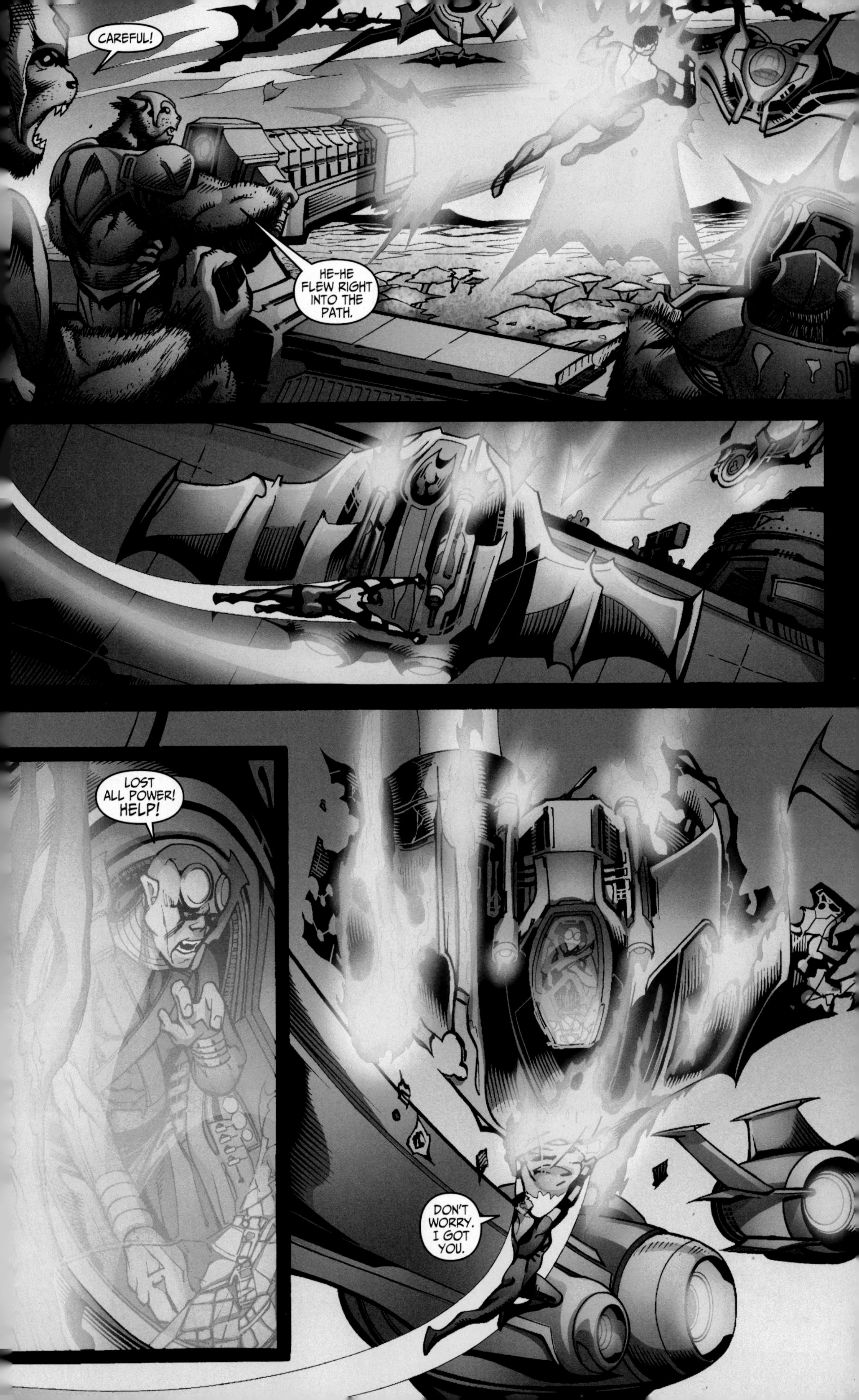
CAREFUL!
HE-HE FLEW RIGHT INTO THE PATH.
LOST ALL POWER! HELP!
DON'T WORRY. I GOT YOU.

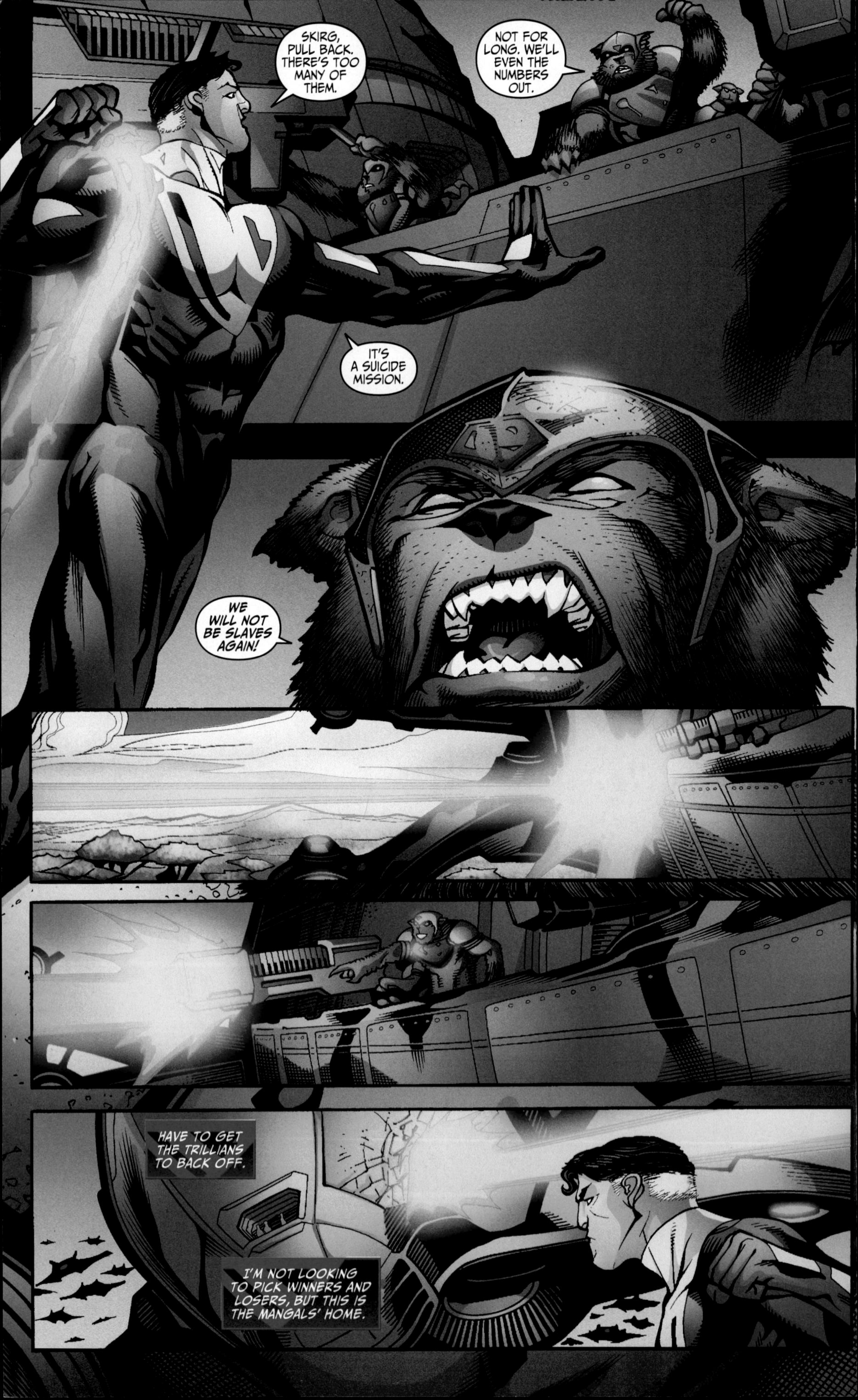
SKIRG, PULL BACK. THERE'S TOO MANY OF THEM.
NOT FOR LONG. WE'LL EVEN THE NUMBERS OUT.
IT'S A SUICIDE MISSION.
WE WILL NOT BE SLAVES AGAIN!
HAVE TO GET THE TRILLIANS TO BACK OFF.
I'M NOT LOOKING TO PICK WINNERS AND LOSERS, BUT THIS IS THE MANGALS' HOME.

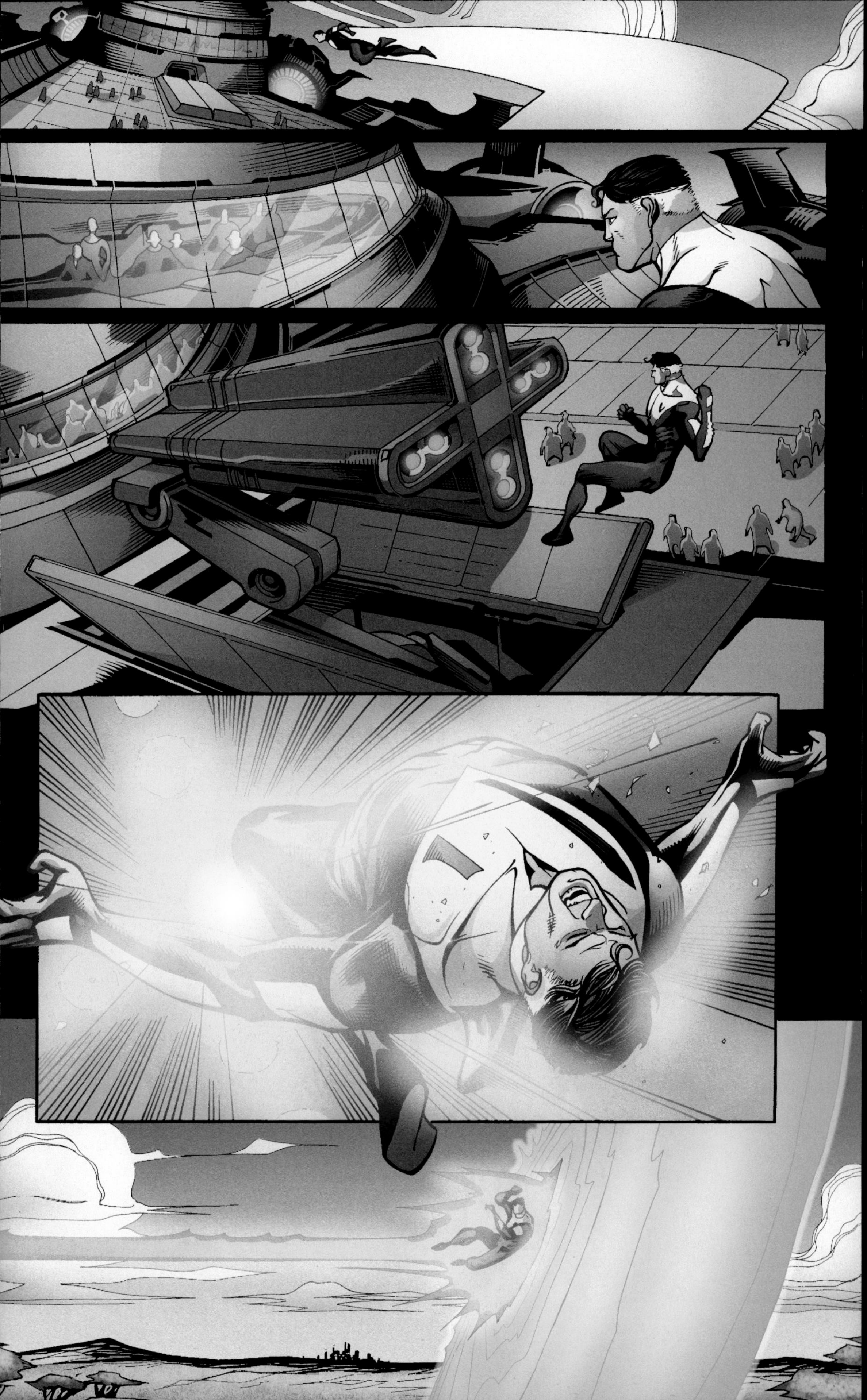

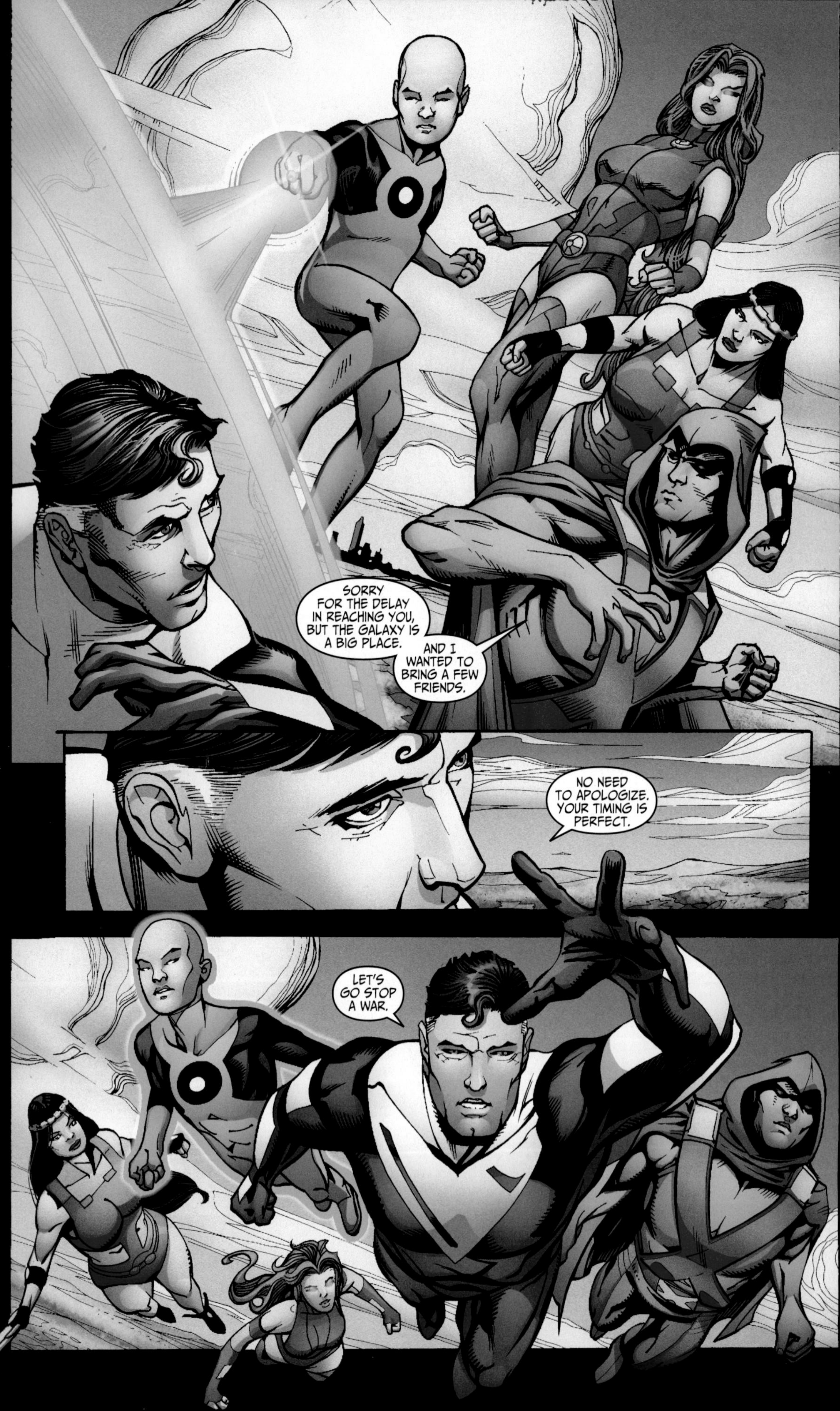
SORRY FOR THE DELAY IN REACHING YOU, BUT THE GALAXY IS A BIG PLACE.
AND I WANTED TO BRING A FEW FRIENDS.
NO NEED TO APOLOGIZE. YOUR TIMING IS PERFECT.
LET'S GO STOP A WAR.

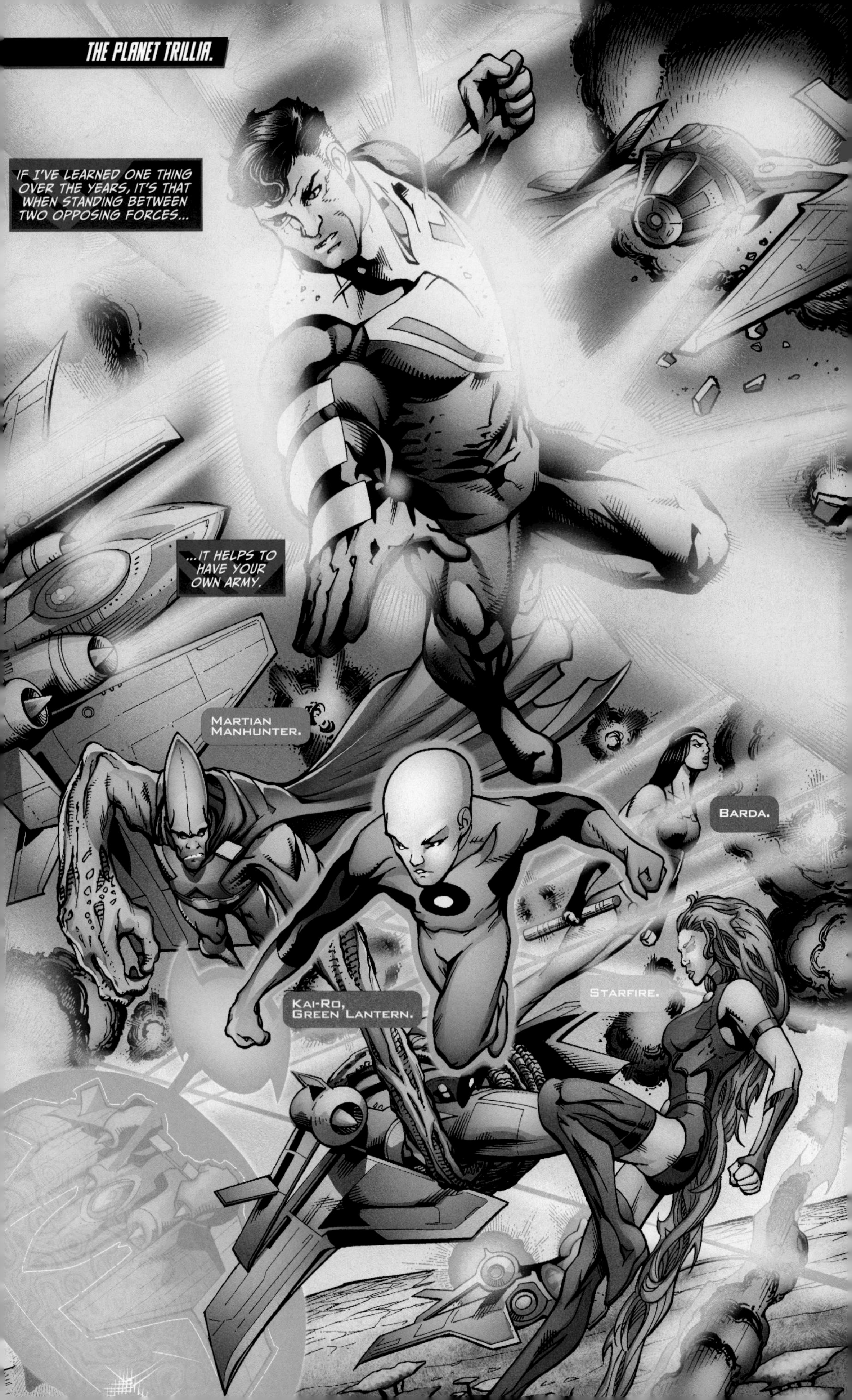
THE PLANET TRILLIA.
IF I'VE LEARNED ONE THING OVER THE YEARS, IT'S THAT WHEN STANDING BETWEEN TWO OPPOSING FORCES...
...IT HELPS TO HAVE YOUR OWN ARMY.
MARTIAN MANHUNTER.
BARDA.
KAI-RO, GREEN LANTERN.
STARFIRE.

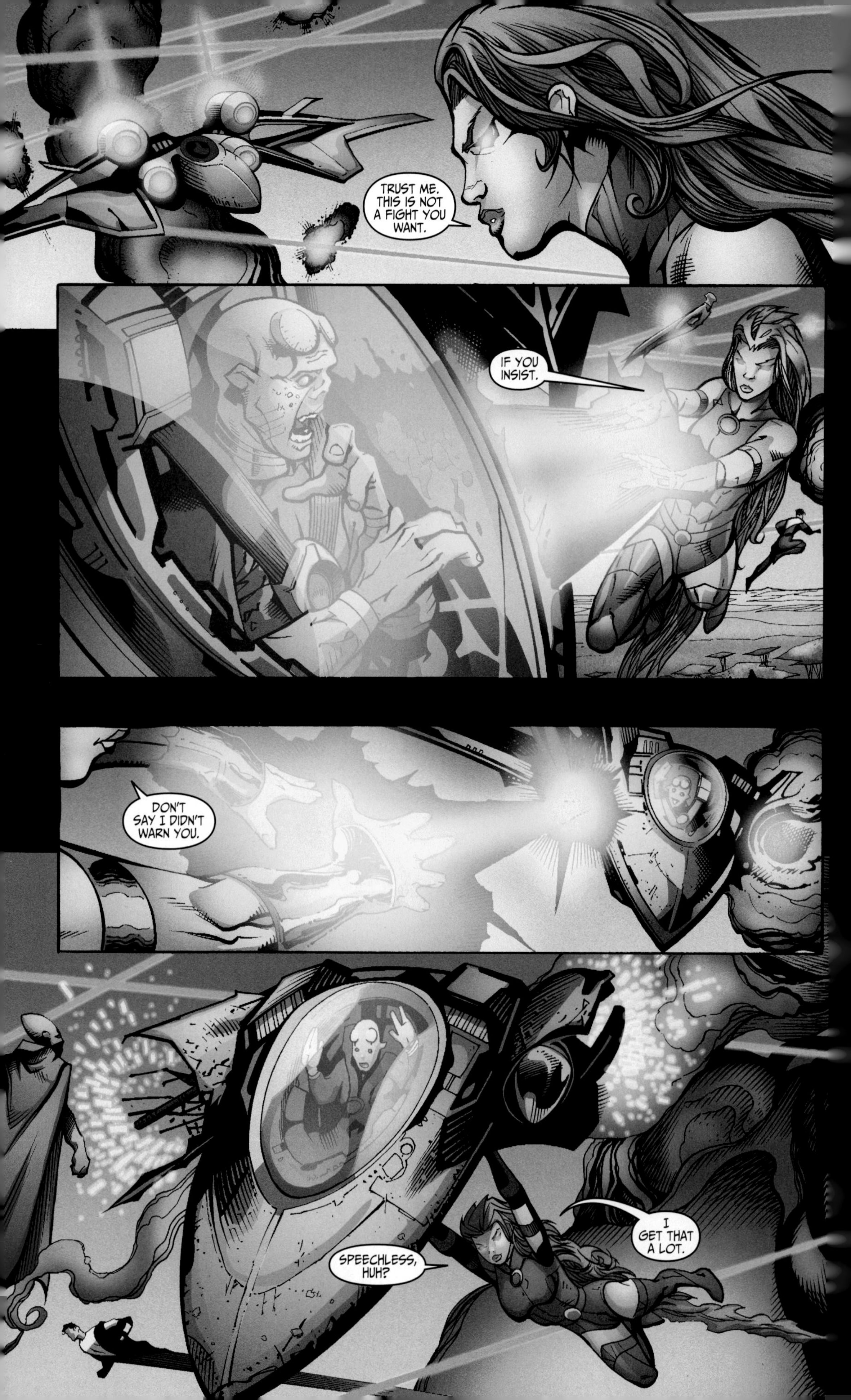
TRUST ME. THIS IS NOT A FIGHT YOU WANT.
IF YOU INSIST.
DON'T SAY I DIDN'T WARN YOU.
SPEECHLESS, HUH?
I GET THAT A LOT.

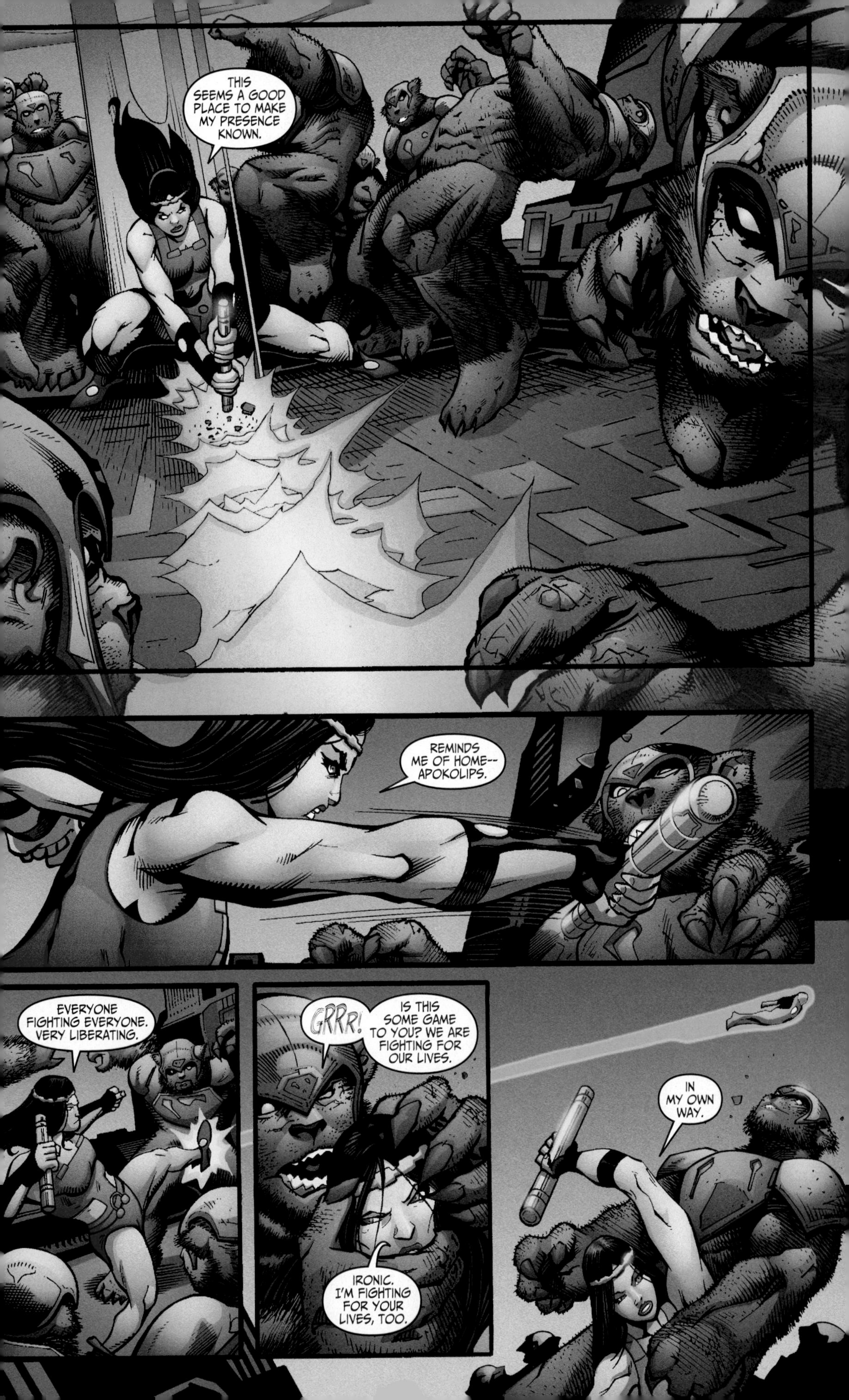
THIS SEEMS A GOOD PLACE TO MAKE MY PRESENCE KNOWN.
REMINDS ME OF HOME-- APOKOLIPS.
EVERYONE FIGHTING EVERYONE. VERY LIBERATING.
GRRR!
IS THIS SOME GAME TO YOU? WE ARE FIGHTING FOR OUR LIVES.
IRONIC. I'M FIGHTING FOR YOUR LIVES, TOO.
IN MY OWN WAY.

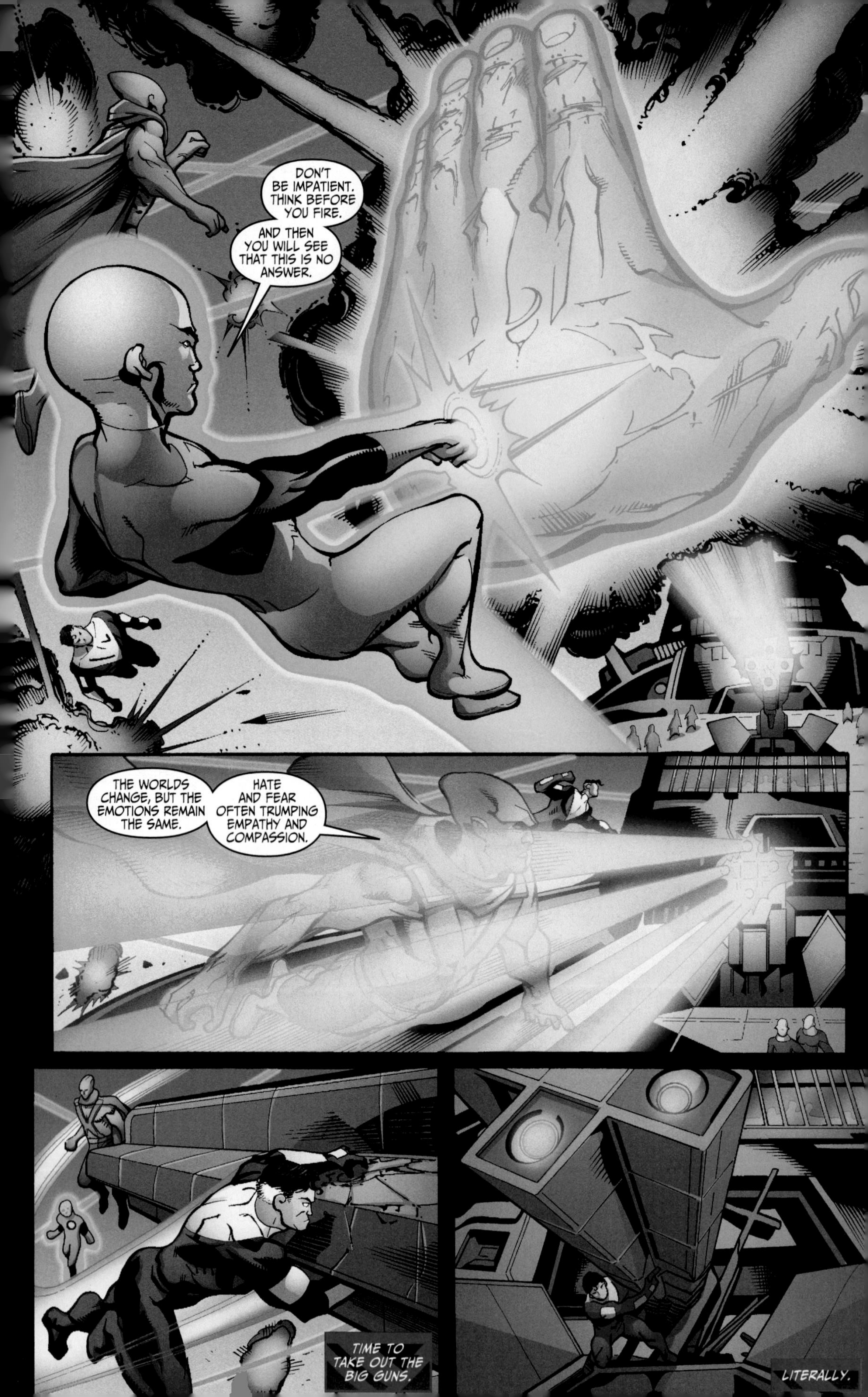
DON'T BE IMPATIENT. THINK BEFORE YOU FIRE.
AND THEN YOU WILL SEE THAT THIS IS NO ANSWER.
THE WORLDS CHANGE, BUT THE EMOTIONS REMAIN THE SAME.
HATE AND FEAR OFTEN TRUMPING EMPATHY AND COMPASSION.
TIME TO TAKE OUT THE BIG GUNS.
LITERALLY.

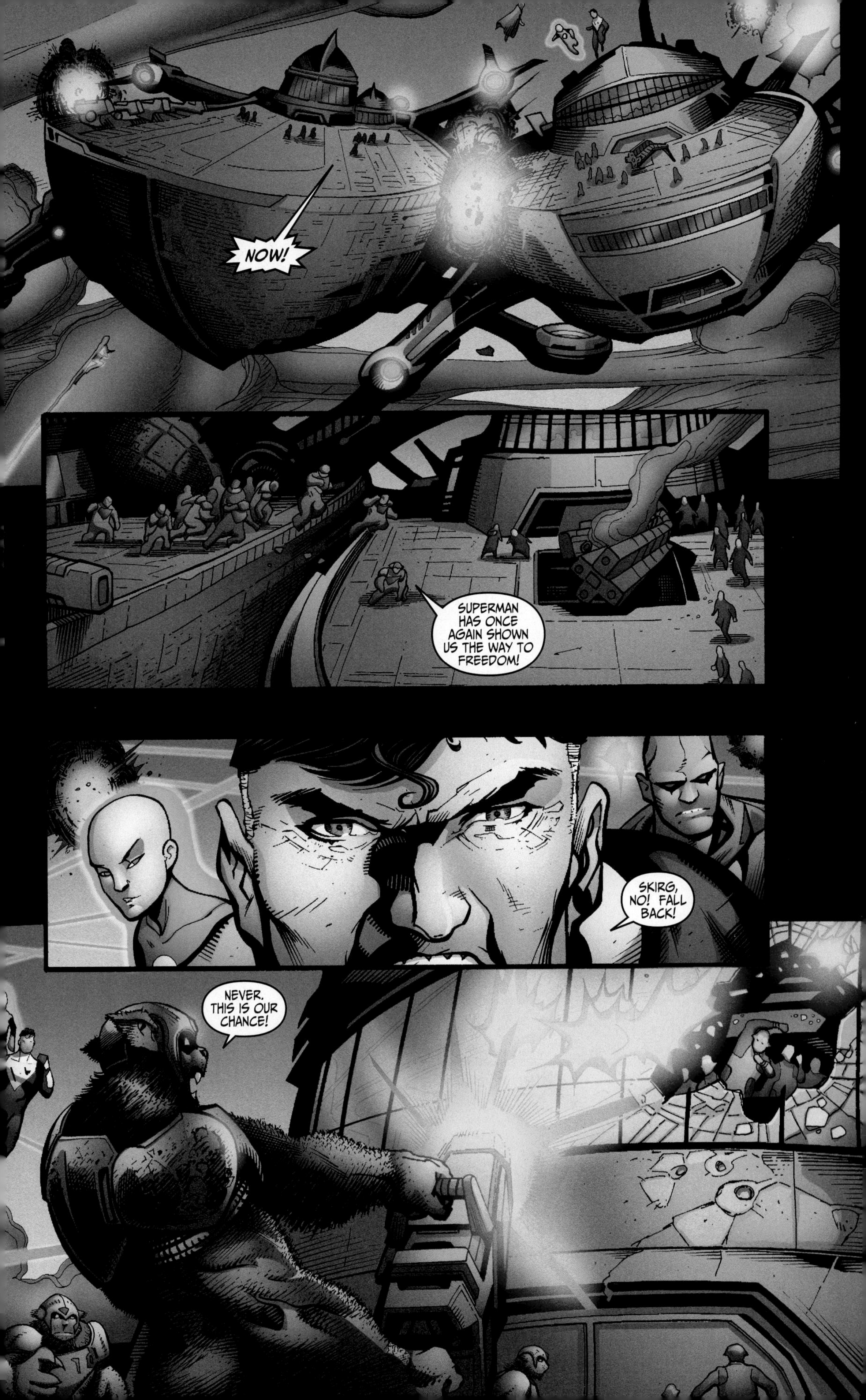
NOW!
SUPERMAN HAS ONCE AGAIN SHOWN US THE WAY TO FREEDOM!
SKIRG, NO! FALL BACK!
NEVER. THIS IS OUR CHANCE!

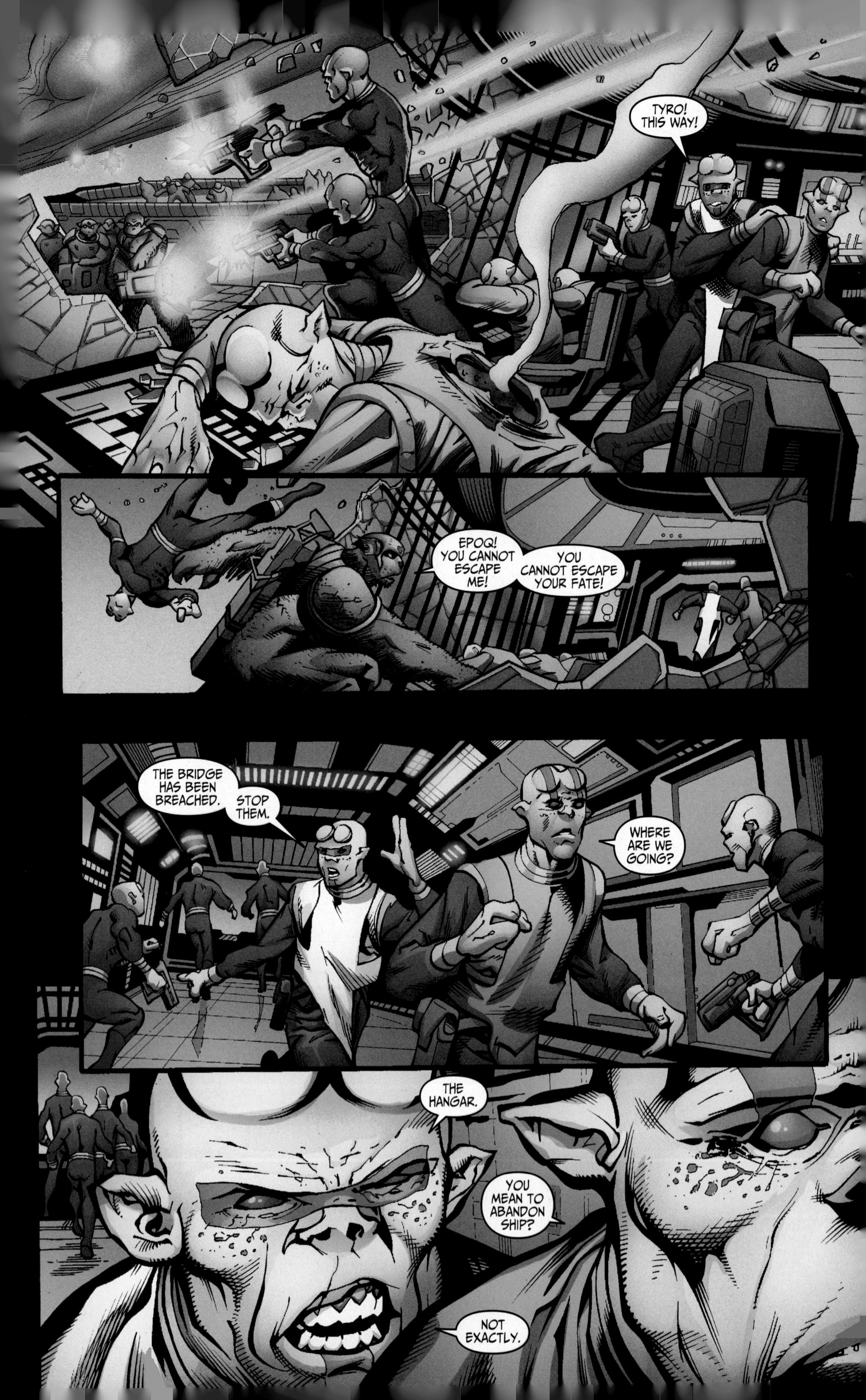
TYRO! THIS WAY!
EPOQ! YOU CANNOT ESCAPE ME!
YOU CANNOT ESCAPE YOUR FATE!
THE BRIDGE HAS BEEN BREACHED.
STOP THEM.
WHERE ARE WE GOING?
THE HANGAR.
YOU MEAN TO ABANDON SHIP?
NOT EXACTLY.

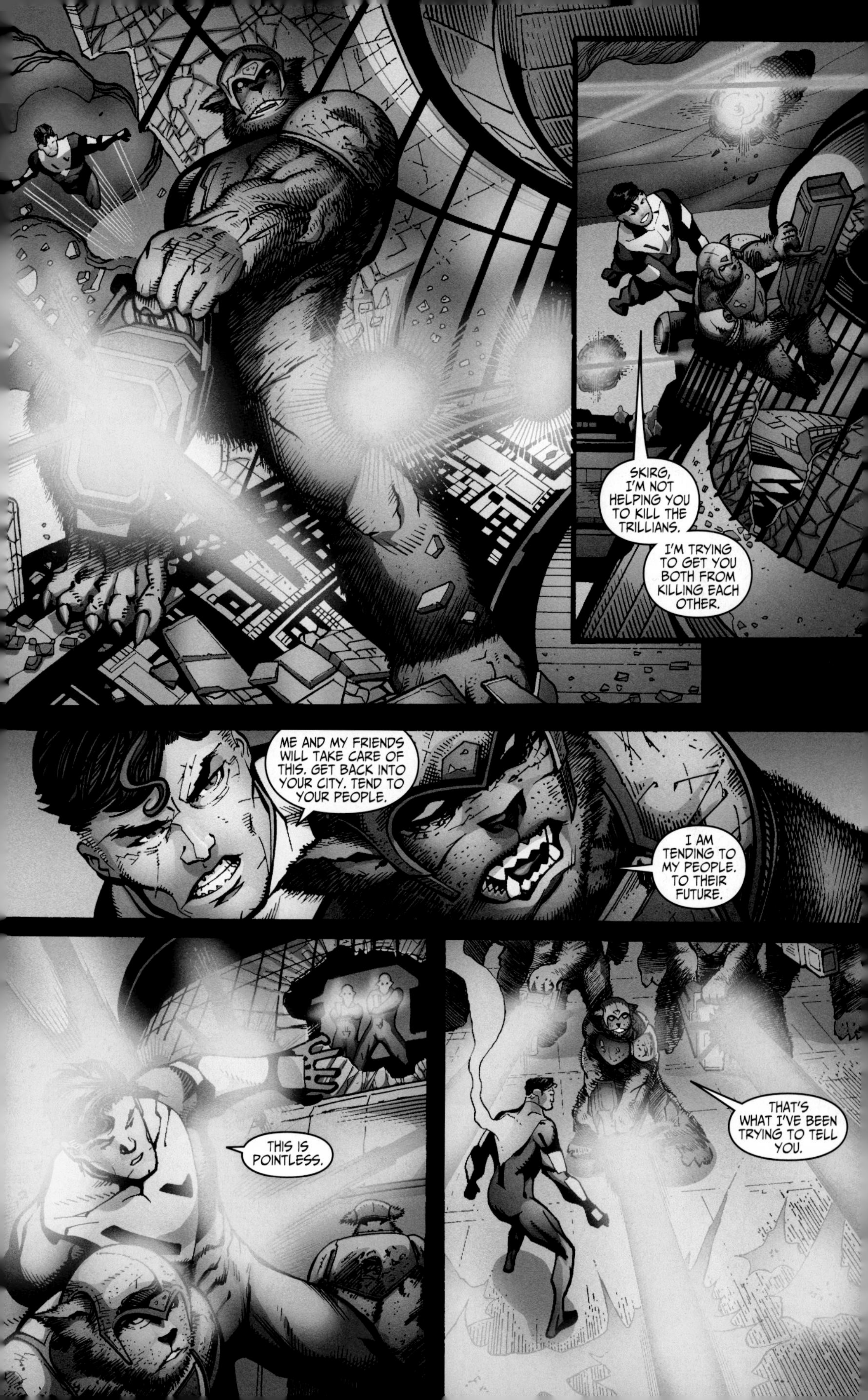
SKIRG, I'M NOT HELPING YOU TO KILL THE TRILLIANS.
I'M TRYING TO GET YOU BOTH FROM KILLING EACH OTHER.
ME AND MY FRIENDS WILL TAKE CARE OF THIS. GET BACK INTO YOUR CITY. TEND TO YOUR PEOPLE.
I AM TENDING TO MY PEOPLE. TO THEIR FUTURE.
THIS IS POINTLESS.
THAT'S WHAT I'VE BEEN TRYING TO TELL YOU.

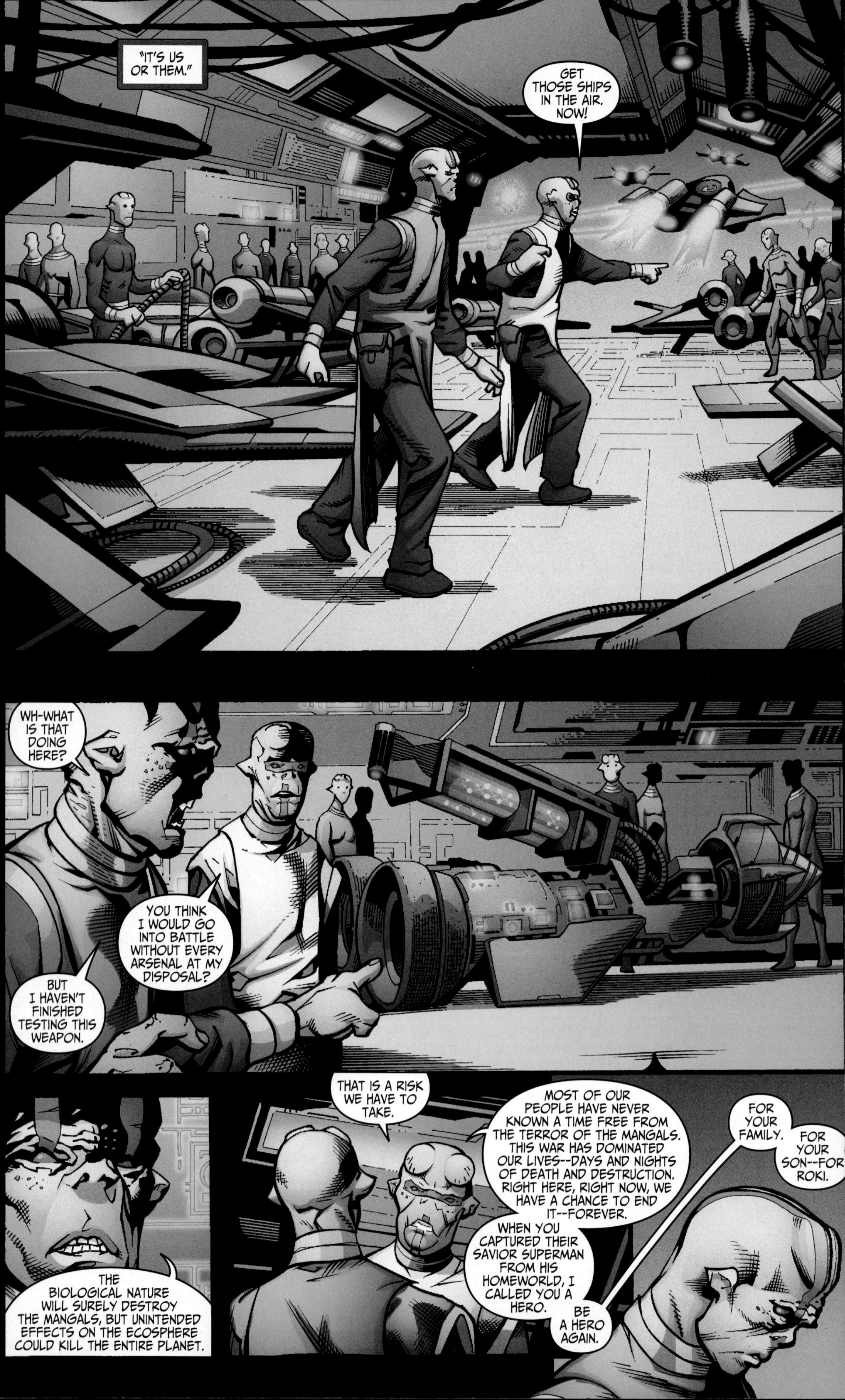
"IT'S US OR THEM."
GET THOSE SHIPS IN THE AIR. NOW!
WH-WHAT IS THAT DOING HERE?
YOU THINK I WOULD GO INTO BATTLE WITHOUT EVERY ARSENAL AT MY DISPOSAL?
BUT I HAVEN'T FINISHED TESTING THIS WEAPON.
THE BIOLOGICAL NATURE WILL SURELY DESTROY THE MANGALS, BUT UNINTENDED EFFECTS ON THE ECOSPHERE COULD KILL THE ENTIRE PLANET.
THAT IS A RISK WE HAVE TO TAKE.
MOST OF OUR PEOPLE HAVE NEVER KNOWN A TIME FREE FROM THE TERROR OF THE MANGALS. THIS WAR HAS DOMINATED OUR LIVES--DAYS AND NIGHTS OF DEATH AND DESTRUCTION. RIGHT HERE, RIGHT NOW, WE HAVE A CHANCE TO END IT--FOREVER.
WHEN YOU CAPTURED THEIR SAVIOR SUPERMAN FROM HIS HOMEWORLD, I CALLED YOU A HERO.
BE A HERO AGAIN.
FOR YOUR FAMILY.
FOR YOUR SON--FOR ROKI.

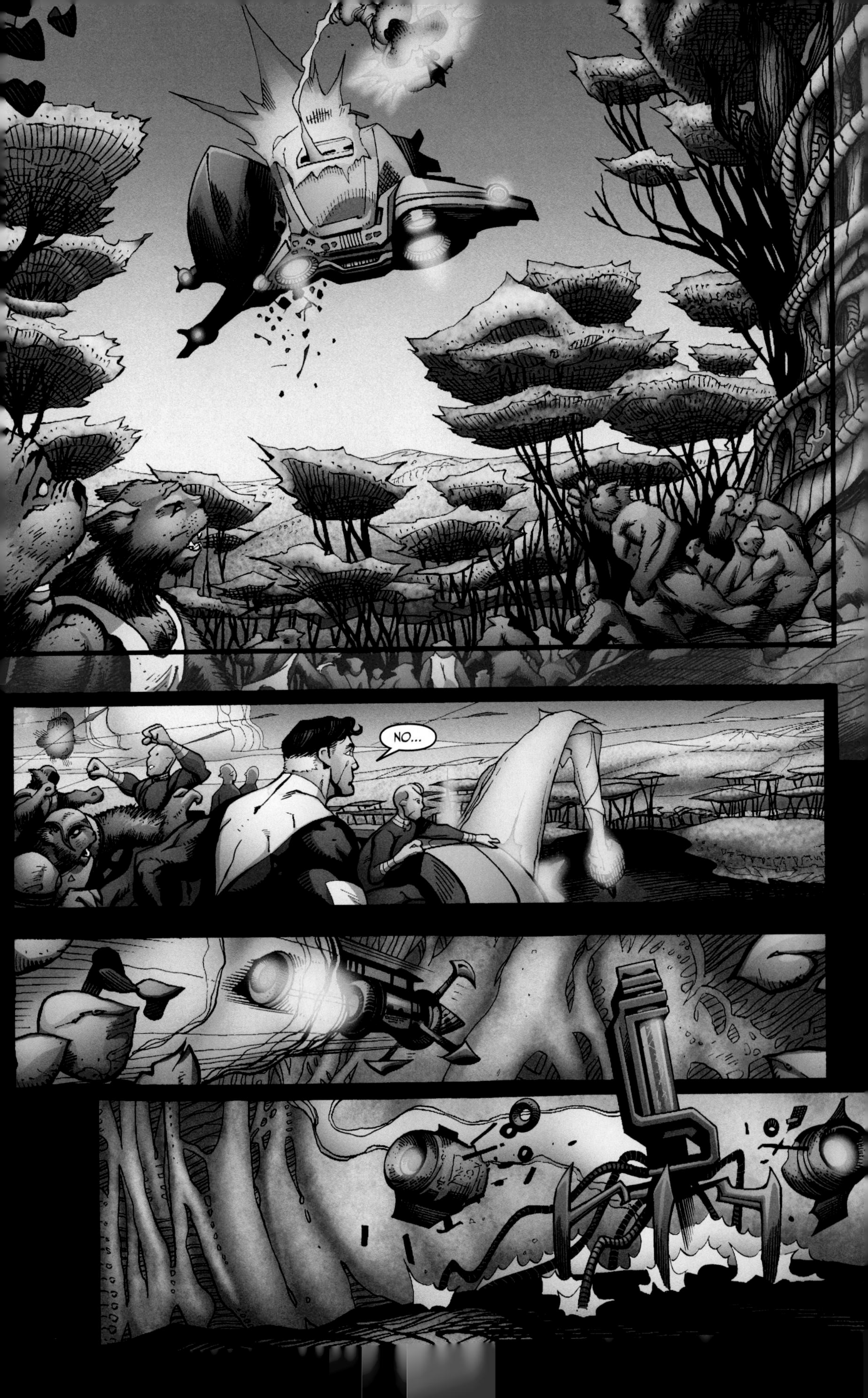
NO...

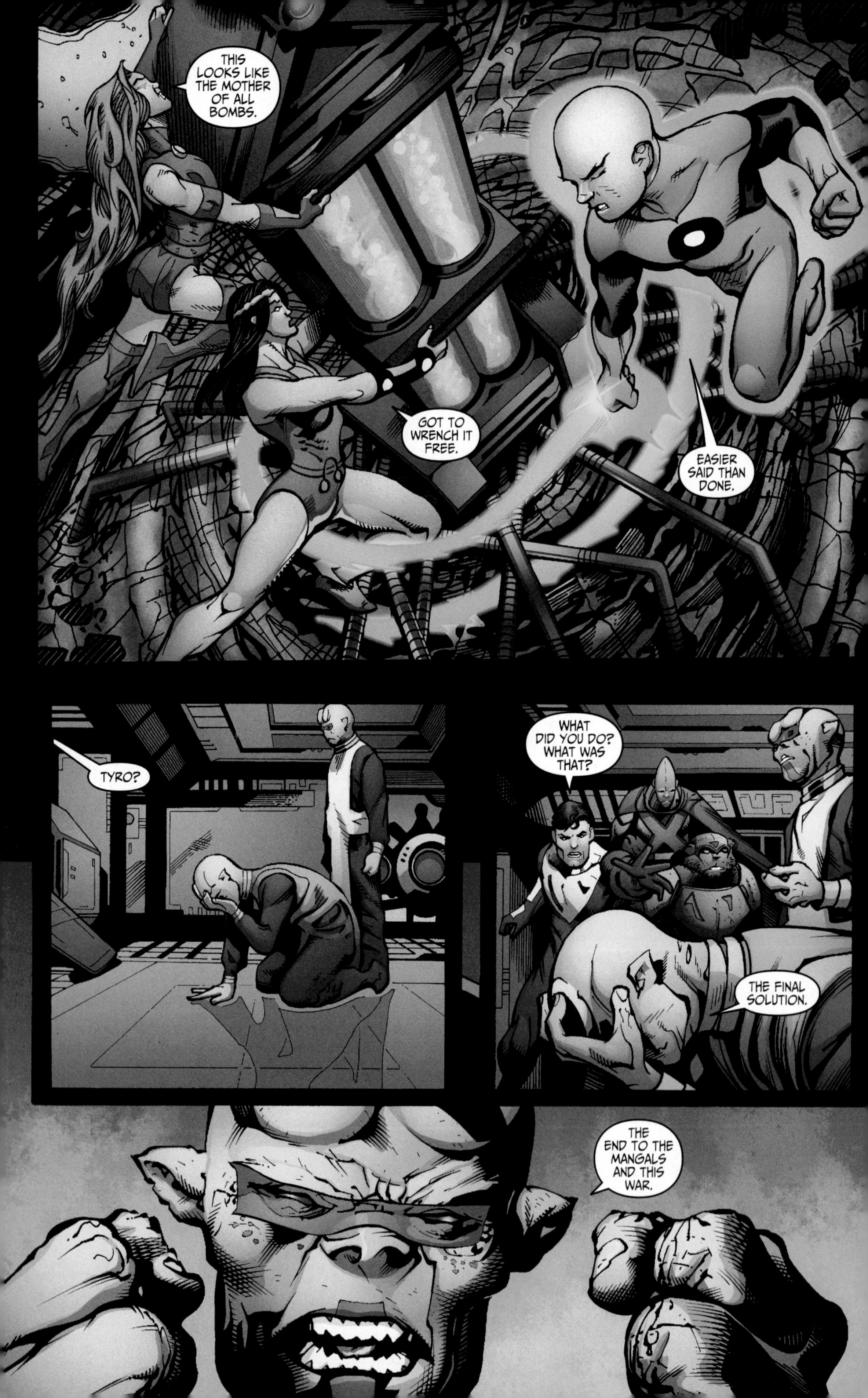
THIS LOOKS LIKE THE MOTHER OF ALL BOMBS.
GOT TO WRENCH IT FREE.
EASIER SAID THAN DONE.
TYRO?
WHAT DID YOU DO? WHAT WAS THAT?
THE FINAL SOLUTION.
THE END TO THE MANGALS AND THIS WAR.

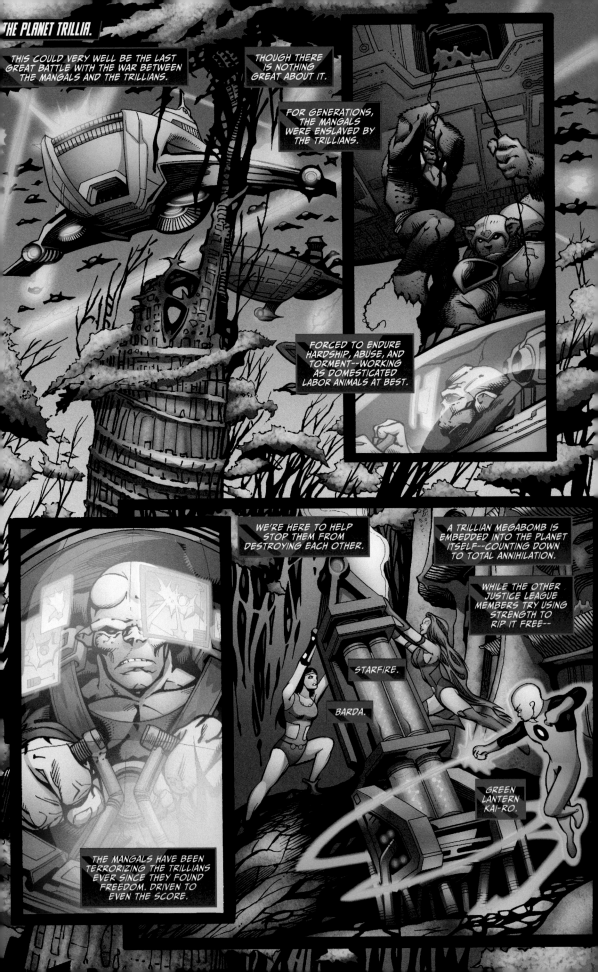

THE PLANET TRILLIA.

THIS COULD VERY WELL BE THE LAST GREAT BATTLE WITH THE WAR BETWEEN THE MANGALS AND THE TRILLIANS.

THOUGH THERE IS NOTHING GREAT ABOUT IT.

FOR GENERATIONS, THE MANGALS WERE ENSLAVED BY THE TRILLIANS.

FORCED TO ENDURE HARDSHIP, ABUSE, AND TORMENT--WORKING AS DOMESTICATED LABOR ANIMALS AT BEST.

WE'RE HERE TO HELP STOP THEM FROM DESTROYING EACH OTHER.

A TRILLIAN MEGABOMB IS EMBEDDED INTO THE PLANET ITSELF--COUNTING DOWN TO TOTAL ANNIHILATION.

WHILE THE OTHER JUSTICE LEAGUE MEMBERS TRY USING STRENGTH TO RIP IT FREE--

STARFIRE.

BARDA.

GREEN LANTERN KAI-RO.

THE MANGALS HAVE BEEN TERRORIZING THE TRILLIANS EVER SINCE THEY FOUND FREEDOM. DRIVEN TO EVEN THE SCORE.

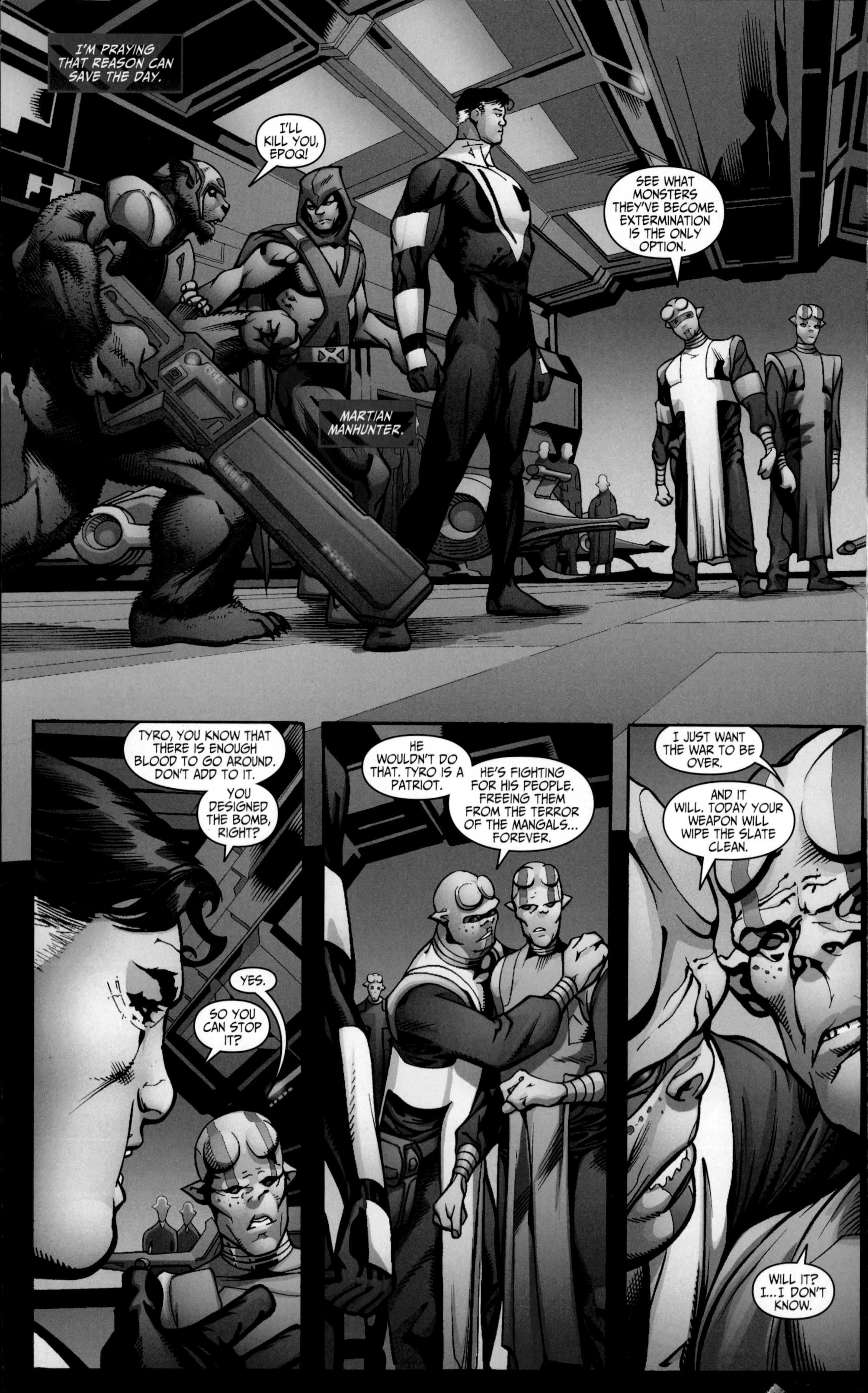
I'M PRAYING THAT REASON CAN SAVE THE DAY.
I'LL KILL YOU, EPOQ!
SEE WHAT MONSTERS THEY'VE BECOME. EXTERMINATION IS THE ONLY OPTION.
MARTIAN MANHUNTER.
TYRO, YOU KNOW THAT THERE IS ENOUGH BLOOD TO GO AROUND. DON'T ADD TO IT.
YOU DESIGNED THE BOMB, RIGHT?
YES.
SO YOU CAN STOP IT?
HE WOULDN'T DO THAT. TYRO IS A PATRIOT.
HE'S FIGHTING FOR HIS PEOPLE. FREEING THEM FROM THE TERROR OF THE MANGALS... FOREVER.
I JUST WANT THE WAR TO BE OVER.
AND IT WILL. TODAY YOUR WEAPON WILL WIPE THE SLATE CLEAN.
WILL IT? I...I DON'T KNOW.

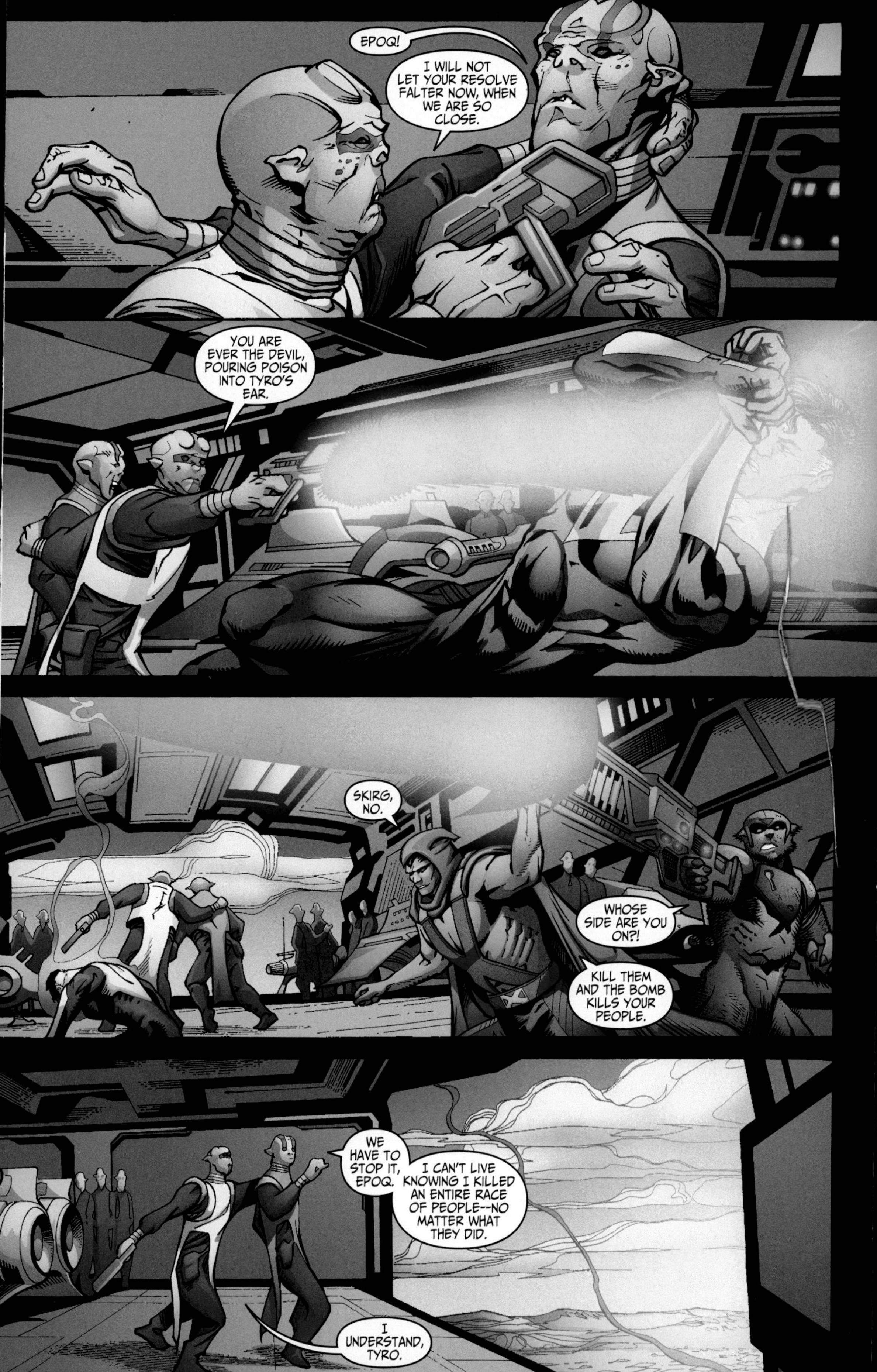
EPOQ!
I WILL NOT LET YOUR RESOLVE FALTER NOW, WHEN WE ARE SO CLOSE.
YOU ARE EVER THE DEVIL, POURING POISON INTO TYRO'S EAR.
SKIRG, NO.
WHOSE SIDE ARE YOU ON?!
KILL THEM AND THE BOMB KILLS YOUR PEOPLE.
WE HAVE TO STOP IT, EPOQ.
I CAN'T LIVE KNOWING I KILLED AN ENTIRE RACE OF PEOPLE--NO MATTER WHAT THEY DID.
I UNDERSTAND, TYRO.

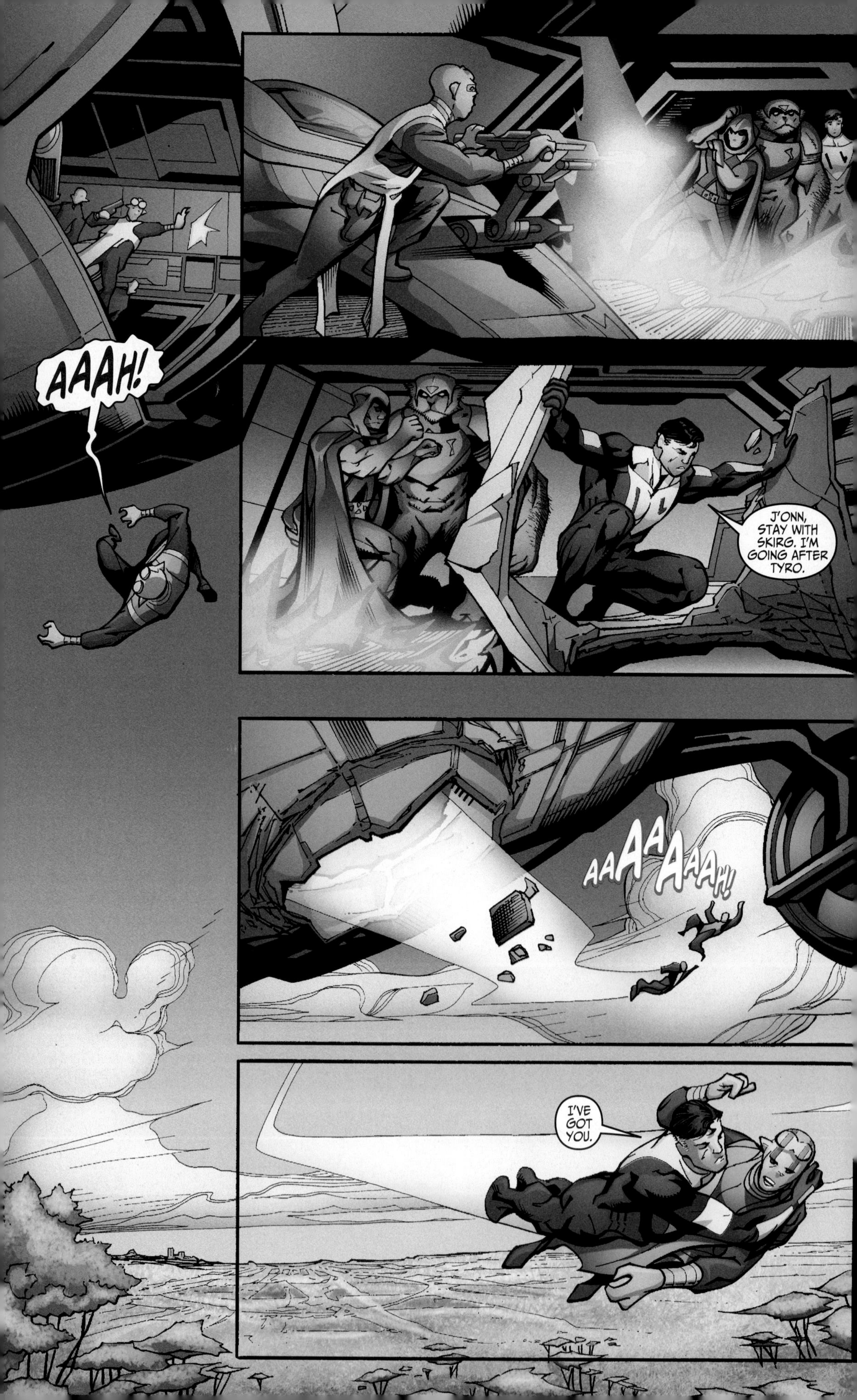
AAAH!
J'ONN, STAY WITH SKIRG. I'M GOING AFTER TYRO.
AAAAAAAH!
I'VE GOT YOU.

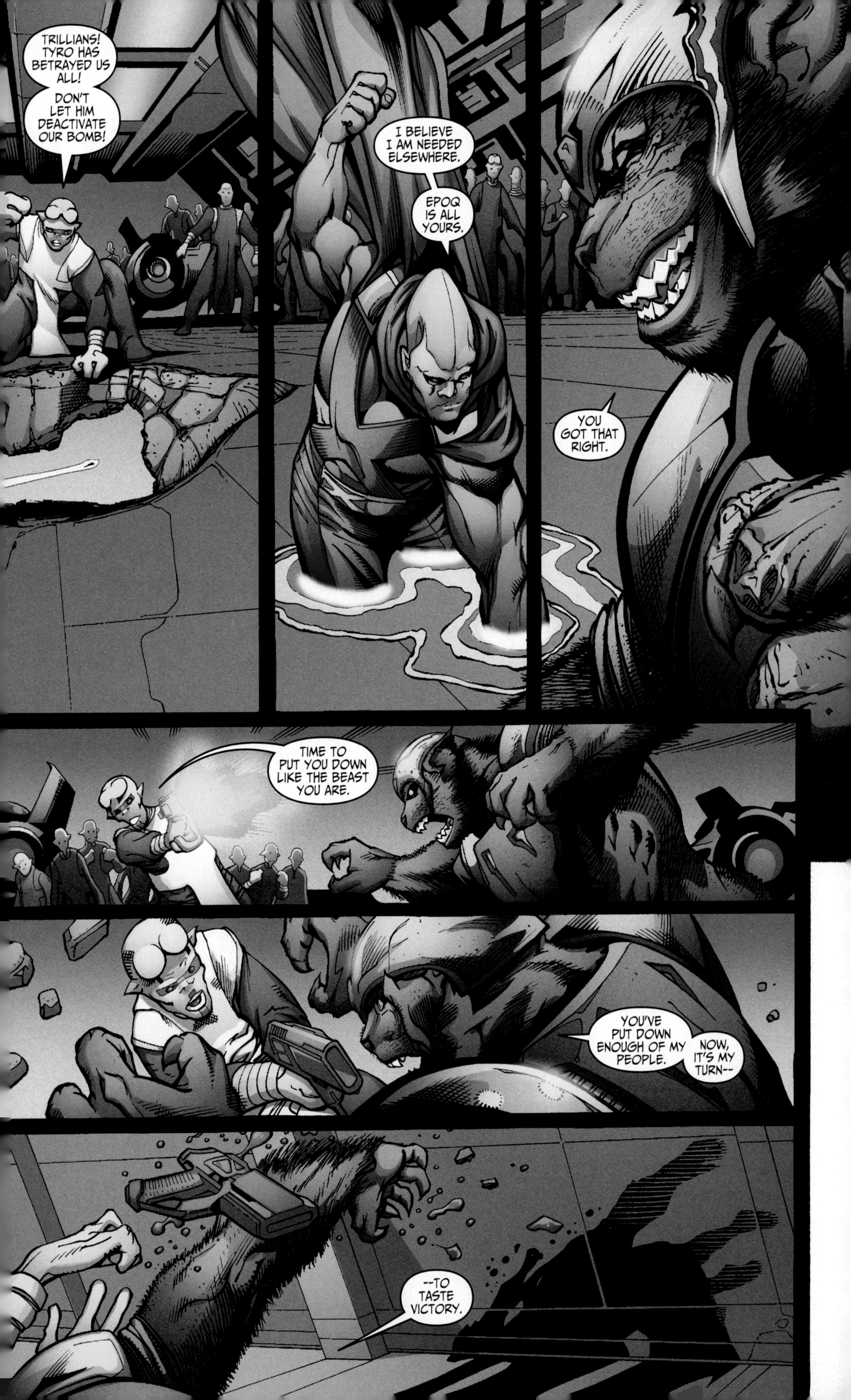
TRILLIANS! TYRO HAS BETRAYED US ALL!
DON'T LET HIM DEACTIVATE OUR BOMB!
I BELIEVE I AM NEEDED ELSEWHERE.
EPOQ IS ALL YOURS.
YOU GOT THAT RIGHT.
TIME TO PUT YOU DOWN LIKE THE BEAST YOU ARE.
YOU'VE PUT DOWN ENOUGH OF MY PEOPLE.
NOW, IT'S MY TURN--
--TO TASTE VICTORY.

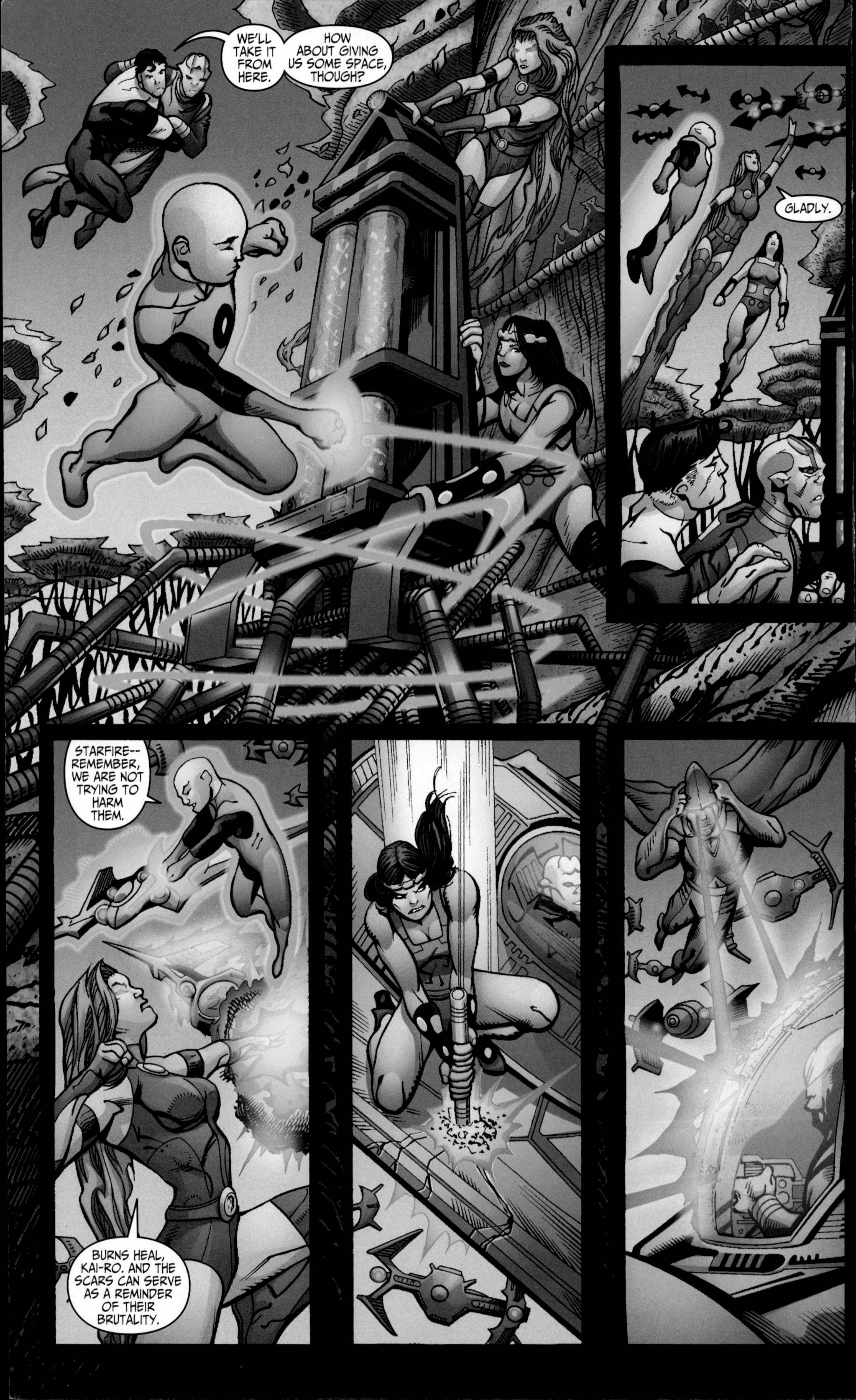
WE'LL TAKE IT FROM HERE.
HOW ABOUT GIVING US SOME SPACE, THOUGH?
GLADLY.
STARFIRE-- REMEMBER, WE ARE NOT TRYING TO HARM THEM.
BURNS HEAL, KAI-RO. AND THE SCARS CAN SERVE AS A REMINDER OF THEIR BRUTALITY.

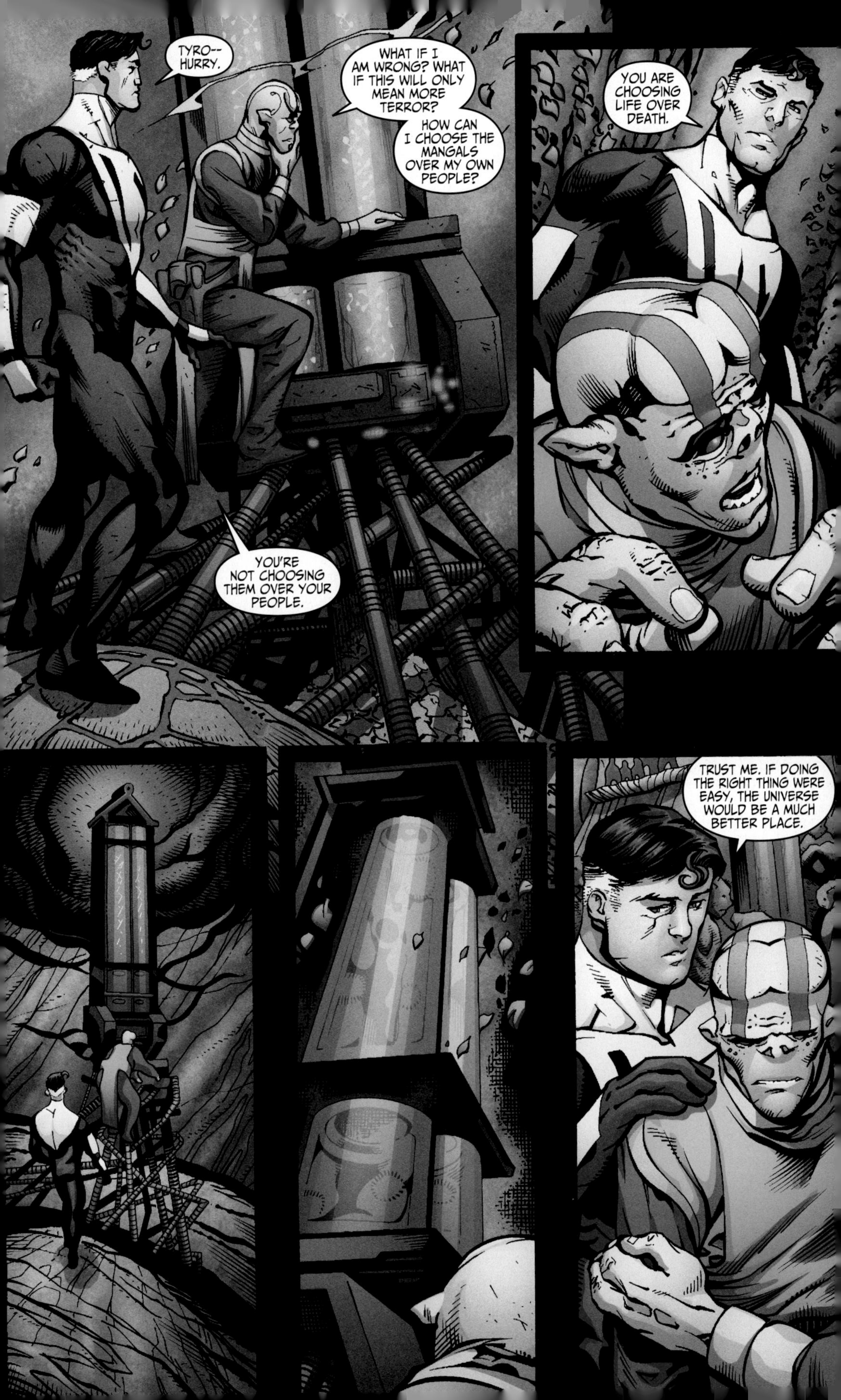
TYRO--
HURRY.
WHAT IF I AM WRONG? WHAT IF THIS WILL ONLY MEAN MORE TERROR?
HOW CAN I CHOOSE THE MANGALS OVER MY OWN PEOPLE?
YOU'RE NOT CHOOSING THEM OVER YOUR PEOPLE.
YOU ARE CHOOSING LIFE OVER DEATH.
TRUST ME. IF DOING THE RIGHT THING WERE EASY, THE UNIVERSE WOULD BE A MUCH BETTER PLACE.

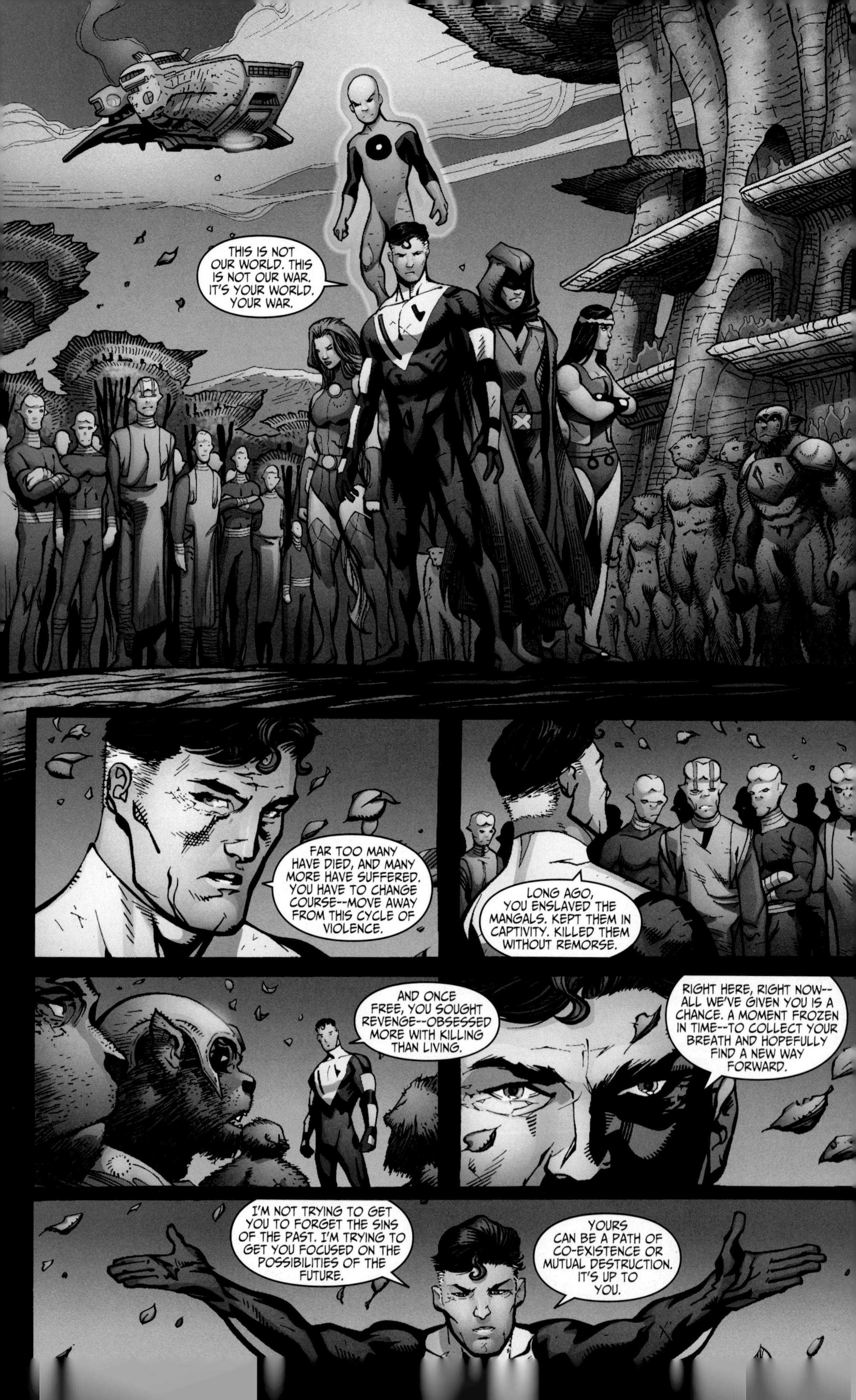
THIS IS NOT OUR WORLD. THIS IS NOT OUR WAR. IT'S YOUR WORLD. YOUR WAR.
FAR TOO MANY HAVE DIED, AND MANY MORE HAVE SUFFERED. YOU HAVE TO CHANGE COURSE--MOVE AWAY FROM THIS CYCLE OF VIOLENCE.
LONG AGO, YOU ENSLAVED THE MANGALS. KEPT THEM IN CAPTIVITY. KILLED THEM WITHOUT REMORSE.
AND ONCE FREE, YOU SOUGHT REVENGE--OBSESSED MORE WITH KILLING THAN LIVING.
RIGHT HERE, RIGHT NOW--ALL WE'VE GIVEN YOU IS A CHANCE. A MOMENT FROZEN IN TIME--TO COLLECT YOUR BREATH AND HOPEFULLY FIND A NEW WAY FORWARD.
I'M NOT TRYING TO GET YOU TO FORGET THE SINS OF THE PAST. I'M TRYING TO GET YOU FOCUSED ON THE POSSIBILITIES OF THE FUTURE.
YOURS CAN BE A PATH OF CO-EXISTENCE OR MUTUAL DESTRUCTION. IT'S UP TO YOU.

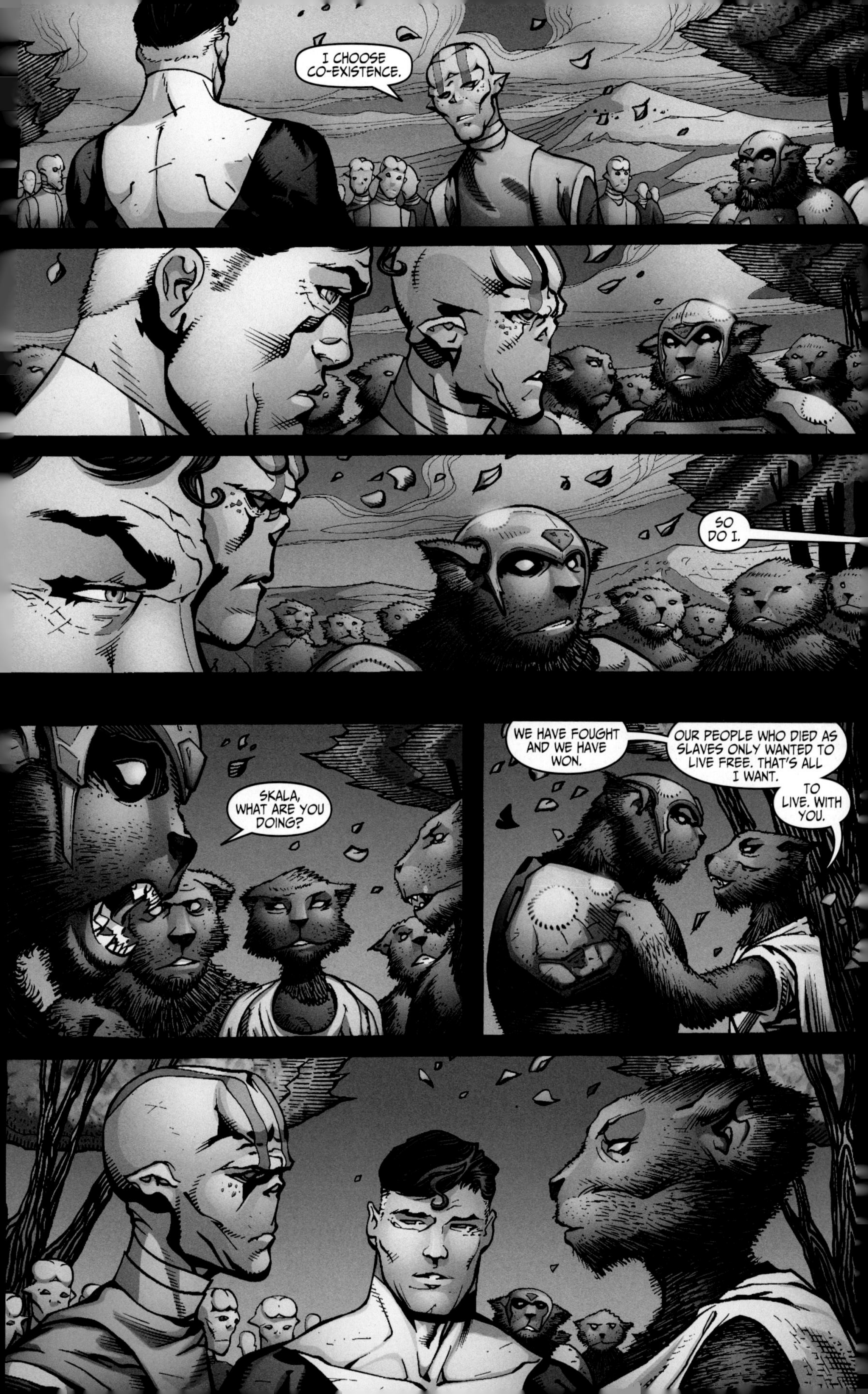
I CHOOSE CO-EXISTENCE.
SO DO I.
SKALA, WHAT ARE YOU DOING?
WE HAVE FOUGHT AND WE HAVE WON.
OUR PEOPLE WHO DIED AS SLAVES ONLY WANTED TO LIVE FREE. THAT'S ALL I WANT.
TO LIVE. WITH YOU.

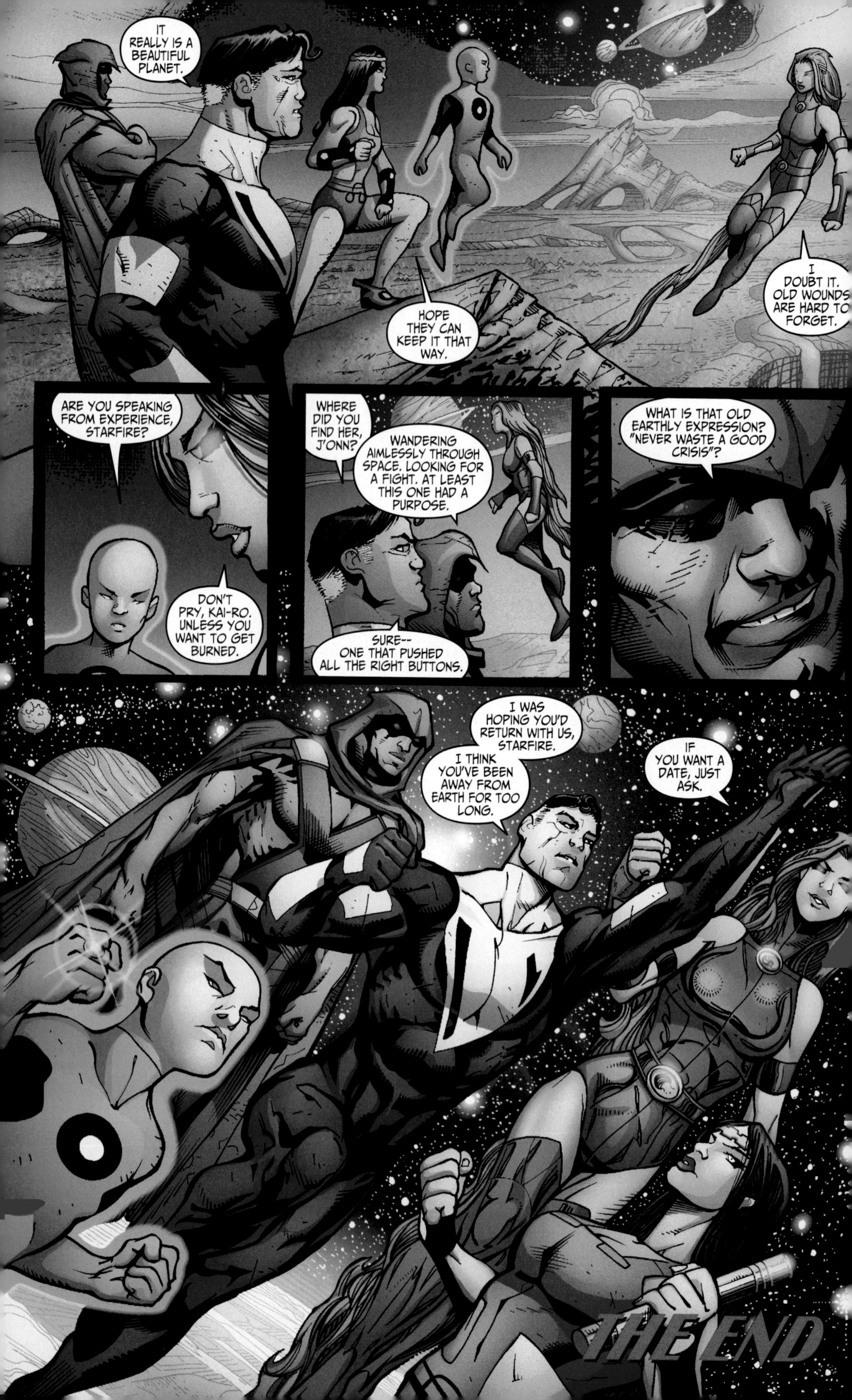
IT REALLY IS A BEAUTIFUL PLANET.
HOPE THEY CAN KEEP IT THAT WAY.
I DOUBT IT. OLD WOUNDS ARE HARD TO FORGET.
ARE YOU SPEAKING FROM EXPERIENCE, STARFIRE?
DON'T PRY, KAI-RO. UNLESS YOU WANT TO GET BURNED.
WHERE DID YOU FIND HER, J'ONN?
WANDERING AIMLESSLY THROUGH SPACE. LOOKING FOR A FIGHT. AT LEAST THIS ONE HAD A PURPOSE.
SURE-- ONE THAT PUSHED ALL THE RIGHT BUTTONS.
WHAT IS THAT OLD EARTHLY EXPRESSION? "NEVER WASTE A GOOD CRISIS"?
I WAS HOPING YOU'D RETURN WITH US, STARFIRE.
I THINK YOU'VE BEEN AWAY FROM EARTH FOR TOO LONG.
IF YOU WANT A DATE, JUST ASK.
THE END

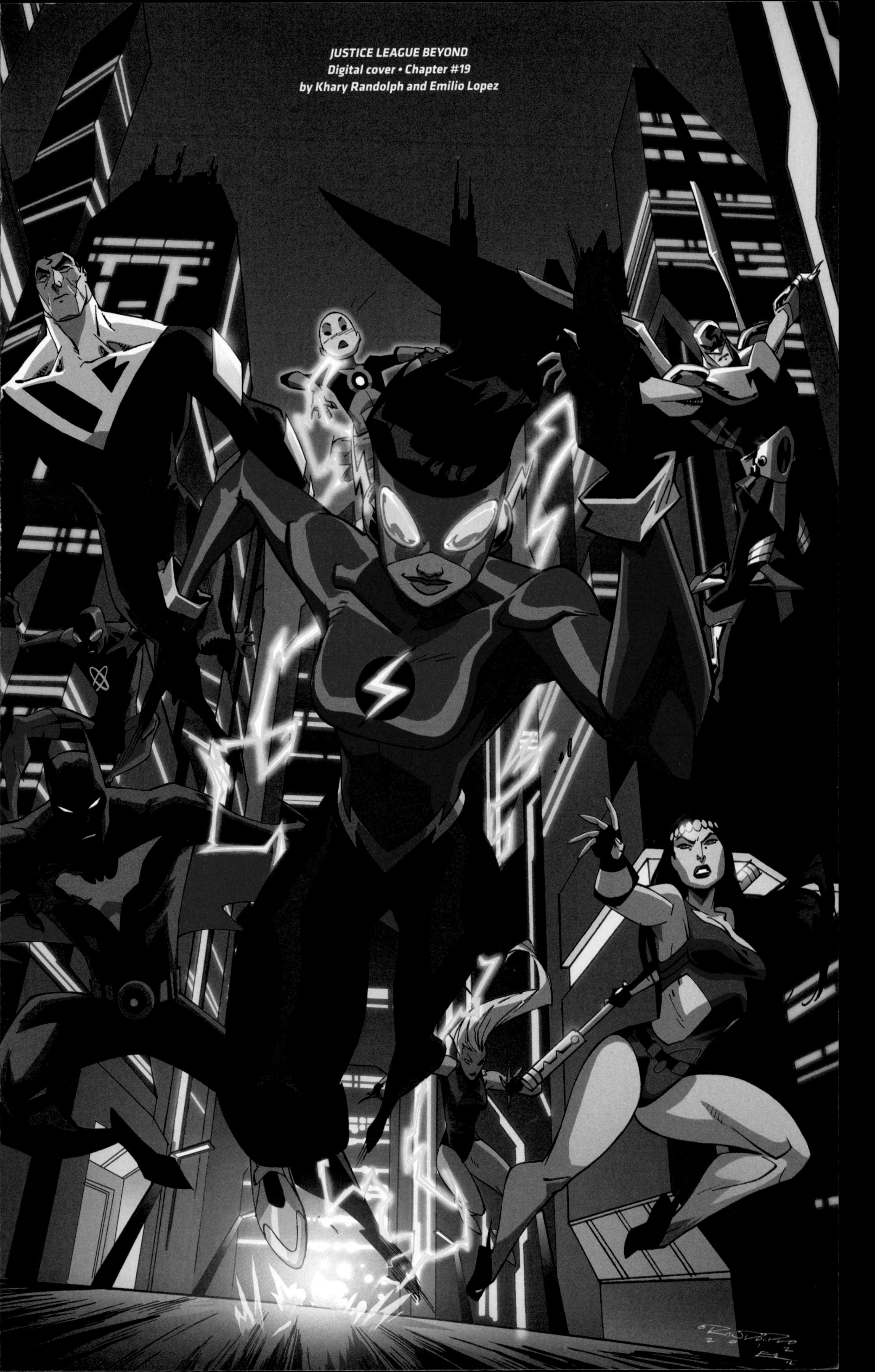

JUSTICE LEAGUE BEYOND
Digital cover • Chapter #19
by Khary Randolph and Emilio Lopez

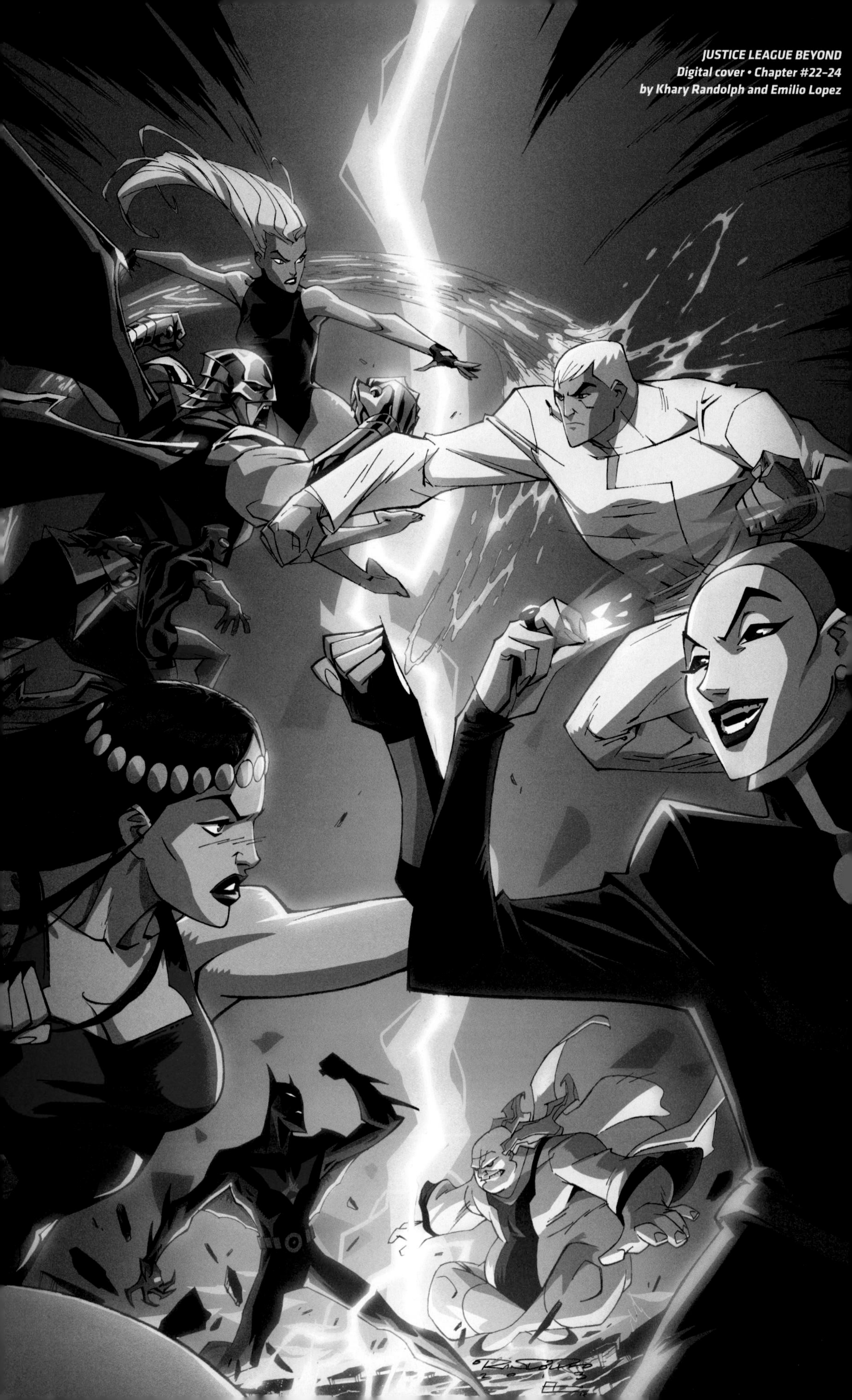

JUSTICE LEAGUE BEYOND
Digital cover • Chapter #22–24
by Khary Randolph and Emilio Lopez

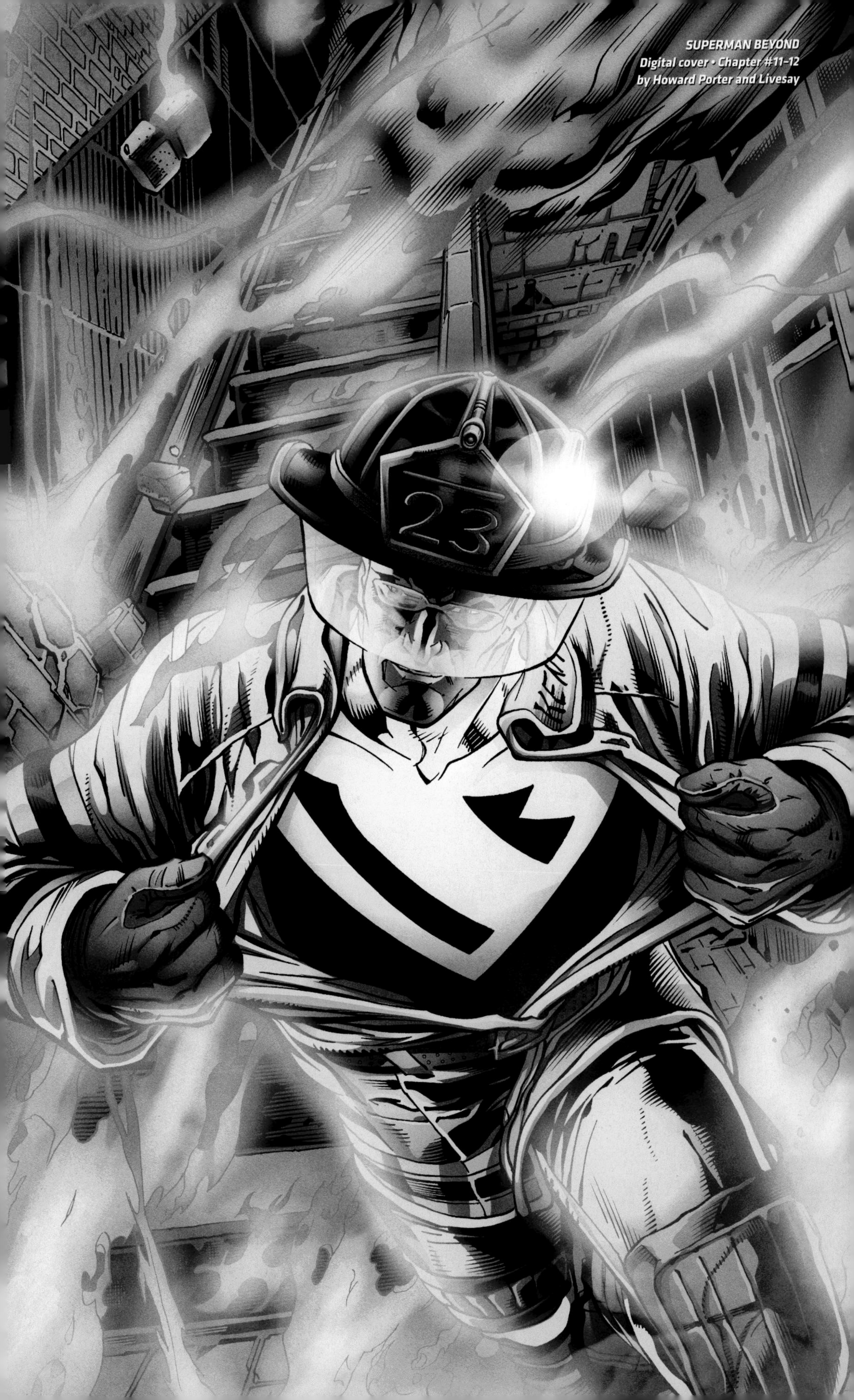
23

SUPERMAN BEYOND
Digital cover • Chapter #11–12
by Howard Porter and Livesay

SUPERMAN BEYOND
Digital cover • Chapter #13–14
by Howard Porter and Livesay

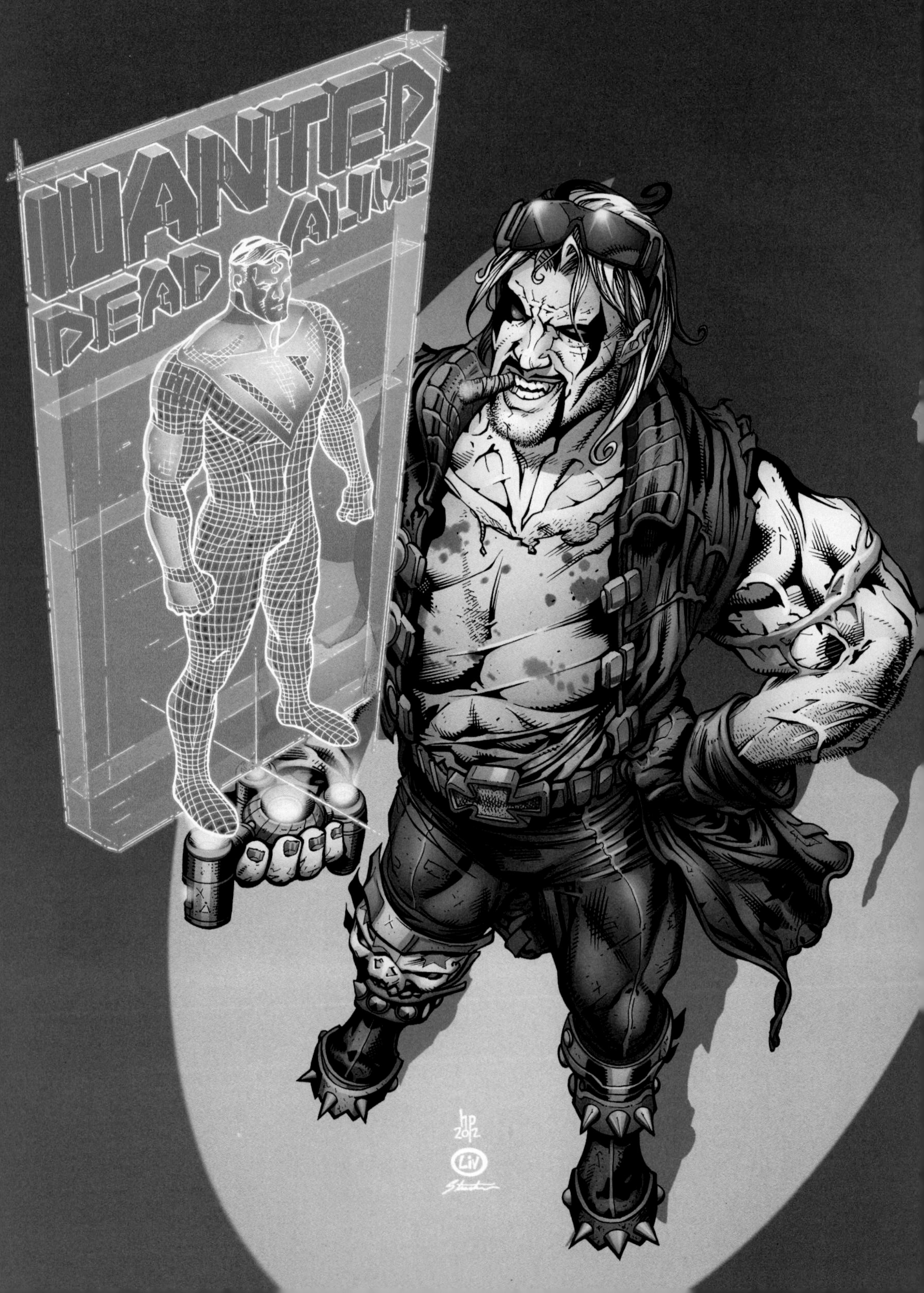

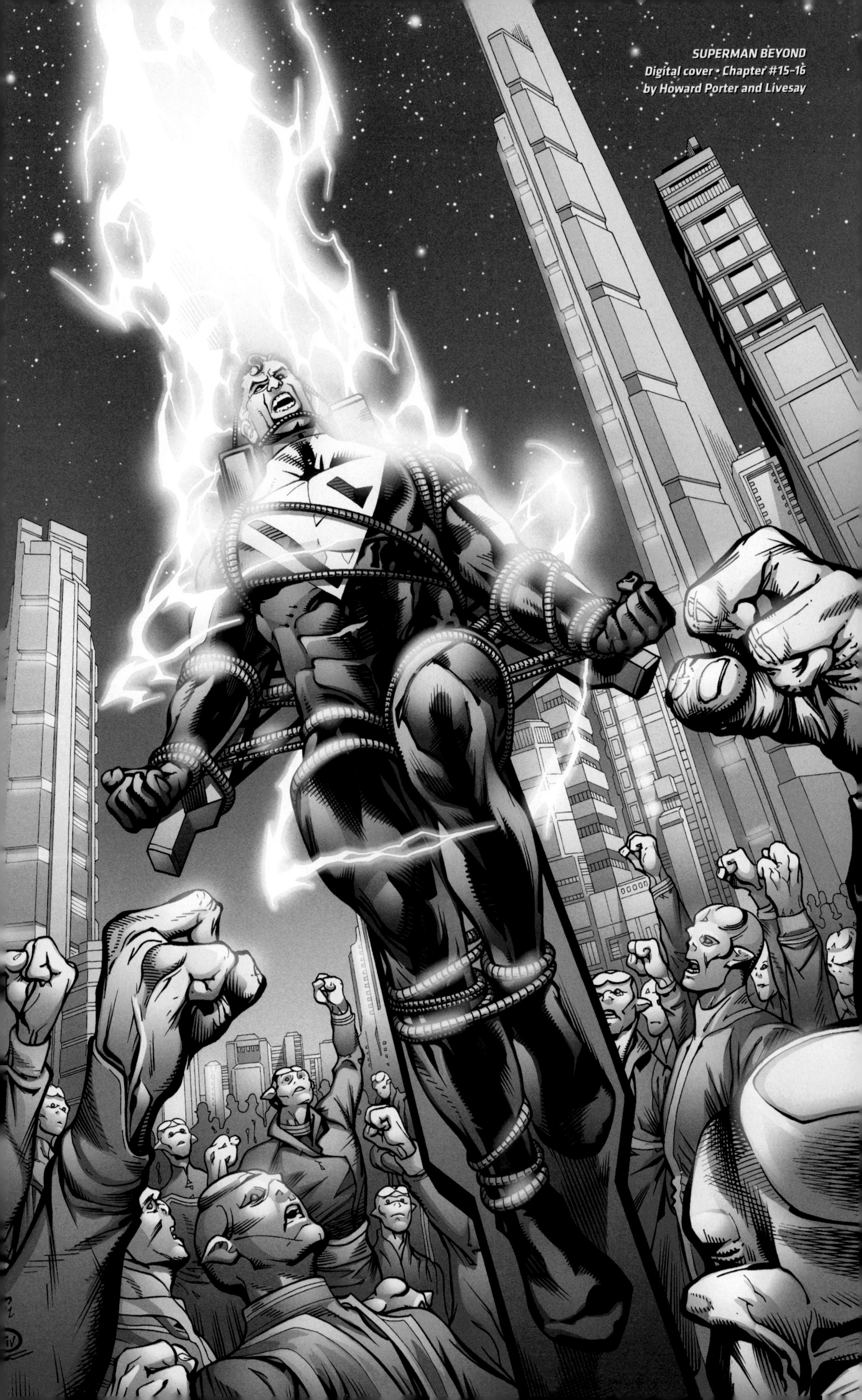

SUPERMAN BEYOND
Digital cover • Chapter #15–16
by Howard Porter and Livesay

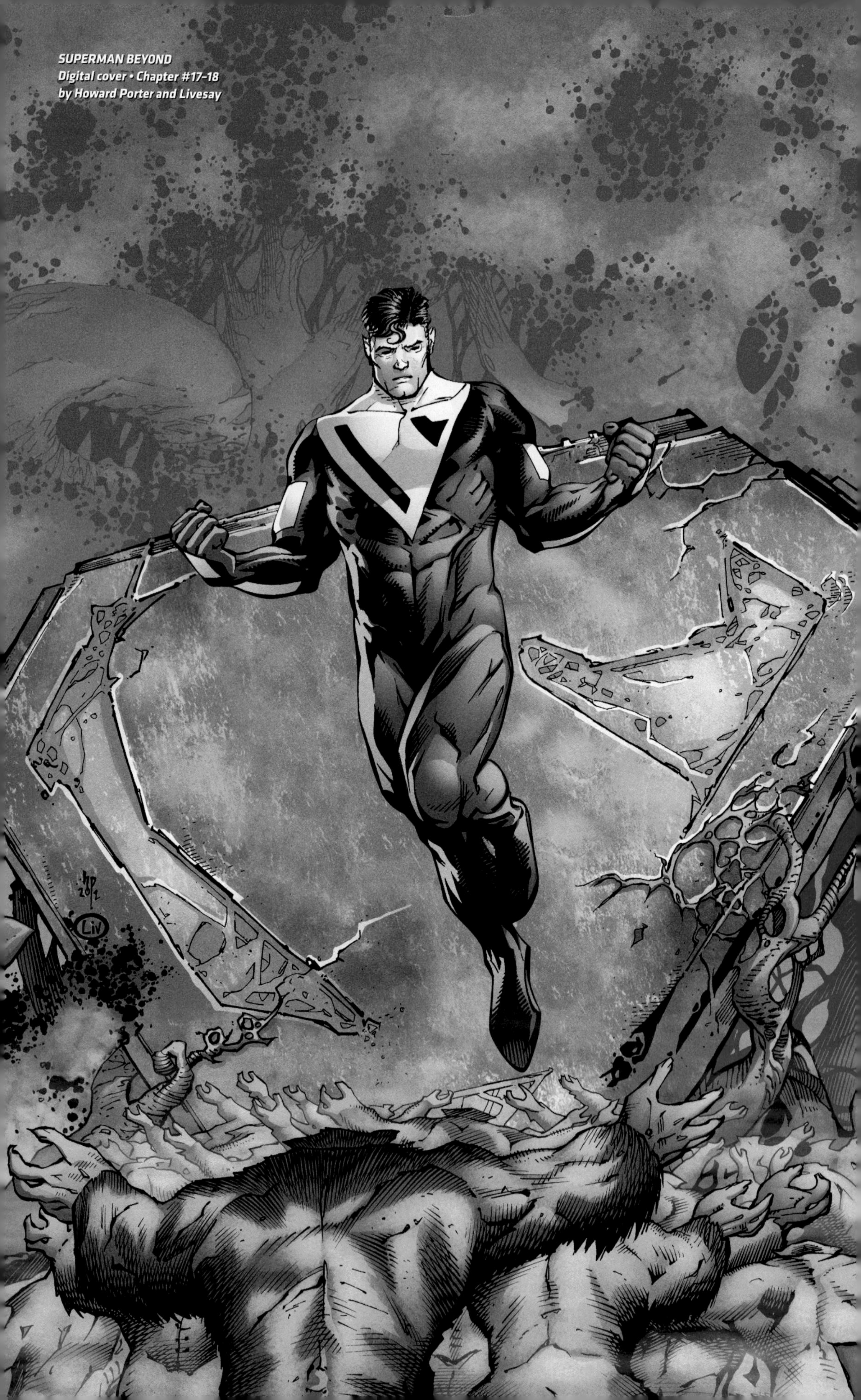

SUPERMAN BEYOND
Digital cover • Chapter #17–18
by Howard Porter and Livesay

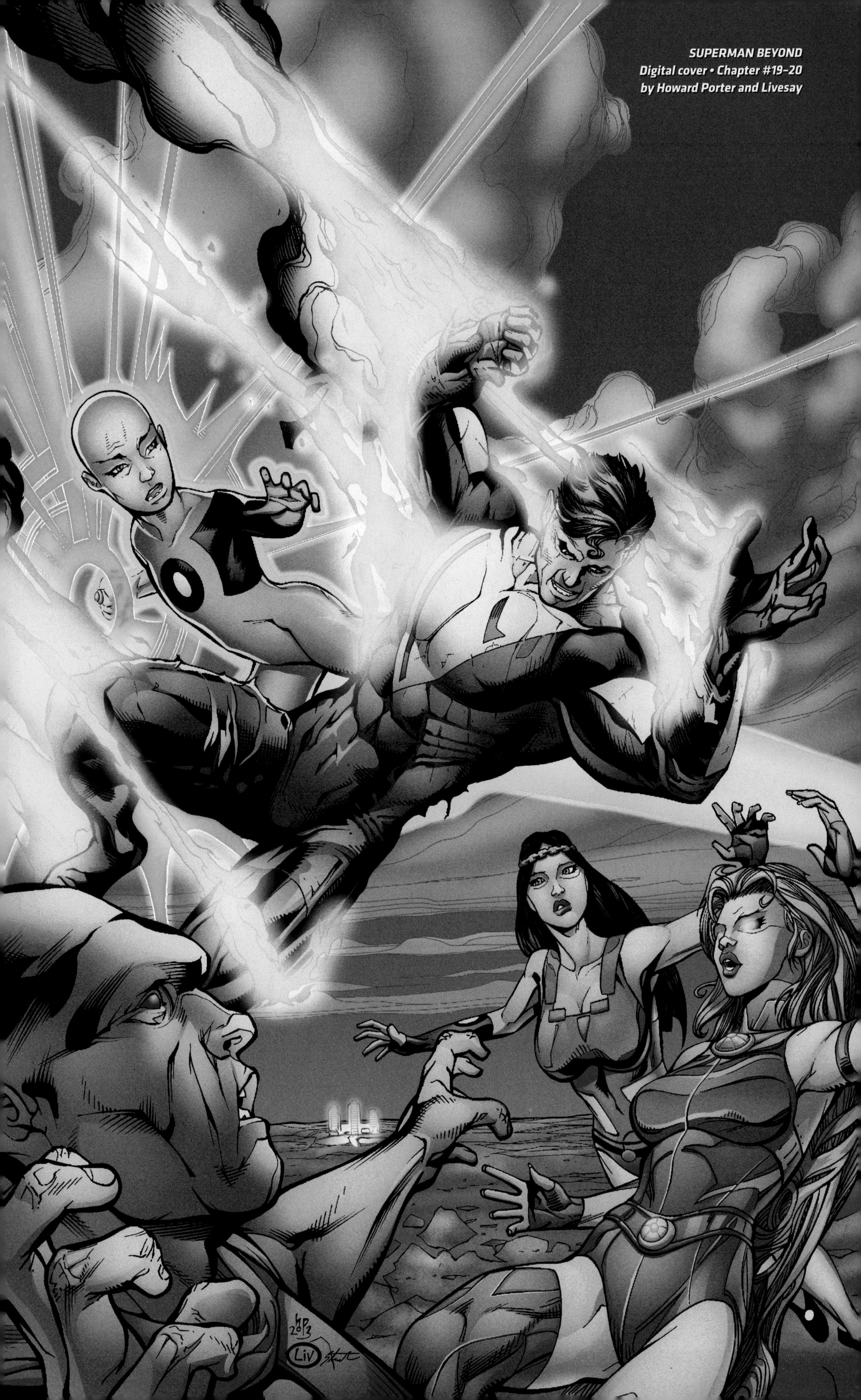

SUPERMAN BEYOND
Digital cover • Chapter #19–20
by Howard Porter and Livesay

JUSTICE LEAGUE BEYOND sketch gallery

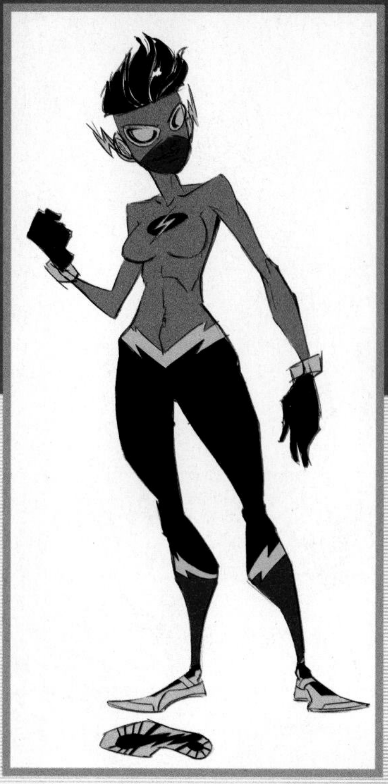

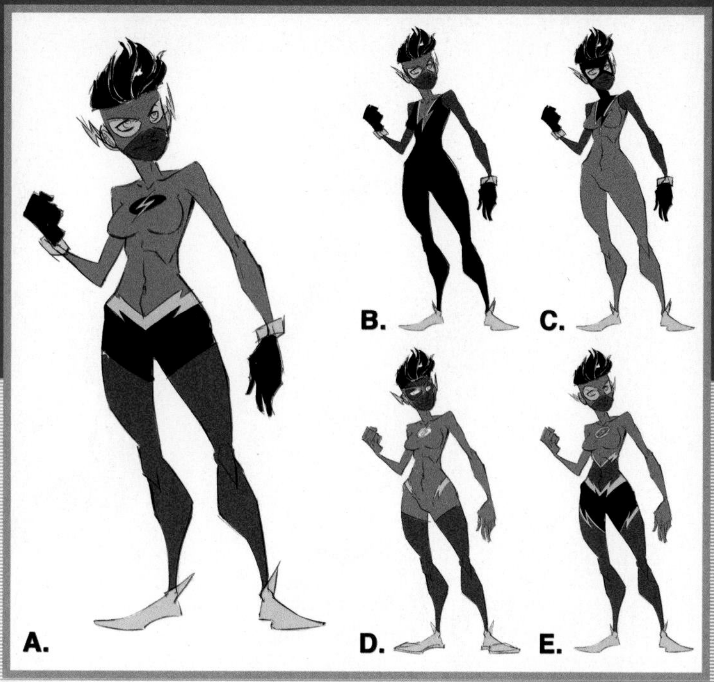
B.
C.
A.
D.
E.

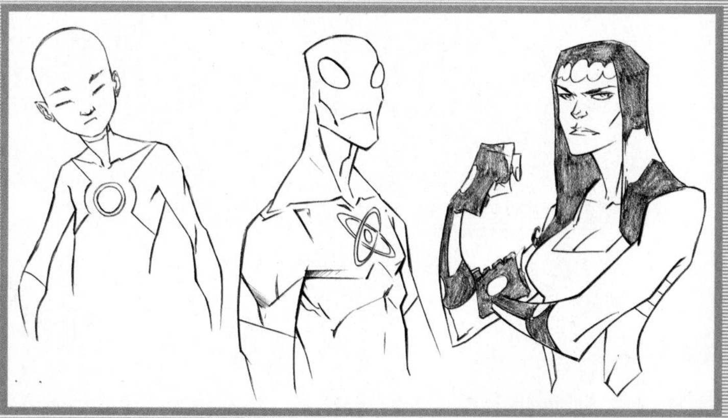

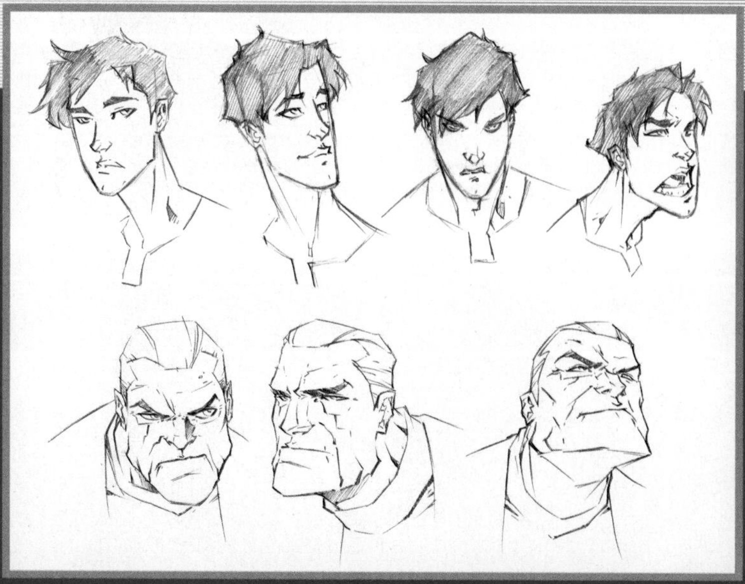

"Flashdrive"
character studies by Jorge Corona

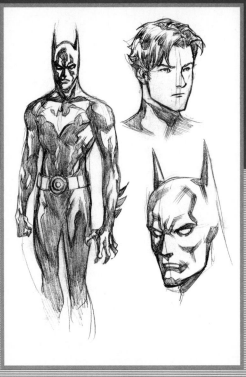

JUSTICE LEAGUE BEYOND
character studies by Marcus To

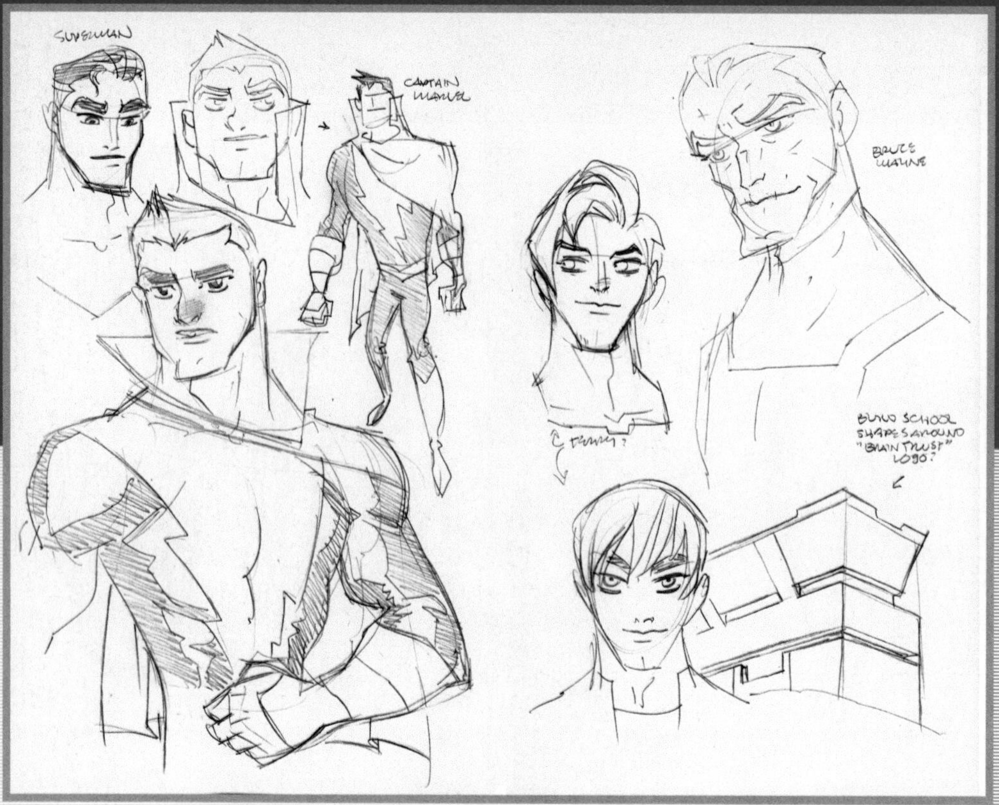
SUPERMAN
CAPTAIN MARVEL
BRUCE WAYNE
BLIND SCHOOL SHAPES AROUND "BRAIN TRUST" LOGO?

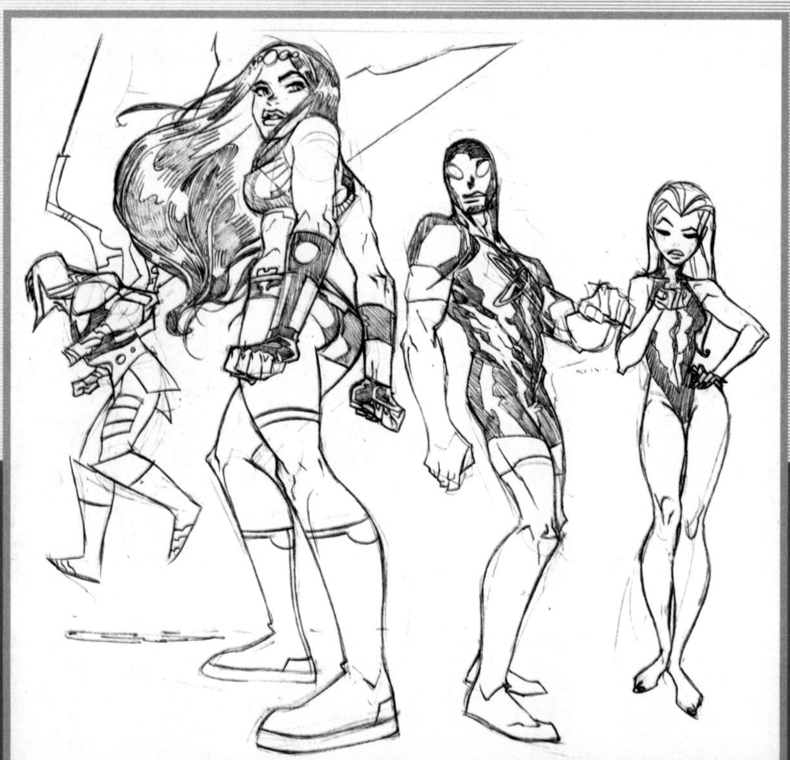

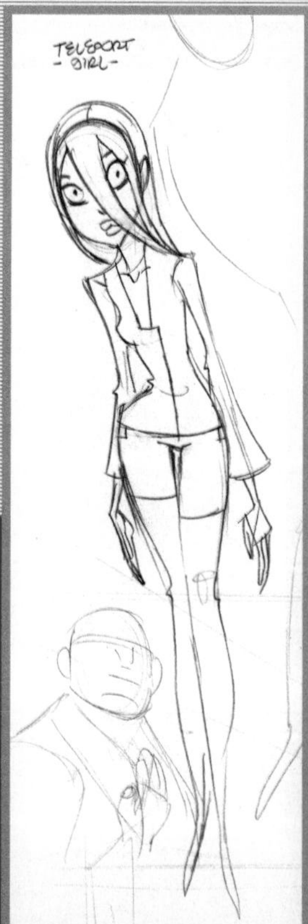
TELEPORT
-GIRL-

"In Gods We Trust" character studies by Ben Caldwell

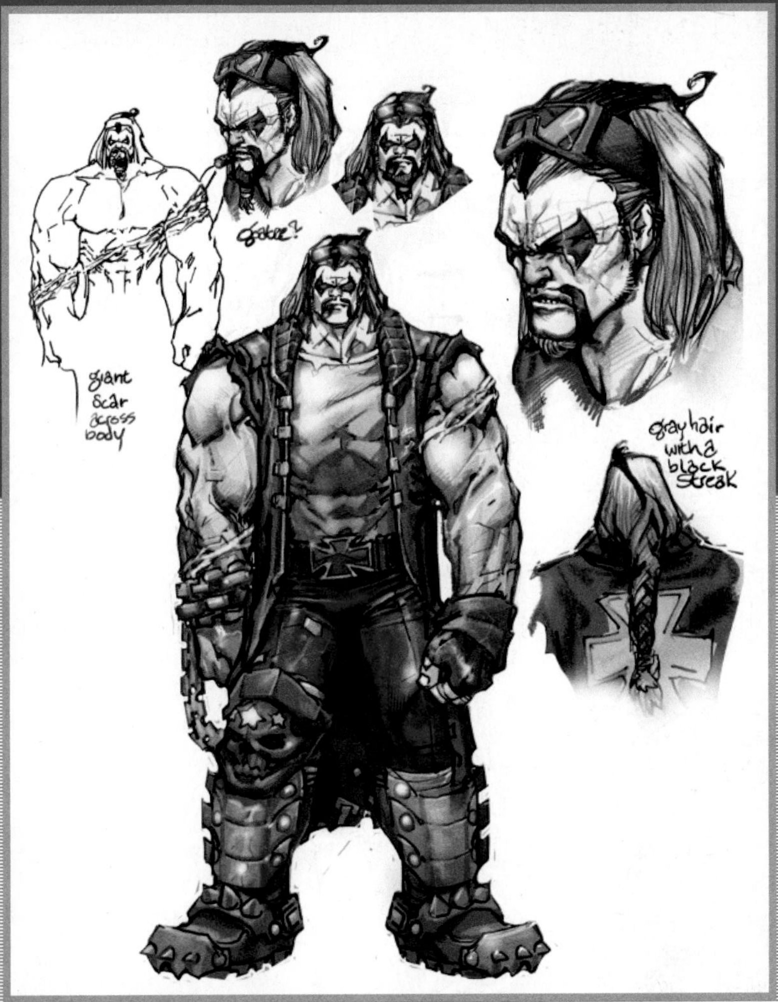
giant scar across body
goatee?
gray hair with a black streak

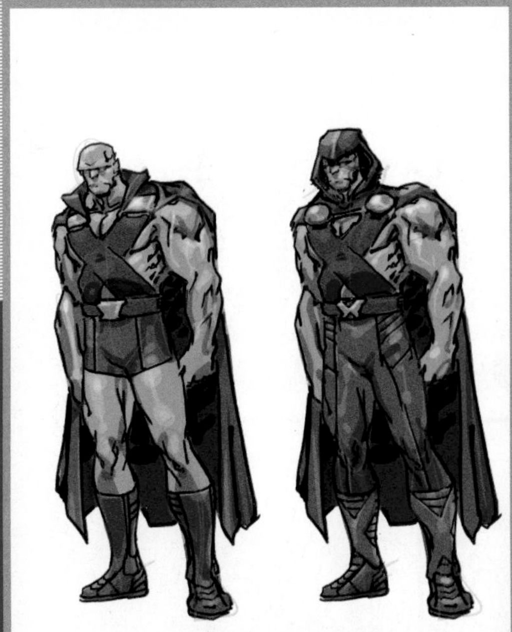
martian manhunter beyond

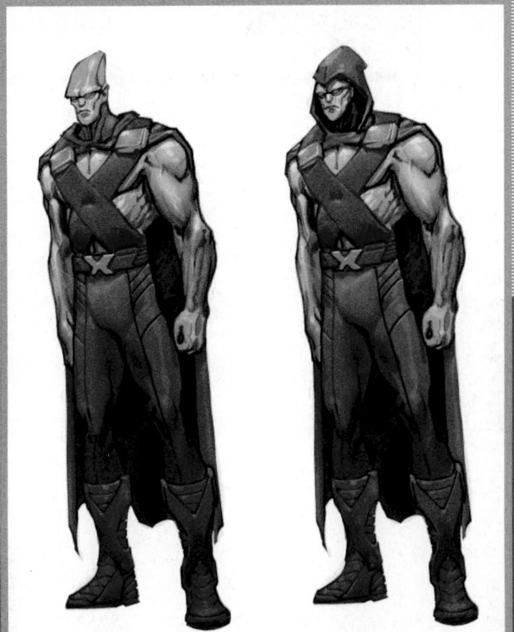
martian manhunter beyond

Lobo and Martian Manhunter character studies by Howard Porter

SUPERMAN BEYOND cover sketches by Howard Porter

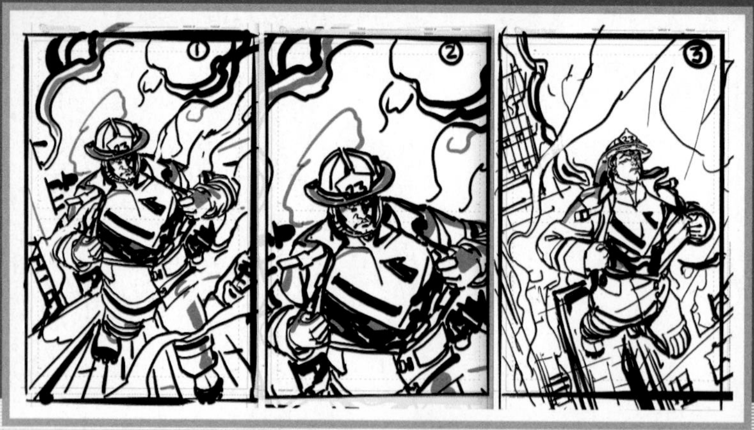
1
2
3

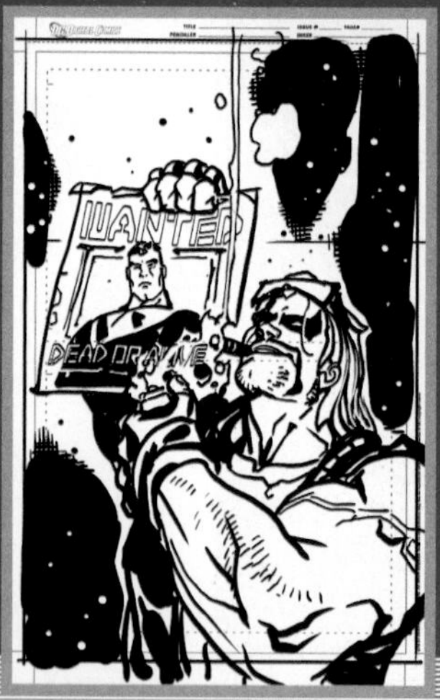
WANTED
DEAD OR ALIVE

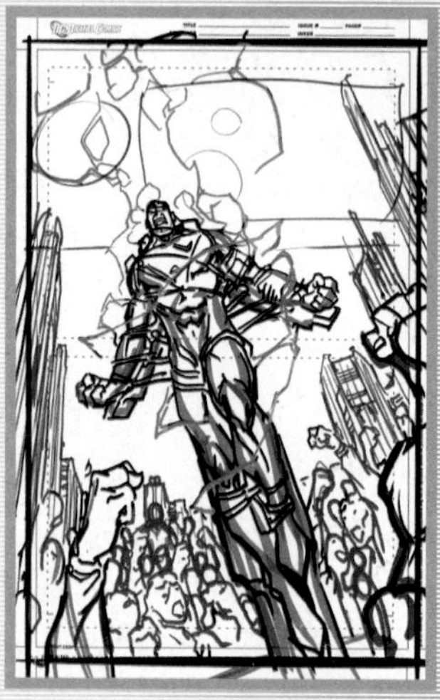

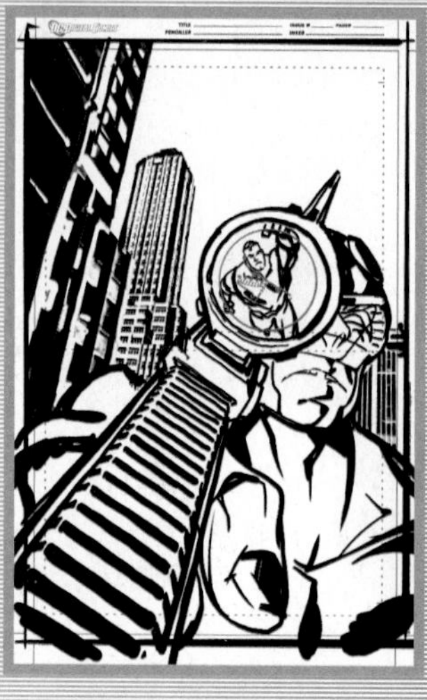

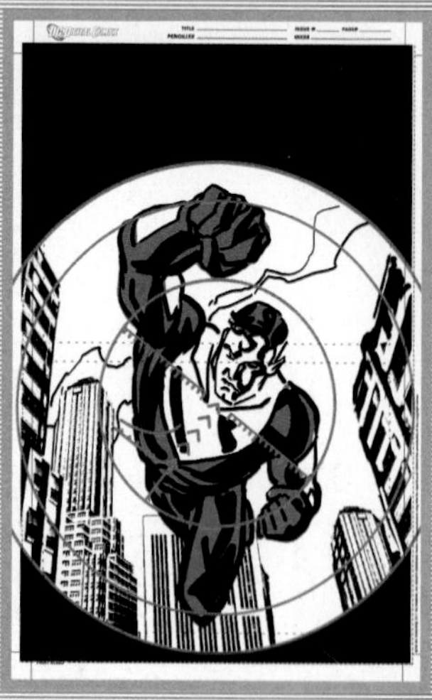

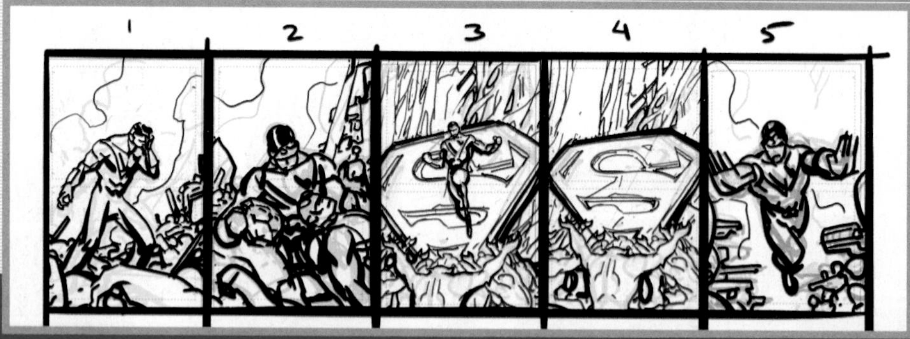
1
2
3
4
5

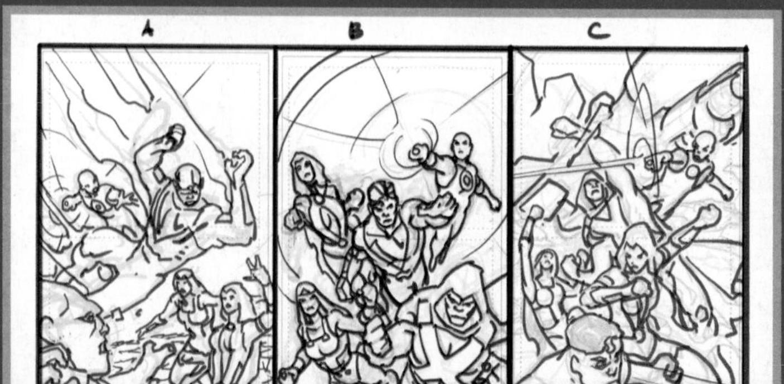
A
B
C